0-89596-205-5     © 1974     Merit Publications/610 N.E. 124th St./North Miami, FL 33161/Copyright

# The Low Carbohydrate, Practical Way To Lose Weight Without Going Hungry

The underlying basis of all diets remains the same as it always has been: to lose weight, one must consume less than one expends. The energy provided by food, as burned by the body, is measured in units called calories. One calorie is the amount of energy necessary to raise the temperature of one gram of water one degree centigrade. Depending upon height, frame structure and general level of physical activity, most women require from about 1625 to about 2600 calories daily and most men from about 1850 to about 3000 calories daily to meet the energy demands of the body. Diets work because, by and large, your body will continue to expend energy, to burn calories, whether or not you consume energy producing substances; that is, whether or not you eat. By reducing the amount you eat to below the expenditure requirements of your body, you will lose weight. This rule never varies, is always true; all safe and successful diet plans are based on this single bit of knowledge, however varied they may appear.

In its simplest and most common form, this has resulted in the so-called "starvation diet." Although calorie-wise the starvation diet is factually sound, it has two major drawbacks: it is unsafe and it rarely works! Starvation diets rarely work for a reason as simple and common as the diet itself: people on starvation diets invariably cheat. They cheat because they get hungry, because this sort of diet is too restrictive. In brief, because when deprived of the pleasures of eating they eat anyway; because this diet makes no allowances for the enjoyment of food.

The low carbohydrate diet, on the other hand, takes into account that food tastes good and that people, regardless of how overweight they are, will eat. The low carbohydrate diet, however, also takes into account that one must eat less to weigh less. The low carbohydrate diet works because when you limit your carbohydrate consumption to 75 grams per day, you will also automatically lower your caloric consumption of proteins and fats; because proteins and fats have a greater satiation or filling value than do carbohydrates. The low carbohydrate diet is a sensible and practical way to both enjoy food and lose weight without ever going hungry!

Nutrients are composed of five items or groups of items: proteins, carbohydrates, fats, minerals and vitamins. Of these, it is the first three— proteins, carbohydrates and fats—from which the body derives its energy.

1

One gram of either protein or carbohydrates (sugars and starches) yields 4 calories; a gram of fat yields 9. To operate healthily, the body requires that certain general balances be maintained. Between protein and fat, that balance should be 60%-80% protein and 40%-20% fat, or about equal calories from either (remember, a gram of fat yields more than twice the calories than does a gram of protein). An overly high fat consumption has been implicated as a major contributing factor to heart attacks and strokes. Especially recommended is the replacement of saturated fats, to a large extent, with unsaturated or preferably polyunsaturated fats. Too much protein consumption can place an excessive burden upon the kidneys in the presence of certain diseases of those organs. So, once again, it is the balance among foods which is significant. With reasonable care, the balance between fat and protein in your diet should cause no real problem.

It is also important to maintain a balance between carbohydrates for the proper utilization of fats as well. Furthermore, carbohydrates are the **only source** from which brain tissue derives its energy. All carbohydrates, whether sugars or starches, are converted into a single simple sugar, glucose. When the carbohydrate consumption is overly reduced, the body will convert protein into glucose; so that, if protein consumption is too low as well, the healthy body tissue protein from the muscles will be sacrificed to the production of glucose. Now, if the body must burn its reserves of fat in addition to healthy tissue to meet its caloric needs, the fats are then incompletely burned. These incompletely burned fats form residual substances, called ketones. Ketones build up in the blood and, if the build-up becomes excessive, an acid state called ketosis develops. In its more severe forms, this toxic condition of ketosis can prove lethal. This explains not only the importance of a good balance between carbohydrates and fats, but also explains the importance of a good balance between fats and proteins. The high protein figure insures against the destruction of muscle tissue and the lower fat figure against the development of ketosis.

Do not reduce your carbohydrate intake to below 75 grams each and every day. Unless your fat-protein ratio is inordinately high, 75 grams of carbohydrate daily will usually prevent the possibility of ketosis from materializing. However, since your body will burn **more than** 75 grams of carbohydrates each day, you will lose and continue to lose weight because, as noted, when your carbohydrate intake is restricted you will naturally consume less protein and fat without feeling hungry.

Much of the early and dramatic weight loss you will experience on the low carbohydrate diet will not actually be from the loss of fat as much as it will be from the loss of water. The low carbohydrate diet has a diuretic effect. That is, it promotes water loss. Excessive water loss can result in a state of dehydration. Water is essential to all human life. In fact, a person can live for long periods without eating any solid food, although he would probably die within a week or so without any water. Because water is so vital and because the low carbohydrate diet does tend to purge the body of considerable quantities of water, you should drink eight (8) glasses of water daily and never allow yourself to become too thirsty at any given time. You may find this also has a positive effect upon weight loss too, for filling up on a glass or two of water can help to reduce the appetite and, furthermore, water is the original diet beverage — it has zero calories.

Most of the success you will achieve through the low carbohydrate diet will come as a result of **reasonable expectations coupled with reasonable eating habits**. It is **not** reasonable to expect to lose in a month or two month's time the excess weight it may have taken you ten years to put on. **It is reasonable**, however, to expect to lose about forty or fifty pounds in the first six months and to reach your desired weight within a year's time… if, of course, you stick to the diet. Being in good physical shape includes not being overweight. Obesity subjects you to many physical hardships and places an undue burden upon your heart. Although it is only through eating less that you will lose unwanted pounds, it is only through eating the right kinds of foods that will insure a good state of nutritional health. Thus it is very crucial that you do not exhaust your 75 gram allowance of carbohydrates on so-called empty-calorie foods. Variety in food is the surest, most reliable single way to make certain that one gets all the nutrients the body needs. To rely exclusively upon vitamin and mineral supplements is unwise. The science of nutrition is yet in its infancy, and it is presumptive and dangerous to equate a vitamin pill with good eating habits. Your diet should always include: meat, poultry, eggs (one or two per week), nuts (such as soy) or fish; milk, cheese or other dairy products; bread, cereal or bran, especially whole grain, to provide you with bulk, indispensible for proper functioning of the digestive tract; soft margarine; fruits, particularly citrus fruits and tomatoes, or the juice from fruits; and an assortment of green, leafy and yellow vegetables as well as other vitamin-rich vegetables, like carrots.

This may sound like a lot to eat, and you may wonder how you will ever lose weight, but the trick is this: you need not eat these foods in quantity to derive the nutritional benefits they bestow. You do, however, have to eat them. As you can see from this book, there is no difficulty in planning perfectly balanced and wholesome meals while limiting your carbohydrate intake to 75 grams per day. Just make certain that you get some good nutrition besides just good taste. For instance, most cans of cola will use up one/half of your daily carbohydrate allowance and do no more than satisfy your sweet tooth for several minutes. It then becomes just **that much more difficult** to obtain your necessary nutrients without exceeding your 75 gram limit; which, needless to say, you must not do. On the other hand, a low calorie diet soda has maybe one or, at the most, two grams of carbohydrates; and, better yet, water has none at all.

Which brings us to alcoholic beverages. While a shot of scotch may have no carbohydrates, it still has 100 calories. If you drink liquor, one or two drinks a day may very well be permissible. Even though the carbohydrate content is absent, the caloric content is not; and, a calorie is a calorie is a calorie. As has been said already, too many calories and weight loss is impossible. Furthermore, too many alcoholic calories and the body runs the heavy risk of liver damage and many other undesirable perils. In any event, two drinks is the limit, liqueurs, sweet wines and beer (a can of beer has about 13 grams of carbohydrates and is not, as is often mistakenly believed, nutritious) are out, or should not exceed a single drink. If you do consume alcohol don't drink every day. Give your liver a rest and a chance to recuperate.

ALL SOUND DIETS, INCLUDING THIS ONE, HAVE BEEN FORMULATED FOR THOSE IN A GOOD STATE OF NORMAL HEALTH. THEY ARE NOT FOR PERSONS WHO HAVE ANY KIND OF OF PERSISTENT OR CHRONIC ILLNESS, SUCH AS—BUT NOT LIMITED TO—HYPERTENSION (HIGH BLOOD PRESSURE), HEART TROUBLE, KIDNEY DISEASE, DIABETES AND SO FORTH. EVEN THOUGH YOU MAY BELIEVE YOU ARE IN GOOD HEALTH, CHECK WITH YOUR PHYSICIAN BEFORE COMMENCING THIS DIET PLAN—OR ANY OTHER, FOR THAT MATTER. If you do have some health problem, it may still be possible for you, with your physician's guidance and recommendations, to take advantage of the LOW CARBOHYDRATE diet with suitable precautions and modifications. This is, in fact, frequently the case.

The book you now hold in your hands contains over 10,000 listings of the carbohydrate contents contained in common household foods and brand name products. Carry it with you when you go out to eat with friends or at restaurants, when you go to the market for grocery shopping and at any time when you prepare meals for yourself or others. The listings in this book represent one of the most complete, thorough and comprehensive compilations currently available in print.

If you have never before been on a weight loss diet, keep these few thoughts in mind: Usually one loses weight dramatically within the first few weeks of the diet. However, this weight loss is predominantly water loss; and, as such, can be misleading. It is an encouraging sign that you are responding to the diet but it should not lull you into a false sense of accomplishment. This beginning period is followed by one in which nothing appears to happen i.e. you do not lose weight, and this may last from a week or two to a bit over a month. It is during this period that your body's metabolism undergoes the essential phase of readjustment. This adjustment period is finally followed by the true weight loss period, a slow but sure period in which the excess fat is lost. This is the time of ultimate reward for your perseverance and persistence in adhering to the LOW CARBOHYDRATE DIET: a trimmer, slimmer, healthier, more vital YOU emerges as fat melts away.

# HOW TO READ THE CARBOHYDRATE CHART

In the following pages we have listed thousands of foods, both common household and brand-name commercial products. The first column lists the food, the second column lists the portion, and the third column lists the carbohydrate count in grams. Here are a few examples:

| | | |
|---|---|---|
| Apples, Raw | 1 Md. | 17 |
| Fish, Blue | 1 Serv. | 0 |
| Potatoes | 4 Ozs. | 21 |

"T" means **trace,** which is a negligable amount of carbohydrates present in that portion.

Brand names are listed in parentheses. An **Average Serving** usually means 4 ounces.

REMEMBER, WHILE ON A LOW CARBOHYDRATE DIET TRY AND RESTRICT YOUR CARBOHYDRATE INTAKE TO 75 GRAMS A DAY.

By checking the following chart, you can easily see at a glance what foods are best for you on this diet and what foods to avoid.

Our handy pocket-size format makes this book an ideal supermarket and restaurant companion. Take it with you wherever you go. *GOOD LUCK!*

| Food | Portion | Carbo Grams |
|---|---|---|
| A-1 Sauce | 1 Tsp. | 0 |
| Abalone | Av. Serv. | 2 |
| Abalone, Broiled | 3-1/2 Ozs. | 3 |
| Abalone (Canned) | 2/3 Cup | 3 |
| Accent | 1 Tsp. | 0 |
| Acidophilus Milk | 1 Cup | 8 |
| Acorn Squash | 1/2 Cup | 12 |
| African Lobster Tail | 4 Ozs. | T |
| After Dinner Choc. Mints | 1 Pc. Sm. | 7 |
| Alabama Rice Fritters | 6 Tbsp. | 36 |
| A La King, Chicken | 1/2 Cup | 4 |
| Alaska, Baked | Av. Serv. | 28 |
| Ale | 1 Cup | 8 |
| Alexander | 1 Cktl. | 1 |
| Alexander, Brandy | Cktl. Gl. | 1 |
| Alexander, Gin | Cktl. Gl. | 1 |
| All-Bran | 1 Cup | 36 |
| Alligator Pears (A-C) | 1/2 Sm. | 3 |
| All Milk Skimmed Coca | 1 Gl. | 10 |
| All Purpose Flour, White | 1 Cup | 84 |
| Allspice | 1/8 Tsp. | 0 |
| Almond Cake | Av. Serv. | 36 |
| Almond Chocolate Bar | 1 Av. | 17 |
| Almond Coffee Cake | Av. Pc. | 33 |
| Almond Cookies | 2 Med. | 9 |
| Almond Extract, Burnt | 2 Tsp. | 0 |
| Almond Fudge | 1 In. Sq. | 22 |
| Almond Joy Candies | Bar | 22 |
| Almond Macaroons | 1 Lg. | 16 |
| Almond Macaroon Cookies | 1 | 16 |
| Almond Souffle | 1 Serv. | 40 |
| Almonds, Choc. Covered | 10 Med. | 17 |
| Almonds, in Shell | 1/2 Cup | 4 |
| Almonds, Roasted: | | |
| (Blue Diamond) | 2 Ozs. | 11 |
| (Planters) | 1 Oz. | 10 |
| Almonds, Salted | 12 Med. | 3 |
| (Blue Diamond) | 2 Ozs. | 11 |
| Almonds, Shelled | 12 Med. | 3 |
| (Blue Diamond) | 1 Oz. | 5 |
| Alphabet Soup Mix: | | |
| (Golden Grain) | 1 Cup | 9 |

| Food | Portion | Carbo Grams |
|---|---|---|
| (Lipton) vegetable | 1 Pkg. | 36 |
| Alpha-bits, Oat Cereal (Post) | 1 Cup | 23 |
| Ambrosia | Av. Serv. | 23 |
| (Kraft) | 4 Ozs. | 18 |
| Am. Cheese | 1 Sl. | T |
| Am. Cheese, Dry & Grated | 4 Ozs. | 2 |
| Am. Cheese, Fresh & Grated | 1 Tsp. | T |
| Am. Cheese Sandwich | 1 Sl. | 24 |
| Am. Cheese & Tomato | 1 Sl. | 27 |
| Am. Fries, Potatoes | 1 Med. | 40 |
| Am. Grog, Hot | 6 Ozs. | 0 |
| Am. Steamed Pudding | Av. Serv. | 25 |
| Anadama Bread | 1 Sl. | 30 |
| Anchovy Butter Spread | 1 Tbsp. | T |
| Anchovy Paste | 1 Tbsp. | 1 |
| (Crosse & Blackwell) | 1 Tbsp. | 1 |
| Anchovy Pizza with Cheese | 1/6-12 In. Diam. | 23 |
| Anchovy Sauce | 3/4 Cup | 2 |
| Anchovies | 6 | T |
| Anchovies (Canned) | 8 Sm. | T |
| Anchovies With Scallions | Av. Serv. | T |
| Angel Food Cake | 2 In. | 22 |
| Angel Food Cake Mix: | | |
| (Betty Crocker): | | |
| Confetti | 1 Oz. | 24 |
| Lemon custard | 1 Oz. | 24 |
| Strawberry | 1 Oz. | 24 |
| (Duncan Hines) | 1 Pc. | 24 |
| (Pillsbury): | | |
| Raspberry Swirl | 1 Oz. | 23 |
| White | 1 Oz. | 23 |
| (Swans Down) | 1 Pc. | 26 |
| Animal Crackers | 6 | 12 |
| Animal Cracker Cookies | 1 | 2 |
| Anise | 1/8 Tsp. | 0 |
| Anise Cookies | 3 Sm. | 9 |
| Aniseed | 1/8 Tsp. | 0 |
| Anisette | 1 Oz. | 9 |
| Anisette Cordial | 1 | 7 |
| Anisette Liqueur: | | |
| (Bois) | 1 Fl. Oz. | 14 |

| FOOD | AMT. | CARB. GRAMS | FOOD | AMT. | CARB. GRAMS |
|---|---|---|---|---|---|
| (Garnier) | 1 Fl. Oz. | 9 | (Diet Delight) | 1 Tbsp. | 1 |
| (Hiram Walker) | 1 Fl. Oz. | 11 | (Kraft) | 1 Tbsp. | 3 |
| (Leroux) | 1 Fl. Oz. | 10 | (Slenderella) | 1 Tbsp. | 5 |
| (Old Mr Boston) 42 proof | 1 Fl. Oz. | 8 | (Tillie Lewis) | 1 Tbsp. | 2 |
| (Old Mr. Boston) 60 proof | 1 Fl. Oz. | 7 | Apple Juice, Fresh | 1/2 Cup | 19 |
| Appetizers, Avocado-Tomato | 1 Serv. | 5 | Apple Juice (Canned) | 1/2 Cup | 17 |
| Appetizers, Chicken Liver de Luxe | 1 | 3 | (Heinz) | 5-1/2-Oz Can | 17 |
| Appetizer, Lobster Canapes | 1 Serv | 6 | (Seneca) | 1/2 Cup | 27 |
| Appetizers, Stuffed Cucumber | 1 | 3 | (White House) | 1/2 Cup | 30 |
| Apple (C) | 1 Sm | 11 | Apple Marney | 4 Ozs | 13 |
| Apples and Apricots | | | Apple on a Stick | 1 | 55 |
| (Canned, Infant) | 4 Ozs. | 20 | Apple Pandowdy | Av Serv | 42 |
| Apples and Apricots Strained | | | Apple Pie | 1/6 | 42 |
| (Canned) | 1 Oz. | 5 | (Tastykake) | 4 Ozs. | 58 |
| Apple Baked  1 Lg. w/2 Tbsp Sugar | | 50 | French apple (Tastykake) | 4 Ozs. | 60 |
| Apple Baked With Sugar | 1 Sm. | 47 | (Banquet) | 4 Ozs. | 40 |
| Apple Baked With Sugar | | | (Morton) | 1 Pc. | 18 |
| & Cream | 1 Sm. | 47 | (Mrs. Smith's) | 1 Pc. | 21 |
| Apple Betty | 1/2 Cup | 34 | (Mrs. Smith's) Dutch apple | 1 Pc. | 25 |
| Apple Brown Betty Pudding | 1/2 Cup | 35 | (Mrs. Smith's) tart | 1 Pc. | 22 |
| Apple Butter | 1 Tbsp. | 9 | Apple Pie A La Mode | 1 Pc. | 58 |
| (White House) | 1 Tbsp. | 7 | Apple Pie, Deep Dish | Av Pc. | 44 |
| Apple Butter Creamy Cake | | | (Lucky Leaf) | 4 Ozs. | 30 |
| Filling | 1 Cup | 14 | Apple Pie, Fr. | Av. Pc. | 45 |
| Apple Cake, Dutch | 1 Av. Pc. | 65 | Apple & Raisin Salad | 1/2 Cup | 25 |
| Apple-Carrot Salad | 1/2 Cup | 11 | Apple Salad, Diced | Av Serv | 18 |
| Apple and Cheese Baked | 1 Serv. | 21 | Apple Sauce Bread | 1 Sl. | 21 |
| Apple Chutney | 5 Tbsp. | 50 | Apple Sauce Cake | 1/8 Cake | 63 |
| Apple Cider, Hard | 3/4 Cup | 13 | Apple Sauce Cake Mix: | | |
| (Indian Summer) | 6 Fl. Ozs. | 19 | Raisin (Duncan Hines) | 1 Pc. | 26 |
| Apple Cider, Soft | 3/4 Cup | 13 | Spice (Pillsbury) | 1 Oz. | 23 |
| Apple Cider, Sweet | 6 Ozs. | 18 | Apple Sauce (Canned) | 1/2 Cup | 13 |
| Apple Cobbler | 1 | 44 | Apple Sauce (Canned, Infant) | 4 Ozs. | 20 |
| Apple, Crab | 2 Ozs. | 8 | Apple Sauce, Strained | | |
| Apple Crisps, (Epicure) | 1 Oz. | 22 | (Canned) | 1/2 Cup | 22 |
| Apple, Crumb Cake | 1 Sl. | 49 | Apple Sauce With Sugar | | |
| Apple, Dried | 2 Ozs. | 32 | (Canned) | 1/2 Cup | 25 |
| Apple Drink, (Hi-C) | 6 Fl. Ozs. | 22 | (Seneca) Cinnamon | 1 Cup | 60 |
| Apple Dumpling Pudding | 1 | 54 | (Seneca) 100% McIntosh | 1 Cup | 60 |
| Apple Dumpling | 1 Med. | 63 | (Stokely-Van Camp) | 1 Cup | 62 |
| Apple Fritters | 1 | 12 | (White House) | 1 Cup | 56 |
| Apple Fruit Roll, frozen | | | Apple Sauce, Unsweetened | | |
| (Chun King) | 1 Oz. | 10 | (Canned) | 1 Cup | 26 |
| Apple & Grapefruit Gelatin | | | (Blue Boy) | 3 Ozs. | 9 |
| Salad | 1 Serv. | 26 | (Diet Delight) | 1 Cup | 21 |
| Applejack Highball | Gl. Av. | 3 | (Lucky Leaf) | 3 Ozs. | 9 |
| Apple Jack | Shot | 0 | (S and W) Nutradiet | 4 Ozs. | 13 |
| Apple Jacks, Cereal (Kellogg's) | 1 Cup | 25 | (Tillie Lewis) | 1 Cup | 24 |
| Apple Jelly | 1 Tbsp. | 13 | (White House) | 1 Cup | 24 |
| Sweetened (White House) | 1 Tbsp. | 13 | Apple Sauce, Fresh | 1/2 Cup | 11 |
| Dietetic or low calorie: | | | Apple Sauce, Fresh With | | |
| (Dia-Mel) | 1 Tbsp. | 5 | Sugar | 1/2 Cup | 23 |

| FOOD | AMT. | CARB. GRAMS | FOOD | AMT. | CARB. GRAMS |
|---|---|---|---|---|---|
| Apple Snow Pudding | 1/2 Cup | 25 | Apricot Nectar, Juice | 1 Cup | 36 |
| Apple Soup | 1 Serv | 18 | Apricot-Orange Pie | | |
| Apple, Stewed | 1 | 29 | (Tastykake) | 1 Pie | 54 |
| Apple Struedel | Av Pc. | 34 | Apricot Pan Boiled | 1/2 Cup | 10 |
| Apple Tapioca | 4 Ozs. | 26 | Apricot Pie | 1/8 | 31 |
| Apple Tart | 1 Med. | 26 | Apricot Pie Filling (Lucky | | |
| Apple Turnover | 1 Med. | 37 | Leaf) | 4 Ozs | 38 |
| (Pepperidge Farm) | 1 Oz. | 10 | Apricot & Pineapple | | |
| Apple Vinegar | 1 Oz. | 0 | Nectar, unsweetened | | |
| Apples, Cinnamon | 1 Serv | 52 | (S and W) Nutradiet | 4 Ozs | 8 |
| Apples, Dehydrated | 2 Ozs. | 52 | Apricot & Pineapple | | |
| Apples, Dried, Cooked, | | | Preserve, low calorie. | | |
| Sweetened | 1 Cup | 62 | (Dia-Mel) | 1 Tbsp. | 5 |
| Apples, Dried, Cooked, | | | (Diet Delight) | 1 Tbsp. | 1 |
| Unsweetened | 1 Cup | 44 | (Tillie Lewis) | 1 Tbsp. | 2 |
| Apples, Frozen, Sweetened | 1/2 Cup | 26 | Apricot Preserve, | | |
| Apples, Raw | 1 Lg. | 25 | low calorie: | | |
| Apples, Raw | 1 Med. | 17 | (Dia-Mel) | 1 Tbsp. | 5 |
| Apples, Raw | 1 Sm. | 11 | (Polaner) | 1 Tbsp. | T |
| Apples, Raw | 1 Cup | 19 | Apricot Puree | 1 Serv. | 33 |
| Apricot-Almond Cream | Av Serv | 4 | Apricot Salad (Lettuce & | | |
| Apricot & Blackberry Jam | 1 Tbsp. | 16 | Fr. Dressing) | 1 Serv. | 7 |
| Apricot Brandy | Cordial | 7 | Apricot Snow | 4 Ozs. | 28 |
| Apricot Butter Preserve | 1 Tbsp. | 8 | Apricot Stuffing | 1/2 Cup | 34 |
| Apricot (Canned, Low Calorie) | 1/2 Cup | 9 | Apricot Whip | Av. Serv. | 24 |
| (Del Monte) | 4 Ozs. | 11 | Apricots (A) | 5 Med. | 22 |
| (Diet Delight) halves | 1 Cup | 16 | Apricots, Candied | 1 Med. | 26 |
| (Diet Delight) whole, peeled | 1 Cup | 14 | Apricots (Canned) | | |
| (Libby's) | 4 Ozs. | 11 | | 4 Halves 2 Tbsps Syrup | 21 |
| (S and W) Nutradiet | 4 Halves | 8 | Apricots (Canned) | 1 Cup w/Syrup | 55 |
| Apricot (Canned, Syrup Pack) | 1 Cup | 55 | Apricots, Strained (Canned) | 1 Oz | 10 |
| (Hunt's) | 4 Ozs. | 25 | Apricots, With Sugar | | |
| (Stokely-Van Camp) | 4 Halves | 27 | (Canned) | 3 Halves | 20 |
| Apricot Cordial | 1 Gl. | 7 | Apricots, No Syrup (Canned) | 3 Halves | 8 |
| Apricot, Dehydrated | | | Apricots (Canned, | | |
| Slices (Vacu-Dry) | 1 Oz. | 24 | Water Packed) | 1 Cup | 20 |
| Apricot Dried | 5 Sm. Halves | 13 | Apricots, Dried-Cooked | 4 Ozs. | 31 |
| Apricot Dried | 1 Cup | 87 | Apricots, Dried (A) | 3 Halves | 11 |
| Apricot Float | 1 Av. | 18 | Apricots, Dried-Cooked | | |
| Apricot Fritters | 1 Serv. | 28 | Sweetened | 1/2 Cup | 51 |
| Apricot Glaze, Fr. | 1/2 Cup | 87 | Apricots, Dried-Cooked | | |
| Apricot Jam | 1 Tbsp. | 14 | Unsweetened | 1/2 Cup | 31 |
| (Slenderella) | 2 Tbsp. | 11 | Apricots, Fresh | 3 Med. | 10 |
| Apricot Juice | 6 Ozs. | 18 | Apricots, Spiced | 4 Med. | 26 |
| Apricot Liqueur: | | | Apricots, Stewed | 4 Ozs. | 31 |
| (Bols) | 1 Fl. Oz. | 9 | Arawak Cocktail | 1 Cktl. Gl. | 5 |
| (Hiram Walker) | 1 Fl. Oz. | 8 | Arrowhead | 1 Tbsp. | 7 |
| (Leroux) | 1 Fl. Oz. | 9 | Arrowroot | 1 Tbsp. | 8 |
| Apricot Meringue Pie | Av. Serv. | 45 | Arrowroot Cookies | 1 | 4 |
| Apricot Nectar | 1 Cup | 34 | Arrowroot Flour | 2 Ozs. | 40 |
| (Heinz) | 1 Can | 19 | Artichoke | 1 Lg. | 11 |
| (Diet Delight) | 1/2 Cup | 5 | Artichoke With Mushrooms | 1 | 11 |

| FOOD | AMT. | CARB. GRAMS | FOOD | AMT. | CARB. GRAMS |
|---|---|---|---|---|---|
| Artichoke Hearts | 1 Med. | 10 | Austrian Cabbage Salad | Av. Serv. | 3 |
| Frozen (Bird's Eye) | 3 Ozs. | 4 | Avocado (B1-C) | 1 Sm. | 8 |
| Artichoke, Jerusalem-Raw | 1 Lg. | 17 | Avocado, California | 1/2 Med. | 6 |
| Artichoke Salad | 1 Serv. | 14 | Avocado, California | 1 Cup Cubes | 9 |
| Artichoke With Tbsp. | | | Avocado Cocktail | 1 Serv. | 8 |
| Hollandaise Sauce | 1 | 11 | Avocado Consomme | 1 Serv. | 5 |
| Artichokes, Bottoms | 1 Lg. | 5 | Avocado Florida | 1 Cup Cubes | 13 |
| Artichokes, Fr. | 1 Lg. | 14 | Avocado-Grapefruit Cocktail | 1 Serv. | 12 |
| Artificial Flavor, | | | Avocado Ice or Sherbet | 1 Serv. | 8 |
| Ice Cream Soda | 10 Ozs. | 71 | Avocado & Lime Gelatin Salad | 1 Serv. | 6 |
| Ash Bread | 1 Pc. | 21 | Avocado Puree Spread | 1 Serv. | 1 |
| Asparagus (C) | 12 Stalks | 4 | Avocado Salad With Dressing | 1/2 Cup | 5 |
| Asparagus | 2/3 Cup Cut Spears | 4 | Avocado Salad (B1-C) | Av. | 10 |
| Asparagus (Canned) | 1 Cup Spears | 6 | Avocado Salad Dressing | 2 Tbsp. | 1 |
| Asparagus (Canned) | 6 Spears | 3 | Avocado-Tomato Appetizers | 1 Serv. | 5 |
| Asparagus: | | | Avocado-Tomato-Cheese | | |
| Green: | | | Salad | Av. Serv. | 9 |
| (Green Giant) | 4 Ozs. | 3 | Awake (Bird's Eye) | 1 Cup | 25 |
| (Stokely-Van Camp) | 4 Spears | 2 | Ayds: | | |
| (Cannon) | 4 Ozs. | 4 | Chocolate or chocolate mint | 1 Pc. | 5 |
| White: | | | Vanilla caramel | 1 Pc. | 5 |
| (Stokely-Van Camp) | 3 Spears | 2 | Bacardi Flip Cocktail | 1 Gl. | 3 |
| Asparagus, Cooked | 6 Stalks | 3 | Bacardi Rum Shot | 1-1/2 Ozs. | 0 |
| Asparagus, Cream of Soup | 1 Cup | 13 | Baco Noir Burgundy Wine | | |
| Condensed (Campbell) | 4 Ozs. | 10 | (Great Western) | 3 Fl. Ozs. | 2 |
| Asparagus Crisps, | | | Bac*O Chips (General Mills) | 1 Oz. | 8 |
| (Epicure) | 1 Oz. | 12 | Bac*O's (General Mills) | 1 Oz. | 4 |
| Asparagus, dietetic: | | | Bacon Bits (McCormick) | 1 Oz. | 8 |
| (Blue Boy) | 4 Ozs. | 3 | Bacon, Crisp | 3 Strips | T |
| (Diet Delight) | 1 Can | 3 | Bacon, Broiled, Crisp | 3 Strips | T |
| (S and W) Nutradiet | 8 Spears | 3 | Bacon, Broiled Or Fried | 1 Lb. | 5 |
| (Tillie Lewis) | 1 Cup | 5 | Bacon, Broiled Or Fried | 2 Strips | T |
| Asparagus, Frozen | 6 Spears | 4 | Bacon, Canadian | 1-1/2 Ozs. | T |
| (Bird's Eye) | 1 Cup | 7 | Bacon, Canadian, Broiled | 4 Ozs. | T |
| (Stokely-Van Camp) | 1 Cup | 6 | Bacon, Canadian, Fried | 4 Ozs. | T |
| (Bird's Eye) | 6 Spears | 4 | (Wilson) | 1 Oz. | T |
| (Green Giant) boil-in-the-bag | 4 Ozs. | 4 | Bacon Cheese Spread | 1 Oz. | 2 |
| Asparagus Omelet | Av. Serv. | 4 | Bacon, Cured: | | |
| Asparagus Salad | 5 Spears | 4 | (Oscar Mayer) | 1 Sl. | 1 |
| Asparagus Tips (Canned) | 12 | 3 | (Wilson) | 4 Ozs. | 1 |
| Asparagus Toast Rolls | 2 | 31 | (Wilson) Corn King | 4 Ozs. | 1 |
| Asparagus Vinaigrette | Av. Serv. | 4 | Bacon-Egg Sandwich | 1 | 24 |
| Aspic, Chicken | 1 Serv. | 2 | Bacon Fat | 1 Tsp. | 1 |
| Aspic Salad, Tomato | 1/2 Cup | 4 | Bacon Pork Cured | 4 Ozs. | 0 |
| Aspic, Seafood | 1 Serv. | 2 | Bacon-Tomato-Lettuce Sandwich | 1 | 30 |
| Aspic, Tomato | Av. Serv. | 9 | Bacon Vinegar Salad Dressing | 1 Tbsp. | 1 |
| Aster Leaves | 4 Ozs. | T | Bagel | 1 | 23 |
| Asti Wine (Gancia) | 4 Fl. Oz. | 24 | Baked Alaska | Av. Serv. | 48 |
| Atlantic Herring | 4 Ozs. | 0 | Baked Apple With Sugar 2 Tbsp. | 1 Lg. | 47 |
| Au Gratin, Macaroni | Av. Serv. | 30 | Baked Apple & Cheese | 1 Serv. | 21 |
| Au Gratin, Potatoes | Av. Serv. | 16 | Baked Apple With Cream | | |
| Au Gratin, Seafood | 1/2 Cup | 12 | & Sugar | 1 Sm. | 47 |

10

| FOOD | AMT. | CARB. GRAMS | FOOD | AMT. | CARB. GRAMS |
|---|---|---|---|---|---|
| Baked Apple Delight | 1 Serv. | 19 | Banana Bread | 1 Sl. | 22 |
| Baked Apple With 2 Ozs. | | | Banana Cake | Av. Serv. | 36 |
| Milk & Sugar | 1 Sm. | 50 | Banana Cake Mix: | | |
| Baked Bananas | 1 Med. | 23 | (Betty Crocker) Chiquita Banana | 1 Oz. | 23 |
| Baked Bass | 4 Ozs. | 0 | (Pillsbury) | 1 Oz. | 22 |
| Baked Beans | 1 Cup | 48 | (Pillsbury) Loaf Cake | 1 Oz. | 22 |
| Baked Beans (Canned) | 1/2 Cup | 24 | Banana Cream Pie | Av. Serv. | 56 |
| Baked Beans With Pork & | | | (Tastykake) | 1 Pc. | 20 |
| Molasses (Canned) | 1/2 Cup | 19 | Frozen (Banquet) | 1 Pc. | 10 |
| Baked Beans With Tomato | | | Frozen (Mrs. Smith's) | 1 Pc. | 11 |
| (Canned) | 1/2 Cup | 24 | Banana Cream Pie Filling Mix | | |
| Baked Bluefish | Av. Serv. | 0 | (Jell-O) | 1/2 Cup | 60 |
| Baked Or Broiled Lobster | Av. Serv. | 1 | Banana Cream Pudding Mix: | | |
| Baked Browned Chicken | | | Instant (Jell-O) | 1 Cup | 61 |
| Breasts | Av. Serv. | 1 | Instant (Royal) | 1 Cup | 60 |
| Baked Butterfish | Av. Serv. | 0 | Regular (Jell-O) | 1 Cup | 62 |
| Baked Cabbage Mountain Style | 4 Ozs. | 5 | Regular (My-T-Fine) | 2 Ozs. | 54 |
| Baked Capon | Av. Serv. | 0 | Banana Crisps (Epicure) | 1 Oz. | 19 |
| Baked Chicken | Av. Serv. | 0 | Banana Custard | Av. Serv. | 24 |
| Baked Clams & Chicken | 1 Serv. | 6 | Banana Custard Pudding | | |
| Baked Clams Italian Style | 8 | 8 | With Meringue | 1/2 Cup | 19 |
| Baked Cod | 4 Ozs. | 0 | Banana Filling | 1 Layer Of Cake | 40 |
| Baked Hake | 1 Serv. | 0 | Banana, Fresh | 1 Lg. | 46 |
| Baked Ham | Av. Serv. | 0 | Banana, Fried | 1 Med. | 35 |
| Baked Lentils | 4 Ozs. | 20 | Banana Fritters | 1 Av. | 12 |
| Baked Pork Chops | 2 | 0 | Banana Liqueur (Leroux): | | |
| Baked Red Snapper | Av. Serv. | 0 | 56 proof | 1 Fl. Oz. | 11 |
| Baked Salmon | 1 Serv. | 0 | 100 proof | 1 Fl. Oz. | 9 |
| Baked Shad | Av. Serv. | 0 | Banana & Nut Salad | 1 Serv. | 15 |
| Baked Summer Squash | 4 Ozs. | 5 | Banana & Orange Salad | 1/2 Each | 23 |
| Baked Sweet Potatoes | 5 Ozs. | 45 | Banana & Peanut Salad | 1 Serv. | 34 |
| Baked Yams | 5 Ozs. | 36 | Banana Pudding Mix | | |
| Bahia Club, Cocktail | 1 Gl. | 5 | Regular (Royal) | 1 Cup | 54 |
| Baking Powder (Royal) | 1/2 Tsp. | T | Banana Salad | 1 Serv. | 15 |
| Baking Powder Biscuits | 1 Lg. | 15 | Banana Scallops | 1 Serv. | 31 |
| Bakon Delites (Wise): | | | Banana Short Cake | Av. Serv. | 44 |
| Regular | 1 Cup | 0 | Bananas, Sliced | 1 Lg. | 30 |
| Barbecue Flavored | 1 Cup | 0 | Banana Soft Drink (Yoo-Hoo): | | |
| Bali Hai Wine (Italian Swiss | | | Regular | 8 Fl. Ozs. | 24 |
| Colony—Gold Medal) | 4 Fl. Ozs. | 12 | High-protein | 8 Fl. Ozs. | 33 |
| Balls, Codfish | 1 Av. | 5 | Banana Split | 1 | 75 |
| Balls, Matzoh | 1 Av. | 17 | Banana Split, Ice Cream Sundae | 1 | 75 |
| Balls, Meat | 1-2 Ozs. | 2 | Banana Split, Royal | 1 Serv. | 75 |
| Balls, Meat & Spaghetti | 2 Av. | 16 | Banana Tea Bread | 1 Sl. | 22 |
| Balls, Popcorn With Syrup | Av. | 12 | Banana Whip Pudding | 1/2 Cup | 15 |
| Balls, Sour | 6-1 Oz. | 28 | Bar, Average Candies | 1 Bar | 7 |
| Balm | 1/8 Tsp. | 0 | Barbados Red Rum Swizzle | 10 Oz. Gl. | 5 |
| Baltimore Cocktail | 1 Gl. | 10 | Barbecue Beef Sandwich | 1 | 24 |
| Bamboo Cocktail | 1 Gl. | 7 | Barbecue Pork Sandwich | 1 | 24 |
| Bamboo Shoots | 2/3 Cup | 5 | Barbecue Sauce | 1 Tbsp. | T |
| Banana (A-C) | 1 Med. | 23 | Barbecue Seasoning (Lawry's): | | |
| Banana, Baked | 1 Med. | 23 | Bar-B-Q | 1 Pkg. | 98 |
| Banana Bread | 1/4 Loaf | 94 | Sweet 'N Sour | 1 Pkg. | 88 |

11

| FOOD | AMT. | CARB. GRAMS | FOOD | AMT. | CARB. GRAMS |
|---|---|---|---|---|---|
| Barbecued Beef | Av. Serv. | 0 | (Heinz) Vegetarian | 1 Cup | 50 |
| Barbecued Chicken | Av. Serv. | 0 | Beans, Baked with Tomato | | |
| Barbecued Lamb | Av. Serv. | 0 | (Canned) | 1/2 Cup | 24 |
| Barbecued Spareribs | 6 | 1 | Beans, Baked With Pork | | |
| Barbecued Steaks | 1 Serv. | T | & Molasses (Canned) | 1/2 Cup | 30 |
| Barbecued Stuffed Patties | 1 Serv. | 3 | Beans, Barbecue | | |
| Barbera Wine | | | (Campbell) | 4 Ozs. | 25 |
| (Louis M. Martini) | 3 Fl. Ozs. | T | Beans, Black-Soup | 1 Cup | 17 |
| Bardolino Wine, Italian red | | | Beans, Butter, Cooked | 1/2 Cup | 23 |
| (Antinori) | 3 Fl. Ozs. | 6 | Beans & Frankfurter (Canned): | | |
| Barley | 1/2 Cup | 80 | (Campbell) | 6 Ozs. | 27 |
| Barley Cereal, Dry | 1/2 Cup | 88 | (Heinz) | 6 Ozs. | 27 |
| Barley & Mushroom Soup | 1 Cup | 13 | Beans & Frankfurter Dinner | | |
| Barley, Pearled, Light, Dry | 1/2 Cup | 80 | Frozen: | | |
| Barley Soup | 1 Cup | 13 | (Banquet) | 1 Dinner | 70 |
| Barracuda | Av. Serv. | 0 | (Morton) | 1 Dinner | 57 |
| Bars, Chocolate | 1 Av. | 23 | (Swanson) | 1 Dinner | 70 |
| Bars, Figs | 2 | 22 | Beans, Lima, Frozen | 3-1/2 Ozs. | 18 |
| Basil | 1/8 Tsp. | 0 | Beans, Green-Cooked | 1 Cup | 3 |
| Bass | 1/4 Lb. | 0 | Beans, Green (Canned) | 1 Cup | 6 |
| Bass, Broiled | 4 Ozs. | 0 | Beans, Green or Snap: | | |
| Bass (Canned) | 4 Ozs. | 0 | (Butter Kernel) | 1 Cup | 9 |
| Bavarian, Orange, Pudding | 1 Serv. | 40 | Blue Lake (Cannon) | 4 Ozs. | 6 |
| B & B Liqueur | | | (Fall River) | 1 Cup | 9 |
| (Julius Wile) | 1 Fl. Oz. | 5 | (Green Giant) | 1 Cup | 9 |
| Bavarian Pie Filling | | | (Stokely-Van Camp) | 1/2 Cup | 5 |
| (Lucky Leaf) | 4 Ozs. | 25 | Dietetic: | | |
| Bavarian Pie or Pudding Mix: | | | (Blue Boy) | 4 Ozs. | 5 |
| Cream (My-T-Fine) | 2 Ozs. | 53 | (Diet Delight) | 1 Cup | 6 |
| Custard, Rice-A-Roni | 1/2 Cup | 21 | (S and W) Nutradiet | 4 Ozs. | 3 |
| Bavarian-Style Vegetables | | | (Tillie Lewis) | 1 Cup | 7 |
| (Birds Eye) Frozen | 1 Pkg. | 36 | Beans, Green-Strained (Canned) | 1 Oz. | 1 |
| Bay Leaf | 1/4 Tsp. | 0 | Beans, Green, Frozen Cut | 3-1/2 Ozs. | 8 |
| Bean Curd | 1 Serv. | 3 | (Birds Eye) | 1 Cup | 10 |
| Bean Soup | 1 Cup | 17 | (Stokely-Van Camp) | 4 Ozs. | 7 |
| Bean Sprouts | 4 Ozs. | 3 | (Birds Eye) | 1 Cup | 10 |
| Bean Sprouts, Mung | 1 Cup | 14 | (Blue Goose) | 4 Ozs. | 6 |
| Bean Sprouts, Soy | 1 Cup | 16 | French-style (Birds Eye) | 1 Cup | 10 |
| Beans, Baked | 1 Cup | 48 | French-style, with Toasted | | |
| Beans, Baked (Canned) | 1/4 Cup | 24 | Almonds (Birds Eye) | 1 Cup | 11 |
| (B & M) | 1 Cup | 60 | French-style, with Sauteed | | |
| (Heinz) | 1 Cup | 60 | Mushrooms (Birds Eye) | 1 Cup | 11 |
| (Campbell) | 4 Ozs. | 21 | In Butter Sauce (Birds Eye) | 1 Cup | 9 |
| (Cannon) | 4 Ozs. | 21 | In Butter Sauce (Green Giant) | 4 Ozs. | 5 |
| (Hunt's) | 4 Ozs. | 21 | In Mushroom Sauce | | |
| (Green Giant) | 1 Cup | 48 | (Green Giant) | 4 Ozs. | 7 |
| (Heinz) Boston-style | 1 Cup | 62 | Beans & Ground Beef | | |
| (Green Giant) With Pork | 1 Cup | 46 | Canned (Campbell) | 4 Ozs. | 17 |
| (Heinz) With Pork | 1 Cup | 42 | Beans, Italian, Frozen: | | |
| With Tomato Sauce: | | | (Birds Eye) | 1 Cup | 10 |
| (Heinz) Campside, | | | In Butter Sauce (Green Giant) | | |
| Smoky Beans | 1 Cup | 50 | Boil-in-the-bag | 4 Ozs. | 5 |

| FOOD | AMT. | CARB. GRAMS | FOOD | AMT. | CARB. GRAMS |
|---|---|---|---|---|---|
| Beans, Jelly | 15 | 24 | Beans, Soy | 1/2 Cup | 6 |
| Beans, Kidney or Red, Canned: | | | Beans, Soy, Dry | 1/2 Cup | 37 |
| (Butter Kernel) | 1 Cup | 40 | Beans, Soy, Flour | 1 Cup | 14 |
| Red (Hunt's) | 4 Ozs. | 18 | Beans, Soy (Immature) | 1/2 Cup | 3 |
| Beans, Kidney | 1 Cup | 37 | Beans, Soy, Sauce | 1 Tsp. | 0 |
| Beans, Kidney, Baked | 1 Cup | 37 | Bean Sprouts, Canned | | |
| Beans, Kidney (Canned) | 1 Cup | 37 | (Chun King) | 3 Ozs. | 2 |
| Red Kidney & Chili Gravy | | | Beans, String (A-B2-C) | 1 Cup | 5 |
| (Nalley's) | 4 Ozs. | 18 | Beans, String (Canned) | 1 Cup | 5 |
| Beans, Kidney, Dried | 1/2 Cup | 64 | Beans, String, Fr. | 1 Cup | 5 |
| Beans, Lima (B1-C) | 1 Cup | 28 | Beans, Wax (Canned) | 1 Cup | 5 |
| Beans, Lima (Canned) | 1/2 Cup | 24 | Beans, Wax, Fresh | 1 Cup | 5 |
| With Ham (Nalley's) | 4 Ozs. | 14 | Beans, White Marrow, Dry | 1/2 Cup | 62 |
| Dietetic (Blue Boy) | 4 Ozs. | 12 | (Sinsheimer) | 2 Ozs. | 35 |
| Beans, Lima, Dried | 1/2 Cup | 38 | (Uncle Ben's) | 1 Cup | 31 |
| Beans, Lima, Frozen: | | | Beans, Yellow (Canned) | 1 Cup | 5 |
| Baby Butter Beans | | | (Butter Kernel) | 1 Cup | 9 |
| (Birds Eye) | 1/2 Cup | 58 | (Green Giant) | 1 Cup | 9 |
| (Birds Eye) | 4 Ozs. | 26 | (Stokely-Van Camp) | 4 Ozs. | 5 |
| (Stokely-Van Camp) | 4 Ozs. | 26 | Dietetic (Blue Boy) | 4 Ozs. | 3 |
| In Butter Sauce | | | Beans, Yellow, Fresh | 1 Cup | 5 |
| (Green Giant) | 4 Ozs. | 18 | Beans, Yellow, Frozen | | |
| Fordhooks (Birds Eye) | 1 Cup | 36 | (Birds Eye) | 1 Cup | 11 |
| Beans, Mung, Dried | 1/2 Cup | 68 | Beaujolais Wine, French Burgundy: | | |
| Beans, Navy (B1-B2) | 1 Cup | 25 | (Barton & Guestier) St. Louis | 4 Fl. Ozs. | T |
| Beans, Navy (Canned) | 1/2 Cup | 19 | (Chanson) St. Vincent | 4 Fl. Ozs. | 8 |
| Beans, Navy, Dry | 1/2 Cup | 48 | Beaune Wine: | | |
| Beans, Navy, Soup | 8 Oz. Cup | 27 | Clos des Feves, French Burgundy | | |
| Beans, Pea, Dried | 1/2 Cup | 18 | (Chanson) | 4 Fl. Ozs. | 8 |
| Beans, Pinto, Dry | 1/2 Cup | 63 | St. Vincent, French Burgundy | | |
| (Sinsheimer) | 1 Oz. | 17 | (Chanson) | 4 Fl. Ozs. | 8 |
| (Uncle Ben's) Quick-cooked, | | | Beautiful Brunch Eggs | 2 | 6 |
| Including Broth | 1 Cup | 34 | Bechamel Sauce | 1/2 Cup | 7 |
| Beans, Pinto, Soup | 8 Ozs. | 17 | Beefaroni, Canned | | |
| Beans, Red Mexican, Dry | 1/2 Cup | 64 | (Chef Boy-Ar-Dee) | 4 Ozs. | 14 |
| Beans, Refried, Canned | | | Beef & Beef Stock | | |
| (Rosarita) | 4 Ozs. | 17 | (Bunker Hill) | 15-Oz. Can | 0 |
| Beans, Snap, Green | | | Beef, Broiled (B2) | Av. Serv. | 0 |
| (Canned) | 8 Oz. Cup | 6 | Beef Bouillon | 1 Cup | 0 |
| Beans, Snap, Green, | | | Beef Bouillon/Broth: | | |
| Fresh | 8 Oz. Cup | 5 | (Croyden House) | 1 Tsp. | 2 |
| Bean Soup, Canned: | | | (Herb-Ox) | 1 Cube | T |
| (Manischewitz) | 4 Ozs. | 8 | (Herb-Ox) Instant | 1 Packet | T |
| With Bacon (Campbell) | 4 Ozs. | 19 | (Maggi) | 1 Cube | T |
| With Smoked Ham (Heinz) | | | (Maggi) Instant | 1 Tsp. | T |
| Great American | 1 Cup | 22 | (Wyler's) | 1 Cube | T |
| With Smoked Pork (Heinz) | 1 Cup | 19 | (Wyler's) Instant | 1 Tsp. | T |
| Bean Soup, Black, Canned: | | | Beef Brains | Av. Serv. | 2 |
| (Campbell) | 4 Ozs. | 13 | Beef Brains, Fried | 6 Ozs. | 2 |
| (Crosse & Blackwell) | 4 Ozs. | 9 | Beef Brains, Scrambled | 6 Ozs. | 2 |
| Bean Soup, Lima, Canned | | | Beef, Brisket | Av. Serv. | 0 |
| (Manischewitz) | 4 Ozs. | 7 | Beef, Broiled (B2) | Av. Serv. | 0 |

| FOOD | AMT. | CARB. GRAMS | FOOD | AMT. | CARB. GRAMS |
|------|------|-------------|------|------|-------------|
| Beef Broth | 1 Cup | 0 | Beef, Porterhouse Steak | Av. Serv. | 0 |
| Beefburgers | 2 Ozs. | 0 | Beef Pot Pie | 4-1/2 in. diam. | 37 |
| Beef (Canned, Infant Food) | 4 Ozs. | 0 | Beef, Pot Roast | Av. Serv. | 0 |
| Beef, Chipped | 3 Ozs. | 0 | Beef Puffs, Hors d'Oeuvre, | | |
| (Armour Star) | 2 Ozs. | 0 | Frozen (Durkee) | 1 Piece | 3 |
| Frozen, Creamed (Banquet) | | | Beef Ragout, | | |
| Cookin' Bag | 4 Ozs. | 10 | Frozen (Swanson) | 1 Pkg. | 13 |
| Beef, Chipped, Creamed | 3 Ozs. | 0 | Beef, Rib Roast-Rolled | Av. Serv. | 0 |
| Beef, Chopped (B2) | 1/4 Lb. | 0 | Beef, Rib Roast | Av. Serv. | 0 |
| Beef, Chopped, Canned | | | Beef, Rib Roast-Standing | Av. Serv. | 0 |
| (Hormel) | 1 Can | 2 | Beef Roast | Av. Serv. | 0 |
| Beef, Chuck (Pot Roast) | Av Serv. | 0 | Beef Roast (Canned) | Av. Serv. | 0 |
| Beef Consomme | 1 Cup | 0 | Beef Roast, Hash | 1/2 Cup | 8 |
| Beef, Corned | 4 Ozs. | 0 | Beef Roast Rump | Av. Serv. | 0 |
| Beef Croquettes | Av. Serv. | 9 | Beef, Round Steak | Av. Serv. | 0 |
| Beef Dinner, Frozen: | | | Beef, Round Steak, | | |
| (Banquet) | Dinner | 20 | Bottom Cooked | Av. Serv. | 0 |
| (Morton) | Dinner | 20 | Beef, Short Ribs, Braised | Av. Serv. | 0 |
| (Swanson) | Dinner | 32 | Beef, Sirloin Tip | Av. Serv. | 0 |
| (Swanson) 3-course | Dinner | 65 | Beef, Sliced, with Barbecue Sauce: | | |
| Chopped (Banquet) | Dinner | 27 | Buffet (Banquet) | 5 Ozs. | 12 |
| Chopped (Swanson) | Dinner | 40 | Cookin' Bag (Banquet) | 5 Ozs. | 12 |
| Stew (Tom Thumb) | 1 Lb. | 27 | Beef Soup, Canned: | | |
| Beef, Dried | 3 Ozs. | 0 | Condensed (Campbell) | 4 Ozs. | 10 |
| Beef Drippings | Av. Serv | 0 | Barley (Manischewitz) | 4 Ozs. | 6 |
| Beef, Filet Mignon (B2) | Av. Serv. | 0 | Barley, Mix (Wyler's) | 1 Cup | 13 |
| Beef, Flank, Cooked | 4 Ozs. | 0 | Broth, Condensed | | |
| Beef Goulash: | | | (Campbell) | 1 Cup | 5 |
| Canned (Heinz) | 8 Ozs. | 18 | Cabbage (Manischewitz) | 1 Cup | 9 |
| Seasoning Mix (Lawry's) | 1 Pkg. | 24 | Noodle, Condensed | | |
| Beef Goulash Elegant | Av. Serv. | 3 | (Campbell) | 1 Cup | 16 |
| Beef Hamburger | 2 Ozs. | 0 | (Heinz) | 1 Cup | 5 |
| Beef Hash, Roast: | | | (Manischewitz) | 1 Cup | 8 |
| Canned (Hormel) | | | With Dumplings (Heinz) | | |
| Mary Kitchen | 15 Ozs. | 18 | Great American | 1 Cup | 10 |
| Frozen (Stouffer's) | 11-1/2 Ozs. | 11 | Vegetable (Manischewitz) | 1 Cup | 9 |
| Beef Heart | 3 Ozs. | T | Beef Soup Mix, Noodle: | | |
| Beef Heart, Baked | Av. Serv. | 0 | (Lipton) | 1 Pkg. | 32 |
| Beef Heart, Broiled | Av. Serv. | 0 | (Wyler's) | 1 Cup | 9 |
| Beef Jerky | | | Beef Steak | Av. Serv. | 0 |
| (Giant Snacks) | 1 Oz. | 0 | Beef Steak, Flank | Av. Serv. | 0 |
| Beef, Kidney (A-B2) | Av. Serv. | 2 | Beef Steak & Kidney Pie | Av. Serv. | 24 |
| Beef, Kidney, Broiled | 1/2 Cup | 1 | Beef Steak, Planked | Av. Serv. | 0 |
| Beef, Liver (A-B1-B2-C) | Av. Serv. | 6 | Beef Stew | 1 Cup | 14 |
| Beef Pie | Av. Serv. | 32 | Canned: | | |
| Frozen: | | | (Armour Star) | 8 Ozs. | 12 |
| (Banquet) | 4 Ozs. | 20 | (Austex) | 8 Ozs. | 16 |
| (Morton) | 4 Ozs. | 18 | (B & M) | 8 Ozs. | 14 |
| (Stouffer's) | 4 Ozs. | 17 | (Bounty) | 8 Ozs. | 16 |
| (Swanson) | 4 Ozs. | 18 | (Bunker Hill) | 8 Ozs. | 9 |
| (Swanson) deep dish | 4 Ozs. | 13 | (Dinty Moore) | 8 Ozs. | 12 |
| Beef, Plate | 4 Sl. | 0 | (Heinz) | 8 Ozs. | 7 |

14

| FOOD | AMT. | CARB. GRAMS | FOOD | AMT. | CARB. GRAMS |
|---|---|---|---|---|---|
| (Nalley's) | 8 Ozs. | 19 | Low Carbohydrate: | | |
| (Wilson) | 8 Ozs. | 16 | Dia-beer | 8 Fl. Ozs. | 3 |
| Dietetic (Claybourne) | 8 Ozs. | 18 | Gablinger's | 8 Fl. Ozs. | T |
| Meatball (Hormel) | 8 Ozs. | 28 | Meister Brau Lite | 8 Fl. Ozs. | 1 |
| Frozen, Buffet (Banquet) | 8 Ozs. | 21 | Beer, Ginger | 6 Ozs. | 28 |
| Beef Stew, Irish | 1 Cup | 15 | Beer, Half & Half | 8 Ozs. | 8 |
| Beef Stew Seasoning Mix: | | | Beer, Lager | 8 Ozs. | 10 |
| (French's) | 1 Pkg. | 14 | Beer, Root | 6 Ozs. | 18 |
| (Lawry's) | 1 Pkg. | 24 | Bee's Kiss Cocktail | 1 Cktl. Gl. | 5 |
| Beef Stroganoff | Av. Serv. | 7 | Beet Borscht | 1 Cup | 6 |
| Beef Suet | 3-1/2 Ozs. | 0 | Beet & Cabbage Relish | Av. Serv. | 8 |
| Beef, Sweetbreads (C) | Sm. Serv. | 0 | Beet Cups | 1/2 Cup | 8 |
| Beef, Swiss Steak | Av. Serv. | 15 | Beet Greens (A-C) Cooked | 1 Cup | 4 |
| Beef Tartar Ala Caesar | Av. Serv. | 5 | Beet Sugar | Tsp. | 4 |
| Beef, T-Bone Steak | Av. Serv. | 0 | Beets | 1/2 Cup | 10 |
| Beef, Tenderloin Steak | Av. Serv. | 0 | Beets, Buttered (1 Tsp.) | 1/2 Cup | 9 |
| Beef Tongue, Broiled | 3 Ozs. | T | Beets (Canned) | 1/2 Cup | 9 |
| Beef Tongue (Canned) | 2 Av. Sl. | 0 | (Butter Kernel) | 1 Cup | 18 |
| Beef Tongue, Fresh | 2 Av. Sl. | 0 | (Comstock-Greenwood) | 4 Ozs. | 10 |
| Beef Tongue, Pickled | 2 Av. Sl. | 0 | (Fall River) | 1 Cup | 18 |
| Beef Tongue, Potted, Deviled | 1 Tbsp. | T | Pickled | | |
| Beef Tripe | Av. Serv. | 0 | (Comstock-Greenwood) | 4 Ozs. | 14 |
| Beef & Vegetable Stew | 1 Cup | 15 | Beets (Canned, Infant) | 4 Ozs. | 8 |
| Beer | 1-12 Oz. Bot. | 13 | Beets, Cooked | 1 Cup | 16 |
| Beer, Birch | 6 Ozs. | 28 | Dietetic: | | |
| Beer, Bock | 8 Ozs. | 15 | Whole (Blue Boy) | 12 Small | 8 |
| Beer, Canned: | | | Diced (Blue Boy) | 4 Ozs. | 5 |
| Buckeye | 8 Fl. Ozs. | 8 | Sliced (Blue Boy) | 15 Slices | 8 |
| Budweiser, 4.9% alcohol | 8 Fl. Ozs. | 8 | Sliced (S & W) Nutradiet | 4 Ozs. | 6 |
| Budweiser, 3.9% alcohol | 8 Fl. Ozs. | 8 | (Tillie Lewis) | 1 Cup | 18 |
| Busch Bavarian, | | | Frozen (Birds Eye) | 1 Cup | 26 |
| 4.9% alcohol | 8 Fl. Ozs. | 8 | Beets, Harvard | Av. Serv. | 9 |
| Busch Bavarian, | | | Beets, Pickled | 1 Cup | 20 |
| 3.9% alcohol | 8 Fl. Ozs. | 8 | Beets, Raw | 2 | 10 |
| Gold Medal | 8 Fl. Ozs. | 6 | Beets, Strained (Canned) | 1 Oz. | 2 |
| Hamm's | 8 Fl. Ozs. | 8 | Bell Peppers | 1 Med. | 3 |
| Knickerbocker | 8 Fl. Ozs. | 8 | Bel Paese Cheese | 1-1/2 Ozs. | T |
| Meister Brau Premium | 8 Fl. Ozs. | 13 | Benedictine | 1 Oz. | 7 |
| Meister Brau Premium | | | Benedictine Cordial | Pony | 7 |
| Draft | 8 Fl. Ozs. | 8 | Benedictine Liqueur | | |
| Michelob, 4.9% alcohol | 8 Fl. Ozs. | 8 | (Julius Wile) | 1 Fl. Oz. | 10 |
| Narragansett, 4.7% alcohol | 8 Fl. Ozs. | 9 | Bermuda Onions, Raw | 1 | 10 |
| North Star, Regular | 8 Fl. Ozs. | 10 | Bernkasteler, German Moselle | | |
| North Star, 3.2 low gravity | 8 Fl. Ozs. | 9 | Wine (Deinhard) | 4 Fl. Ozs. | 1 |
| Pfeifer, Regular | 8 Fl. Ozs. | 10 | Bernkasteler Doktor, German | | |
| Pfeifer, 3.2 low gravity | 8 Fl. Ozs. | 9 | Moselle Wine (Deinhard) | 4 Fl. Ozs. | 1 |
| Rheingold | 8 Fl. Ozs. | 9 | Berry, Blueberries, Fresh | 1/2 Cup | 7 |
| Schmidt, Regular | 8 Fl. Ozs. | 10 | Berry, Charlotte | 1 Serv. | 46 |
| Schmidt, Extra Special, | | | Berry Jams | 1 Tbsp. | 14 |
| Regular | 8 Fl. Ozs. | 10 | Berry Pie | Av. Pc. | 57 |
| Schmidt, 3.2 low gravity | 8 Fl. Ozs. | 9 | Best Beef Stew | Av. Serv. | 14 |
| Yuengling Premium | 8 Fl. Ozs. | 10 | Bev., Apricot Champagne | 1 Gl. | 3 |

15

| FOOD | AMT. | CARB. GRAMS |
|---|---|---|
| Bev., Black Stripe (Honey) | 1 Gl. | 15 |
| Bev., Bloody Mary | 4 Ozs. | 5 |
| Bev., Carbonated | Av. | 21 |
| Bev., Caribbean Hot Swizzle | 12 Oz. Gl. | 7 |
| Bev., Champagne Cup | 1 Gl. | 11 |
| Bev., Chaud Vin | 1 Serv. | 37 |
| Bev., Chocolate With Milk | 1 Cup | 17 |
| Bev., Comfort, Southern Mint Julep | 1 Gl. | 0 |
| Bev., Cutter Fog | 14 Oz. Gl. | 7 |
| Bev., Diablo El Mexican | 10 Ozs. | 13 |
| Bev., Falkland Island Warmer | 1 Gl. | 4 |
| Bev., Flamingo | 12 Ozs. | 21 |
| Bev., Fruit Buttermilk | 1 Serv. | 25 |
| Bev., Haole Pikia | 10 Ozs. | T |
| Bev., Hot Benefactor | 1 Serv. | 8 |
| Bev., Hot Buttered Rum Batter | 1 Tsp. | 4 |
| Bev., Hot Egg Nog | 1 Serv. | 17 |
| Bev., Mahukona | 10 Ozs. | 4 |
| Bev., Martinique Swizzle | 14 Ozs. | 5 |
| Bev., Bloody Mary | 4 Ozs. | 5 |
| Bev., Mojito | 10 Ozs. | 7 |
| Bev., Mojito Criollo | 8 Ozs. | 11 |
| Bev., North Side Special | 12 Ozs. | 28 |
| Bev., Pickup Rum | 10 Ozs. | 2 |
| Bev., Pino Frio | 14 Ozs. | 4 |
| Bev., Puerto Rico Swizzle | 14 Ozs. | 10 |
| Bev., Punch, Thanksgiving | 4 Ozs. | 26 |
| Bev., Queen's Park Swizzle | 14 Ozs. | 11 |
| Bev., Rum Float | 6 Ozs. | 7 |
| Bev., Rum Mocha | 14 Ozs. | 28 |
| Bev., Shingle Stain | 12 Ozs. | 3 |
| Bev., Squash Bourbon | 14 Ozs. | 15 |
| Bev., Tortuga | 14 Ozs. | 3 |
| Bev., Wahine | 1 Serv. | 4 |
| Bianca Della Costa Toscana, Italian White Wine (Antinori) | 3 Fl. Ozs. | 6 |
| Bif (Wilson), Canned Luncheon Meat | 3 Ozs. | 1 |
| Bing Cherries Charmaine | 1 Serv. | 33 |
| Bing Cherries, In Syrup (Canned) | 1 Cup | 59 |
| Birch Beer, Soft Drink: | | |
| (Canada Dry) | 3 Fl. Ozs. | 10 |
| (Yukon Club) | 3 Fl. Ozs. | 11 |
| Bird's Nest Norge | Av. Serv. | 14 |
| Birds, Veal | 2 Av. | 22 |
| Biscuit, Canape Bases | 1 Med. | 23 |
| Biscuit Mix: | | |
| Bisquick (Betty Crocker) | 1 Lb. | 304 |
| New Bisquick (Betty Crocker) | 1 Lb. | 300 |
| Biscuit, Shredded Wheat | 1 | 14 |
| Biscuit, Tortoni | 1 Sm. | 14 |
| Biscuit, Yeast | 1 Lg. | 15 |
| Biscuits | 1 Sm. | 14 |
| Biscuits (Baking Powder) | 1 Lg. | 15 |
| Biscuit, Buttermilk | 1 Lg. | 15 |
| Biscuits, Cream | 1 Sm. | 14 |
| Biscuits, Egg (Stella D'oro): | | |
| Dietetic | 1 Piece | 6 |
| Roman | 1 Piece | 19 |
| Biscuit Dough: | | |
| (Pillsbury) Ballard, ovenready | 4 Ozs. | 52 |
| (Pillsbury) Baking Powder: | | |
| Regular | 4 Ozs. | 44 |
| Buttermilk | 4 Ozs. | 44 |
| (Pillsbury) Buttermilk: | | |
| Regular | 4 Ozs. | 52 |
| Extra Light | 4 Ozs. | 48 |
| Hungry Jack, Regular | 4 Ozs. | 48 |
| Hungry Jack, Flaky | 4 Ozs. | 44 |
| Tenderflake | 4 Ozs. | 44 |
| (Pillsbury) Country Style | 4 Ozs. | 51 |
| (Pillsbury) Hungry Jack: | | |
| Butter Tastin' | 4 Ozs. | 42 |
| Flaky | 4 Ozs. | 42 |
| (Pillsbury) Tenderburst | 4 Ozs. | 44 |
| Biscuits, Short Cake | 1 | 27 |
| Biscuits, Sour Milk | 1 Sm. | 14 |
| Biscuits, Southern Beaten | 1 Med. | 20 |
| Bishop's Cooler Rum | 10 Ozs. | 15 |
| Bisque, Chicken | 1 Serv. | 6 |
| Bisquick Flour | 1/2 Cup | 84 |
| Bitter Chocolate | 1 Oz. | 8 |
| Bitter Lemon, Soft Drink: | | |
| (Canada Dry) | 8 Fl. Ozs. | 28 |
| (Hoffman) | 8 Fl. Ozs. | 28 |
| (Schweppes) | 8 Fl. Ozs. | 31 |
| Bitter Orange, Soft Drink: | | |
| (Schweppes) | 8 Fl. Ozs. | 30 |
| Bitters (Angostura) | 1 Tsp. | 2 |
| Blackberry & Apricot Jam | 1 Tbsp. | 10 |
| Blackberry Brandy | Shot | 0 |
| Blackberry Cordial | Pony | 7 |
| Blackberry Crisps (Epicure) | 1 Oz. | 21 |
| Blackberry Jam | 1 Tbsp. | 13 |
| Blackberry Jam, Diatetic: | | |
| (Dia-Mel) | 1 Tbsp. | 5 |
| (Diet Delight) | 1 Tbsp. | 1 |
| Blackberry Jelly | Tbsp. | 13 |
| Low Calorie (Slenderella) | 1 Tbsp. | 5 |
| Blackberry Juice | 6 Ozs. | 12 |
| Blackberry Liqueur: | | |
| (Bols) | 1 Fl. Oz. | 0 |

| FOOD | AMT. | CARB. GRAMS |
|------|------|-------------|
| (Hiram Walker) | 1 Fl. Oz. | 12 |
| Blackberry Pie | Av. Serv. | 38 |
| (Tastykake) | 4 Ozs. | 60 |
| Frozen (Banquet) | 4 Ozs. | 44 |
| Blackberry Pie Filling | | |
| (Lucky Leaf) | 4 Ozs. | 31 |
| Blackberry Preserves | Tbsp. | 13 |
| Blackberry Wine | | |
| (Mogen David) | 3 Fl. Ozs. | 18 |
| Blackberries (Canned), | | |
| Low Cal. | 1 Cup | 18 |
| Blackberries, Syrup (Canned) | 1 Cup | 44 |
| Blackberries (Canned, | | |
| Water Packed) | 1 Cup | 13 |
| Blackberries, Fresh | 1 Cup | 13 |
| Blackberries, Fresh | | |
| With 2 Tbsp. Cream | 1 Cup | 16 |
| Black Coffee | 1 Cup | T |
| Black Currant Juice | 1 Cup | 34 |
| Black-Eye Peas, | | |
| Drained (Canned) | 1/2 Cup | 17 |
| Black Raspberries | 1 Cup | 16 |
| Black Stripe Bev., Honey | 1 Gl. | 15 |
| Black Stripe Bev., Molasses | 1 Gl. | 15 |
| Blackstrap Molasses | 1 Tbsp. | 11 |
| Black Walnuts | 11 Halv. | 8 |
| Black & White Soda (Cola) | 8 Ozs. | 27 |
| Blanc Mange | 1/2 Cup | 20 |
| Blanc Mange | | |
| Chocolate Pudding | 1/2 Cup | 23 |
| Blanc Mange Vanilla Pudding | 1/2 Cup | 20 |
| Bleu Cheese | 1-1/2 Ozs. | T |
| Blintzes, Cheese | 1 Av. | 8 |
| Blintzes, Jelly | 1 Av. | 35 |
| Bloody Mary Bev. | 4 Ozs. | 5 |
| Bloody Mary Mix | | |
| (Bartender's) | 1 Serv. | 5 |
| Blossom, Orange | 3 Ozs. | 8 |
| Blueberries (Canned) | 1/2 Cup | 26 |
| Blueberries, (Canned, Low Cal.) | 1 Cup | 17 |
| Blueberries (Canned, | | |
| Water Pack) | 1/2 Cup | 9 |
| Blueberries, Fresh | 1 Cup | 17 |
| Blueberries, Frozen, Sweetened | 1 Cup | 60 |
| Blueberries, Frozen, | | |
| Unsweetened | 3 Ozs. | 11 |
| Blueberry Cake | Av. Pc. | 20 |
| Blueberry Crisp | 1 Serv. | 46 |
| Blueberry Cream Pie | 1 Pc. | 56 |
| Blueberry Griddle Cakes | 1-4 in. diam. | 12 |
| Blueberry Jam | 1 Tbsp. | 13 |
| Blueberry Muffins | 1 Aver. | 23 |

| FOOD | AMT. | CARB. GRAMS |
|------|------|-------------|
| Blueberry Pie | 1 Pc. | 38 |
| (Tastykake) | 1 Pie | 58 |
| Frozen (Banquet) | 5 Ozs. | 58 |
| (Mrs. Smith's) | 1 Pc. | 20 |
| Blueberry Pie Filling: | | |
| (Lucky Leaf) | 4 Ozs. | 30 |
| Blueberry Preserve, Diatetic | | |
| (Die-Mel) | 1 Tbsp. | 5 |
| Blueberry Syrup, Diatetic | | |
| (Die-Mel) | 1 Tbsp. | 5 |
| Blueberry Tarts | 1 Med. | 21 |
| Blueberry Waffles | 1 Med. | 43 |
| Blue Cheese | 1-1/2 Ozs. | T |
| Blue Cheese Salad Dressing | Av. Serv. | 1 |
| Bluefish | Av. Serv. | 0 |
| Bluefish, Baked | Av. Serv. | 0 |
| Bluefish, Broiled | Av. Serv. | 0 |
| Bluefish, Fried | Av. Serv. | 0 |
| Blue Point (Oysters) | 12 | 7 |
| Blue Point Oysters, Raw | 12 | 7 |
| Bock Beer | 8 Oz. Gl. | 15 |
| Boiled Beef (B2) | Av. Serv. | 0 |
| Boiled Brussels Sprouts | Av. Serv. | 6 |
| Boiled Cabbage | 1 Cup | 7 |
| Boiled Chicken | 1 Serv. | 0 |
| Boiled Chicken (Cold) | 1/2 Sm. | 0 |
| Boiled Eggs (A-B1-B2) | 1 Av. | T |
| Boiled Pig's Feet | 4 Ozs. | 0 |
| Boiled Potato, Peeled | 1 | 23 |
| Bologna | 8 Sl. | 9 |
| Bologna | 1/8 In. Sl. | 1 |
| (Vienna) | 3 Ozs. | 2 |
| (Wilson) | 3 Ozs. | 2 |
| Bologna & Cheese | | |
| Canape Spread | 1 Serv. | 1 |
| Bologna Cups Meat | 2 | 2 |
| Bologna Sandwich | 1 | 26 |
| Bombay Cocktail | 1 | 7 |
| Bon-bon Candies | 1 | 9 |
| Borscht: | | |
| (Manischewitz) | 4 Ozs. | 8 |
| Bosco (Best Foods) | 1 Tbsp. | 10 |
| Boston Bread (Degermed Meal) | 1 Sl. | 22 |
| Boston Brown Bread | 3/4 Sl. | 24 |
| Boston Cookies | 1 | 22 |
| Boston Cream Pie | | |
| Mix (Betty Crocker) | 1 Oz. | 24 |
| Bouillabaisse | 1 Serv. | 13 |
| Bouillabaisse-Table Top | 1 Serv. | 6 |
| Bouillon-Braised Celery | Av. Serv. | 3 |
| Bouillon, Clear (Condensed) | 4 Ozs. | 0 |
| Bouillon Cubes | 1 Cube | 0 |

| FOOD | AMT. | CARB. GRAMS | FOOD | AMT. | CARB. GRAMS |
|---|---|---|---|---|---|
| Bourbon Squash Bev. | 14 Ozs. | 15 | (Leroux) Polish | 1 Fl. Oz. | 8 |
| Bourbon Whiskey, Peach Flavored | | | (Old Mr. Boston) | 1 Fl. Oz. | 8 |
| (Old Mr. Boston) | 1 Fl. Oz. | 8 | (Mr. Boston's) blackberry | | |
| Bourguignonne Snails | 6 Ozs. | 2 | & brandy | 1 Fl. Oz. | 8 |
| Boysenberries, Frozen, | | | Cherry: | | |
| Sweetened | 1 Cup | 54 | (Garnier) | 1 Fl. Oz. | 7 |
| Boysenberries, Frozen, | | | (Hiram Walker) | 1 Fl. Oz. | 7 |
| Unsweetened | 1 Cup | 26 | (Leroux) | 1 Fl. Oz. | 8 |
| Boysenberry Crisps (Epicure) | 1 Oz. | 21 | (Old Mr. Boston) | | |
| Boysenberry Jam | | | wild cherry | 1 Fl. Oz. | 8 |
| Low Calorie (Slenderella) | 1 Tbsp. | 5 | (Mr. Boston's) wild cherry | | |
| Boysenberry Pie, Frozen | | | & brandy | 1 Fl. Oz. | 8 |
| (Banquet) | 1 Oz. | 11 | Coffee: | | |
| Boysenberry Preserve | | | (Garnier) | 1 Fl. Oz. | 7 |
| Low Cal. (Tillie Lewis) | 1 Tbsp. | 2 | (Old Mr. Boston) | 1 Fl. Oz. | 1 |
| Braids Rolls | 1 | 13 | (Leroux) coffee | | |
| Braised Celery | Av. Serv. | 4 | & brandy | 1 Fl. Oz. | 8 |
| Braised Chicken | 1 Serv. | 7 | Ginger: | | |
| Braised Chicken With Dressing | 1 Serv. | 29 | (Garnier) | 1 Fl. Oz. | 4 |
| Braised Heart, Beef | 3 Ozs. | 1 | (Hiram Walker) | 1 Fl. Oz. | 3 |
| Braised Lettuce | 1 Serv. | 4 | (Leroux) | 1 Fl. Oz. | 4 |
| Bran Cereal | 1/2 Cup | 39 | (Leroux) sharp | 1 Fl. Oz. | 4 |
| Bran Breakfast Cereal, | | | (Old Mr. Boston) | 1 Fl. Oz. | 1 |
| Plain: | | | (Mr. Boston's) ginger | | |
| All-Bran (Kellogg's) | 1 Cup | 43 | & brandy | 1 Fl. Oz. | 8 |
| Bran-Buds (Kellogg's) | 1 Cup | 45 | Peach: | | |
| 40% Bran Flakes (Kellogg's) | 1 Cup | 30 | (Garnier) | 1 Fl. Oz. | 7 |
| 40% Bran Flakes (Post) | 1 Cup | 31 | (Hiram Walker) | 1 Fl. Oz. | 7 |
| 100% Bran (Nabisco) | 1 Cup | 41 | (Leroux) | 1 Fl. Oz. | 9 |
| & Prune Flakes (Post) | 1 Cup | 29 | (Old Mr. Boston) | 1 Fl. Oz. | 8 |
| Raisin: | | | (Mr. Boston's) peach | | |
| (Kellogg's) | 1 Cup | 33 | & brandy | 1 Fl. Oz. | 8 |
| (Post) | 1 Cup | 42 | Brandy Fruit Cake | 1 Pc. | 64 |
| Chex (Ralston) | 1 Cup | 29 | Brandy (Imported) | 1 Fl. Oz. | 0 |
| Bran Raisin Bread | 1 Sl. | 17 | Brandy Refrigerated Cake | 1 Pc. | 87 |
| Bran Raisin Cereal | 4 Ozs. | 16 | Brandy Sour | 6 Ozs. | 10 |
| Bran, Whole Cereal | 1/2 Cup | 16 | Braunschweiger | | |
| Brandy, California | 3 Ozs. | 0 | (Wilson) | 1 Oz. | T |
| Brandy Cocktail | 3 Ozs. | 5 | Brazil Nuts—In Shell | 10 | 5 |
| Brandy, Flavored: | | | Brazil Nut No Flour Cake | 1 Sl. | 23 |
| Apricot: | | | Brazil Nuts | 1 Med. | T |
| (Bols) | 1 Fl. Oz. | 7 | Brazil Nuts, Shelled | 1/2 Cup | 8 |
| (Garnier) | 1 Fl. Oz. | 7 | Bread, Apricot Fritters | 1 Serv. | 38 |
| (Hiram Walker) | 1 Fl. Oz. | 7 | Bread, Ash | 1 Pc. | 21 |
| (Leroux) | 1 Fl. Oz. | 8 | Bread, Banana | 1 Sl. | 22 |
| (Old Mr. Boston) | 1 Fl. Oz. | 8 | Bread, Banana Tea | 1 Sl. | 22 |
| (Mr. Boston's) apricot | | | Bread, Boston Brown | 3/4 Sl. | 21 |
| & brandy | 1 Fl. Oz. | 8 | Bread, Boston (Degermed Meal) | 1 Sl. | 22 |
| Blackberry: | | | Bread, Bran Raisin | 1 Sl. | 17 |
| (Garnier) | 1 Fl. Oz. | 7 | Bread, Brown Nut | 1 Sl. | 27 |
| (Hiram Walker) | 1 Fl. Oz. | 7 | Bread, Buckwheat | 1 Sl. | 11 |
| (Leroux) | 1 Fl. Oz. | 8 | Bread, Buttermilk | 1 Sl. | 12 |

| FOOD | AMT. | CARB. GRAMS |
|---|---|---|
| Bread & Butter Pickles | 6 Sm. Sl. | 8 |
| Bread & Butter Pudding | 1 Pc. | 28 |
| Bread, Cinnamon | 1 Sl. | 16 |
| Cinnamon Raisin (Thomas') | 1 Sl. | 12 |
| Bread, Cocoa | 1 Sl. | 13 |
| Bread, Continental | 1 Sl. | 10 |
| Bread, Corn and Molasses | | |
| (Pepperidge Farm) | 1 Sl. | 13 |
| Bread, Corn Crisps | 1 Pc. | 21 |
| Bread, Corn, Southern Style | 2 in. sq. | 22 |
| Bread, Cracked Wheat | | |
| (Pepperidge Farm) | 1 Sl. | 12 |
| Bread Crumbs, Dry | 1 Tbsp. | 4 |
| (Wonder) | 1 Oz. | 20 |
| Bread, Daffodil Farm | | |
| (Wonder) | 1 Sl. | 9 |
| Bread, Date-Nut Loaf | | |
| (Thomas') | 1 Sl. | 19 |
| Bread, Dutch Egg | | |
| (Arnold) | 1 Sl. | 13 |
| Bread Fingers, Coconut | 1 | 9 |
| Bread, Flat Norwegian | | |
| (Ideal) | 1 Dble. Wafer | 5 |
| Bread, Fr. | 1/4 Lb. | 59 |
| Brown & Serve | | |
| (Pepperidge Farm) | 1 Sl. | 14 |
| Bread, Ginger With Hot Water | 1 Sq. | 27 |
| Bread, Ginger With Sour Milk | 1 Sq. | 27 |
| Bread, Glutogen Gluten | | |
| (Thomas') | 1 Sl. | 5 |
| Bread, Graham | 1/4 Lb. | 55 |
| Bread, Hollywood | | |
| Dark or Light | 1 Sl. | 10 |
| Bread, Italian | 1/4 Lb. | 61 |
| Brown & Serve | | |
| (Pepperidge Farm) | 1 Sl. | 14 |
| Bread, Melba Toast | 1 Sl. | 4 |
| Bread, Oatmeal: | | |
| (Arnold) | 1 Sl. | 10 |
| (Pepperidge Farm) | 1 Sl. | 12 |
| Bread, Orange Raisin | | |
| (Arnold) | 1 Sl. | 12 |
| Bread, Profile (Wonder) | 1 Sl. | 10 |
| Bread, Protogen Protein | | |
| (Thomas') | 1 Sl. | 8 |
| Bread, Pumpernickel | 1 Sl. | 16 |
| (Levy's) | 1 Sl. | 12 |
| Family (Pepperidge Farm) | 1 Sl. | 15 |
| Bread, Raisin | 1/4 Lb. | 67 |
| Tea (Arnold) | 1 Sl. | 11 |
| With Cinnamon | | |
| (Pepperidge Farm) | 1 Sl. | 14 |

| FOOD | AMT. | CARB. GRAMS |
|---|---|---|
| Rite Diet (Thomas') | 1 Sl. | 9 |
| Roman Light | 1 Sl. | 10 |
| Bread, Roman Meal | 1 Sl. | 14 |
| Bread, Rye-Light | 1/4 Lb. | 60 |
| Delicatessen (Arnold) | 1 Sl. | 10 |
| Family (Pepperidge Farm) | 1 Sl. | 17 |
| Westchester (Levy's) | 1 Sl. | 12 |
| Bread, Rye & Wheat | 1 Sl. | 12 |
| Bread, Sally Lunn | 1 Sq. | 22 |
| Bread, Slender Key | | |
| (Arnold) | 1 Sl. | 10 |
| Bread, Soft Sandwich | | |
| 1-1/2 Lb. Loaf (Arnold) | 1 Sl. | 10 |
| Bread, Soya | 1 Sl. | 17 |
| Bread Sticks | 1 | 8 |
| Cheese (Keebler) | 1 Pc. | 2 |
| Garlic (Keebler) | 1 Pc. | 2 |
| Onion (Keebler) | 1 Pc. | 2 |
| Salt (Keebler) | 1 Pc. | 2 |
| Salt Free (Stella D'oro) | 1 Pc. | 6 |
| Bread, Stuffing | 1/2 Cup | 28 |
| Bread, Swedish Health | 1 Sl. | 16 |
| Bread, Vienna | 1/4 Lb. | 59 |
| Bread, Wheat Germ | | |
| (Pepperidge Farm) | 1 Sl. | 11 |
| Bread, White | 1/4 Lb. | 59 |
| Brick Oven (Arnold) | | |
| 1-Lb. Loaf | .8-Oz. Sl. | 10 |
| 2-Lb. Loaf | 1.1-Oz. Sl. | 13 |
| English Tea Loaf | | |
| (Pepperidge Farm) | 1 Sl. | 12 |
| Hearthstone (Arnold) | | |
| 1-Lb. Loaf | 1 Sl. | 12 |
| 30-Oz. Loaf | 1 Sl. | 14 |
| 2-Lb. Loaf | 1 Sl. | 13 |
| Large Loaf (Pepperidge Farm) | 1 Sl. | 12 |
| Oven-Crust (Levy's) | 1 Sl. | 12 |
| Sandwich (Pepperidge Farm) | 1 Sl. | 11 |
| (Thomas') | 1 Sl. | 12 |
| (Wonder) | 1 Sl. | 12 |
| Bread, Whole Wheat | 1/4 Lb. | 55 |
| Brick Oven, 1-Lb. Loaf | | |
| (Arnold) | 8-Oz. Sl. | 10 |
| (Pepperidge Farm) | 1 Sl. | 11 |
| (Thomas') | 1 Sl. | 11 |
| Bread, Whole Wheat Raisin | 1 Sl. | 15 |
| Bread, Zwiebac | 1 Sl. | 5 |
| Bread, Canned: | | |
| Banana Nut (Dromedary) | 1 Sl. | 11 |
| Brown with Raisins (B & M) | 1 Sl. | 16 |
| Chocolate Nut (Crosse & Blackwell) | 1 Sl. | 14 |

| FOOD | AMT. | CARB. GRAMS | FOOD | AMT. | CARB. GRAMS |
|---|---|---|---|---|---|
| Chocolate Nut (Dromedary) | 1 Sl. | 13 | Broiled Squabs | Av. Serv. | 0 |
| Date & Nut (Crosse & Blackwell) | 1 Sl. | 12 | Broiled Stuffed Clams | Av. Serv. | 8 |
| Date & Nut (Dromedary) | 1 Sl. | 11 | Broiled Turkey Sauterne | Av. Serv. | 4 |
| Fruit & Nut (Crosse & Blackwell) | 1 Sl. | 13 | Bronx Cocktail | 1 | 21 |
| | | | Broth & Seasoning: | | |
| Orange Nut (Crosse & Blackwell) | 1 Sl. | 15 | Beef (Maggi) | 1 Oz. | 4 |
| Orange Nut (Dromedary) | 1 Sl. | 13 | Chicken (Maggi) | 1 Oz. | 5 |
| Spice Nut (Crosse & Blackwell) | 1 Sl. | 13 | Clam (Maggi) | 1 Oz. | 5 |
| Breaded Veal Cutlets | 1 Med. | 16 | Golden (George Washington) | 1 Pkt. | 1 |
| Breakfast Food, Mixed Corn | | | Onion (Maggi) | 1 Oz. | 5 |
| Soy Grits | 1/2 Cup | 14 | Rich Brown | | |
| Brewer's Dry Yeast | 1 Tbsp. | 3 | (George Washington) | 1 Pkt. | 1 |
| Brioche, Fr. | 1 | 21 | Vegetable (Maggi) | 1 Oz. | 4 |
| Brisket Beef | 3 Sl. | 0 | Broth, Clam | 1 Serv. | T |
| Brittany Sauce | 1 Tbsp. | 2 | Brown Nut Bread | 1 Sl. | 27 |
| Brittle Nut | 1 | 10 | Brown Sauce | 1 Tbsp. | 1 |
| Broccoli | 4 Ozs | 6 | Brown Rice With Cheese | Av. Serv. | 20 |
| Broccoli, Frozen | 3 Spears | 4 | Brown Stock | Av. Serv. | 3 |
| (Birds Eye) | 1/2 Cup | 7 | Brown Sugar Corn | | |
| In Cream Sauce | | | Flakes Kisses | 1 Kiss | 11 |
| (Birds Eye) | 1/2 Cup | 19 | Brown Sugar Fruit Cake | 1 Sl. | 22 |
| Broccoli, Frozen, Chopped | 1/2 Cup | 4 | Brown Sugar Fudge Candies | 1 Pc. | 23 |
| Broccoli, Spears: | | | Brugal Cocktail | 1 Cktl. Gl. | 3 |
| (Stokely-Van Camp) | 4 Ozs. | 6 | Brussels Sprouts, Frozen | 3-1/2 Ozs. | 7 |
| Baby Spears (Birds Eye) | 1 Pkg. | 11 | (Birds Eye) | 1 Cup | 11 |
| In Butter Sauce | | | In Butter Sauce (Green Giant) | 4 Ozs. | 7 |
| (Birds Eye) | 1 Cup | 8 | Buckwheat Bread | 1 Sl. | 11 |
| (Green Giant) Boil-in-the-bag | 4 Ozs. | 7 | Buckwheat Flour, Dark Sifted | 2 Ozs. | 41 |
| In Cheese Sauce (Green Giant) | 4 Ozs. | 10 | Buckwheat Groats: | | |
| In Hollandaise Sauce | | | (Birkett) | 1 Oz. | 20 |
| (Birds Eye) | 1 Cup | 6 | (Pocono) | 1 Oz. | 22 |
| Broccoli Soup | Av. Serv. | 5 | Buckwheat Pancakes | 1 | 21 |
| Broiled Abalone | 3-1/2 Ozs. | 3 | Buffalo Meat | 4 Ozs. | 0 |
| Broiled or Baked Lobster | Av. Serv. | 1 | Buns, Cinnamon Raisin | 1 | 29 |
| Broiled Bass | Av. Serv. | 0 | Buns, Pecan | 1 | 37 |
| Broiled, Beef Kidney | 1/2 Cup | 1 | Burgundy Beef Loaf | Av. Serv. | 0 |
| Broiled Butterfish | Av. Serv. | 0 | Burgundy Cup, Cold | Av. | 39 |
| Broiled Calf Kidney | Av. Serv. | 1 | Burgundy Orangeade | 1 Gl. | 12 |
| Broilers, Chicken Raw | 4 Ozs. | 0 | Burgundy Pineapple Punch | 1 Gl. | 55 |
| Broiled Clams | 6 | 5 | Burgundy Punch | 1 Gl. | 62 |
| Broiled Duckling | Av. Serv. | 0 | Burgundy Wine: | | |
| Broiled or Fried Bacon | 1 Lb. | 5 | (Gallo) | 3 Fl. Ozs. | 1 |
| Broiled or Fried Bacon | 2 Strips | T | (Gallo) Hearty | 3 Fl. Ozs. | 1 |
| Broiled Game Birds | Av. Serv. | 0 | (Gold Seal) | 3 Fl. Ozs. | T |
| Broiled Lamb Chops | Av. Serv. | 0 | (Italian Swiss Colony | | |
| Broiled Lettuce | Av. Serv. | 1 | -Gold Medal) Napa-Sonoma | | |
| Broiled Liver | Av. Serv. | 6 | -Mendocino | 3 Fl. Ozs. | 1 |
| Broiled, Lobster | 1 | 1 | (Italian Swiss Colony- | | |
| Broiled Rock Cornish | | | Gold Medal) | 3 Fl. Ozs. | T |
| Game Hens | Av. Serv. | 0 | (Italian Swiss Colony- | | |
| Broiled Scallops | 4 Ozs. | 4 | Private Stock) | 3 Fl. Ozs. | T |
| | | | (Louis M. Martini) | 3 Fl. Ozs. | T |

20

| FOOD | AMT. | CARB. GRAMS | FOOD | AMT. | CARB. GRAMS |
|---|---|---|---|---|---|
| (Mogen David) American | 3 Fl. Ozs. | 2 | Butterscotch Pudding, | | |
| (Taylor) | 3 Fl. Ozs. | T | Sugar-Free | 1/2 Cup | 9 |
| Burgundy Wine, Sparkling: | | | Butterscotch Pudding Mix: | | |
| (Barton & Guestier) | | | Sweetened | | |
| French Red | 3 Fl. Ozs. | 2 | Instant (Jell-O) | 1 Cup | 60 |
| (Chanson) French Red | 3 Fl. Ozs. | 3 | Instant (My-T-Fine) | 1 Oz. | 20 |
| (Gold Seal) | 3 Fl. Ozs. | 2 | Instant (Royal) | 1 Cup | 59 |
| (Great Western) | 3 Fl. Ozs. | 5 | Regular (My-T-Fine) | 1 Oz. | 27 |
| (Italian Swiss Colony- | | | Regular (Royal) | 1 Cup | 62 |
| Private Stock) | 3 Fl. Ozs. | 2 | (Thank You) | 1 Cup | 59 |
| (Lejon) | 3 Fl. Ozs. | 2 | Low Calorie | | |
| (Taylor) | 3 Fl. Ozs. | 2 | With Whole Milk | | |
| Butter (A-D) | Aver. Pat. | T | (D-Zerta) | 1/2 Cup | 24 |
| Butter Almond Ice Cream | 1 Cup | 40 | With Nonfat Milk | | |
| Butter Cake | 1 Sl. | 36 | (D-Zerta) | 1/2 Cup | 24 |
| Butter, Guava | 1 Tbsp. | 13 | Butter Spread, Anchovy | 1 Tbsp. | T |
| Butter, Salt | 1 Tbsp. | T | Butter Spread, Catsup | 1 Tbsp. | 3 |
| (Breakstone) | 1 Tbsp. | T | Butter Spread, Caviar | 1 Tbsp. | T |
| (Hotel Bar) | 1 Tbsp. | T | Butter Spread, Cheese | 1 Tbsp. | T |
| (Land O'Lakes) | 1 Tbsp. | T | Butter Spread, Chili | 1 Tbsp. | T |
| (Sealtest) | 1 Tbsp. | T | Butter Spread, Egg | 1 Tbsp. | T |
| Whipped (Breakstone) | 4 Ozs. | T | B-V (Wilson) | 1 Tsp. | 1 |
| Butter, (A-D) Sweet | Aver. Pat. | T | Cabbage & Beet Relish | 1 Serv. | 6 |
| Butter Cheese Noodles | 1 Serv. | 10 | Cabbage, Canned, Red | | |
| Butterfish, Baked or Broiled | 4 Ozs. | 0 | (Comstock-Greenwood) | 1 Oz. | 4 |
| Buttermilk | 8 Ozs. | 12 | Cabbage & Carrot Garnish | 1 | 2 |
| Buttermilk Bread | 1 Sl. | 12 | Cabbage, Celery or Chinese, | | |
| Buttermilk, Cultured | 8 Ozs. | 12 | Fresh | 1 Cup | 2 |
| Buttermilk Frosting | Av. | 13 | Cabbage, Chinese | 1 Cup | 2 |
| Buttermilk, Fruit Bev. | 1 Serv. | 25 | Cabbage, Chinese-Cooked | 1 Cup | 5 |
| Buttermilk Soup | 1 Serv. | 10 | Cabbage, Cole Slaw | 1 Cup | 14 |
| Buttermilk Spice Cake | 1 Sl. | 27 | Cabbage & Frankfurter | | |
| Butterscotch Candy | 1 Oz. | 24 | Casserole | 1 Serv. | 28 |
| Butterscotch Cookies | 1 | 15 | Cabbage & Raisin Salad | 4 Ozs. | 20 |
| Butterscotch Custard | 1 Serv. | 12 | Cabbage Rolls | | |
| Butterscotch Ice Cream | 1/2 Cup | 14 | (Holloway House) | 1 Roll | 61 |
| Butterscotch, Ice Cream | | | Cabbage, Shredded | 1 Cup | 5 |
| Sundae | Av. Serv. | 56 | Cabbage, Swamp | 4 Ozs. | 5 |
| Butterscotch Morsels | | | Cabernet Sauvignon Wine | | |
| (Nestle's) | 4 Ozs. | 68 | (Louis M. Martini) | 3 Fl. Ozs. | T |
| Butterscotch Pie | | | Cactus Cooler, Soft Drink | | |
| Frozen, Cream (Banquet) | 1 Oz. | 10 | (Canada Dry) | 8 Fl. Ozs. | 29 |
| Butterscotch Pie Filling Mix: | | | Cake, Almond Coffee | 1 Sl. | 33 |
| With Whole Milk, Low Calorie | | | Cake, Apple Crumb | 1 Sl. | 49 |
| (D-Zerta) | 1 Cup | 19 | Cake, Brandy Fruit | 1 Pc. | 64 |
| With Nonfat Milk, Low Calorie | | | Cake, Brandy Refrigerated | 1 Pc. | 87 |
| (D-Zerta) | 1 Cup | 20 | Cake, Brazel Nut—No Flour | 1 Pc. | 23 |
| (My-T-Fine) | 1 Oz. | 27 | Cake, Buttermilk Spice | 1 Pc. | 27 |
| Butterscotch Pudding: | | | Cake, Butter | 1 Pc. | 36 |
| (Betty Crocker) | 1 Oz. | 6 | Cake, Butter, Iced | 1 Sq. | 46 |
| (Bounty) | 1 Oz. | 7 | Cake, Caramel Iced | 1 Pc. | 44 |

| FOOD | AMT. | CARB. GRAMS | FOOD | AMT. | CARB. GRAMS |
|---|---|---|---|---|---|
| Cake, Cheese Pineapple | 1 Pc. | 34 | Dark Chocolate Fudge, | | |
| Cake, Chocolate Layer, | | | Creamy (Betty Crocker) | 4 Ozs. | 85 |
| No Icing | 1 Pc. | 54 | Dole Pineapple, Creamy | | |
| Cake, Chocolate Layer, | | | (Betty Crocker) | 4 Ozs. | 102 |
| With Icing | 1 Pc. | 64 | Fudge (Dromedary) | 4 Ozs. | 8 |
| Cake, Chocolate Iced | 1 Pc. | 45 | Fudge Nugget, Creamy | | |
| Cake, Chocolate Loaf | 1 Pc. | 54 | (Betty Crocker) | 4 Ozs. | 98 |
| Cake, Cocoanut Iced | 1 Pc. | 50 | Sour Cream, Chocolate Fudge, | | |
| Cake, Cocoa Fruit | 1 Sl. | 22 | Creamy (Betty Crocker) | 4 Ozs. | 96 |
| Cake, Coffee Iced With Nuts | 1 Pc. | 33 | Spice, Creamy (Betty Crocker) | 4 Ozs. | 98 |
| Cake, Cup Plain | 1 | 33 | Sunkist Lemon, Creamy | | |
| Cake, Date Torte | 1 Serv. | 38 | (Betty Crocker) | 4 Ozs. | 100 |
| Cake Decorator, Canned, | | | Sunkist Lemon Fluff | | |
| (Pillsbury) | 2 Ozs. | 42 | (Betty Crocker) | 4 Ozs. | 108 |
| Cake, English Tea | 1 Serv. | 53 | Sunkist Orange, Creamy | | |
| Cakes, Fish | 1 | 10 | (Betty Crocker) | 4 Ozs. | 98 |
| Cake Flour | 1 Cup | 85 | White, Creamy (Betty Crocker) | 4 Ozs. | 100 |
| Cake, Foundation | Av. Sl. | 30 | White, Fluffy (Betty Crocker) | 4 Ozs. | 108 |
| Cake, Ginger | 1 Sl. | 26 | Cake, Layer | 1 Pc. | 55 |
| Cake, Gingerbread | 1 Sq. | 21 | Cake, Lemon Sponge | 1 Pc. | 54 |
| Cake, Gold | 1 Sl. | 32 | Cake Mix, Ginger Bread | 1 Sq. | 27 |
| Cake Icing: | | | Cake Mix: | | |
| Butterscotch (Betty Crocker) | 4 Ozs. | 80 | White: | | |
| Chocolate (Betty Crocker) | 4 Ozs. | 72 | (Betty Crocker) | 1 Oz. | 22 |
| Dark Dutch Fudge | | | Party White (Crutchfield's) | 1 Oz. | 17 |
| (Betty Crocker) | 4 Ozs. | 71 | (Duncan Hines) | 1 Pc. | 32 |
| Milk Chocolate (Betty Crocker) | 4 Ozs. | 79 | (Pillsbury) | 1 Oz. | 21 |
| Sunkist Lemon (Betty Crocker) | 4 Ozs. | 81 | Loaf (Pillsbury) | 1 Oz. | 22 |
| Vanilla (Betty Crocker) | 4 Ozs. | 81 | Whipping Cream (Pillsbury) | 1 Oz. | 21 |
| Cake Icing Mix: | | | (Swans Down) | 1 Pc. | 36 |
| Butter Brickle, Creamy | | | Yellow: | | |
| (Betty Crocker) | 4 Ozs. | 104 | (Betty Crocker) | 1 Oz. | 23 |
| Caramel, Creamy (Betty | | | Butter Recipe | | |
| Crocker) | 4 Ozs. | 100 | (Betty Crocker) | 1 Oz. | 23 |
| Cherry, Creamy (Betty Crocker) | 4 Ozs. | 100 | Party Yellow (Crutchfield's) | 1 Oz. | 16 |
| Cherry Fluff (Betty Crocker) | 4 Ozs. | 108 | (Duncan Hines) | 1 Pc. | 32 |
| Cherry Fudge, Creamy | | | Golden Butter | | |
| (Betty Crocker) | 4 Ozs. | 96 | (Duncan Hines) | 1 Pc. | 36 |
| Chiquita Banana, Creamy | | | (Pillsbury) | 1 Oz. | 22 |
| (Betty Crocker) | 4 Ozs. | 102 | Butter Flavor (Pillsbury) | 1 Oz. | 22 |
| Chocolate, Fluffy (Betty | | | Loaf (Pillsbury) | 1 Oz. | 21 |
| Crocker) | 4 Ozs. | 92 | (Swans Down) | 1 Pc. | 54 |
| Chocolate Fudge, Creamy | | | Cake, Sponge Prepared Mix | 1 Pc. | 22 |
| (Betty Crocker) | 4 Ozs. | 96 | Cake, New England Spice | 1 Sl. | 27 |
| Chocolate Malt, Creamy | | | Cake, Orange Sponge | 1 Pc. | 12 |
| (Betty Crocker) | 4 Ozs. | 98 | Cake, Pineapple Upside-Down | 1 Pc. | 38 |
| Chocolate, Walnut, Creamy | | | Cake, Prune Nut | 1 Pc. | 9 |
| (Betty Crocker) | 4 Ozs. | 98 | Cake, Rich Sherry Nut | 1 Serv. | 51 |
| Coconut-Pecan, Creamy | | | Cake, Round Layer With Icing | 1 Pc. | 61 |
| (Betty Crocker) | 4 Ozs. | 84 | Cake, Silver 3 Layer | 1 Pc. | 50 |
| Coconut, Toasted, Creamy | | | Cake, Sunshine | 1 Pc. | 36 |
| (Betty Crocker) | 4 Ozs. | 98 | Cake, Three Layer With Icing | 1 Pc. | 72 |

| FOOD | AMT. | CARB. GRAMS |
|---|---|---|
| Cake, Two Layer With Icing | 1 Pc. | 41 |
| Cake, Vanilla No Icing | 1 Pc. | 31 |
| Calf's Liver Divine | 1 Serv. | 5 |
| Calf Heart | 3 Ozs. | 1 |
| Calf Heart (Infant) | 4 Ozs. | 1 |
| California Avocado | 1/2 Med. | 6 |
| California Brandy | 3 Ozs. | 0 |
| California Celery | 1 Serv. | 11 |
| California Salad | 1 Serv. | 10 |
| Calves Liver | 1 Serv. | 4 |
| Canadian Whiskey | 1 Oz. | T |
| Canadian Whiskey Highball | 8 Ozs. | T |
| Canape Biscuit | 1 Med. | 23 |
| Canape, Lobster | 1 Serv. | 4 |
| Canape Spread, Cheese & Bologna | 1 Serv. | 1 |
| Canape Spread, Chicken Liver | 1 Serv. | T |
| Canape Spread, Deviled Ham | 1 Serv. | T |
| Canape Spread Liverwurst | 1 Serv. | T |
| Candied Apricots | 1 Med. | 26 |
| Candied Cherries | 1 Lg. | 4 |
| Candied Citron | 1 Oz. | 22 |
| Candies, Almond Joy | 10c Size | 22 |
| Candies, Bonbon | 1 | 9 |
| Candies, Brown Sugar Fudge | 1 Pc. | 23 |
| Candies, Caramel | 1 Med. | 8 |
| Candies, Caramel Choc. Nut | 1 Pc. | 16 |
| Candies, Choc. Bar | 2 Ozs. | 32 |
| Candies, Choc. Bar With Nuts | 1 Oz. | 17 |
| Candies, Choc. Bitter Grated | 1 Cup | 42 |
| Candies, Choc. Butter | 1 Oz. | 8 |
| Candies, Choc. Cherry | 1 | 8 |
| Candies, Choc.-Covered Almonds | 6 | 9 |
| Candies, Choc. Cream | 1 Oz. | 20 |
| Candies, Choc. Kisses | 1 | 2 |
| Candies, Choc. Milk | 1 Oz. | 16 |
| Candies, Choc. Milk With Almonds | 1 Oz. | 17 |
| Candies, Choc. Sweet | 1 Oz. | 18 |
| Candies, Clark Bar | 5c Bar | 22 |
| Candies, Cocoanut Cream | 1 Sq. | 20 |
| Candies, Cream Mint | 2 Sm. | 3 |
| Candies, Date Cream | 1 Oz. | 20 |
| Candies, Divinity | 1 Pc. | 23 |
| Candies, Fondant | 1 Pc. | 10 |
| Candies, Fruit Drops | 3 | 10 |
| Candies, Fudge With Nuts | 1 Oz. | 23 |
| Candies, Glazed Fruit | 1 Pc. | 8 |
| Candies, Packaged | 2 Rolls | 60 |
| Candy, Butterscotch | 1 Oz. | 24 |
| Candy, Chocolate Cream Peppermints | 1 | 8 |

| FOOD | AMT. | CARB. GRAMS |
|---|---|---|
| Candy, Commercial: | | |
| Almond Cluster (Peter Paul) | 10c Bar | 20 |
| Almond Joy (Peter Paul) | 10c Bar | 24 |
| Almonds, Chocolate Covered: | | |
| (Hershey's) | 1 Oz. | 16 |
| (Kraft) | 1 Pc. | 1 |
| Baby Ruth (Curtiss) | 1 Oz. | 21 |
| Baffie Bar (Cardinet's) | 1 Bar | 11 |
| Brazil Nuts, Chocolate Covered: | | |
| (Kraft) | 1 Pc. | 1 |
| Bridge Mix: | | |
| Almond (Kraft) | 1 Pc. | 1 |
| Caramelette (Kraft) | 1 Pc. | 2 |
| Jelly (Kraft) | 1 Pc. | 2 |
| Malted Milk Ball (Kraft) | 1 Pc. | 1 |
| Mintette (Kraft) | 1 Pc. | 2 |
| Peanut (Kraft) | 1 Pc. | 2 |
| Peanut Crunch (Kraft) | 1 Pc. | 3 |
| Raisin (Kraft) | 1 Pc. | T |
| (Nabisco) | 1 Pc. | 1 |
| Butter Chip Bar (Hershey's) | 1 Oz. | 18 |
| Butterfinger (Curtiss) | 1 Oz. | 21 |
| Butternut (Hollywood) | 1 Oz. | 16 |
| Candy Corn (Brach's) | 1 Pc. | 1 |
| Candy Corn, Caramel: | | |
| (Curtiss) | 1 Oz. | 24 |
| Caramelette (Kraft) | 1 Pc. | 2 |
| Chocolate (Kraft) | 1 Pc. | 6 |
| Chocolate Covered (Brach's) | 1 Pc. | 6 |
| Coconut Chocolate (Kraft) | 1 Pc. | 5 |
| Coconut Vanilla (Kraft) | 1 Pc. | 5 |
| Milk Maid (Brach's) | 1 Pc. | 8 |
| Treets (Kraft) | 1 Pc. | 6 |
| Vanilla, Plain (Kraft) | 1 Pc. | 6 |
| Vanilla, Chocolate Covered (Kraft) | 1 Pc. | 6 |
| Caravelle (Peter Paul) | 10c Bar | 28 |
| Cashew Crunch, Canned (Planter's) | 1 Oz. | 14 |
| Cherry, Chocolate Covered: | | |
| (Brach's) | 1 Pc. | 13 |
| Dark (Nabisco) | 1 Pc. | 14 |
| Milk (Nabisco) | 1 Pc. | 15 |
| Chewees (Curtiss) | 1 Oz. | 24 |
| Chocolate Bar: | | |
| Milk Chocolate: | | |
| (Ghirardelli) | 10c Bar | 20 |
| (Hershey's) | 10c Bar | 27 |
| (Hershey's) | 1 Oz. | 16 |
| (Nestle's) | 1 Oz. | 13 |
| (Nestle's) Gala Plain | 1 Oz. | 14 |

23

| FOOD | AMT | CARB. GRAMS |
|---|---|---|
| Sweet | 1 Oz. | 14 |
| Mint Chocolate (Ghirardelli) | 10c Bar | 20 |
| Semisweet (Hershey's) | 1 Oz. | 17 |
| Semisweet (Nestle's) | 1 Oz. | 17 |
| Chocolate Bar With Almonds, | | |
| (Ghirardelli) | 10c Bar | 19 |
| (Hershey's) | 10c Bar | 22 |
| (Hershey's) | 1 Oz. | 14 |
| (Nestle's) | 1 Oz. | 15 |
| Chocolate Blocks, Milk. | | |
| (Ghirardelli) | 1 Sq. | 19 |
| (Hershey's) | 1 Oz. | 18 |
| Chocolate Crisp Bar | | |
| (Ghirardelli) | 10c Bar | 20 |
| Chocolate Crunch Bar (Nestle's) | 1 Oz. | 18 |
| Chocolate Drops (Nabisco) | 1 Pc. | 10 |
| Chuckles | 1 Oz. | 23 |
| Circlets (Curtiss) | 1 Oz. | 26 |
| Circus Peanuts (Brach's) | 1 Pc. | 6 |
| Cluster: | | |
| Almond (Kraft) | 1 Pc. | 4 |
| Cashew, Chocolate Covered | | |
| (Kraft) | 1 Pc. | 5 |
| Crispy (Nabisco) | 1 Pc. | 13 |
| Peanut, Chocolate Covered | | |
| (Brach's) | 1 Pc. | 7 |
| (Kraft) | 1 Pc. | 5 |
| Royal Clusters (Nabisco) | 1 Pc. | 10 |
| Coconut: | | |
| (Welch's) | 1 Pc. | 21 |
| Bar (Curtiss) | 1 Oz. | 21 |
| Bon Bons (Brach's) | 1 Pc. | 12 |
| Cream Egg (Hershey's) | 1 Oz. | 20 |
| Neapolitan (Brach's) | 1 Pc. | 8 |
| Squares (Nabisco) | 1 Pc | 12 |
| Dainties, Semisweet Chocolate | | |
| (Hershey's) | 1 Oz. | 17 |
| Eagle Bar (Ghirardelli) | 1 Sq. | 16 |
| Frappe (Welch's) | 1 Pc. | 21 |
| Fruit 'n Nut Chocolate Bar | | |
| (Nestle's) | 1 Oz. | 16 |
| Fudge: | | |
| Bar (Nabisco) | 1 Pc. | 23 |
| Fudgies (Kraft) | 1 Pc. | 6 |
| Nut, Bar (Nabisco) | 1 Pc. | 3 |
| Nut, Square (Nabisco) | 1 Pc. | 3 |
| Hard Candy: | | |
| (H-B) | 1 Pc. | 3 |
| (Peerless Maid) | 1 Pc. | 5 |
| Butterscotch: | | |
| Disks (Brach's) | 1 Pc. | 5 |
| Skimmers (Nabisco) | 1 Pc. | 5 |

| FOOD | AMT | CARB. GRAMS |
|---|---|---|
| Cherry, Wild, Drops, | | |
| Old-Fashioned (Nabisco) | 1 Pc. | 2 |
| Honey & Horehound Drops, | | |
| Old-Fashioned (Nabisco) | 1 Pc. | 2 |
| Lemon Drops (Brach's) | 1 Pc. | 4 |
| Pops, Assorted (Brach's) | 1 Pc. | 5 |
| Sherbit (F&F) | 1 Pc. | 2 |
| Sour Balls (Brach's) | 1 Pc. | 5 |
| Hershey-Ets, Candy-Coated | 1 Oz. | 21 |
| Hollywood | 1-1/2 Ozs. | 24 |
| Jelly Beans (Brach's) | 1 Pc. | 3 |
| Big Ben Jellies (Brach's) | 1 Pc. | 7 |
| Iced Jelly Cones (Brach's) | 1 Pc. | 3 |
| Nougats (Brach's) | 1 Pc. | 10 |
| Jube Jels (Brach's) | 1 Pc. | 2 |
| Kisses, Milk Chocolate | | |
| (Hershey's) | 1 Pc. | 5 |
| Krackel Bar (Hershey's) | 1 Oz. | 15 |
| Licorice | 1 Oz. | 24 |
| Licorice Twist (American Licorice Co.): | | |
| Black | 1 Pc. | 6 |
| Red | 1 Pc. | 7 |
| Life Savers (Beech-Nut): | | |
| Cl-O-Ve | 1 Pc. | 1 |
| Pep-O-Mint | 1 Pc. | 1 |
| Spear-O-Mint | 1 Pc. | 1 |
| Wint-O-Green | 1 Pc. | 1 |
| All Other Flavors | 1 Pc. | 2 |
| Lollipop | 1 Med. | 28 |
| Lozenges, Mint or Wintergreen | | |
| (Brach's) | 1 Pc. | 3 |
| Mallo Cup (Boyer) | 5c Size | 15 |
| Mallo Cup (Boyer) | 10c Size | 24 |
| Mallo Cup (Boyer) | 15c Size | 32 |
| Malted Milk Balls, Milk | | |
| Chocolate Covered (Brach's) | 1 Pc. | 1 |
| Malted Milk Crunch (Welch's) | 1 Pc. | 1 |
| Maple Nut Goodies (Brach's) | 1 Pc. | 4 |
| Mars Almond Bar | | |
| (M&M/Mars) | 1 Oz. | 17 |
| Mars Milky Way | 1 Bar | 58 |
| Mars Three Musketeers | 1 Bar | 35 |
| Marshmallow: | | |
| (Campfire) | 1 Pc. | 6 |
| Royal Marshmallow (Curtiss) | 1 Oz. | 22 |
| Chocolate (Kraft) | 1 Pc. | 4 |
| Chocolate-Covered (Kraft) | 1 Pc. | 4 |
| Jet Puff (Kraft): | | |
| Plain | 1 Pc. | 4 |
| Chocolate-Covered | 1 Pc. | 4 |
| Flavored | 1 Pc. | 4 |
| Macaroon | 1 Pc. | 5 |

| FOOD | AMT | CARB. GRAMS | FOOD | AMT | CARB. GRAMS |
|---|---|---|---|---|---|
| Miniature | 1 Pc. | T | Peanut Brittle. | | |
| Mary Jane (Miller). | | | (Kraft) | 1 Bar | 23 |
| 1c Size | 1 Pc. | 5 | Coconut (Kraft) | 1 Oz. | 22 |
| 5c Size | 1 Pc. | 22 | Jumbo Peanut Block Bar | | |
| Milk Shake (Hollywood) | 1-1/4 Ozs. | 26 | (Planters) | 1 Oz. | 14 |
| Milky Way, Milk or Dark | | | Peanut Butter Cup. | | |
| Chocolate (M&M/Mars) | 1 Oz. | 17 | (Boyer) | 5c Size | 11 |
| Mint: | | | (Boyer) | 10c Size | 18 |
| Anise, Midget (Kraft) | 1 Pc. | 1 | (Boyer) | 15c Size | 23 |
| Anise, Regular (Kraft) | 1 Pc. | 2 | (Reese's) | 1 Oz. | 15 |
| Buttermint (Kraft) | 1 Pc. | 2 | Smoothie (Boyer) | 5c Size | 11 |
| Candy-Coated Mint | | | Smoothie (Boyer) | 10c Size | 18 |
| Chocolate (Hershey's) | 1 Oz | 21 | Smoothie (Boyer) | 15c Size | 23 |
| Chocolate-Covered Bar | | | Peanut Butter Egg (Reese's) | 1 Oz. | 12 |
| (Brach's) | 1 Pc. | 23 | Penny Candy | 2 Ozs. | 28 |
| Colored, Mints, Midget (Kraft) | 1 Pc. | 1 | Pom Poms (Nabisco) | 1 Pc. | 2 |
| Regular (Kraft) | 1 Pc. | 2 | Poppycock | 1 Oz. | 22 |
| Dessert (Brach's) | 1 Pc. | 1 | Raisin, Chocolate-Covered. | | |
| Jamaica Mints (Nabisco) | 1 Pc. | 5 | (Brach's) | 1 Pc. | T |
| Liberty Mints (Nabisco) | 1 Pc. | 5 | (Nabisco) | 1 Pc. | T |
| Pattie, Chocolate-Covered: | | | Bar (Ghirardelli) | 10c Bar | 21 |
| (Brach's) | 1 Pc. | 9 | Raisinets (B & B) | 5c Box | 15 |
| Junior Mint Pattie | | | Saf-T-Pops (Curtiss) | 1 Oz. | 26 |
| (Nabisco) | 1 Pc. | 2 | Snickers (M & M/Mars) | 1 Oz. | 15 |
| Peppermint Pattie | | | Snowball | 1 | 10 |
| (Nabisco) | 1 Pc. | 13 | Spearmint Leaves (Brach's) | 1 Pc. | 6 |
| Sherbit Pressed Mints (F&F) | 1 Pc | 2 | Spicettes (Brach's) | 1 Pc. | 2 |
| Starlight Mints (Brach's) | 1 Pc. | 4 | Sprigs, Sweet Chocolate | | |
| Swedish (Brach's) | 1 Pc. | 2 | (Hershey's) | 1 Oz. | 18 |
| Thin (Nabisco) | 1 Pc. | 8 | Sprint, Chocolate Wafer Bar | | |
| White, Midget (Kraft) | 1 Pc. | 1 | (M & M/Mars) | 1 Oz. | 16 |
| White, Regular (Kraft) | 1 Pc. | 2 | Stark Wafer Roll | 5c Roll | 33 |
| Mounds (Peter Paul) | 10c Pkg. | 26 | Stars, Chocolate: | | |
| M & M's (M & M/Mars): | | | (Brach's) | 1 Pc. | 1 |
| Chocolate | 1 Oz. | 18 | (Nabisco) | 1 Pc. | 1 |
| Peanut | 1 Oz. | 17 | Sugar Babies (Nabisco) | 1 Pc. | 1 |
| Mr. Goodbar (Hershey's) | 1 Oz. | 12 | Sugar Daddy (Nabisco): | | |
| North Pole (F & F) | 1 Bar | 31 | Giant Sucker | 1 Lb. | 398 |
| Nutty Crunch, Bar (Nabisco) | 1 Pc. | 3 | Junior Sucker | 1 Pc. | 9 |
| Nutty Crunch, Squares (Nabisco) | 1 Pc. | 10 | Chocolate Flavored | 1 Pc. | 9 |
| OH Henry | 1 Bar | 40 | Nugget | 1 Pc. | 5 |
| $100,000 Bar (Nestle's) | 1 Oz. | 19 | Sucker | 1 Pc. | 28 |
| Orange Slices (Brach's) | 1 Pc. | 14 | Sugar Mama, Pop (Nabisco) | 1 Pc. | 22 |
| Payday (Hollywood) | 1 Oz. | 20 | Sugar Wafer (F & F) | 1 Oz. | 22 |
| Peanut, Chocolate-Covered: | | | Taffy: | | |
| (BB) | 1 Oz. | 6 | Salt Water (Brach's) | 1 Pc. | 6 |
| (Brach's) | 1 Pc. | 1 | Turkish (Bonomo): | | |
| (Hershey's) Candy-coated | 1 Oz. | 18 | Bite-size | 1 Pc. | 4 |
| (Kraft) Bite-size | 1 Pc. | 7 | Miniatures | 1 Pc. | 5 |
| (Kraft) Boxed | 1 Pc. | 1 | Nibbles, Chocolate-covered | 1 Pc. | 1 |
| (Nabisco) | 1 Pc. | 1 | Pop | 1 Pc. | 11 |
| French Burnt (Brach's) | 1 Pc. | T | Roll | 1c Size | 5 |

| FOOD | AMT. | CARB. GRAMS | FOOD | AMT. | CARB. GRAMS |
|---|---|---|---|---|---|
| Taffy Molasses | 1 | 10 | Coffee (Barton's) | 1 Pc. | 1 |
| Tan Bark | 1 | 14 | Coffee (Estee) | 1 Pc. | 3 |
| 3 Musketeers Bar (M & M/Mars) | 1 Oz. | 19 | Lollipops (Estee) | 1 Pop | 3 |
| Toffee: | | | Licorice (Dia-Mel) | 1 Pc. | 0 |
| Almond (Kraft) | 1-Oz. Bar | 8 | Marshmallow (Dia-Mel) | 1 Pc. | 3 |
| Almond, Chocolate-Covered | | | Mint: | | |
| (Kraft) | 1 Pc. | 6 | Butterscotch (Estee) | 1 Pc. | 1 |
| Assorted (Brach's) | 1 Pc. | 5 | Chocolate (Estee) | 1 Pc. | 1 |
| Chocolate (Kraft) | 1 Pc. | 5 | Fruit Flavors (Estee) | 1 Pc. | 1 |
| Coffee (Kraft) | 1 Pc. | 5 | Peppermint (Estee) | 1 Pc. | 1 |
| Rum Butter (Kraft) | 1 Pc. | 5 | Peppermint Chocolette (Estee) | 1 Pc. | 1 |
| Vanilla (Kraft) | 1 Pc. | 5 | Peppermint Cream (Estee) | 1 Pc. | 3 |
| Tootsie Rolls, Regular: | | | Thin (Estee) | 1 Pc. | 1 |
| 1c Size or Midgee | 1 Pc. | 5 | Nut, Milk Chocolate | | |
| 2c Size | 1 Pc. | 8 | Covered (Estee) | 1 Pc. | 3 |
| 5c Size | 1 Pc. | 21 | Nut Cluster (Estee) | 1 Pc. | 4 |
| 10c Size | 1 Pc. | 37 | Peanut Butter Cup (Estee) | 1 Cup | 2 |
| Vending-machine Size | 1 Pc. | 4 | Peanutette (Estee) | 1 Pc. | T |
| Pop | 1 Pc. | 13 | Petit Fours (Estee) | 1 Pc. | 4 |
| Pop-drop | 1 Pc. | 4 | Raisin, Chocolate Covered | | |
| Triple Decker Bar (Nestle's) | 1 Oz. | 17 | (Estee) | 1 Pc. | T |
| U-No (Cardinet's) | 1 Bar | 9 | Soft Jells (Dia-Mel) | 1 Pc. | 0 |
| Walnut Hill (F & F) | 1 Bar | 29 | Stick, Filled (Estee) | 1 Pc. | 4 |
| Whirligigs (Nabisco) | 1 Pc. | 3 | Tri-Pack, Chocolate Covered | | |
| Candy, Dietetic: | | | Assorted Bars (Dia-Mel) | 3-Oz. Pkg. | 34 |
| Almondettes (Estee) | 1 Pc. | 1 | Truffle, Chocolate (Estee) | 1 Pc. | 2 |
| Banana Wafer Chocolate | | | TV Mix (Estee) | 1 Pc. | 1 |
| Bar (Estee) | 1 Bar | 10 | Wafer Bar (Estee): | | |
| Chocolate, Assorted: | | | Bittersweet Choc. Covered | 1 Bar | 10 |
| Bittersweet (Estee) | 1 Pc. | 3 | Milk Choc. Covered | 1 Bar | 10 |
| Milk (Estee) | 1 Pc. | 3 | Candied Pineapple | 1 Sl. | 30 |
| Miniatures (Dia-Mel) | 1 Pc. | 4 | Cane, Black Strap Molasses | 1 Tbsp. | 11 |
| Chocolate Bar With | | | Cane, Light Molasses | 1 Tbsp. | 13 |
| Almonds (Estee) | 1 Section | 1 | Cane Molasses (Barbados) | 1 Tbsp. | 11 |
| Chocolate Bar Bittersweet | | | Cane Molasses Syrups Light | 1 Tbsp. | 13 |
| (Estee) | 1 Bar | 10 | Canned Abalone | 1 Serv. | 3 |
| Chocolate Bar, Milk | | | Canned Anchovies | 8 Sm. | T |
| (Estee) | 1 Section | 5 | Canned Apples & Apricots | 1 Oz. | 5 |
| With Peppermint (Estee) | 1 Bar | 8 | Canned Apple Sauce | 1 Oz. | 6 |
| Chocolettes, Almond (Estee) | 1 Pc. | 1 | Canned Apple Sauce | | |
| Chocolettes, Milk (Estee) | 1 Pc. | 1 | Unsweetened | 1 Cup | 26 |
| Coconut Chocolate Bar | | | Canned Apricots | 4 | 21 |
| (Estee) | 1 Bar | 8 | Canned Apricots Syrup Pack | 5 | 25 |
| Coffee Beans, Milk Chocolate- | | | Canned Apricots Water Pack | 1 Cup | 20 |
| Covered (Estee) | 1 Pc. | T | Canned Apricots With Syrup | 1 Cup | 55 |
| Creams, Assorted (Estee) | 1 Pc. | 3 | Canned Asparagus | 6 | 3 |
| Gum Drops: | | | Canned Asparagus | 1 Cup | 6 |
| (Dia-Mel) | 1 Pc. | 0 | Canned Atlantic Mackerel | 1 Serv. | 0 |
| All Flavors (Estee) | 1 Pc. | T | Canned Bass | 1 Serv. | 0 |
| Hard Candy: | | | Canned Beef (Infant) | 4 Ozs. | 0 |
| All Flavors (Estee) | 1 Pc. | 3 | Canned Bing Cherries In Syrup | 1 Cup | 59 |
| Assorted Flavors (Barton's) | 1 Pc. | 3 | Canned Blueberries Low-Cal | 1 Cup | 17 |

| FOOD | AMT. | CARB. GRAMS | FOOD | AMT. | CARB. GRAMS |
|------|------|-------------|------|------|-------------|
| Canned Boned Chicken | 3 Ozs. | T | Canned Red Sour Cherries | 1 Cup | 24 |
| Canned Beef (Strained) | 1 Oz. | 2 | Canned Rhubarb, Low-Cal. | 1 Cup | 5 |
| Canned Blackberries Low-Cal | 1 Cup | 18 | Canned Rhubarb | 4 Ozs. | 8 |
| Canned Carrots | 4 Ozs. | 7 | Canned Royal Anne Cherries | | |
| Canned Carrots (Infant) | 4 Ozs. | 8 | In Syrup | 1 Cup | 49 |
| Canned Carrots (Strained) | 1 Oz. | 2 | Canned Shrimp, Dry Pack | 3 Ozs. | T |
| Canned Clams | 4 Ozs. | 3 | Canned Shrimp, Wet Pack | 3 Ozs. | T |
| Canned Clams (Drained) | 1/2 Cup | 2 | Canned Spinach (Infant) | 4 Ozs. | 8 |
| Canned Drained Potatoes | 4 Ozs. | 19 | Canned Strained Apricots | 4 Ozs. | 10 |
| Canned Drained Shrimp | 4 Ozs. | T | Canned Strained Liver | 1 Oz. | 5 |
| Canned Crab | 8 Ozs. | 3 | Canned Strained Peaches | 1 Oz. | 5 |
| Canned Crabmeat | 2/3 Cup | 1 | Canned Strained Liver | 3-1/2 Ozs. | 2 |
| Canned Drained Tuna | 3 Ozs. | 0 | Canned Tangerine Juice | | |
| Canned Figs | 3 | 36 | (Unsweetened) | 1 Cup | 25 |
| Canned Figs, Low-Cal | 1/2 Cup | 14 | Canned Veal (Infant) | 4 Ozs. | 0 |
| Canned Fried Noodles | 1 Oz. | 17 | Canned Vienna Sausage | 8 Ozs. | 1 |
| Canned Fruit Cocktail | 1/2 Cup | 19 | Cantaloupe, Dried | 1 Cup | 11 |
| Canned Grapefruit Sweetened | 1/2 Cup | 22 | Cantaloupe Fruit | 1/4 Melon | 4 |
| Canned Green Beans | 1 Cup | 6 | Cantaloupe, Pineapple & | | |
| Canned Green Peas (Infant) | 4 Ozs. | 8 | Cherry Salad | 1 Serv. | 13 |
| Canned Green Peas | 4 Ozs. | 14 | Canton Cocktail | 1 Cktl. | T |
| Canned Ham, Boneless | 3 Ozs. | 0 | Canton Pork With Cabbage | 1 Serv. | 4 |
| Canned Ham Deviled | 1 Tbsp. | T | Canton Sauce With | | |
| Canned Ham Spiced | 2 Ozs. | 0 | Fried Shrimp | 1 Serv. | 42 |
| Canned Instant Custard | 4 Ozs. | 23 | Cape Cod Oysters, Raw | 6 Med. | 5 |
| Canned Lamb (Infant) | 4 Ozs. | 0 | Caper Sauce | 1 Tbsp. | T |
| Canned Liver (Infant) | 4 Ozs. | 4 | Capers (Crosse & Blackwell) | 1 Oz. | 1 |
| Canned Low-Cal. Apricot | 1/2 Cup | 9 | Cap'n Crunch, Cereal | | |
| Canned Low-Cal. Bing Cherries | 1 Cup | 22 | (Quaker) | 1 Cup | 30 |
| Canned, Orange Juice, | | | Cappella Wine (Italian Swiss | | |
| Unsweetened | 1 Cup | 28 | Colony-Gold Medal) | 3 Fl. Ozs. | 1 |
| Canned Mixed Vegetables | 4 Ozs. | 15 | Captain's Blood Cocktail | 1 Gl. | 1 |
| Canned Peaches (Infant) | 4 Ozs. | 20 | Caramel Cake Mix: | | |
| Canned Peach Nectar Juice | 1 Cup | 34 | (Duncan Hines) | 1 Pc. | 22 |
| Canned Pears With Syrup | 2 Halves | 17 | Pudding (Betty Crocker) | 1 Oz. | 24 |
| Canned Pears, Strained | 1 Oz. | 4 | Caramel Cake With Icing | 1 Sl. | 44 |
| Canned Pears (Infant) | 4 Ozs. | 18 | Caramel Candies | 1 Med. | 8 |
| Canned Pears Low-Cal. | 1 Cup | 14 | Caramel Choc. Nut Candy | 1 Pc. | 16 |
| Canned Pears Water Pack | 1 Cup | 20 | Caramel Ice Cream | 1/2 Cup | 28 |
| Canned Peas, Strained | 1 Oz. | 4 | Caramel Nut Pudding, | | |
| Canned Pimento | 1 Med. | 2 | Instant (Royal) | 1 Cup | 61 |
| Canned Pineapple Low-Cal. | 1/2 Cup | 11 | Caramel Pudding | 1/2 Cup | 29 |
| Canned Pineapple With Syrup | 1/2 Cup | 14 | Caramel Sauce | 1 Tbsp. | 46 |
| Canned Plums, Low-Cal. | 1/2 Cup | 10 | Caramels With Nuts | 1 Bar | 9 |
| Canned Plums | 6 Halves | 25 | Carbonated Soda, Sweet | 8 Ozs. | 28 |
| Canned Potatoes With Liquid | 4 Ozs. | 10 | Carbonated Water, Seltzer | 4 Ozs. | 0 |
| Canned Potatoes | 4 Sm. | 19 | Caribbean Hot Swizzle | | |
| Canned Prunes With Juice | 1 Cup | 46 | Beverage | 12 Ozs. | 7 |
| Canned Prunes, Strained | 1 Oz. | 7 | Carousel Wine (Gold Seal): | | |
| Canned Pumpkin | 1 Cup | 18 | Pink or White | 3 Fl. Ozs. | 10 |
| Canned Raspberries, | | | Red | 3 Fl. Ozs. | 5 |
| Water Pack | 1 Cup | 6 | Carrot: | | |
| | | | (Butter Kernel) | 1 Cup | 14 |

| FOOD | AMT. | CARB. GRAMS |
|---|---|---|
| (Fall River) | 1 Cup | 14 |
| (Stokely-Van Camp) | 4 Ozs. | 7 |
| Canned, Dietetic: | | |
| Diced (Blue Boy) | 4 Ozs. | 5 |
| Slices (S and W) Nutradiet | 4 Ozs. | 5 |
| (Tillie Lewis) | 4 Ozs. | 5 |
| Frozen (Birds Eye): | | |
| Slices in Butter Sauce | 1 Cup | 7 |
| With Brown Sugar Glaze | 1 Cup | 15 |
| Carrot & Cabbage Garnish | 1 | 2 |
| Carrots (Canned) | 4 Ozs. | 7 |
| Carrots (Canned, Infant) | 4 Ozs. | 8 |
| Carrots (Canned) Strained | 1 Oz. | 2 |
| Carrots de Luxe | 1 Serv. | 8 |
| Carrots, Frozen | 1/2 Cup | 5 |
| Carrots Glazed With Peas | 1 Serv. | 12 |
| Carrot Juice | 1 Cup | 50 |
| Carrot-Raisin Salad | 3 Tbsp. | 28 |
| Carrots, Raw Grated | 1 Cup | 10 |
| Carrots, Raw Sticks | 3 | 3 |
| Carrot Soup | 1 Serv. | 10 |
| Cassava, Common-Bitter | 4 Ozs. | 84 |
| Cashew Nuts | 1 Oz. | 8 |
| Dry Roasted (Planters) | 1 Oz. | 8 |
| Dry Roasted (Skippy) | 1 Oz. | 8 |
| Oil Roasted (Planters) | 1 Oz. | 8 |
| Oil Roasted (Skippy) | 1 Oz. | 7 |
| Casserole Soup | 1 Serv. | 18 |
| Catawba Wine: | | |
| (Gold Seal) | 3 Fl. Ozs. | 5 |
| (Great Western) Pink | 3 Fl. Ozs. | 11 |
| (Mogen David) Pink | 3 Fl. Ozs. | 11 |
| (Mogen David) Red | 3 Fl. Ozs. | 11 |
| Catsup: | | |
| (Heinz) | 1 T. | 5 |
| (Hunt's) | 1 T. | 3 |
| (Nalley's) | 1 T. | 3 |
| Dietetic: | | |
| (Diet Delight) | 1 T. | 1 |
| (Tillie Lewis) | 1 T. | 1 |
| Catsup Butter Spread | 1 Tbsp. | 3 |
| Cauliflower | 1 Cup | 5 |
| Cauliflower, Frozen | 1 Cup | 8 |
| (Birds Eye) | 1 Cup | 6 |
| (Stokely-Van Camp) | 4 Ozs. | 5 |
| Au Gratin (Stouffer's) | 4 Ozs. | 7 |
| Buds, in Butter Sauce (Green Giant) Boil-in-the-Bag | 4 Ozs. | 6 |
| In Cheese Sauce (Green Giant) | 4 Ozs. | 8 |
| Cauliflower Crisps (Epicure) | 1 Oz. | 16 |
| Cauliflower Soup | 1 Serv. | 8 |

| FOOD | AMT. | CARB. GRAMS |
|---|---|---|
| Cauliflower, Sweet Pickled (Smucker's) | 1 Oz. | 11 |
| Caviar, Sturgeon: | | |
| Pressed | 1 Oz. | 1 |
| Whole Eggs | 1 Oz. | 1 |
| Caviar Butter Spread | 1 Tbsp. | T |
| Caviar Cocktail | 1 Oz. | T |
| Cedar Leaves | 4 Ozs. | 0 |
| Celeriac, Vegetable | 1 Serv. | 13 |
| Celeriac | 5 Roots | 9 |
| Celery (Dried) | 1 Cup | 4 |
| Celery | 1 Lg. | 2 |
| Celery & Meat Salad | 1 Serv. | 9 |
| Celery & Olives | 1 Serv. | 2 |
| Celery au Gratin | 1 Serv. | 6 |
| Celery, Cabbage Or Chinese, Fresh | 1 Cup | 2 |
| Celery, Stuffed With Cottage Cheese | 2 Med. | 2 |
| Center Cut Loin Pork Chops | 4 Ozs. | 0 |
| Cereal, Barley (Dry) | 1/2 Cup | 88 |
| Cereal, Cheerios | 4 Ozs. | 9 |
| Cereal, Corn Soya | 1/2 Cup | 13 |
| Cereal, Cooked Average | 4 Ozs. | 14 |
| Cereal, Cooked Wheat Rolled | 4 Ozs. | 23 |
| Cereal, Dry | 1/2 Cup | 15 |
| Cereal, Corn & Soy Grits Mixed | 1/2 Cup | 14 |
| Cereal, Cornflakes | 1 Cup | 21 |
| Cereal, Corn Puffed | 3/4 Cup | 25 |
| Cereal, Corn Soya | 4 Ozs. | 16 |
| Cereal, Force | 4 Ozs. | 11 |
| Cereal, Grape Nut Flakes | 3/4 Cup | 23 |
| Cereal, Infant's Dry Precooked | 1 Oz. | 20 |
| Cereal, Instant Dry Precooked | 1 Oz. | 20 |
| Cereal, Kellogg's Concentrate | 1/2 Cup | 7 |
| Cereal, Kellogg's Special "K" | 1 Cup | 23 |
| Cereal, Kix | 4 Ozs. | 10 |
| Cereal, Krispies | 3/4 Cup | 25 |
| Cereal, Krumbles | 4 Ozs. | 24 |
| Cereal, Maltex, Cooked | 3/4 Cup | 24 |
| Cereal, Maypo Oat, Cooked | 3/4 Cup | 32 |
| Cereal, Meal Wheat | 1/2 Cup | 20 |
| Cereal, Mixed Corn & Soy Grits | 1/2 Cup | 13 |
| Cereal, Mixed Wheat & Malt Bar | 3/4 Cup | 21 |
| Cereal, Muffets | 1 | 18 |
| Cereal, Pablum | 4 Ozs. | 17 |
| Cereal, Pep | 1 Cup | 23 |
| Cereal, Post Toasties | 4 Ozs. | 12 |
| Cereal, Raisin Bran | 1 Cup | 16 |

| FOOD | AMT. | CARB. GRAMS |
|---|---|---|
| Cereal, Ralston Cooked | 2/3 Cup | 20 |
| Cereal, Ralston Wheat Bite Size | 1 Oz. | 15 |
| Cereal, Ralston Wheat Chex | 1/2 Cup | 23 |
| Cereal, Ready To Eat Oat | 4 Ozs. | 13 |
| Cereal, Rice Flakes | 4 Ozs. | 56 |
| Cereal, Rye Flakes | 1/2 Cup | 14 |
| Cereal, Shredded Wheat Malt, Sugar & Salt Added | 4 Ozs. | 81 |
| Cereal, Stirred Wheat Germ | 4 Ozs. | 56 |
| Cereal, Sugar Krisps | 1 Cup | 26 |
| Cereal, Triscuits | 1 | 3 |
| Cereal, Wheat & Barley | 1/2 Cup | 17 |
| Cereal, Wheat & Malted Barley | 3/4 Cup | 21 |
| Cereal, Wheat, Puffed, Sweetened | 1 Oz. | 18 |
| Cereal, Wheat, Whole Meal, Cooked | 4 Ozs. | 20 |
| Cereal, Whole Bran | 1/2 Cup | 16 |
| Certs (Warner-Lambert) | 1 Pc. | 1 |
| Cervelat | 4 Ozs. | 1 |
| Cervelat Sandwich | 1 | 24 |
| Cervelat Sausage | 4 Ozs. | 1 |
| Chablis Wine: | | |
| (Barton & Guestier) | 3 Fl. Ozs. | 1 |
| (Chanson) St. Vincent | 3 Fl. Ozs. | 6 |
| (Gallo) | 3 Fl. Ozs. | 1 |
| (Gallo) Pink | 3 Fl. Ozs. | 3 |
| (Gold Seal) | 3 Fl. Ozs. | T |
| (Great Western) | 3 Fl. Ozs. | 1 |
| (Italian Swiss Colony-Gold Medal) | 3 Fl. Ozs. | T |
| (Italian Swiss Colony-Gold Medal) Napa-Sonoma-Mendocino | 3 Fl. Ozs. | 1 |
| (Italian Swiss Colony-Private Stock) | 3 Fl. Ozs. | T |
| (Italian Swiss Colony-Gold Medal) Gold or Pink | 3 Fl. Ozs. | 3 |
| (Louis M. Martini) | 3 Fl. Ozs. | T |
| Cooked Cereal, Average | 4 Ozs. | 14 |
| Champagne-Apricot Bev. | 1 Gl. | 3 |
| Champagne Cocktail | 6 Ozs. | 10 |
| Champagne Cup Bev. | 1 Gl. | 11 |
| Champagne, Renault Amer. | 1 Gl. | 4 |
| Champagne: | | |
| (Bollinger) | 3 Fl. Ozs. | 3 |
| (Gold Seal) Brut | 3 Fl. Ozs. | 1 |
| (Gold Seal) Brut C. F. | 3 Fl. Ozs. | T |
| (Gold Seal) Pink Extra Dry | 3 Fl. Ozs. | 2 |
| (Great Western) Brut | 3 Fl. Ozs. | 3 |
| (Great Western) Extra Dry | 3 Fl. Ozs. | 4 |
| (Great Western) Pink | 3 Fl. Ozs. | 4 |
| (Great Western) Special Reserve | 3 Fl. Ozs. | 3 |
| (Italian Swiss Colony-Private Stock) | 3 Fl. Ozs. | 2 |
| (Italian Swiss Colony-Private Stock) Pink | 3 Fl. Ozs. | 2 |
| (Lejon) Extra Dry | 3 Fl. Ozs. | 2 |
| (Lejon) Pink | 3 Fl. Ozs. | 2 |
| (Mogen David) American Concord Red | 3 Fl. Ozs. | 9 |
| (Mogen David) American Dry | 3 Fl. Ozs. | 4 |
| (Mumm's) Cordon Rouge Brut | 3 Fl. Ozs. | 1 |
| (Mumm's) Extra Dry | 3 Fl. Ozs. | 5 |
| (Taylor) Brut | 3 Fl. Ozs. | 1 |
| (Taylor) Dry | 3 Fl. Ozs. | 2 |
| (Taylor) Pink | 3 Fl. Ozs. | 3 |
| (Veuve Clicquot) | 3 Fl. Ozs. | T |
| Chaparral Cocktail | 1 Cktl. | 5 |
| Chard Leaves, Cooked | 1 Cup | 2 |
| Charlotte Berry | 1 Serv. | 46 |
| Charlotte Russe Dessert | 1 Serv. | 33 |
| Charmaine, Bing Cherries | 1 Serv. | 33 |
| Chartreuse | 1 Oz. | 7 |
| Chateau Cheese | 1 Oz. | 1 |
| Chateau La Garde Claret, French Red Bordeaux (Chanson) | 3 Fl. Ozs. | 6 |
| Chateauneuf-Du-Pape, French Red Rhone: | | |
| (Barton & Guestier) | 3 Fl. Ozs. | T |
| (Chanson) | 3 Fl. Ozs. | 6 |
| Chateau Olivier Blanc, French White Graves (Chanson) | 3 Fl. Ozs. | 6 |
| Chateau Olivier Rouge, French Red Graves (Chanson) | 3 Fl. Ozs. | 6 |
| Chateau Rausan Segla, French Red Bordeaux (Chanson) | 3 Fl. Ozs. | 6 |
| Chateau St. Germain, French Red Bordeaux (Chanson) | 3 Fl. Ozs. | 6 |
| Chateau Voigny, French Sauternes (Chanson) | 3 Fl. Ozs. | 7 |
| Cheddar Cheese, Grated | 1 Cup | 2 |
| Cheddar Cheese Processed | 4 Ozs. | 2 |
| Cheddar Cheese Processed | 1 Sl. | T |
| Cheddar Cheese Soup, Condensed (Campbell) | 4 Ozs. | 9 |
| Cheerios, Cereal (General Mills) | 1 Cup | 16 |
| Cheese, American Dry & Grated | 4 Ozs. | 2 |

| FOOD | AMT. | CARB. GRAMS | FOOD | AMT. | CARB. GRAMS |
|------|------|------|------|------|------|
| Cheese, American: | | | Cheese, Cottage | 1/2 Cup | 2 |
| Natural: | | | Cheese, Cottage, Creamed | 1 Cup | 6 |
| (Borden) | 2 Ozs. | 1 | (Borden) | 1 Cup | 6 |
| (Kraft) | 2 Ozs. | 1 | Lite Line, Low Fat (Borden) | 1 Cup | 7 |
| (Sealtest) | 2 Ozs. | 1 | California (Breakstone) | 4 Ozs. | 3 |
| Sharp Cheddar (Gerber) | 2 Ozs. | 3 | Tangy Small Curd | | |
| Process: | | | (Breakstone) | 4 Ozs. | 3 |
| (Borden) | 2 Ozs. | 1 | Tangy Small Curd | | |
| (Breakstone) | 2 Ozs. | 1 | (Breakstone) | 1 T. | T |
| Loaf or Slice (Kraft) | 2 Ozs. | 1 | Tiny Soft Curd | | |
| (Sealtest) | 2 Ozs. | 1 | (Breakstone) | 4 Ozs. | 3 |
| With Brick (Kraft) | 2 Ozs. | 1 | Tiny Soft Curd | | |
| With Monterey (Kraft) | 2 Ozs. | 1 | (Breakstone) | 2 Ozs. | 2 |
| With Muenster (Kraft) | 2 Ozs | 1 | (Foremost Blue Moon) | 2 Ozs. | 1 |
| Cheese & Bologna | | | (Kraft) | 2 Ozs. | 2 |
| Canape Spread | 1 Serv. | 1 | (Sealtest) | 1 Cup | 5 |
| Cheese & Corn Rabbit | 1 Serv. | 26 | Light n' Lively, Low Fat | | |
| Cheese & Olive Salad | 1 Serv. | 4 | (Sealtest) | 1 Cup | 6 |
| Cheese & Olive Sand. | 1 | 25 | Chive (Breakstone) | 4 Ozs. | 3 |
| Cheese & Rice | 1 Serv. | 20 | Chive (Breakstone) | 2 Ozs. | T |
| Cheese Asiago (Frigo) | 2 Ozs. | 1 | Pineapple (Breakstone) | 4 Ozs. | 3 |
| Cheese, Baked & Apple | 1 Serv. | 21 | Pineapple (Breakstone) | 2 Ozs. | 2 |
| Cheese, Bakers Special (Kraft) | 2 Ozs. | 14 | Pineapple (Sealtest) | 1 Cup | 13 |
| Cheese, Blue: | | | Spring Garden Salad | | |
| (Borden) | 2 Ozs. | 1 | (Sealtest) | 1 Cup | 8 |
| (Foremost Blue Moon) | 2 Ozs. | T | Uncreamed: | | |
| (Frigo) | 2 Ozs. | 1 | (Borden) | 1 Cup | 6 |
| (Gerber) | 2 Ozs. | 3 | (Kraft) | 2 Ozs. | 1 |
| Natural (Kraft) | 2 Ozs. | 1 | (Sealtest) | 1 Cup | 1 |
| (Stella) | 2 Ozs. | 1 | Pot Style (Breakstone) | 2 Ozs. | 1 |
| Cheese, Bond-Ost, Natural | | | Skim Milk, No Salt | | |
| (Kraft) | 2 Ozs. | 1 | Added (Breakstone) | 2 Ozs. | 1 |
| Cheese, Brick: | | | Cheese, Cream: | | |
| Natural (Kraft) | 2 Ozs. | T | Plain, Unwhipped: | | |
| Process, Slices (Kraft) | 2 Ozs. | 1 | (Borden) | 2 Ozs. | 2 |
| Cheeseburger Sand. | 1 | 22 | (Breakstone) | 2 Ozs. | 1 |
| Cheese Butter Spread | 1 Tbsp. | T | Glass or Loaf (Kraft) | 2 Ozs. | 1 |
| Cheese, Camembert Sand. | 1 | 24 | (Sealtest) | 2 Ozs. | 1 |
| Cheese, Camembert, Domestic: | | | Plain, Whipped (Breakstone), | | |
| (Borden) | 2 Ozs. | 1 | Temp-Tee | 2 Ozs. | 1 |
| (Kraft) | 2 Ozs. | 1 | Flavored, Unwhipped (Kraft): | | |
| Cheese, Caraway, Natural | | | Bacon & Horseradish, Glass | 2 Ozs. | 1 |
| (Kraft) | 2 Ozs. | 1 | Chive, Glass or Loaf | 2 Ozs. | 1 |
| Cheese, Chantelle, Natural | | | Olive-Pimento, Glass | 2 Ozs. | 1 |
| (Kraft) | 2 Ozs. | T | Pimento, Glass or Loaf | 2 Ozs. | 1 |
| Cheese, Chateau | 1 Oz. | 1 | Pineapple | 2 Ozs. | 5 |
| Cheese, Cheddar, Grated | 1 Cup | 2 | Relish, Loaf | 2 Ozs. | 5 |
| Cheese Cheddar, Processed | 4 Ozs. | 2 | Roquefort, Glass | 2 Ozs. | 1 |
| Cheese, Cheddar Sand. | 1 | 26 | Flavored, Whipped (Kraft): | | |
| Cheese, Ched-ett, Process, | | | Catalina | 2 Ozs. | 2 |
| Cold Pack (Kraft) | 2 Ozs. | 4 | Bacon & Horseradish | 2 Ozs. | 1 |
| Cheese, Colby, Natural | | | Blue Cheese | 2 Ozs. | 1 |
| (Kraft) | 2 Ozs. | 1 | Chive | 2 Ozs. | 2 |

| FOOD | AMT. | CARB. GRAMS | FOOD | AMT. | CARB. GRAMS |
|---|---|---|---|---|---|
| Onion | 2 Ozs. | 3 | Natural (Kraft) | 2 Ozs. | 1 |
| Pimento | 2 Ozs. | 2 | Cheese, Jack-Dry, Natural | | |
| Roquefort Cheese | 2 Ozs. | 2 | (Kraft) | 2 Ozs. | T |
| Salami | 2 Ozs. | 2 | Cheese, Jack-Fresh, Natural | | |
| Smoked Salmon | 2 Ozs. | 3 | (Kraft) | 2 Ozs. | T |
| Cheese, Dry Grated | 1 Tbsp. | T | Cheese, Lagerkase, Natural | | |
| Cheese, Edam: | | | (Kraft) | 2 Ozs. | T |
| (House of Gold) | 2 Ozs. | T | Cheese, Leyden, Natural | | |
| Natural (Kraft) | 2 Ozs. | T | (Kraft) | 2 Ozs. | 1 |
| Cheese, Farmer, Packaged | | | Cheese, Leiderkranz (Borden) | 2 Ozs. | T |
| (Breakstone) | 2 Ozs. | 3 | Cheese, Limburger | 1-1/2 Ozs. | T |
| Cheese, Feta | 1 Oz. | 1 | Natural (Kraft) | 2 Ozs. | T |
| Cheese Filled Ravioli | 4 | 24 | Cheese, MacLaren's, Process, | | |
| Cheese Fondue | 1 Serv. | 9 | Cold Pack (Kraft) | 2 Ozs. | 1 |
| Cheese Food | 1 Oz. | T | Cheese, Monterey Jack: | | |
| American: | | | (Frigo) | 2 Ozs. | T |
| (Borden) | 1 Oz. | 2 | Natural (Kraft) | 2 Ozs. | T |
| Grated, Used In Kraft | | | Cheese, Mozzarella: | | |
| Dinner | 1 Oz. | 8 | (Frigo) | 2 Ozs. | T |
| Slices (Kraft) | 1 Oz. | 2 | Natural, Low Moisture, | | |
| (Foremost Blue Moon) | 1 Oz. | 1 | Part Skim: | | |
| With Bacon (Kraft) | 1 Oz. | T | (Kraft) | 2 Ozs. | T |
| Blue, Cold Pack (Kraft) | 1 Oz. | 2 | Pizza (Kraft) | 2 Ozs. | T |
| Cheddar, Cold Pack (Kraft) | 1 Oz. | 2 | Cheese, Muenster: | | |
| Links: | | | Natural (Kraft) | 2 Ozs. | T |
| Bacon, Garlic or | | | Process, Slices (Kraft) | 2 Ozs. | 1 |
| Jalapeno (Kraft) | 1 Oz. | 2 | Cheese, Neufchatel: | | |
| Nippy (Kraft) | 1 Oz. | 2 | (Borden) Eagle Brand | 2 Ozs. | 2 |
| Smokelle (Kraft) | 1 Oz. | 2 | Loaf (Kraft) | 2 Ozs. | 1 |
| Swiss (Kraft) | 1 Oz. | 1 | Natural (Kraft) Calorie-Wise | 2 Ozs. | 1 |
| Loaf: | | | Swankyswigs (Kraft): | | |
| Munst-ett (Kraft) | 1 Oz. | 1 | Olive-Pimento | 2 Ozs. | 2 |
| Pimento Velveeta (Kraft) | 1 Oz. | 2 | Pimento | 2 Ozs. | 2 |
| Pizzalone (Kraft) | 1 Oz. | T | Pineapple | 2 Ozs. | 5 |
| Sharp (Kraft) | 1 Oz. | 1 | Relish | 2 Ozs. | 6 |
| Super Blend (Kraft) | 1 Oz. | 1 | Roka | 2 Ozs. | 1 |
| Super Blend With | | | Cheese, Nippy Whipped | | |
| Caraway (Kraft) | 1 Oz. | 1 | (Kraft) | 2 Ozs. | 2 |
| Velveeta, California | | | Cheese, Nuworld (Kraft) | 2 Ozs. | 1 |
| Only (Kraft) | 1 Oz. | 2 | Cheese, Old English Loaf, | | |
| Cheese, Fontina (Stella) | 2 Ozs. | 1 | Process, Slices (Kraft) | 2 Ozs. | 1 |
| Cheese, Frankenmuth, Natural | | | Cheese Omelet | 2 Eggs | 1 |
| (Kraft) | 2 Ozs. | 1 | Cheese, Pabst-ett | 1 Oz. | 2 |
| Cheese, Gjetost, Natural | | | Cheese, Parmesan, | | |
| (Kraft) | 2 Ozs. | 26 | Fresh Grated | 4 Ozs. | 2 |
| Cheese, Gorgonzola: | | | Cheese, Parmesan, | | |
| (Foremost Blue Moon) | 2 Ozs. | T | Dry Grated | 4 Ozs. | 2 |
| Natural (Kraft) | 2 Ozs. | T | Cheese, Parmesan: | | |
| Cheese, Gouda: | | | Natural: | | |
| Baby (Foremost Blue Moon) | 2 Ozs. | T | (Frigo) | 2 Ozs. | 1 |
| Natural (Kraft) | 2 Ozs. | 1 | (Kraft) | 2 Ozs. | 1 |
| Cheese, Gruyere: | | | (Stella) | 2 Ozs. | 2 |
| (Gerber) | 2 Ozs. | | | | |

31

| FOOD | AMT. | CARB. GRAMS | FOOD | AMT. | CARB. GRAMS |
|------|------|-------------|------|------|-------------|
| Grated: | | | Cheese, Scamorze: | | |
| (Borden) | 1 Tbsp. | T | (Frigo) | 2 Ozs. | T |
| (Buitoni) | 1 Tbsp. | 1 | Natural (Kraft) | 2 Ozs. | T |
| (Frigo) | 1 Tbsp. | T | Cheese Souffle | 1/2 Cup | 6 |
| (Kraft) | 2 Ozs. | 2 | Frozen (Stouffer's) | 4 Ozs. | 12 |
| Shredded (Kraft) | 2 Ozs. | 2 | Cheese Soup | 1 Serv. | 8 |
| Cheese, Parmesan & Romano, | | | Cheese Spread: | | |
| Grated (Borden) | 2 Ozs. | 2 | American: | | |
| Cheese, Pepato (Frigo) | 2 Ozs. | 1 | Process (Borden) | 1 Oz. | 2 |
| Cheese Pie (Tastykake) | 4 Ozs. | 51 | Process (Kraft) | | |
| Cheese, Pimento American | | | Swankyswig | 1 Oz. | 1 |
| Process: | | | (Nabisco) Snack Mate | 1 Oz. | 2 |
| (Borden) | 2 Ozs. | 1 | Bacon | 1 Oz. | 2 |
| Loaf or Slices (Kraft) | 2 Ozs. | T | Cheddar (Nabisco) Snack Mate | 1 Oz. | 2 |
| Cheese Pineapple Cake | 1 Pc. | 34 | Cheese & Bacon | | |
| Cheese, Pizza: | | | (Kraft) Swankyswig | 1 Oz. | T |
| (Frigo) | 2 Ozs. | T | Cheez Whiz, Process (Kraft) | 1 Oz. | 1 |
| (Kraft) | 2 Ozs. | T | Garlic, Process (Kraft) | | |
| Shredded (Kraft) | 2 Ozs. | T | Swankyswig | 1 Oz. | 2 |
| Cheese, Port du Salut, | | | Imitation (Kraft): | | |
| (Foremost Blue Moon) | 2 Ozs. | T | Calorie-Wise | 1 Oz. | 3 |
| Natural (Kraft) | 2 Ozs. | T | Tasty Loaf | 1 Oz. | 3 |
| Cheese Prim-Ost, Natural | | | Limburger (Kraft) | 1 Oz. | T |
| (Kraft) | 2 Ozs. | 26 | Neufchatel: | | |
| Cheese, Provolone (Frigo) | 2 Ozs. | 1 | Bacon & Horseradish | | |
| Cheese, Provolone or Provoloncini, | | | (Kraft) Party Snacks | 1 Oz. | T |
| Natural (Kraft) | 2 Ozs. | 1 | Chipped Beef (Kraft) | | |
| Cheese Puff, Hors D'Oeuvres, | | | Party Snacks | 1 Oz. | 1 |
| Frozen (Durkee) | 1 Pc. | 3 | Chive (Kraft) Party | | |
| Cheese Puff Balls | 1 Serv. | 2 | Snacks | 1 Oz. | 1 |
| Cheese, Ricotta (Sierra) | 2 Ozs. | 2 | Clam (Kraft) Party | | |
| Cheese, Romano: | | | Snacks | 1 Oz. | 1 |
| Natural: | | | Onion Soup (Kraft) | | |
| (Frigo) | 2 Ozs. | 1 | Party Snacks | 1 Oz. | 1 |
| (Kraft) | 2 Ozs. | 1 | Pimento (Kraft) Party | | |
| (Stella) | 2 Ozs. | 1 | Snacks | 1 Oz. | 1 |
| Grated: | | | Old English | 1 Oz. | 2 |
| (Buitoni) | 2 Ozs. | 6 | (Kraft) Swankyswig | 1 Oz. | T |
| (Frigo) | 2 Ozs. | 1 | Olive Pimento | 1 Oz. | 2 |
| (Kraft) | 2 Ozs. | 2 | Onion Flavor, French | | |
| Shredded (Kraft) | 2 Ozs. | 2 | (Nabisco) Snack Mate | 1 Tsp. | T |
| Cheese, Roquefort, Natural: | | | Pimento | 1 Oz. | 2 |
| (Borden) | 2 Ozs. | 1 | (Sealtest) | 1 Oz. | 1 |
| (Kraft) | 2 Ozs. | 1 | (Nabisco) Snack Mate | 1 Oz. | 2 |
| Cheese Salad, Frozen | 1 Serv. | T | Cheez Whiz (Kraft) | 1 Oz. | 1 |
| Cheese, Sap Sago, | | | Neufchatel (Kraft) | 1 Oz. | 1 |
| Natural (Kraft) | 2 Ozs. | 3 | Process (Kraft): | | |
| Cheese, Sardo Romano, | | | Swankyswig | 1 Oz. | 1 |
| Natural (Kraft) | 2 Ozs. | 1 | Velveeta | 1 Oz. | 2 |
| Cheese Sauce | 1/2 Cup | 5 | Pineapple | 1 Oz. | 2 |
| Cheese Sauce Casserole Base | | | Roka Bleu | 1 Oz. | 2 |
| (Pennsylvania Dutch) | 1 Cup | 36 | Sharpie, Process (Kraft) | 1 Oz. | T |

| FOOD | AMT. | CARB. GRAMS | FOOD | AMT. | CARB. GRAMS |
|---|---|---|---|---|---|
| Smokelle Swankyswig, Process (Kraft) | 1 Oz. | T | (White Rose) | 6 Ozs. | 22 |
| Velveeta, Process (Kraft) | 1 Oz. | 2 | (Yes Madame) | 1 Cup | 28 |
| Cheese Straws | 3 | 3 | Cherries (Canned), Royal Anne In Syrup | 1 Cup | 28 |
| (Durkee) | 1 Pc. | 1 | Cherries, Fresh Pitted | 1 Cup | 20 |
| Cheese, Swiss, Domestic: | | | Cherries, Frozen, With Syrup, | | |
| Natural: | | | Quick Thaw (Birds Eye) | 1 Cup | 84 |
| (Foremost Blue Moon) | 2 Ozs. | 2 | Cheerios, Cereal | 4 Ozs. | 9 |
| (Kraft) | 2 Ozs. | 1 | Cherry & Cheese Salad | 1 Serv. | 17 |
| (Sealtest) | 2 Ozs. | 1 | Cherry, Black, Soft Drink: | | |
| Process: | | | Sweetened: | | |
| (Borden) | 2 Ozs. | 1 | (Canada Dry) | 8 Fl. Ozs. | 32 |
| Loaf (Kraft) | 2 Ozs. | 1 | (Dr. Brown's) | 8 Fl. Ozs. | 27 |
| Slices (Kraft) | 2 Ozs. | 1 | (Hoffman) | 8 Fl. Ozs. | 30 |
| With American (Kraft) | 2 Ozs. | 1 | (Key Food) | 8 Fl. Ozs. | 27 |
| With Muenster (Kraft) | 2 Ozs. | 1 | (Kirsch) | 8 Fl. Ozs. | 29 |
| Washed Curd, Natural | | | (Shasta) | 8 Fl. Ozs. | 29 |
| (Kraft) | 2 Ozs. | 1 | (Waldbaum) | 8 Fl. Ozs. | 27 |
| Cheese, Swiss Fondue | | | Unsweetened or Low Calorie: | | |
| With Toast | 1 Serv. | 14 | (Dr. Brown's) Slim-Ray | 8 Fl. Ozs. | 1 |
| Cheese, Swiss Gruyere | 4 Ozs. | 2 | (Hoffman) | 8 Fl. Ozs. | 1 |
| Cheese, Swiss Processed | 4 Ozs. | 1 | (No-Cal) | 8 Fl. Ozs. | 0 |
| Cheese, Swiss Sandwich | 1 | 24 | (Shasta) | 8 Fl. Ozs. | T |
| Cheese, Tomato Rabbit | 1 Serv. | 20 | Cherry Cake Mix: | | |
| Cheese, Velveeta | 4 Ozs. | 2 | (Duncan Hines) | 1 Pc. | 36 |
| Cheese, With Brown Rice | 1 Serv. | 21 | Chip (Betty Crocker) | 1 Oz. | 27 |
| Cheesy Snap Beans | 1 Serv. | 5 | Cherry Chiffon Pie | 1 Pc. | 46 |
| Chef's Salad Bowl | 1 Serv. | 24 | Cherry Conserve | 1 Oz. | 32 |
| Chelois Wine | | | Cherry Drink: | | |
| (Great Western) | 3 Fl. Ozs. | 2 | (Hi-C) | 8 Fl. Ozs. | 30 |
| Chenin Blanc Wine | | | (Wyler's) | 8 Fl. Ozs. | 21 |
| (Louis M. Martini) Dry | 3 Fl. Ozs. | T | Cherry Fruit Roll, | | |
| Cheri Suisse, Swiss | | | Frozen (Chun King) | 1 Oz. | 10 |
| Liqueur (Leroux) | 1 Fl. Oz. | 10 | Cherry Gelatin Mold | 1 Serv. | 19 |
| Cherries, Candied | 1 Lg. | 4 | Cherry Heering, Danish | | |
| (Liberty) | 1 Oz. | 22 | Liqueur | 1 Fl. Oz. | 10 |
| Cherries, Candied | | | Cherry Ice | 1/2 Cup | 27 |
| Choc. Covered | 2 Ozs | 43 | Cherry Jelly (Slenderella) | 1 T. | 6 |
| Cherries (Canned), | | | Cherry Karise, | | |
| Bing Low-Cal. | 1 Cup | 22 | Liqueur (Leroux) | 1 Fl. Oz. | 7 |
| (Blue Boy) | 4 Ozs. | 10 | Cherry Kijafa, | | |
| Dark (Yes Madame) | 1 Cup | 22 | Danish Wine | 3 Fl. Ozs. | 15 |
| Cherries (Canned), | | | Cherry Liqueur: | | |
| Bing In Syrup | 1 Cup | 59 | (Bols) | 1 Fl. Oz. | 9 |
| Cherries (Canned), | | | (Hiram Walker) | 1 Fl. Oz. | 8 |
| Bing In Water | | | (Leroux) | 1 Fl. Oz. | 7 |
| (Stokely-Van Camp) | 1/2 Cup | 12 | Cherry, Maraschino (Liberty) | 5 Aver. | 8 |
| Cherries (Canned), Red Sour | 1 Cup | 24 | Cherry Marmalade | 1 Tbsp. | 14 |
| Cherries (Canned), Royal Anne | 1 Cup | 21 | Cherry Pie: | | |
| (Diet Delight) | 1 Cup | 22 | Cherry-Apple (Tastykake) | 4 Ozs. | 56 |
| Unsweetened (S and W) | | | Frozen: | | |
| Nutradiet | 12 Cherries | 8 | (Banquet) | 4 Ozs. | 40 |

33

| FOOD | AMT. | CARB. GRAMS | FOOD | AMT. | CARB. GRAMS |
|---|---|---|---|---|---|
| (Morton) | 4 Ozs. | 9 | Peppermint (Amurol) | 1 Stick | 2 |
| (Mrs. Smith's) | 1 Pc. | 26 | Chianti Wine: | | |
| Cherry Pie Filling | | | (Antinori): | | |
| (Lucky Leaf) | 8 Ozs. | 29 | Classico | 3 Fl. Ozs. | 6 |
| Cherry-Plum Danish Dessert | | | 1955 | 3 Fl. Ozs. | 6 |
| (Junket) | 1/2 Cup | 67 | Vintage | 3 Fl. Ozs. | 6 |
| Cherry Preserve (Dia-Mel) | 1 T. | 5 | Brolio Classico | 3 Fl. Ozs. | T |
| Cherry Rum Fizz | 12 Ozs. | 5 | (Italian Swiss Colony): | | |
| Cherry, Soft Drink | 8 Ozs. | 28 | Gold Medal | 3 Fl. Ozs. | 1 |
| (Canada Dry) | 8 Fl. Ozs. | 29 | Private Stock, Tipo | 3 Fl. Ozs. | T |
| Fanta | 8 Fl. Ozs. | 28 | (Louis M. Martini) | 3 Fl. Ozs. | T |
| (Hires) | 8 Fl. Ozs. | 27 | Chicken & Baked Clams | 1 Serv. | 6 |
| (Nedick's) | 8 Fl. Ozs. | 27 | Chicken & Rice, Puerto Rican | 1 Serv. | 31 |
| (Yoo-Hoo) | 8 Fl. Ozs. | 24 | Chicken & Sherried | | |
| High-Protein (Yoo-Hoo) | 8 Fl. Ozs. | 32 | Mushrooms | 1 Serv. | 16 |
| (Yukon Club) | 8 Fl. Ozs. | 29 | Chicken & Spaghetti | 1 Serv. | 16 |
| Cherry Stone Clams | 6 | 5 | Chicken A La King: | | |
| Cherry Syrup, Dietetic: | | | Canned (College Inn) | 4 Ozs. | 2 |
| (Dia-Mel) | 1 Tbsp. | 5 | Canned (Richardson & | | |
| (No-Cal) Black | 1 Tbsp. | T | Robbins) | 1/2 Cup | 3 |
| Cherry Tapioca | 1 Serv. | 47 | Frozen (Banquet) | | |
| Cherry Wine | | | Cookin' Bag | 4 Ozs. | 7 |
| (Mogen David) | 3 Fl. Ozs. | 17 | Chicken Aspic | 1 Serv. | 2 |
| Chestnuts | 2 Lg. | 7 | Chicken Baronet (Lipton) | 1 Pkg. | 90 |
| Chestnut Creamed | 1 Serv. | 33 | Chicken Bisque | 1 Serv. | 6 |
| Chestnut & Red Cabbage | 1 Serv. | 30 | Chicken Bouillon/Broth: | | |
| Chestnut Souffle | 1 Serv. | 15 | (Croyden House) | 1 Tsp. | 2 |
| Chestnut Stuffing | 1/2 Cup | 26 | (Herb-Ox) | 1 Cube | T |
| Chewing Gum: | | | (Maggi) | 1 Cube | 1 |
| Sweetened: | | | (Wyler's) | 1 Cube | 1 |
| Bazooka, Bubble, 1c Size | 1 Pc. | 4 | Chicken, Braised | | |
| Bazooka, Bubble, 5c Size | 1 Pc. | 21 | With Dressing | 1 Serv. | 29 |
| Beechies | 1 Tablet | 2 | Chicken, Braised | 1 Serv. | 7 |
| Beech-Nut | 1 Stick | 2 | Chicken, Boiled | 1 Serv. | 0 |
| Beemans | 1 Stick | 2 | Chicken Cacciatore (Hormel) | 1-Lb. Can | 8 |
| Black Jack | 1 Stick | 2 | Chicken, Canned Boned | 3 Ozs. | T |
| Chiclets | 1 Pc. | 1 | (College Inn) | 4 Ozs. | 0 |
| Cinnamint | 1 Stick | 2 | (Lynden) | 4 Ozs. | 0 |
| Clove | 1 Stick | 2 | (Richardson & Robbins) | 4 Ozs. | 1 |
| Dentyne | 1 Pc. | 1 | Whole (College Inn) | 4 Ozs. | 0 |
| Doublemint | 1 Stick | 2 | Chicken Croquettes | 1 Med. | 9 |
| Fruit Punch | 1 Stick | 2 | Chicken, Creamed | 1/2 Cup | 6 |
| Juicy Fruit | 1 Stick | 2 | Frozen (Stouffer's) | 11-1/2 Ozs. | 16 |
| Peppermint (Clark) | 1 Stick | 2 | Chicken Dinner: | | |
| Sour Lemon (Clark) | 1 Stick | 2 | Canned: | | |
| Spearmint (Wrigley's) | 1 Stick | 2 | Noodle (Heinz) | 8 Ozs. | 16 |
| Teaberry | 1 Stick | 2 | Frozen: | | |
| Unsweetened: | | | Chicken & Dumplings | | |
| All Flavors (Clark) | 1 Stick | 1 | Buffet (Banquet) | 2 Lbs. | 111 |
| All Flavors (Estee) | 1 Stick | 1 | (Tom Thumb) | 3-Lb. 8 Ozs. | 112 |
| Bazooka, Bubble, Sugarless | 1 Pc. | T | Fried: | | |
| Bubble (Estee) | 1 Pc. | 0 | (Banquet) | Dinner | 48 |
| (Harvey's) | 1 Stick | 1 | (Morton) | Dinner | 22 |

| FOOD | AMT. | CARB. GRAMS |
|---|---|---|
| Smokelle Swankyswig, Process (Kraft) | 1 Oz. | T |
| Velveeta, Process (Kraft) | 1 Oz. | 2 |
| Cheese Straws | 3 | 3 |
| (Durkee) | 1 Pc. | 1 |
| Cheese, Swiss, Domestic: | | |
| Natural: | | |
| (Foremost Blue Moon) | 2 Ozs. | 2 |
| (Kraft) | 2 Ozs. | 1 |
| (Sealtest) | 2 Ozs. | 1 |
| Process: | | |
| (Borden) | 2 Ozs. | 1 |
| Loaf (Kraft) | 2 Ozs. | 1 |
| Slices (Kraft) | 2 Ozs. | 1 |
| With American (Kraft) | 2 Ozs. | 1 |
| With Muenster (Kraft) | 2 Ozs. | 1 |
| Washed Curd, Natural (Kraft) | 2 Ozs. | 1 |
| Cheese, Swiss Fondue With Toast | 1 Serv. | 14 |
| Cheese, Swiss Gruyere | 4 Ozs. | 2 |
| Cheese, Swiss Processed | 4 Ozs. | 1 |
| Cheese, Swiss Sandwich | 1 | 24 |
| Cheese, Tomato Rabbit | 1 Serv. | 20 |
| Cheese, Velveeta | 4 Ozs. | 2 |
| Cheese, With Brown Rice | 1 Serv. | 21 |
| Cheesy Snap Beans | 1 Serv. | 5 |
| Chef's Salad Bowl | 1 Serv. | 24 |
| Chelois Wine (Great Western) | 3 Fl. Ozs. | 2 |
| Chenin Blanc Wine (Louis M. Martini) Dry | 3 Fl. Ozs. | T |
| Cheri Suisse, Swiss Liqueur (Leroux) | 1 Fl. Oz. | 10 |
| Cherries, Candied | 1 Lg. | 4 |
| (Liberty) | 1 Oz. | 22 |
| Cherries, Candied Choc. Covered | 2 Ozs | 43 |
| Cherries (Canned), Bing Low-Cal. | 1 Cup | 22 |
| (Blue Boy) | 4 Ozs | 18 |
| Dark (Yes Madame) | 1 Cup | 22 |
| Cherries (Canned), Bing In Syrup | 1 Cup | 59 |
| Cherries (Canned), Bing In Water (Stokely-Van Camp) | 1/2 Cup | 12 |
| Cherries (Canned), Red Sour | 1 Cup | 24 |
| Cherries (Canned), Royal Anne | 1 Cup | 21 |
| (Diet Delight) | 1 Cup | 22 |
| Unsweetened (S and W) Nutradiet | 12 Cherries | 8 |
| (White Rose) | 6 Ozs. | 22 |
| (Yes Madame) | 1 Cup | 28 |
| Cherries (Canned), Royal Anne In Syrup | 1 Cup | 28 |
| Cherries, Fresh Pitted | 1 Cup | 20 |
| Cherries, Frozen, With Syrup, Quick Thaw (Birds Eye) | 1 Cup | 84 |
| Cheerios, Cereal | 4 Ozs. | 9 |
| Cherry & Cheese Salad | 1 Serv. | 17 |
| Cherry, Black, Soft Drink: | | |
| Sweetened: | | |
| (Canada Dry) | 8 Fl. Ozs. | 32 |
| (Dr. Brown's) | 8 Fl. Ozs. | 27 |
| (Hoffman) | 8 Fl. Ozs. | 30 |
| (Key Food) | 8 Fl. Ozs. | 27 |
| (Kirsch) | 8 Fl. Ozs. | 29 |
| (Shasta) | 8 Fl. Ozs. | 29 |
| (Waldbaum) | 8 Fl. Ozs. | 27 |
| Unsweetened or Low Calorie: | | |
| (Dr. Brown's) Slim-Ray | 8 Fl. Ozs. | 1 |
| (Hoffman) | 8 Fl. Ozs. | 1 |
| (No-Cal) | 8 Fl. Ozs. | 0 |
| (Shasta) | 8 Fl. Ozs. | T |
| Cherry Cake Mix: | | |
| (Duncan Hines) | 1 Pc. | 36 |
| Chip (Betty Crocker) | 1 Oz. | 27 |
| Cherry Chiffon Pie | 1 Pc. | 46 |
| Cherry Conserve | 1 Oz. | 32 |
| Cherry Drink: | | |
| (Hi-C) | 8 Fl. Ozs. | 30 |
| (Wyler's) | 8 Fl. Ozs. | 21 |
| Cherry Fruit Roll, Frozen (Chun King) | 1 Oz. | 10 |
| Cherry Gelatin Mold | 1 Serv. | 19 |
| Cherry Heering, Danish Liqueur | 1 Fl. Oz. | 10 |
| Cherry Ice | 1/2 Cup | 27 |
| Cherry Jelly (Slenderella) | 1 T. | 6 |
| Cherry Karise, Liqueur (Leroux) | 1 Fl. Oz. | 7 |
| Cherry Kijafa, Danish Wine | 3 Fl. Ozs. | 15 |
| Cherry Liqueur: | | |
| (Bols) | 1 Fl. Oz. | 9 |
| (Hiram Walker) | 1 Fl. Oz. | 8 |
| (Leroux) | 1 Fl. Oz. | 7 |
| Cherry, Maraschino (Liberty) | 5 Aver. | 8 |
| Cherry Marmalade | 1 Tbsp. | 14 |
| Cherry Pie: | | |
| Cherry-Apple (Tastykake) | 4 Ozs. | 56 |
| Frozen: | | |
| (Banquet) | 4 Ozs. | 40 |

| FOOD | AMT. | CARB. GRAMS |
|---|---|---|
| (Morton) | 4 Ozs. | 9 |
| (Mrs. Smith's) | 1 Pc. | 26 |
| Cherry Pie Filling | | |
| (Lucky Leaf) | 8 Ozs. | 29 |
| Cherry-Plum Danish Dessert | | |
| (Junket) | 1/2 Cup | 67 |
| Cherry Preserve (Dia-Mel) | 1 T. | 5 |
| Cherry Rum Fizz | 12 Ozs. | 5 |
| Cherry, Soft Drink | 8 Ozs. | 28 |
| (Canada Dry) | 8 Fl. Ozs. | 29 |
| Fanta | 8 Fl. Ozs. | 28 |
| (Hires) | 8 Fl. Ozs. | 27 |
| (Nedick's) | 8 Fl. Ozs. | 27 |
| (Yoo-Hoo) | 8 Fl. Ozs. | 24 |
| High-Protein (Yoo-Hoo) | 8 Fl. Ozs. | 32 |
| (Yukon Club) | 8 Fl. Ozs. | 29 |
| Cherry Stone Clams | 6 | 5 |
| Cherry Syrup, Dietetic: | | |
| (Dia-Mel) | 1 Tbsp. | 5 |
| (No-Cal) Black | 1 Tbsp. | T |
| Cherry Tapioca | 1 Serv. | 47 |
| Cherry Wine | | |
| (Mogen David) | 3 Fl. Ozs. | 28 |
| Chestnuts | 2 Lg. | 7 |
| Chestnut Creamed | 1 Serv. | 33 |
| Chestnut & Red Cabbage | 1 Serv. | 30 |
| Chestnut Souffle | 1 Serv. | 15 |
| Chestnut Stuffing | 1/2 Cup | 26 |
| Chewing Gum: | | |
| Sweetened: | | |
| Bazooka, Bubble, 1c Size | 1 Pc. | 4 |
| Bazooka, Bubble, 5c Size | 1 Pc. | 21 |
| Beechies | 1 Tablet | 1 |
| Beech-Nut | 1 Stick | 2 |
| Beemans | 1 Stick | 2 |
| Black Jack | 1 Stick | 2 |
| Chiclets | 1 Pc. | 1 |
| Cinnamint | 1 Stick | 2 |
| Clove | 1 Stick | 2 |
| Dentyne | 1 Pc. | 1 |
| Doublemint | 1 Stick | 2 |
| Fruit Punch | 1 Stick | 2 |
| Juicy Fruit | 1 Stick | 2 |
| Peppermint (Clark) | 1 Stick | 2 |
| Sour Lemon (Clark) | 1 Stick | 2 |
| Spearmint (Wrigley's) | 1 Stick | 2 |
| Teaberry | 1 Stick | 2 |
| Unsweetened: | | |
| All Flavors (Clark) | 1 Stick | 1 |
| All Flavors (Estee) | 1 Stick | 1 |
| Bazooka, Bubble, Sugarless | 1 Pc. | T |
| Bubble (Estee) | 1 Pc. | 0 |
| (Harvey's) | 1 Stick | 1 |

| FOOD | AMT. | CARB. GRAMS |
|---|---|---|
| Peppermint (Amurol) | 1 Stick | 2 |
| Chianti Wine: | | |
| (Antinori): | | |
| Classico | 3 Fl. Ozs. | 6 |
| 1955 | 3 Fl. Ozs. | 6 |
| Vintage | 3 Fl. Ozs. | 6 |
| Brolio Classico | 3 Fl. Ozs. | T |
| (Italian Swiss Colony): | | |
| Gold Medal | 3 Fl. Ozs. | 1 |
| Private Stock, Tipo | 3 Fl. Ozs. | T |
| (Louis M. Martini) | 3 Fl. Ozs. | T |
| Chicken & Baked Clams | 1 Serv. | 6 |
| Chicken & Rice, Puerto Rican | 1 Serv. | 31 |
| Chicken & Sherried | | |
| Mushrooms | 1 Serv. | 16 |
| Chicken & Spaghetti | 1 Serv. | 16 |
| Chicken A La King: | | |
| Canned (College Inn) | 4 Ozs. | 2 |
| Canned (Richardson & | | |
| Robbins) | 1/2 Cup | 3 |
| Frozen (Banquet) | | |
| Cookin' Bag | 4 Ozs. | 7 |
| Chicken Aspic | 1 Serv. | 2 |
| Chicken Baronet (Lipton) | 1 Pkg. | 90 |
| Chicken Bisque | 1 Serv. | 6 |
| Chicken Bouillon/Broth: | | |
| (Croyden House) | 1 Tsp. | 2 |
| (Herb-Ox) | 1 Cube | T |
| (Maggi) | 1 Cube | 1 |
| (Wyler's) | 1 Cube | 1 |
| Chicken, Braised | | |
| With Dressing | 1 Serv. | 29 |
| Chicken, Braised | 1 Serv. | 7 |
| Chicken, Boiled | 1 Serv. | 0 |
| Chicken Cacciatore (Hormel) | 1-Lb. Can | 8 |
| Chicken, Canned Boned | 3 Ozs. | T |
| (College Inn) | 4 Ozs. | 0 |
| (Lynden) | 4 Ozs. | 0 |
| (Richardson & Robbins) | 4 Ozs. | 1 |
| Whole (College Inn) | 4 Ozs. | 0 |
| Chicken Croquettes | 1 Med. | 9 |
| Chicken, Creamed | 1/2 Cup | 6 |
| Frozen (Stouffer's) | 11-1/2 Ozs. | 16 |
| Chicken Dinner: | | |
| Canned: | | |
| Noodle (Heinz) | 8 Ozs. | 16 |
| Frozen: | | |
| Chicken & Dumplings | | |
| Buffet (Banquet) | 2 Lbs. | 111 |
| (Tom Thumb) | 3-Lb. 8 Ozs. | 112 |
| Fried: | | |
| (Banquet) | Dinner | 48 |
| (Morton) | Dinner | 22 |

34

| FOOD | AMT. | CARB. GRAMS | FOOD | AMT. | CARB. GRAMS |
|---|---|---|---|---|---|
| (Swanson) | Dinner | 46 | Chicken Sand. Sliced | 1 | 21 |
| (Swanson) 3-Course | Dinner | 91 | Chicken, Sauteed | 1 Serv. | 5 |
| Chicken Fats | 1 Oz. | 0 | Chicken Saute' Chasseur | 1 Serv. | 7 |
| Chicken Fricassee, Canned: | | | Chicken (Stewed) | 1/2 Med. | 0 |
| (College Inn) | 4 Ozs. | 3 | Chicken Soup | 1 Cup | 2 |
| (Richardson & Robbins) | 1 Cup | 5 | Chicken Soup, Canned: | | |
| Chicken, Fried | | | Barley (Manischewitz) | 4 Ozs. | 6 |
| Frozen (Swanson) | 4 Ozs. | 18 | Broth: | | |
| Chicken Giblets | 1 Serv. | T | (Campbell) | 4 Ozs. | 1 |
| Chicken Giblets Fricassee | 1 Serv. | 6 | Diet, Condensed | | |
| Chicken Gizzard | 4 Ozs. | 0 | (Claybourne) | 1 Cup | 0 |
| Chicken Gravy | 2 Ozs. | 4 | (College Inn) | 4 Ozs. | T |
| Chicken Gumbo | 1 Cup | 6 | Low Calorie | | |
| Chicken Heart | 3 Ozs. | 1 | (College Inn) | 4 Ozs. | T |
| Chicken (Infant) | 4 Ozs. | T | (Richardson & Robbins) | 1 Cup | T |
| Chicken Livers | 1 Oz. | T | With Noodles | | |
| Chicken Liver ala Chelsea | 1 Serv. | 1 | (College Inn) | 4 Ozs. | 1 |
| Chicken Liver & Poached | | | With Rice: | | |
| Eggs | 1 Serv. | 2 | (College Inn) | 4 Ozs. | 3 |
| Chicken Liver Canape | | | (Richardson & Robbins) | 1 Cup | 1 |
| Spread | 1 Serv. | T | Cream of: | | |
| Chicken Liver de Luxe, | | | Condensed (Campbell) | 4 Ozs. | 7 |
| Appetizers | 1 | 3 | (Heinz) | 1 Cup | 9 |
| Chicken Liver de Luxe | 1 Serv. | 3 | Great American | 1 Cup | 8 |
| Chicken Liver Kebobs | 1 Serv. | 5 | & Dumplings: | | |
| Chicken Liver Puff, Hors | | | Condensed (Campbell) | 4 Ozs. | 5 |
| D'Oeuvres, Frozen (Durkee) | 1 Pc. | 3 | Gumbo: | | |
| Chicken Liver, Raw | 4 Ozs | 3 | Condensed (Campbell) | 4 Ozs. | 8 |
| Chicken Liver Sand. | 1 | 26 | & Matzoth Balls | 1 Cup | 34 |
| Chicken Noodle Soup | 1 Cup | 8 | & Noodle: | | |
| Chicken & Noodles, Frozen | | | Condensed (Campbell) | 4 Ozs. | 8 |
| Escalloped (Stouffer's) | 8 Ozs. | 36 | Noodle-O's (Campbell) | 4 Ozs. | 9 |
| (Swanson) | 8 Ozs. | 17 | (Heinz) | 1 Cup | 8 |
| Chicken Paprika | 1 Serv. | 0 | (Manischewitz) | 4 Ozs. | 2 |
| Chicken Pie | 1 Serv. | 20 | (Tillie Lewis) Dietetic | 1 Cup | 4 |
| Frozen: | | | With Dumplings (Heinz) | | |
| (Banquet) | 4 Ozs. | 38 | Great American | 1 Cup | 8 |
| (Morton) | 4 Ozs. | 37 | With Stars: | | |
| (Stouffer's) | 4 Ozs. | 44 | Condensed (Campbell) | 4 Ozs. | 7 |
| (Swanson) | 4 Ozs. | 53 | (Heinz) | 1 Cup | 7 |
| Chicken Pot Pie | 4 Ozs | 20 | & Rice: | | |
| Chicken Puff, Hors D'Oeuvres, | | | Condensed (Campbell) | 4 Ozs. | 5 |
| Frozen (Durkee) | 1 Pc. | 3 | (Heinz) | 1 Cup | 7 |
| Chicken Ravioli (Lyden) 14-1/2 Oz Can | | 53 | (Manischewitz) | 4 Ozs. | 3 |
| Chicken, Raw (Broilers) | 4 Ozs. | 0 | With Mushrooms (Heinz) | | |
| Chicken, Raw (Friers) | 4 Ozs. | 0 | Great American | 1 Cup | 10 |
| Chicken, Raw (Roasters) | 4 Ozs. | 0 | Vegetable: | | |
| Chicken, Raw | | | Condensed (Campbell) | 4 Ozs. | 8 |
| (Stewing Hens) | 4 Ozs. | 0 | (Manischewitz) | 4 Ozs. | 4 |
| Chicken Rice Soup | 1 Cup | 5 | (Heinz) | 1 Cup | 10 |
| Chicken Roast | 1 Serv. | 0 | With Kasha (Manischewitz) | 4 Ozs. | 3 |
| Chicken Salad | 4 Ozs. | 3 | Chicken Soup, Condensed | 4 Ozs | 2 |
| Chicken Salad Sand. | 1 | 25 | | | |

| FOOD | AMT. | CARB. GRAMS |
|---|---|---|
| Chicken Soup, Creamed, Canned | 1 Cup | 12 |
| Chicken Soup Mix: | | |
| & Noodle: | | |
| (Golden Grain) | 1 Cup | 8 |
| (Lipton) | 2 Ozs. | 29 |
| With Diced Chicken (Lipton) | 1 Pkg. | 27 |
| (Wyler's) | 4 Fl. Ozs. | 3 |
| & Rice: | | |
| (Lipton) | 3 Ozs. | 47 |
| Rice-A-Roni | 1 Cup | 11 |
| (Wyler's) | 8 Fl. Ozs. | 8 |
| Vegetable: | | |
| (Lipton) | 2 Ozs. | 30 |
| (Wyler's) | 4 Fl. Ozs. | 3 |
| Chicken Spread (Underwood) | 1 T. | 3 |
| Chicken Stew: | | |
| Canned: | | |
| (B & M) | 1 Cup | 14 |
| (Bounty) | 4 Ozs. | 7 |
| With Dumplings (Heinz) | 4 Ozs. | 8 |
| Frozen, In White Wine Cream Sauce (Swanson) | 6-Oz. Pkg. | 3 |
| Chicken Tetrazzini | 1 Serv | 16 |
| Chicken Timbales | 1 Serv. | 6 |
| Chicken T. V. Dinner | 1 | 42 |
| Chicken With Celery Salad | 1/2 Cup | 2 |
| Chicken Won Ton | 4 Av. | 7 |
| Chick Peas (Garbanzos) | 4 Ozs. | 64 |
| Chick Peas, Dry | 1/2 Cup | 64 |
| Chicory | 1 Serv. | 1 |
| Chiffonade Salad Dressing | 1 Tbsp. | 1 |
| Chiffon Pie, Lemon | 1 Pc. | 35 |
| Chiffon Pie, Lime | 1 Pc. | 34 |
| Chiffon Pie, Strawberry | 1 Pc. | 34 |
| Chili Butter Spread | 1 Tbsp. | 4 |
| Chili Con Carne | 1/2 Cup | 6 |
| Chili Con Carne With Beans | 1 Cup | 14 |
| Chili or Chili Con Carne: | | |
| Canned, With Beans: | | |
| (Armour Star) | 8 Ozs. | 30 |
| (Austex) | 8 Ozs. | 28 |
| (Bounty) | 8 Ozs. | 21 |
| (Chef Boy-Ar-Dee) | 8 Ozs. | 25 |
| (College Inn) | 8 Ozs. | 18 |
| (Heinz) | 8 Ozs. | 23 |
| (Hormel) | 8 Ozs. | 17 |
| (Rosarita) | 8 Ozs. | 27 |
| (Silver Skillet) | 8 Ozs. | 19 |
| (Stokely-Van Camp) | 1 Cup | 30 |

| FOOD | AMT. | CARB. GRAMS |
|---|---|---|
| (Wilson) | 8 Ozs. | 21 |
| Canned, Without Beans: | | |
| (Armour Star) | 8 Ozs. | 12 |
| (Austex) | 8 Ozs. | 12 |
| (Chef Boy-Ar-Dee) | 8 Ozs. | 14 |
| (Hormel) | 8 Ozs. | 8 |
| (Nalley's) | 8 Ozs. | 13 |
| (Stokely-Van Camp) | 1 Cup | 14 |
| (Wilson) | 8 Ozs. | 13 |
| Frozen, With Beans: | | |
| Cookin' Bag (Banquet) | 8 Ozs. | 21 |
| Dinner (Swanson) | Dinner | 58 |
| Chili Beef Soup: | | |
| Condensed (Campbell) | 8 Ozs. | 41 |
| (Heinz) | 1 Cup | 19 |
| (Heinz) Great American | 1 Cup | 20 |
| Chili Con Carne Mix: | | |
| With Meat and Beans (Durkee) | 1 Cup | 33 |
| Without Meat and Beans: | | |
| (Durkee) | 1 Cup | 30 |
| (Chili Products) | 1 Oz. | 15 |
| (Mexene) | 1 Oz. | 16 |
| Chili Con Carne, Northern Style | 1 Serv. | 20 |
| Chili Dog Sauce Mix (McCormick) | 1 Oz. | 4 |
| Chili Powder | 1 Tbsp. | T |
| Chili Sauce | 1 Tbsp. | 4 |
| (Heinz) | 1 T. | 4 |
| (Hunt's) | 1 T. | 3 |
| Chili Seasoning Mix: | | |
| Chilli-O (French's) | 1 Pkg. | 24 |
| (Lawry's) | 1 Pkg. | 23 |
| (Wyler's) | 1 Pkg. | 22 |
| Chilled Cucumber Soup | 1 Serv. | 16 |
| Chinatown Turkey Soup | 1 Serv. | 2 |
| Chinese Cabbage | 1 Cup | 2 |
| Chinese Dinner, Frozen (Swanson) | Dinner | 41 |
| Chinese Emperor's Salad | 1 Serv. | 10 |
| Chinese Fried Rice | 1 Cup | 22 |
| Chinese Fried Rice With Chicken | 1 Cup | 22 |
| Chinese Fried Rice With Pork | 1 Cup | 22 |
| Chinese Radishes | 4 Ozs. | T |
| Chip Beef (B1-B2) | 6 Sls. | 0 |
| Chipped Beef With Melons | 1 Serv. | 8 |
| Chitterlings, Fried | 1 Serv. | 0 |
| Chives | 1/2 Cup | 4 |

| FOOD | AMT. | CARB. GRAMS | FOOD | AMT. | CARB. GRAMS |
|---|---|---|---|---|---|
| Chocolate Almond Candies | 1 Oz. | 17 | Chocolate Cookies | 3 Sm. | 9 |
| Choco Fizz (Dia-Mel) | 1 Tbsp. | 2 | Chocolate Cookies, Refrigerator | 1 | 6 |
| Chocolate, Baking: | | | Chocolate Cornstarch | 1 Tbsp. | 7 |
| Bitter or Unsweetened: | | | Chocolate Covered Almond | | |
| (Baker's) | 1 Oz. | 7 | Candies | 6 | 9 |
| Pre-Melted, Choco-Bake | 1 Oz. | 10 | Chocolate Covered Graham | | |
| (Hershey's) | 1 Oz. | 6 | Crackers | 1 | 7 |
| Sweetened: | | | Chocolate Covered Ice Cream | | |
| German's Sweet (Baker's) | 1 Oz. | 15 | Popsicle | 1 | 14 |
| Semisweet (Baker's) | 1 Oz. | 18 | Chocolate Cream Cookies | 1 Oz. | 20 |
| Chips, Milk (Hershey's) | 1 Oz. | 16 | Chocolate Cream Peppermint | | |
| Chips, Semisweet: | | | Candies | 1 | 8 |
| (Baker's) | 1 Oz. | 18 | Chocolate Creams | 1 Av. | 12 |
| (Ghirardelli) | 1/3 Cup | 35 | Chocolate Cream Pie | 1 Pc. | 47 |
| (Hershey's) | 1 Oz. | 17 | Chocolate Cup Cakes | 1 | 20 |
| Morsels, Milk (Nestle's) | 1 Oz. | 17 | Chocolate Custard Sauce | 1 Tbsp. | 2 |
| Morsels, Semisweet: | | | Chocolate Drink (Borden): | | |
| (Nestle's) | 1 Oz. | 18 | Dutch | 1 Pt. | 53 |
| Mint (Nestle's) | 1 Oz. | 18 | Dutch, Canned | 1 Can | 32 |
| Chocolate Bar Candies | 2 Ozs. | 32 | Chocolate Drink Mix: | | |
| Chocolate Bar With | | | Dutch, Instant (Borden): | | |
| Nuts Candies | 1 Oz. | 17 | With Water | 3 Fl. Ozs. | 9 |
| Chocolate Beverage With | | | With Skim Milk | 3 Fl. Ozs. | 13 |
| Milk | 1 Cup | 17 | With Whole Milk | 3 Fl. Ozs. | 13 |
| Chocolate, Bitter | 1 Bar | 8 | Hot (Hershey's) | 1 Oz. | 20 |
| Chocolate Butter Frosting | 1 Tbsp. | 6 | Quik (Nestle's) | | |
| Chocolate Cake Mix: | | | Regular or Fudge | 1 Tbsp. | 16 |
| Chocolate Pudding | | | Chocolate Eclair (Custard) | 1 | 20 |
| (Betty Crocker) | 4 Ozs. | 90 | Chocolate Eclair (Cream) | 1 | 15 |
| Chocolate Loaf (Pillsbury) | 1 Oz. | 22 | Chocolate Flavored Ice Cream | | |
| Chocolate Malt | | | Soda | 1 | 71 |
| (Betty Crocker) | 4 Ozs. | 48 | Chocolate Flavored Milk | 1 Cup | 25 |
| Deep Chocolate | | | Chocolate Flavored Skim Milk | 1 Cup | 26 |
| (Duncan Hines) | 1 Pc. | 32 | Chocolate Filling | 1 Serv. | 25 |
| German Chocolate (Pillsbury) | 1 Oz. | 22 | Chocolate Finger Cookies | 1 | 6 |
| German Chocolate | | | Chocolate Frosting Boiled | 1 Serv. | 18 |
| (Swans Down) | 1 Pc | 35 | Chocolate Frosting, | | |
| German Chocolate | | | Marshmallow | 1 Serv | 16 |
| (Betty Crocker) | 1 Oz. | 23 | Chocolate Fudge | 1 Sq. | 23 |
| Milk Chocolate | | | Chocolate Gaiety Cream | | |
| (Betty Crocker) | 1 Oz. | 22 | Sandwich Cookie | 1 | 16 |
| Swiss Chocolate | | | Chocolate, Ground | | |
| (Duncan Hines) | 1 Pc. | 32 | (Ghirardelli) | 1 Cup | 120 |
| Chocolate Cake, Iced | 1 Sl. | 45 | Chocolate, Hot With | | |
| Chocolate Candies, Sweet | 1 Oz. | 18 | Whipped Cream | 1 Cup | 26 |
| Chocolate Cheese Frosting | 1 Serv. | 11 | Chocolate Ice Cream: | | |
| Chocolate Cherry Candies | 1 | 8 | (Sealtest) | 1 Cup | 35 |
| Chocolate Chip Pie | 1 Pc. | 30 | French (Prestige) | 1 Cup | 56 |
| Chocolate Chiffon, Whipped | | | Chocolate Ice Cream Mix | | |
| Cream Pie | 1 Pc. | 33 | (Junket) | 1 Oz. | 24 |
| Chocolate Chip Cookies | 3 Sm. | 15 | Chocolate Ice Cream Soda | 10 Oz. | 71 |
| Chocolate Chip Ice Cream | 1 Serv. | 14 | Chocolate Ice Cream Sundae | 1 | 54 |

| FOOD | AMT. | CARB. GRAMS | FOOD | AMT. | CARB. GRAMS |
|------|------|------------|------|------|------------|
| Chocolate Layer Cake | 1 Pc. | 64 | Tapioca (Royal) | 1 Cup | 59 |
| Chocolate Layer Cake, | | | Sweetened, Instant: | | |
| No Frosting | 1 Pc. | 54 | (Jell-O) | 1 Cup | 60 |
| Chocolate Loaf Cake | 1 Pc. | 54 | (My-T-Fine) | 1 Oz. | 23 |
| Chocolate Marshmallow Cookies | 1 | 9 | (Royal) | 1 Cup | 64 |
| Chocolate Marshmallow | | | Dark 'N' Sweet | 1 Cup | 65 |
| Pudding | 1 Serv. | 37 | Shake-A-Pudd'N | 1 Cup | 80 |
| Chocolate Meringue Pie | 1 Pc. | 32 | Fudge (Jell-O) | 1 Cup | 61 |
| Chocolate Milk, 1/2 Water, | | | Malt (Royal) | | |
| 1/2 Milk | 8 Ozs. | 11 | Shake-A-Pudd'N | 1 Cup | 80 |
| Chocolate Milk, All Milk | 8 Ozs. | 25 | Nut (My-T-Fine) | 1 Oz. | 23 |
| Chocolate Milk Candies | | | Low Calorie or Dietetic: | | |
| With Almonds | 1 Oz. | 17 | With Nonfat Milk: | | |
| Chocolate Milkshake | 10 Ozs. | 57 | (Dia-Mel) | 4 Ozs. | 8 |
| Chocolate Milkshake, Malted | 10 Ozs. | 70 | (D-Zerta) | 1 Cup | 24 |
| Chocolate Milk, Skimmed | 1 Gl. | 26 | With Whole Milk: | | |
| Chocolate Milk Candies | 1 Oz. | 16 | (Dia-Mel) | 4 Ozs. | 8 |
| Chocolate Mints | 8 Sm. | 21 | (D-Zerta) | 1 Cup | 24 |
| Chocolate Mints, Cream | 1 Bar | 23 | Chocolate Kisses, Candies | 1 | 2 |
| Chocolate Mint Sauce | 1 Serv. | 53 | Chocolate Roll | 1 Sl. | 13 |
| Chocolate Nut Caramel | 1 Av. | 16 | Chocolate Sauce | 1 Tbsp. | 5 |
| Chocolate Pancakes | 1 Serv. | 26 | Chocolate, Semi-Sweet | 1 Bar | 17 |
| Chocolate Pie: | | | Chocolate, Skim Milk Pudding | 1/2 Cup | 30 |
| Nut (Tastykake) | 1 Pie | 64 | Chocolate Soda | 1 Serv. | 15 |
| Frozen, Cream: | | | Chocolate Soft Drink: | | |
| (Banquet) | 2 Ozs. | 22 | (Yoo-Hoo) | 8 Fl. Ozs. | 24 |
| (Morton) | 2 Ozs. | 22 | High-Protein (Yoo-Hoo) | 8 Fl. Ozs. | 32 |
| (Mrs. Smith's) | 1 Pc. | 19 | Chocolate Sundae | Av. | 54 |
| Chocolate Pie Filling: | | | Chocolate Sundae Fancy | | |
| Regular, Fudge (Jell-O) | 1 Oz. | 6 | With Nuts | 1/2 Cup | 33 |
| Cream (Jell-O) | 1 Pc. | 42 | Chocolate Sweet Milk | | |
| (My-T-Fine) | 1 Oz. | 25 | With Nuts | 1 Bar | 25 |
| Almond (My-T-Fine) | 1 Oz. | 25 | Chocolate, Sweet Milk | 1 Bar | 16 |
| Fudge (My-T-Fine) | 1 Oz. | 25 | Chocolate Syrup | 1 Tbsp. | 10 |
| Low Calorie (D-Zerta): | | | Sweetened (Hershey's) | 1 Oz. | 16 |
| With Whole Milk | 1 Cup | 18 | Low Calorie, Choco Sip | | |
| With Nonfat Milk | 1 Cup | 19 | (Dia-Mel) | 1 Oz. | 7 |
| Chocolate Pudding | 1/2 Cup | 31 | Chocolate, Unsweetened | | |
| Canned: | | | Candies | 1 Bar | 8 |
| (Betty Crocker) | 4 Ozs. | 26 | Chocolate & Vanilla | | |
| Dutch (Bounty) | 4 Ozs. | 31 | Ice Cream Soda | 10 Ozs. | 71 |
| Fudge (Betty Crocker) | 4 Ozs. | 26 | Chocolate Wafer Cookie | 1 | 6 |
| Chocolate Pudding Mix: | | | Chocolate Waffles | 1 | 48 |
| Sweetened, Regular: | | | Chocolate With Icing Cake | 1 Pc. | 64 |
| (Jell-O) | 1 Cup | 62 | Chop Suey, Beef | 1/2 Cup | 4 |
| (My-T-Fine) | 1 Oz. | 25 | Chop Suey, Chicken | 1/2 Cup | 4 |
| (Royal) | 1 Cup | 61 | Chop Suey, Pork | 1/2 Cup | 4 |
| Dark 'N' Sweet | 1 Cup | 61 | Chop Suey, Vegetable | 1/2 Cup | 4 |
| (Thank You) | 1 Cup | 59 | Chop Suey: | | |
| Almond (My-T-Fine) | 1 Oz. | 25 | Canned: | | |
| Fudge (Jell-O) | 1 Cup | 62 | Chicken (Hung's) | 1 Cup | 12 |
| Fudge (My-T-Fine) | 1 Oz. | 25 | Meatless (Hung's) | 1 Cup | 11 |

| FOOD | AMT. | CARB. GRAMS |
|---|---|---|
| Vegetable (Hung's) | 1 Cup | 6 |
| Chop Suey Vegetables, Canned (Chun King) | 4 Ozs. | 3 |
| Chops, Lamb, Broiled | 4 Ozs. | 0 |
| Chops, Lamb, Loin Fried | 4 Ozs. | 0 |
| Chops, Pork, Broiled | 1 Med. | 0 |
| Chops, Pork, Fried | 1 Med. | 0 |
| Chops or Roast Mutton | 4 Ozs. | 0 |
| Chops, Veal | 1 Med. | 0 |
| Chops, Veal, Breaded-Baked | 1 Med. | 6 |
| Chops, Veal, Fried | 1 Med. | 0 |
| Chow Chow (Crosse & Blackwell) | 1 Oz. | 2 |
| Chow-Chow Pickles, Sour | 2 Ozs. | 2 |
| Chow-Chow Pickles, Sweet | 2 Ozs. | 13 |
| Chow Mein | 1/2 Cup | 4 |
| Chow Mein, Beef | 1/2 Cup | 4 |
| Chow Mein, Chicken | 1/2 Cup | 4 |
| (Chun King) | 8 Ozs. | 12 |
| (Hung's) | 8 Ozs. | 7 |
| Chow Mein, Chicken Sub Gum | 1/2 Cup | 4 |
| Chow Mein, Meatless: | | |
| (Chun King) | 8 Ozs. | 12 |
| (Hung's) | 8 Ozs. | 6 |
| Chow Mein, Frozen | | |
| Chicken (Chun King) | 8 Ozs. | 10 |
| Meatless (Chun King) | 8 Ozs. | 15 |
| Shrimp (Chun King) | 8 Ozs. | 13 |
| Chow Mein, Pork | 1/2 Cup | 4 |
| Chowder, Fish | 1 Serv. | 13 |
| Christmas Star Cookies | 1 | 28 |
| Chuck Steak With Bone | 1 Serv. | 0 |
| Chutney | 1 Tsp. | 6 |
| Major Grey's (Crosse & Blackwell) | 1 Oz. | 13 |
| Chutney, Apple | 5 Tbsp. | 50 |
| Chutney, Tomato | 5 Tbsp. | 40 |
| Cider | 1 Cup | 25 |
| Cider, Apple | 3/4 Cup | 13 |
| Cider, Apple Hard | 3/4 Cup | 13 |
| Cider, Cherry | 6 Ozs. | 13 |
| Cider Cup Cocktail | 1 Serv | 20 |
| Cider, Mulled | 1/2 Cup | 18 |
| Cider, Sweet Apple | 1 Cup | 22 |
| Cinnamon | 1/8 Tsp. | 0 |
| Cinnamon Apples | 1 Serv. | 20 |
| Cinnamon Bread | 1 Sl. | 16 |
| Cinnamon Bun | 1 | 19 |
| Cinnamon Cake | 1 Pc. | 28 |
| Cinnamon Muffin | 1 | 23 |
| Cinnamon Raisin-Buns | 1 | 29 |

| FOOD | AMT. | CARB. GRAMS |
|---|---|---|
| Cinnamon Roll | 1 | 11 |
| Cinnamon Stick | 1 | 0 |
| Frozen (Aunt Jemima) | 1 Pc. | 22 |
| Cinnamon Toast | 1 Sl. | 29 |
| Citron, Candied | 1 Oz. | 22 |
| (Liberty) | 1 Oz. | 22 |
| Citron, Dried | 4 Ozs. | 12 |
| Citrus Cooler (Hi-C) | 6 Fl. Ozs. | 22 |
| Citrus Soft Drink, Low Calorie (No-Cal) | 6 Fl. Ozs. | 0 |
| Clam Broth | 6 Ozs. | T |
| Clam Chowder, Boston | 1 Serv. | 22 |
| Clam Chowder, Manhattan | 1 Cup | 8 |
| Condensed (Campbell) | 8 Ozs. | 21 |
| (Crosse & Blackwell) | 1/2 Can | 13 |
| Clam Chowder, New England | 1 Serv. | 6 |
| Canned (Crosse & Blackwell) | 1/2 Can | 10 |
| Frozen, Condensed (Campbell) | 8 Ozs. | 20 |
| Clam Cocktail (Sau-Sea) | 4 Ozs. | 19 |
| Clam Dip, Sour Cream | 3 Tsp. | T |
| Clam Fritters | 3-1/2 Ozs. | 31 |
| Clam Juice | 6 Ozs. | 0 |
| Clam Juice Cocktail | 1 Serv. | 5 |
| Clam Pie | 1 Serv. | 12 |
| Clam Stew, Frozen (Mrs. Paul's) | 4 Ozs. | 10 |
| Clam Tomato Broth | 1 Serv. | 8 |
| Clam and Tomato Soup | 1 Serv. | 9 |
| Clams | 12 Med. | 3 |
| Clams, Baked With Spaghetti | 1 Serv. | 17 |
| Clams, Broiled | 6 | 5 |
| Clams, Broiled Stuffed | 1 Serv. | 8 |
| Clams, Canned, Chopped: | | |
| Solids & Liquid (Doxsee) | 4 Ozs. | 3 |
| Meat Only (Doxsee) | 4 Ozs. | 2 |
| Clams, (Canned) Drained | 1/2 Cup | 2 |
| Clams, Cherry Stone | 6 | 5 |
| Clams & Chicken Baked | 1 Serv. | 6 |
| Clams, Fried | 6 | 5 |
| Clams, Littleneck | 6 | 5 |
| Clams, Raw (Meat Only) | 5-10 | 3 |
| Clams, Roasted | 6 | 5 |
| Clams & Scalloped Cod | 1 Serv. | 8 |
| Clams, Steamed | 12 Med. | 4 |
| Clams, Stuffed Deviled | 6 | 10 |
| Clams, Stuffed Baked | 2 | 10 |
| Claret Punch | 1 Serv. | 31 |
| Claret Wine | 1 Gl. | 2 |
| (Gold Seal) | 3 Fl. Ozs. | T |

| FOOD | AMT. | CARB. GRAMS | FOOD | AMT. | CARB. GRAMS |
|------|------|-------------|------|------|-------------|
| (Italian Swiss Colony-Gold Medal) | 3 Fl. Ozs. | T | Cocktail, Crabmeat | 1/2 Cup | 1 |
| (Louis M. Martini) | 3 Fl. Ozs. | T | Cocktail, Cuban Presidente | 1 Serv. | 1 |
| Claret Wine Lemonade | 1 Gl. | 22 | Cocktail, Devil's Leap | 1 Serv. | 0 |
| Claristine Liqueur | | | Cocktail, Doctor's | 1 Serv. | 4 |
| (Leroux) | 1 Fl. Oz. | 10 | Cocktail, Dry Martini | 1 Serv. | T |
| Clark Bar | 1 | 22 | Cocktail, Florida Special | 1 Serv. | 5 |
| Clay Morgan's Cooler | 1 Gl. | 26 | Cocktail, Frankfurters | 1/4 Lb. | 1 |
| Clear Condensed Bouillon | 4 Oz. | 1 | Cocktail, Fruit (Canned) | 1 Serv. | 19 |
| Clear Consomme (As Served) | 4 Ozs. | 0 | Cocktail, Fruit, Fresh | 1 Serv. | 12 |
| Clear Soup | 4 Ozs. | 3 | Cocktail, Gilded Lily | 1 Serv. | 3 |
| Clorets:- | | | Cocktail, Havana | 1 Serv. | 5 |
| Chewing Gum | 1 Pc. | 1 | Cocktail, Havana Beach | 1 Serv. | 8 |
| Mint | 1 Pc. | 1 | Cocktail, Hibiscus | 1 Serv. | 2 |
| Clover Leaf Rolls | 1 | 20 | Cocktail, Honi Honi | 1 Serv. | 2 |
| Cloves | 1/8 Tsp. | 0 | Cocktail, Huapala | 1 Serv. | 2 |
| Club Sandwiches | 1 | 39 | Cocktail, Jabon Candido | 1 Serv. | 5 |
| Club Sandwiches, 3 Decker | 1 | 42 | Cocktail, Jack Rose | 1 Serv. | 17 |
| Cobbler, Apple | 1 | 44 | Cocktail, Kailua | 1 Serv. | 7 |
| Cobbler, Black Raspberry | 1 Av. | 44 | Cocktail, Kingston | 1 Serv. | 6 |
| Cobbler, Cherry | 1 Av. | 44 | Cocktail, Kona | 1 Serv. | 5 |
| Cobbler, Fruit | 1 Av. | 44 | Cocktail, LaFlordia Rum Daisy | 1 Serv. | 13 |
| Cobbler, Peach | 1 Av. | 44 | Cocktail, Lobster | 1/2 Cup | T |
| Cobbler, Peached (Canned) | 1 Av. | 44 | Cocktail, Lobster, With Sauce | 1/2 Cup | 8 |
| Cobbler, Plum | 1 Av. | 44 | Cocktail, Lobster With | | |
| Cobbler, Raisin | 1 Av. | 44 | Mayonnaise | 1/2 Cup | 2 |
| Cobbler, Sherry | 1 Av. | 44 | Cocktail, Lobster, With | | |
| Coca Cola | 8 Ozs. | 27 | Lemon Wedge | 1/2 Cup | 1 |
| Cocktail, Alexander Brandy | 3 Ozs. | 4 | Cocktail, Manhattan | 1 Serv. | 3 |
| Cocktail, Arawak | 1 Cktl. | 5 | Cocktail, Miguel Ligero | 1 Serv. | 4 |
| Cocktail, Avocado | 1 Serv. | 6 | Cocktail, Mofuco | 1 Serv. | 7 |
| Cocktail, Avocado-Grapefruit | 1 Serv. | 12 | Cocktail, O'Hara, Scarlett | 1 Serv. | 4 |
| Cocktail, Bacardi Flip | 1 Gl. | 3 | Cocktail, Oyster (Raw) | 6 | 6 |
| Cocktail, Bamboo | 1 Gl. | 7 | Cocktail, Peking | 1 Serv. | 2 |
| Cocktail, Bahia Club | 1 Serv. | 5 | Cocktail, Pikaki | 1 Serv. | 12 |
| Cocktail, Batista | 1 Serv. | 6 | Cocktail, Plantation | 1 Serv. | 5 |
| Cocktail, Bee's Kiss | 1 Serv. | 5 | Cocktail, Puerto Rican | 1 Serv. | 4 |
| Cocktail Biltmore | 1 Serv. | 10 | Cocktail, Ron-Cacao | 1 Serv. | 5 |
| Cocktail, Bombay | 1 Serv. | 7 | Cocktail, Rumba | 1 Serv. | 2 |
| Cocktail, Brandy | 3 Ozs. | 5 | Cocktail, Rum Daisy | 1 Serv. | 3 |
| Cocktail, Brouse | 1 Serv. | 21 | Cocktail, Rum Old Fashioned | 1 Serv. | 7 |
| Cocktail, Brugal | 1 Serv. | 3 | Cocktail, Rum Manhattan | 1 Serv. | 3 |
| Cocktail, Canton | 1 Serv. | T | Cocktail, Rum Ramsey | 1 Serv. | 3 |
| Cocktail, Captain's Blood | 1 Serv. | 1 | Cocktail, Santiago | 1 Serv. | 3 |
| Cocktail, Captain Kidd | 1 Serv. | 3 | Cocktail, Sausages, Pork | 1/4 Lb. | T |
| Cocktail, Caviar | 1 Oz. | 1 | Cocktail, Seafood | 1/2 Cup | 1 |
| Cocktail, Champagne | 6 Ozs. | 10 | Cocktail, Shrimp With Sauce | 6 Med. | 1 |
| Cocktail, Chaparra | 1 Serv. | 5 | Cocktail, Sloe Gin | 1 Serv. | 3 |
| Cocktail, Cider Cup | 1 Serv. | 20 | Cocktail, Small Dinger | 1 Serv. | 0 |
| Cocktail, Clam | 6 Med. | 2 | Cocktail, Southern Cross | 1 Serv. | 8 |
| Cocktail, Clam Juice | 1 Serv. | 6 | Cocktail, South Sea | 1 Serv. | 6 |
| Cocktail, Coffee | 1 Serv. | 28 | Cocktail, Tahitian Honey Bee | 1 Serv. | 6 |
| Cocktail, Coronation | 1 Serv. | 16 | Cocktail, Tomato Juice (A-C) | 6 Ozs. | 7 |
| | | | Cocktail, Whiskey | 1-1/2 Ozs. | 0 |

| FOOD | AMT. | CARB. GRAMS | FOOD | AMT. | CARB. GRAMS |
|---|---|---|---|---|---|
| Cocoa, All Milk, Skimmed | 1 Gl. | 12 | Coconut Ice Cream | 1 Scp. | 20 |
| Cocoa Bread | 1 Sl. | 13 | Coconut Macaroons | 1 Lg. | 14 |
| Cocoa Corn Flake Macaroons | 1 | 8 | Coconut Milk | 1 Cup | 10 |
| Cocoa-Cream Soft Drink: | | | Coconut Pie: | | |
| (Hoffman) | 6 Fl. Ozs. | 22 | Cream: | | |
| (Yukon Club) | 6 Fl. Ozs. | 22 | (Tastykake) | 4 Ozs. | 48 |
| Cocoa Fruit Cake | 1 Sl. | 22 | Frozen (Banquet) | 5 Ozs. | 48 |
| Cocoa Krispies, Cereal | | | (Mrs. Smith's) | 1/6 Pie | 24 |
| (Kellogg's) | 1 Cup | 24 | Custard, Frozen: | | |
| Cocoamalt | 1 Cup | 22 | (Banquet) | 5 Ozs. | 40 |
| Cocoa Mix: | | | (Mrs. Smith's) | 1/6 Pie | 31 |
| Sweet Milk Cocoa | | | Coconut Pie Filling Mix: | | |
| (Hershey's) | 1 Oz. | 20 | Cream (Jell-O) | 1 Cup | 60 |
| (Nestle's Ever Ready) | 1 Oz. | 38 | Cream (Jell-O) | 1 Pc. | 42 |
| Instant (Hershey's) | 1 Oz. | 25 | Coconut Pudding Mix: | | |
| Instant (Swiss Miss) | 1 Oz. | 20 | Cream (Jell-O) | 1 Cup | 62 |
| Cocoa, Powdered | 1-1/2 Tbsp. | 13 | Cream, Instant (Jell-O) | 1 Cup | 61 |
| Unsweetened (Droste) | 1 T. | 3 | Toasted, Instant (Royal) | 1 Cup | 56 |
| (Hershey's) | 1 Cup | 11 | Coconut Soft Drink: | | |
| Cocoa Powder, Dry With | | | (Yoo-Hoo): | | |
| Milk & Sugar | 3 Tbsp. | 52 | Regular | 8 Fl. Ozs. | 24 |
| Cocoa, Powdered With | | | High Protein | 8 Fl. Ozs. | 32 |
| Dry Milk | 3 Tbsp. | 7 | Cod, Frozen: | | |
| Cocoa Puffs, Cereal | | | Fillets (Taste O'Sea) | 8 Ozs. | 0 |
| (General Mills) | 1 Cup | 25 | Alaska (Van de Kamp's) | 1 Pkg. | 0 |
| Cocoa With 1/2 Milk & | | | Codfish | 1 Serv. | 0 |
| 1/2 Water | 1 Cup | 18 | Codfish Balls | 1 Av. | 5 |
| Cocoa With Milk | 1 Cup | 18 | Codfish, Creamed | 1/2 Cup | 8 |
| Cocoa, Skim Milk | 3/4 Cup | 9 | Cod Liver Oil (A) | 1 Tbsp. | 0 |
| Cocoa Syrup | 1 Tbsp. | 12 | Coffee Almond Cake | 1 Sl. | 33 |
| Coconut: | | | Coffee, Black | 1 Cup | T |
| Dried, Canned: | | | Coffee Break, Cream | | |
| Angel Flake (Baker's) | 1 Cup | 44 | Substitute (Seneca) | 1 Oz. | 4 |
| Shred & Cookie (Baker's) | 1 Cup | 46 | Coffee Cake | 1 Pc. | 14 |
| Coconut Bread Fingers | 1 | 9 | (Drake's) | 1 Pkg. | 52 |
| Coconut Bar, Cookie | 1 | 9 | Coffee Cake Iced With Nuts | 1 Pc. | 33 |
| Coconut Cake | 1 Sl. | 29 | Coffee Cake Mix | | |
| Coconut Cake Mix: | | | (Aunt Jemima) | 1 Pc. | 20 |
| Toasted (Betty Crocker) | 4 Ozs. | 90 | Coffee Cocktail | 1 Serv. | 28 |
| (Duncan Hines) | 1 Pc. | 36 | Coffee Cream | 1 Tbsp. | 1 |
| Coconut Cake, Iced | 1 Sl. | 50 | Coffee Custard | 1/2 Cup | 14 |
| Coconut Covered Ice | | | Coffee Eclair | 1 Av. | 30 |
| Cream Pop | 1 | 18 | Coffee, Expresso | 1 Cup | 18 |
| Coconut Cream Candies | 1 Sq. | 20 | Coffee Flavoring, Low | | |
| Coconut Cream Pie | 1 Sl. | 50 | Calorie (Coffee Time) | 1 Fl. Oz. | T |
| Coconut Creams | 1 Sl. | 9 | Coffee Ice Cream | 1 Scp. | 14 |
| Coconut Custard Pie | 1 Pc. | 50 | Coffee Ice Cream | 1/4 Pt. | 16 |
| Coconut, Dried | 2 Tbsp. | 4 | Coffee Ice Cream Parfait | 1 | 20 |
| Coconut, Dried, Shredded, | | | Coffee, Iced, No Sugar | | |
| Sweetened | 1 Cup | 33 | or Cream | 1 Cup | T |
| Coconut Fingers | 1 | 27 | Coffee, Instant | 1 Cup | T |
| Coconut, Fresh-Shredded | 1 Cup | 22 | Coffee-Mate, Cream | | |
| Coconut Fudge | 1 Sq. | 22 | Substitute | 1 Tsp. | 1 |

| FOOD | AMT. | CARB. GRAMS | FOOD | AMT. | CARB. GRAMS |
|---|---|---|---|---|---|
| Coffee-Rich, Cream Substitute | 1 Oz. | 3 | Pepsi-Cola | 8 Fl. Ozs. | 26 |
| Coffee Royal (With 2 Tbsp. Cream 1 Tsp. Sugar) | 1 Cup | 10 | (Shasta) | 8 Fl. Ozs. | 26 |
| | | | (Waldbaum) | 8 Fl. Ozs. | 27 |
| Coffee Soft Drink, Low Calorie (No-Cal) | 6 Fl. Ozs. | T | Cherry (Shasta) | 8 Fl. Ozs. | 26 |
| | | | Low Calorie: | | |
| Coffee Southern, Liqueur | 1 Fl. Oz. | 7 | Diet Pepsi-Cola | 8 Fl. Ozs. | 9 |
| Coffee Toffee | 1 Pc. | 8 | (Dr. Brown's) Slim-Ray | 8 Fl. Ozs. | 2 |
| Coffee, Turkish With 5 Tsp. Sugar | 1 Cup | 20 | (Hoffman) | 8 Fl. Ozs. | 2 |
| | | | (No-Cal) | 8 Fl. Ozs. | T |
| Coffee, Viennese With 1 Tbsp. Whipped Cream & 2 Tsp. Sugar | 1 Cup | 8 | (Shasta) | 8 Fl. Ozs. | T |
| | | | Cherry (Shasta) | 8 Fl. Ozs. | T |
| Coffee With Cream | 1 Cup | 1 | Tab | 8 Fl. Ozs. | T |
| Coffee With Sugar | 1 Cup | 4 | Cola Syrup, Dietetic | | |
| Coffee With Sugar & Cream | 1 Cup | 5 | (No-Cal) | 1 Tsp. | T |
| Coffee With 1 Tbsp. Condensed Milk | 1 Cup | 8 | Cold Burgundy Cup | 1 Serv. | 39 |
| | | | Cold Duck Wine (Italian Swiss Colony-Private Stock) | 3 Fl. Ozs. | 4 |
| Coffee With 1 Tbsp. Evaporated Milk | 1 Cup | 2 | Cold Hors d'Oeuvres | 4 Ozs. | T |
| Coffee With 1 Tbsp. Milk | 1 Cup | T | Cole Slaw, Cabbage | 1 Cup | 14 |
| Coffee With 1 Tbsp. Skim Milk | 1 Cup | T | Collards | 1/2 Cup | 5 |
| Coffee: | | | Chopped (Birds Eye) | 1 Pkg. | 13 |
| Regular: | | | Collins, Rum | 10 Ozs. | 9 |
| (Maxwell House) | 1 Cup | T | Collins Mix (Bar-Tender's) | 1 Oz. | 26 |
| (Yuban) | 1 Cup | T | Colonel's Big Opu | | |
| Instant: | | | Beverage, The | 14 Ozs. | 5 |
| (Chase & Sanborn) | 1 Cup | T | Combination Vegetable Salad | 1/2 Cup | 16 |
| (Maxwell House) | 1 Cup | T | Commercial Mayonnaise Type Salad Dressing | 1 Tbsp. | T |
| Nescafe | 1 Tbsp. | 2 | Compote, Apricot-Apple | 1 Serv. | 12 |
| (Yuban) | 1 Cup | T | Condensed Milk (B1-C) | 1 Tbsp. | 8 |
| Decaffeinated: | | | Condensed Milk Sweetened | 4 Ozs. | 48 |
| Decaf | 1 Tbsp. | 2 | Condensed Milk Unsweetened | 1 Gl | 24 |
| Sanka | 1 Cup | T | Condensed Chicken Soup, Regular | 4 Ozs. | 5 |
| Siesta | 1 Cup | T | | | |
| Freeze-Dried: | | | Concentrate, Cereal (Kellogg's) | 1 Oz. | 15 |
| Maxim | 1 Cup | 1 | Concentrated Orange Juice (Canned) | 1/2 Cup | 40 |
| Taster's Choice | 1 Tbsp. | 2 | | | |
| Coffee Parfait | 1 Serv. | 14 | Concentrated Orange Juice, Diluted | 1/2 Cup | 10 |
| Cognac | Shot | 0 | Concord Wine: | | |
| Cola | 6 Ozs. | 18 | (Gold Seal) | 3 Fl. Ozs. | 10 |
| Cola Soft Drink: | | | (Mogen David) | 3 Fl. Ozs. | 16 |
| Sweetened: | | | (Mogen David) Dry | 3 Fl. Ozs. | 2 |
| (Canada Dry) | 8 Fl. Ozs. | 27 | Conserve Cherry | 1 Oz. | 32 |
| (Clicquot Club) | 8 Fl. Ozs. | 27 | Consomme | 1 Cup | 0 |
| Coca-Cola | 8 Fl. Ozs. | 24 | Consomme, Clear (As Served) | 1 Cup | 0 |
| (Cott) | 8 Fl. Ozs. | 27 | Consomme Madrilene | 1 Cup | 1 |
| (Dr. Brown's) | 8 Fl. Ozs. | 27 | Canned, Clear or Red (Crosse & Blackwell) | 1/2 Can | 2 |
| (Hoffman) | 8 Fl. Ozs. | 27 | | | |
| (Key Food) | 8 Fl. Ozs. | 27 | Continental Bread | 1 Sl. | 10 |
| (Kirsch) | 8 Fl. Ozs. | 27 | Converted Cooked Rice | 3/4 Cup | 24 |
| (Mission) | 8 Fl. Ozs. | 27 | Converted Rice (Raw) | 2 Ozs. | 44 |
| Mr. Cola | 8 Fl. Ozs. | 27 | | | |

| FOOD | AMT. | CARB. GRAMS | FOOD | AMT. | CARB. GRAMS |
|---|---|---|---|---|---|
| Cooked Beets | 1 Cup | 16 | Pecan Fudge (Keebler) | 1 Pkg. | 28 |
| Cooked Currants | 4 Ozs. | 9 | Brown Sugar (Nabisco) | | |
| Cooked Corn Grits Degermed | 1/2 Cup | 14 | Family Favorites | 1 Pc. | 3 |
| Cooked Cow Peas | 4 Ozs. | 13 | Brussels (Pepperidge Farm) | 1 Pc. | 4 |
| Cooked Dried Apples, | | | Butter: | | |
| Sweetened | 1 Cup | 77 | (Nabisco) | 1 Pc. | 5 |
| Cooked Dried Apricots, | | | (Sunshine) | 1 Pc. | 3 |
| Sweetened | 1/2 Cup | 51 | Buttercup (Keebler) | 1 Pc. | 3 |
| Cooked Green Beans | 1 Cup | 3 | Butterscotch Fudgies | | |
| Cooked Macaroni (Enriched) | 1/2 Cup | 16 | (Tastykake) | 1 Pkg. | 35 |
| Cooked Meal Rolled Oats | 4 Ozs. | 13 | Capri (Pepperidge Farm) | 1 Pc. | 6 |
| Cooked Oatmeal | 1/2 Cup | 14 | Caramel Peanut Logs | | |
| Cooked Prunes (No Sugar) | 4 Ozs. | 40 | (Nabisco) Hey Days | 1 Pc. | 13 |
| Cooked Prunes Sugar Added | 1/3 Cup | 20 | Chocolate & Chocolate Covered: | | |
| Cooked Raisins, Sweetened | 1/2 Cup | 36 | Kings (Sunshine) | 1 Pc. | 19 |
| Cooked Rolled Oatmeal | 1/2 Cup | 11 | Melody (Nabisco) | 1 Pc. | 5 |
| Cooked Rolled Wheat | 4 Ozs. | 13 | Nuggets (Sunshine) | 1 Pc | 3 |
| Cooked Scotch Oatmeal | 4 Ozs. | 10 | Peanut Bars (Nabisco) | | |
| Cooked Spaghetti | 4 Ozs. | 23 | Ideal | 1 Pc. | 10 |
| Cookie Commercial: | | | Pin Wheel Cakes | | |
| Angelica Goodies | | | (Nabisco) | 1 Pc. | 21 |
| (Stella D'oro) | 1 Pc. | 14 | Puffs (Sunshine) | 1 Pc. | 10 |
| Angel Puffs, Dietetic | | | Snaps (Nabisco) | 1 Pc. | 2 |
| (Stella D'oro) | 1 Pc. | 1 | Wafers (Nabisco) Famous | 1 Pc. | 4 |
| Anginetti (Stella D'oro) | 1 Pc. | 1 | Wafers (Sunshine) | 1 Pc. | 2 |
| Animal Cracker: | | | Wafers (Sunshine) | | |
| (Nabisco) Barnum's | 1 Pc. | 2 | Ice Box | 1 Pc. | 5 |
| (Sunshine) | 1 Pc. | 2 | Chocolate Chip: | | |
| Anisette Sponge | | | (Nabisco) | 1 Pc. | 7 |
| (Stella D'oro) | 1 Pc. | 8 | (Nabisco) Chips Ahoy | 1 Pc. | 7 |
| Anisette Toast | | | (Nabisco) Family Favorites | 1 Pc. | 4 |
| (Stella D'oro) | 1 Pc. | 7 | Snaps (Nabisco) | 1 Pc. | 3 |
| Applesauce (Sunshine) | 1 Pc. | 4 | Old Fashioned (Pepperidge | | |
| Applesauce, Iced (Sunshine) | 1 Pc. | 14 | Farm) | 1 Pc. | 6 |
| Apple Strudel (Nabisco) | 1 Pc. | 7 | (Sunshine) | 1 Pc. | 5 |
| Assortments: | | | Coconut (Sunshine) | 1 Pc. | 10 |
| (Nabisco) Famous | 1 Pc. | 9 | Choc-O-Chip (Tastykake) | 1 Pc. | 9 |
| (Nabisco) Pride Sandwich | 1 Pc. | 7 | Cinnamon, Old Fashioned | | |
| (Sunshine) Lady Joan | | | (Pepperidge Farm) | 1 Pc. | 8 |
| Party Assortment | 1 Pc. | 6 | Cinnamon Wafers | | |
| Bordeaux (Pepperidge Farm) | 1 Pc. | 5 | (Sunshine) | 1 Pc. | 3 |
| Breakfast Treats | | | Clover Leaves (Sunshine) | 1 Pc. | 3 |
| (Stella D'oro) | 1 Pc. | 15 | Coco Creme (Wise) | 1 Pc. | 6 |
| Brown Edge Wafers | | | Coconut Bar | 1 | 9 |
| (Nabisco) | 1 Pc. | 4 | Bars (Nabisco) | 1 Pc. | 6 |
| Brownie: | | | Bars (Sunshine) | 1 Pc | 7 |
| (Tastykake) | 1 Pkg. | 34 | Chocolate Chip | | |
| Chocolate Nut, Old Fash- | | | (Nabisco) | 1 Pc. | 9 |
| ioned (Pepperidge Farm) | 1 Pc. | 6 | Chocolate Drop | | |
| Nut Fudge (Nab) | | | (Keebler) | 1 Pc. | 8 |
| Bake Shop | 1 Oz. | 17 | Coconut Kiss (Tastykake) | 1 Pc. | 33 |
| Peanut Butter (Tastykake) | 1 Pkg. | 32 | Family Favorites (Nabisco) | 1 Pc. | 2 |

43

| FOOD | AMT. | CARB. GRAMS | FOOD | AMT. | CARB. GRAMS |
|---|---|---|---|---|---|
| Como Delight (Stella D'oro) | 1 Pc. | 18 | Ladyfinger | 1 | 5 |
| Cowboys and Indians | | | Lemon: | | |
| (Nabisco) | 1 Pc. | 2 | Creme Sandwich (Keebler) | 1 Pc. | 12 |
| Creme Wafer Stick: | | | Jumble Rings (Nabisco) | 1 Pc. | 11 |
| (Dutch Twin) | 1 Pc. | 6 | Nut Crunch, Old Fashioned | | |
| (Nabisco) | 1 Pc. | 6 | (Pepperidge Farm) | 1 Pc. | 6 |
| Crests Cakes (Nabisco) | 1 Pc. | 10 | Snaps (Nabisco) | 1 Pc. | 3 |
| Cup Custard (Sunshine) | 1 Pc. | 10 | Lido (Pepperidge Farm) | 1 Pc. | 10 |
| Danish Swirls (Nabisco) | 1 Pc. | 7 | Lisbon (Pepperidge Farm) | 1 Oz. | 18 |
| Danish Wedding (Keebler) | 1 Pc. | 5 | Lorna Doone | 1 | 5 |
| Date and Nut (Sunshine) | 1 Pc. | 14 | Macaroon: | | |
| Devil's Food Cake: | | | (Sunshine) | 1 Pc. | 12 |
| (Nab) | 1 Pc. | 38 | Almond (Tastykake) | 1 Pc. | 12 |
| (Nabisco) | 1 Pc. | 11 | Butter Flavored | | |
| (Sunshine) | 1 Pc. | 11 | (Sunshine) | 1 Pc. | 5 |
| Dresden (Pepperidge Farm) | 1 Pc. | 2 | Coconut (Nabisco) | | |
| Dutch Apple (Keebler) | 1 Pc. | 4 | Bake Shop | 1 Pc. | 12 |
| Dutch Crunch (Keebler) | 1 Pc. | 6 | Coconut (Sunshine) | 1 Pc. | 13 |
| Fig Bar: | | | Sandwich (Nabisco) | 1 Pc. | 9 |
| (Keebler) | 1 Pc. | 14 | Marshmallow: | | |
| (Nab) Fig Newton | 1 Pc. | 70 | Mallomar (Nabisco) | 1 Pc. | 8 |
| (Nabisco) Fig Newton | 1 Pc. | 11 | Mallo Puff (Sunshine) | 1 Pc. | 13 |
| (Sunshine) | 1 Pc. | 9 | Puffs (Nabisco) | 1 Pc. | 12 |
| Frosted Cake (Sunshine) | 1 Pc. | 15 | Sandwich (Nabisco) | 1 Pc. | 5 |
| Fruit: | | | Twirls (Nabisco) | 1 Pc. | 22 |
| California Fruit Bar | | | Margherite: | | |
| (Stella D'oro) | 1 Pc. | 11 | Chocolate (Stella D'oro) | 1 Pc. | 10 |
| Golden Fruit (Sunshine) | 1 Pc. | 16 | White (Stella D'oro) | 1 Pc. | 10 |
| Iced Fruit (Nabisco) | 1 Pc. | 14 | Marquisette (Pepperidge Farm) | 1 Oz. | 17 |
| Fudge: | | | Milano (Pepperidge Farm) | 1 Pc. | 7 |
| Chip, Old Fashioned | | | Milco, Dandies (Sunshine) | 1 Pc. | 12 |
| (Pepperidge Farm) | 1 Pc. | 7 | Milco, Sugar Wafers | | |
| Eton Fudge Stick | | | (Sunshine) | 1 Pc. | 10 |
| (Keebler) | 1 Pc. | 6 | Minarets (Nabisco) | 1 Pc. | 5 |
| Fudge Stripes (Keebler) | 1 Pc. | 7 | Minarets Cakes (Nab) | 1 Oz. | 18 |
| Penguin Fudge (Keebler) | 1 Pc. | 14 | Mint Sandwich, Cocoa | | |
| Gaiety Creme Sandwich | 1 | 14 | Covered (Nabisco) | 1 Pc. | 10 |
| Gaiety Cream Sandwich, | | | Molasses | 1 | 5 |
| Chocolate | 1 | 16 | Nabisco Devil | 1 | 12 |
| Gingersnap | 1 Lg. | 6 | Naples, Plain | | |
| Large (Sunshine) | 1 Pc. | 5 | (Pepperidge Farm) | 1 Oz. | 18 |
| Old Fashioned (Nabisco) | 1 Pc. | 5 | Naples, Enriched | | |
| Small (Sunshine) | 1 Pc. | 2 | (Pepperidge Farm) | 1 Oz. | 17 |
| Zu Zu (Nabisco) | 1 Pc. | 3 | Nassau (Pepperidge Farm) | 1 Pc. | 9 |
| Graham Cracker, Chocolate | | | Nut Sundae (Sunshine) | 1 Pc. | 12 |
| Covered | 1 | 7 | Oatmeal: | | |
| Hermit | 1 | 7 | (Drake's) | 1 Pc. | 12 |
| Hermit Bar, Frosted | | | (Nabisco) Family Favorites | 1 Pc. | 3 |
| (Tastykake) | 1 Pkg. | 61 | (Nabisco) Home Style | 1 Pc. | 9 |
| Hydrox (Sunshine) | 1 Pc. | 6 | (Sunshine) | 1 Pc. | 9 |
| Iced | 1 | 10 | Iced (Keebler) | 1 Pc. | 13 |
| Jumble (Drake's) | 1 Pc. | 12 | Irish, Old Fashioned | | |
| Kreemlined Wafers (Sunshine) | 1 Pc. | 6 | (Pepperidge Farm) | 1 Pc. | 7 |

| FOOD | AMT. | CARB. GRAMS | FOOD | AMT. | CARB. GRAMS |
|------|------|-------------|------|------|-------------|
| Old Fashioned (Keebler) | 1 Pc. | 11 | Scotch Shortbread | 1 | 5 |
| Raisin (Nabisco) | | | Sesame, Regina (Stella D'oro) | 1 Pc. | 6 |
| Bake Shop | 1 Pc. | 11 | Shortbread or Shortcake: | | |
| Raisin Bar (Tastykake) | 1 Pkg. | 47 | (Nabisco) Dandy | 1 Pc. | 7 |
| Raisin, Iced (Nabisco) | 1 Pc. | 8 | Lorna Doone (Nab) | 1 Pc. | 5 |
| Raisin, Old Fashioned | | | Lorna Doone (Nabisco) | 1 Pc. | 4 |
| (Pepperidge Farm) | 1 Pc. | 7 | Pecan (Nabisco) | 1 Pc. | 8 |
| Oreo Creme Sand. | 1 | 8 | Scottie (Sunshine) | 1 Pc. | 5 |
| Orleans (Pepperidge Farm) | 1 Pc. | 4 | Striped (Nabisco) | 1 Pc. | 6 |
| Peanut | 1 | 9 | Vanilla (Tastykake) | 1 Pc. | 7 |
| Peanut & Peanut Butter: | | | Smack Wafers (Sunshine) | 1 Pc. | 1 |
| (Sunshine) | 1 Pc. | 4 | Social Tea | 1 | 4 |
| Bars, Cocoa-Covered | | | Social Tea Biscuit | | |
| (Nabisco) Crowns | 1 Pc. | 10 | (Nabisco) | 1 Pc. | 3 |
| Crunch (Sunshine) | 1 Pc. | 8 | Spiced Wafers (Nabisco) | 1 Pc. | 6 |
| Creme Patties: | | | Sprinkles (Sunshine) | 1 Pc. | 13 |
| (Nab) | 1 Pc. | 4 | Sugar Cookie | 1 | 7 |
| (Nabisco) | 1 Pc. | 4 | Brown, Old Fashioned | | |
| Cocoa-Covered | | | (Pepperidge Farm) | 1 Pc. | 7 |
| (Nabisco) Fancy | 1 Pc. | 6 | Old Fashioned: | | |
| Creme Sticks, Cocoa- | | | (Keebler) | 1 Pc. | 12 |
| Covered (Nabisco) | 1 Pc. | 6 | (Pepperidge Farm) | 1 Pc. | 7 |
| Patties (Sunshine) | 1 Pc. | 4 | Rings (Nabisco) | 1 Pc. | 10 |
| Pecan Krunch (Sunshine) | 1 Pc. | 8 | Sugar Wafer | 1 | 2 |
| Pecan Sandies (Keebler) | 1 Pc. | 9 | (Nab) | 1 Pc. | 5 |
| Pirouettes, Vanilla | | | (Nabisco) Biscos | 1 Pc. | 2 |
| (Pepperidge Farm) | 1 Pc. | 4 | (Sunshine) | 1 Pc. | 7 |
| Pitter Patter (Keebler) | 1 Pc. | 11 | Assorted (Dutch Twin) | 1 Pc. | 4 |
| Plain | 1 | 7 | Chocolate (Keebler) | 1 Pc. | 3 |
| Raisin: | | | Krisp Kreem (Keebler) | 1 Pc. | 3 |
| Bar, Iced (Keebler) | 1 Pc. | 11 | Regent (Sunshine) | 1 Pc. | 3 |
| Fruit Biscuit (Nabisco) | 1 Pc. | 12 | Strawberry (Keebler) | 1 Pc. | 3 |
| Rich 'n' Chips (Keebler) | 1 Pc. | 9 | Vanilla (Keebler) | 1 Pc. | 3 |
| Sandwich, Creme: | | | Swedish Kreme (Keebler) | 1 Pc. | 12 |
| Cameo (Nabisco) | 1 Pc. | 10 | Tahiti (Pepperidge Farm) | 1 Pc. | 8 |
| Chocolate Fudge: | | | Toll House | 1 | 7 |
| (Keebler) | 1 Pc. | 13 | Toy (Sunshine) | 1 Pc. | 2 |
| (Nabisco) Cookie Break | 1 Pc. | 7 | Vanilla Creme (Wise) | 1 Pc. | 6 |
| (Sunshine) | 1 Pc. | 9 | Vanilla Snap (Nabisco) | 1 Pc. | 2 |
| Empire (Keebler) | 1 Pc. | 11 | Vanilla Wafer | 1 | 4 |
| Lemon (Keebler) | 1 Pc. | 12 | (Keebler) | 1 Pc. | 2 |
| Orbit (Sunshine) | 1 Pc. | 7 | Nilla (Nabisco) | 1 Pc. | 3 |
| Oreo (Nab) | 1 Pc. | 6 | (Sunshine) | 1 Pc. | 2 |
| Oreo (Nabisco) | 1 Pc. | 7 | Venice (Pepperidge Farm) | 1 Pc. | 6 |
| Oreo & Swiss (Nab) | 1 Pc. | 5 | Waffle Cream | 1 | 7 |
| Oreo & Swiss Creme | | | (Dutch Twin) | 1 Pc. | 6 |
| (Nabisco) | 1 Pc. | 7 | (Nabisco) Biscos | 1 Pc. | 5 |
| Social Tea (Nabisco) | 1 Pc. | 7 | Yums Yums (Sunshine) | 1 Pc. | 10 |
| Swiss (Nab) | 1 Pc. | 5 | Cookie, Dietetic: | | |
| Vanilla (Nabisco) | | | Almond Chocolate Wafer | | |
| Cookie Break | 1 Pc. | 7 | (Estee) | 1 Wafer | 2 |
| Vanilla, French (Keebler) | 1 Pc. | 13 | Apple Pastry | | |
| Vienna Finger (Sunshine) | 1 Pc. | 11 | (Stella D'oro) | 1 Pc. | 15 |

45

| FOOD | AMT. | CARB. GRAMS |
|---|---|---|
| Assorted (Estee) | 1 Pc. | 3 |
| Assorted Filled Wafers (Estee) | 1 Pc. | 3 |
| Belgian Treats (Estee) | 1 Pc. | 3 |
| Chocolate Chip: | | |
| (Dia-Mel) | 1 Pc. | 3 |
| (Estee) | 1 Pc. | 4 |
| Chocolate Holland-Filled Wafer (Estee) | 1 Pc. | 2 |
| Chocolate Mint Wafer (Dia-Mel) | 1 Pc. | 3 |
| Chocolate & Vanilla Wafer (Estee) | 1 Pc. | 3 |
| Coconut Tea (Dia-Mel) | 1 Pc. | 2 |
| Expresso Wafers (Estee) | 1 Pc. | 2 |
| Fig Pastry (Stella D'oro) | 1 Pc. | 16 |
| Fruit Flavored Wafer (Estee) | 1 Pc. | 2 |
| Fudge Nut (Estee) | 1 Pc. | 1 |
| Kichel (Stella D'oro) | 1 Pc. | T |
| Metrecal (Drackett) | | |
| Any Flavor | 1 Pc. | 3 |
| Monties (Estee) | 1 Pc. | 3 |
| Oatmeal Raisin: | | |
| (Dia-Mel) | 1 Pc. | 2 |
| (Estee) | 1 Pc. | 4 |
| Peach-Apricot Pastry (Stella D'oro) | 1 Pc. | 15 |
| Prune Pastry (Stella D'oro) | 1 Pc | 15 |
| Ripple Supreme (Dia-Mel) | 1 Pc. | 4 |
| Royal Nuggets (Stella D'oro) | 1 Pc. | T |
| Sandwich (Dia-Mel) | 1 Pc. | 3 |
| Sandwich (Estee) | 1 Pc | 4 |
| Vanilla Filled Wafer (Estee) | 1 Pc. | 3 |
| Vanilla Holland-Filled Wafer (Estee) | 1 Pc. | 2 |
| Cookie Dough (Pillsbury). | | |
| Brownie | 1 Oz. | 17 |
| Butterscotch Nut | 1 Oz. | 15 |
| Chocolate Chip | 1 Oz. | 17 |
| Fudge Nut | 1 Oz. | 16 |
| Oatmeal Raisin | 1 Oz. | 17 |
| Peanut Butter | 1 Oz. | 16 |
| Sugar | 1 Oz. | 16 |
| Cookies, Almond | 1 Oz. | 9 |
| Cookies, Animal Crackers | 1 | 2 |
| Cookies, Anise | 3 Sm. | 9 |
| Cookies, Arrowroot | 1 | 4 |
| Cookies, Boston | 1 | 22 |

| FOOD | AMT. | CARB. GRAMS |
|---|---|---|
| Cookies, Butter | 6 | 19 |
| Cookies, Butterscotch | 1 | 15 |
| Cookies, Chocolate | 3 Sm. | 9 |
| Cookies, Chocolate Chip | 3 Sm. | 15 |
| Cookies, Chocolate Fingers | 1 | 6 |
| Cookies, Chocolate Marshmallow | 1 | 9 |
| Cookies, Chocolate Refrigerator | 1 | 6 |
| Cookies, Chocolate Wafer | 1 | 6 |
| Cookies, Christmas Star | 1 | 28 |
| Cookies, Dasheens | 1 | 6 |
| Cookies, Date | 2 | 15 |
| Cookies, Devil Food Sq. | 1 | 12 |
| Cookies, Hermit | 1 | 7 |
| Cookies, Honey | 1 | 23 |
| Cookies, Ice Box (Butterscotch) | 1 | 11 |
| Cookies, Mix: | | |
| Brownies: | | |
| Family Size (Duncan Hines) | 1 Pc. | 30 |
| Regular Size (Duncan Hines) | 1 Pc. | 20 |
| Butterscotch (Betty Crocker) | 1 Oz | 21 |
| Butterscotch, Chocolate Chip (Betty Crocker) | 1 Oz. | 21 |
| Fudge (Betty Crocker) | 1 Oz. | 21 |
| Fudge (Pillsbury) | 1 Oz | 21 |
| Fudge, With Chocolate Chip (Betty Crocker) | 1 Oz | 21 |
| German Chocolate (Betty Crocker) | 1 Oz. | 22 |
| Walnut (Betty Crocker) | 1 Oz. | 20 |
| Walnut (Pillsbury) | 1 Oz. | 21 |
| Date Bar (Betty Crocker) | 1 Oz. | 15 |
| Macaroon, Coconut (Betty Crocker) | 1 Oz. | 14 |
| Vienna Dream Bar (Betty Crocker) | 1 Oz. | 14 |
| With Morsels (Nestle's) | 1 Oz. | 17 |
| Without Morsels (Nestle's) | 1 Oz. | 19 |
| Cookies, Oatmeal | 1 | 15 |
| Cookies, Raisin | 1/4 Lb. | 90 |
| Cookies, Soya | 1 | 6 |
| Cookies, Wafer | 4 | 16 |
| Cookies, Walnut | 2 Ozs | 32 |
| Cooking Fats | 1 Tbsp. | 0 |
| Cooking Fat Vegetable: | | |
| Snowdrift | 1 Cup | 0 |
| Spry | 1 Cup | 0 |
| Cooking Oil (Vegetable): | | |
| Buttery Flavor (Wesson) | 1 Tbsp. | 0 |
| Corn (Mazola) | 1 Tbsp. | 0 |
| Cottonseed, Winterized (Kraft) | 1 Tbsp. | 0 |

| FOOD | AMT. | CARB. GRAMS | FOOD | AMT. | CARB. GRAMS |
|------|------|-------------|------|------|-------------|
| Peanut (Planters) | 1 Tbsp. | 0 | (Stokely-Van Camp) | 1 Cup | 36 |
| Safflower (Kraft) | 1 Tbsp. | 0 | White, Whole Kernel: | | |
| Safflower (Saff-O-Life) | 1 Tbsp. | 0 | (Fall River) | 1 Cup | 33 |
| (Saffola) | 1 Tbsp. | 0 | Dietetic: | | |
| (Wesson) | 1 Tbsp. | 0 | (Blue Boy) | 4 Ozs. | 16 |
| Cool Cool Salad | 1 Serv. | 2½ | (Diet Delight) | 4 Ozs. | 15 |
| Cooler, Apricot | 1 Av. | 16 | (S and W) Nutradiet | 4 Ozs. | 12 |
| Cooler, Clay Morgans | 1 Serv. | 26 | (Tillie Lewis) | 4 Ozs. | 13 |
| Cooler, Grape | 1 Serv. | 16 | Cream Style: | | |
| Cooler, Lemon | 1 Serv. | 13 | (Butter Kernel) | 4 Ozs. | 22 |
| Cooler, Orange | 1 Serv. | 20 | Golden (Fall River) | 4 Ozs. | 22 |
| Cooler, Rum | 8 Ozs. | 19 | White (Fall River) | 4 Ozs. | 22 |
| Cooler, Vermouth | 1 Serv. | 15 | White or Golden | | |
| Cooler, Vin Rouge | 1 Serv. | 24 | (Stokely-Van Camp) | 4 Ozs. | 50 |
| Cooler, Wine | 1 Serv. | 11 | Cream Style, Dietetic: | | |
| Cooper's Ranch Punch | 12 Ozs. | 60 | (Blue Boy) | 4 Ozs. | 20 |
| Cordial, Anisette | 1 Serv. | 7 | (S and W) Nutradiet | 4 Ozs. | 19 |
| Cordial, Apricot | 1 Serv. | 7 | Frozen, On the Cob: | | |
| Cordial, Benedictine | 1 Serv. | 7 | (Birds Eye) | 4 Ozs. | 23 |
| Cordial, Blackberry | 1 Serv. | 7 | Frozen, Kernel: | | |
| Cordial, Chartreuse | 1 Serv. | 7 | (Birds Eye) | 4 Ozs. | 20 |
| Cordial, Cherry | 1 Serv. | 7 | (Blue Goose) | 4 Ozs. | 20 |
| Cordial, Creme de Cocoa | 1 Serv. | 7 | (Stokely-Van Camp) | 4 Ozs. | 22 |
| Cordial, Creme de Menthe | 1 Serv. | 7 | Frozen, In Butter Sauce: | | |
| Cordial, Peach | 1 Serv. | 7 | (Birds Eye) | 4 Ozs. | 17 |
| Cordial, Raspberry | 1 Serv. | 7 | Niblets (Green Giant) | | |
| Cordon D'Alsace, | | | Boil-in-the-Bag | 4 Ozs. | 18 |
| Alsatian Wine | 3 Fl. Ozs. | 3 | White Shoe Peg (Green Giant) | | |
| Cordon De Bordeaux, French, | | | Boil-in-the-Bag | 4 Ozs. | 17 |
| Red or White (Chanson) | 3 Fl. Ozs. | 6 | Mexicorn (Green Giant) | | |
| Cordon De Bourgogne, French | | | Boil-in-the-Bag | 4 Ozs. | 16 |
| White Burgundy (Chanson) | 3 Fl. Ozs. | 6 | Frozen, Cream Style: | | |
| Cordon Du Rhone, French | | | (Birds Eye) | 4 Ozs. | 21 |
| Red Rhone Wine | | | (Green Giant) | | |
| (Chanson) | 3 Fl. Ozs. | 6 | Boil-in-the-Bag | 4 Ozs. | 24 |
| Corinander | 1/8 Tsp. | 0 | With Peas & Tomatoes | | |
| Coronation Cocktail | 1 Serv. | 16 | (Birds Eye) | 4 Ozs. | 16 |
| Coronel Batista Cocktail | 1 Med. Gl. | 6 | Corn Cereal-Puffed | 3/4 Cup | 25 |
| Corn, Fresh | 4 Ozs. | 24 | Corn Chowder, Creamed | 1 Serv. | 19 |
| Corn | 1 Ear | 24 | Corn, Cream of Soup | 1 Cup | 18 |
| Corn Bread | 2 In. Sq. | 22 | Corn Crisps Bread | 1 Pc. | 21 |
| Corn Sticks, Frozen | | | Cornflakes | 1 Oz. | 34 |
| (Aunt Jemima) | 1 Oz. | 13 | Corn Flakes Cereal | 1 Cup | 21 |
| Combread Mix: | | | Country (General Mills) | 1 Cup | 18 |
| (Aunt Jemima) | 4 Ozs. | 56 | (Kellogg's) | 1 Cup | 18 |
| (Pillsbury) Ballard | 4 Ozs. | 80 | (Ralston Purina) | 1 Cup | 24 |
| Corn (Canned) | 1/2 Cup | 21 | (Van Brode) | 1 Cup | 24 |
| Golden or Yellow, Whole Kernel: | | | Dietetic (Van Brode) | 1 Cup | 25 |
| (Butter Kernel) | 1 Cup | 36 | Corn Flour, Dry Sifted | 1/2 Cup | 85 |
| (Cannon) | 4 Ozs. | 22 | Corn, Fresh, Frozen | 1 Cup | 46 |
| (Fall River) | 1 Cup | 36 | Corn Fritters | 1 | 43 |
| (Green Giant) | 1 Cup | 36 | Frozen (Mrs. Paul's) | 4 Ozs. | 45 |

47

| FOOD | AMT. | CARB. GRAMS | FOOD | AMT. | CARB. GRAMS |
|---|---|---|---|---|---|
| Corn Grits, Dry | 1/4 Cup | 28 | Cottage Cheese, Creamed | 4 Ozs. | 3 |
| (Aunt Jemima) | 1 Oz. | 23 | Cottage Cheese In Green | | |
| (Quaker) | 1 Oz. | 23 | Peppers | 1 Serv. | 5 |
| Corn Grits, Degermed | 1/4 Cup | 14 | Cottage Cheese (Jewish) | 1/2 Cup | 9 |
| Corn, Grits, Degermed, | | | Cottage Cheese and Salmon | | |
| Cooked, Enriched | 1/2 Cup | 14 | Mold | 1 Serv. | 5 |
| Corn Meal | 1/2 Cup | 45 | Cottage Cheese (Skim Milk) | 1 Cup | 5 |
| (Albers) | 1 Cup | 25 | Cottage Creamed Cheese | 1 Cup | 6 |
| Enriched (Aunt Jemima) | 1 Cup | 28 | Cottage Pudding With | | |
| Enriched (Quaker) | 1 Cup | 28 | Lemon Sauce | 1 Serv. | 61 |
| Corn Meal Flour | 1/2 Cup | 45 | Cottage Pudding | 1 Serv. | 44 |
| Corn Meal Muffins | 1 | 18 | Cotton Seed Oil | 1 Tbsp. | 0 |
| Corn, Mexican Style | 1/2 Cup | 16 | Cone, Ice Cream | | |
| Corn, Niblets | 1/2 Cup | 21 | (Cone Alone) | 1 | 7 |
| Corn Oil | 1 Tbsp. | 0 | Cough Drop: | | |
| Corn On the Cob | 1 Ear | 19 | (Beech-Nut) | 1 Drop | 2 |
| Corn Pone | 1 Sq. | 20 | (H-B) | 1 Drop | 2 |
| Corn Pudding, Southern | 1/2 Cup | 13 | (Luden's) Menthol | 1 Drop | 2 |
| Corn Souffle, Frozen | | | (Pine Bros.) | 1 Drop | 2 |
| (Stouffer's) | 4 Ozs. | 19 | (Smith Brothers) | 1 Drop | 2 |
| Corn Starch | 1 Tbsp. | 9 | Cow Peas, Dry | 4 Ozs. | 14 |
| (Argo) | 1 Oz. | 14 | Cow Peas, Cooked | 4 Ozs. | 13 |
| (Kingford's) | 1 Oz. | 14 | Crab Apple | 2 Ozs. | 8 |
| (Duryea's) | 1 Oz. | 14 | Crab Apple Jelly | 1 Tbsp. | 13 |
| Cornstarch, Butterscotch | | | Crab, Canned | 8 Ozs. | 3 |
| Pudding | 1/2 Cup | 37 | (Harris Atlantic) | 4 Ozs. | 1 |
| Corn Starch Pudding | 1/2 Cup | 24 | Alaska King (Icy Point) | 4 Ozs. | 1 |
| Corn Starch, Vanilla Pudding | 1/2 Cup | 20 | Alaska King (Pillar Rock) | 4 Ozs. | 1 |
| Corn Soya Cereals | 4 Ozs. | 16 | Frozen, Alaska King | | |
| Corn Soya Shreds Cereals | 1 Oz. | 21 | (Wakefield's) | 4 Ozs. | T |
| Corn Soya Grits | 1/2 Cup | 13 | Crab Cocktail, | | |
| Corn & Soy Grits Cereals, | | | King Crab (Sau-Sea) | 4 Ozs. | 18 |
| Mixed | 1/2 Cup | 14 | Crab, Deviled | 1 Med. | 1 |
| Corn Syrup | 2 Tbsp. | 24 | Frozen (Mrs. Paul's) | 4 Ozs. | 15 |
| Corned Beef | 4 Ozs. | 0 | Crab, Fresh (Epicure) | 1/2 Cup | T |
| (Vienna) | 4 Ozs. | T | Crab, Hard Shell (Atlantic) | 3 Ozs. | T |
| Corned Beef Hash | 1/2 Cup | 8 | Crab Jambalaya | 1 Serv. | 16 |
| Canned: | | | Crab, Louis With Dressing | 1 Serv. | 18 |
| (Armour Star) | 4 Ozs. | 9 | Crab Meat | 1/2 Cup | T |
| (Austex) | 4 Ozs. | 12 | Crab Meat (Canned) | 2/3 Cup | 1 |
| (Bounty) | 4 Ozs. | 12 | Crabmeat Sandwich | 1 | 25 |
| (Hormel) | 4 Ozs. | 8 | Crab Newburg, Alaska King, | | |
| (Nalley's) | 4 Ozs. | 9 | Frozen (Stouffer's) | 12-Oz. Pkg. | 13 |
| (Silver Skillet) | 4 Ozs. | 11 | Crab Paste | 1 Tsp. | T |
| (Wilson) | 4 Ozs. | 8 | Crab Salad With Celery | 1/2 Cup | 3 |
| Corned Beef Hash Dinner | | | Crab, Soft Shelled | 1 Med. | T |
| Frozen (Swanson) | Dinner | 27 | Crab Soup | | |
| Corned Beef Sandwich | 1 | 24 | (Crosse & Blackwell) | 1 Can | 16 |
| Corned Beef Spread | | | Cracked Wheat Bread | 1 Sl. | 12 |
| (Underwood) | 1 Tbsp. | T | Cracked Wheat Hearts Raw | 3/4 Cup | 75 |
| Corned Rabbit & Cheese | 1 Serv. | 28 | Cracked Wheat Hearts | | |
| Cottage Cheese | 1 Cup | 5 | Cooked | 6 Tbsp. | 19 |

| FOOD | AMT. | CARB. GRAMS | FOOD | AMT. | CARB. GRAMS |
|---|---|---|---|---|---|
| Cracked Wheat Toasted | 1 Sl. | 12 | Thins, Dietetic (Estee) | 1 Pc. | T |
| Crackerjack Popcorn | 1 Box | 48 | Tid Bit (Nab) | 1 Pkg. | 29 |
| Cracker Meal | 1 Tbsp. | 7 | Tid Bit (Nabisco) | 1 Pc. | T |
| Cracker, Triscuit | 1 | 3 | Toast (Keebler) | 1 Pc. | 2 |
| Cracker, Uneeda | 1 | 4 | Twists (Nalley's) | 1 Oz. | 14 |
| Cracker, Water | 1 | 3 | Waffles (Old London) | 1 Oz. | 13 |
| Cracker, Wheat Thin | 1 | 1 | Cheese & Peanut Butter Sand.: | | |
| Crackers, Puffs and Chips: | | | (Austin's) | 1 Pc. | 4 |
| Animal | 6 | 12 | (Nab) O-So-Gud | 1 Oz. | 17 |
| Appeteasers (Nabisco): | | | (Nab) Squares | 1 Pc. | 7 |
| Crescent Roll Shaped | 1 Pc. | T | (Nab) Variety Pack | 1 Pc. | 12 |
| Ham Tasting, Shaped | 1 Pc. | T | (Wise) | 1 Pc. | 3 |
| Onion Shaped | 1 Pc. | T | Chicken in a Biscuit | | |
| Arrowroot Biscuit: | | | (Nabisco) | 1 Pc. | 1 |
| (Nabisco) | 1 Pc. | 3 | Chippers (Nabisco) | 1 Pc. | 2 |
| (Sunshine) | 1 Pc. | 3 | Chipsters (Nabisco) | 1 Pc. | T |
| Bacon Flavored Thins | | | Cinnamon Crisp (Keebler) | 1 Sect. | 2 |
| (Nabisco) | 1 Pc. | 1 | Club (Keebler) | 1 Sect. | 2 |
| Bacon Toast (Keebler) | 1 Pc. | 2 | Corn Chips: | | |
| Barbecue Snack Wafer | | | (Fritos) | 1 Oz. | 15 |
| (Sunshine) | 1 Pc. | 2 | (Old London) | 1 Oz. | 14 |
| Barbecue Vittles | | | (Wise) | 1 Oz. | 14 |
| (General Mills) | 1 Pc. | T | Barbecue Flavored (Wise) | 1 Oz. | 15 |
| Bows (General Mills) | 1 Pc. | T | Crown Pilot (Nabisco) | 1 Pc. | 12 |
| Bugles (General Mills) | 1 Pc. | T | Dipsy Doodles (Old London) | 1 Oz. | 14 |
| Butter | 3 Sm. | 7 | Doo Dads (Nabisco) | 1 Oz. | 18 |
| Butter Thins (Nabisco) | 1 Pc. | 1 | Duet (Nabisco) | 1 Pc. | 2 |
| Buttons (General Mills) | 1/2 Oz. | T | Flings, Cheese-Flavored | | |
| Cheese | 3 Sm. | 7 | Curls (Nabisco) | 1 Pc. | T |
| Cheese Flavored: | | | Flings, Swiss- & Ham-Flavored | | |
| Cheese 'n Bacon Sandwich | | | Curls (Nabisco) | 1 Pc. | 1 |
| (Nab) | 3 Pcs. | 18 | French Fried Potato Crisps | | |
| Cheese-N-Cheese (Wise) | 1 Pc. | 4 | (General Mills) | 15 Pcs. | 7 |
| Cheese-Nips (Nab) | 1 Pkg. | 28 | Goldfish (Pepperidge Farm): | | |
| Cheese-Nips (Nabisco) | 1 Pc. | T | Cheese | 1 Oz. | 18 |
| Cheese on Rye | | | Lightly Salted | 1 Oz. | 19 |
| Sandwich (Nab) | 1 Pc. | 3 | Graham | 3 Med. | 15 |
| Chee-Tos, Cheese-Flavored | | | (Nabisco) | 1 Pc. | 5 |
| Puffs | 1 Oz. | 15 | (Sunshine) | 1 Pc. | 3 |
| Cheez Doodles | | | Graham, Chocolate or | | |
| (Old London) | 1 Oz. | 17 | Cocoa-Covered: | | |
| Cheez-It (Sunshine) | 1 Pc. | T | (Keebler) Deluxe | 1 Pc. | 5 |
| Che-zo (Keebler) | 1 Pc. | T | (Nabisco) | 1 Pc. | 7 |
| Cheese Pixies (Wise) | 1 Oz. | 14 | (Nabisco) Fancy | 1 Pc. | 9 |
| Ritz Cheese (Nabisco) | 1 Pc. | 2 | (Nabisco) Pantry | 1 Pc. | 8 |
| Sesame Cheese Snack | | | (Sunshine) Delito | 1 Pc. | 5 |
| (Sunshine) | 1 Pc. | 2 | Graham, Sugar Honey-Coated: | | |
| Shapies, Dip Delights | | | (Keebler) | 1 Pc. | 3 |
| (Nabisco) | 1 Pc. | T | (Nabisco) Honey Maid | 1 Pc. | 5 |
| Shapies, Shells (Nabisco) | 1 Pc. | T | (Sunshine) | 1 Pc. | 5 |
| Skinny Dips (Keebler) | 1 Pc. | T | Hi-Ho (Sunshine) | 1 Pc. | 2 |
| Thins (Pepperidge Farm) | 1 Pc. | 1 | Holland Rusk | 1 | 9 |

| FOOD | AMT. | CARB. GRAMS |
|---|---|---|
| Krispy, Salted Tops (Sunshine) | 1 Pc. | 2 |
| Krispy, Unsalted Tops (Sunshine) | 1 Pc. | 2 |
| Matzoth | 1 | 17 |
| Regular (Manischewitz) | 1 | 26 |
| Diet-10's (Goodman's) | 1 | 23 |
| Diet Thins (Manischewitz) | 1 | 23 |
| Egg 'n Onion (Manischewitz) | 1 | 23 |
| Egg, Passover (Manischewitz) | 1 | 26 |
| Midgetea (Goodman's) | 1 | 8 |
| Round Tea (Goodman's) | 1 | 14 |
| Tasteas (Manischewitz) | 1 | 20 |
| Thin Tea (Manischewitz) | 1 | 24 |
| Unsalted (Goodman's) | 1 | 23 |
| Unsalted (Horowitz-Margareten) | 1 | 28 |
| Whole Wheat, Passover (Manischewitz) | 1 | 24 |
| Melba | 1 | 3 |
| Milk Lunch (Nabisco) Royal Lunch | 1 Pc. | 8 |
| New Daisys (General Mills) | 28 Pcs. | 9 |
| Oatmeal | 3 | 15 |
| Onion-Flavored: | | |
| French (Nabisco) | 1 Pc. | 1 |
| Rings (Old London) | 1 Oz. | 21 |
| Rings (Wise) | 1 Oz. | 22 |
| Skinny Dips (Keebler) | 1 Pc. | T |
| Toast (Keebler) | 1 Pc. | 2 |
| Onion Waffies (Old London) | 1 Oz. | 13 |
| OTC (Original Trenton Cracker) | | |
| Regular or Wine | 1 Pc. | 4 |
| Oyster | 1/2 Cup | 10 |
| (Keebler) | 1 Pc. | T |
| Oysterettes (Nabisco) | 1 Pc. | T |
| Soup & Oyster (Nabisco) Dandy | 1 Pc. | T |
| (Sunshine) | 1 Pc. | T |
| Party Toast (Keebler) | 1 Pc. | 2 |
| Peanut Butter Sandwich: | | |
| & Jelly Flavored (Nabisco) | 1 Pc. | 4 |
| Malted Milk (Nab) | 1 Pkg. | 4 |
| Toast (Wise) | 1 Pc. | 3 |
| Pizza Spins (General Mills) | 1 Oz. | 16 |

| FOOD | AMT. | CARB. GRAMS |
|---|---|---|
| Pretzels | 1 Lg. | 13 |
| Ritz (Nabisco) | 1 Pc. | 2 |
| Ry-Krisp | 1 | 10 |
| Rye Thins (Pepperidge Farm) | 1 Pc. | 2 |
| Rye Toast (Keebler) | 1 Sect. | 2 |
| Rye-Wafer | 1 | 2 |
| Saltines | 6 | 36 |
| Regular (Flavor-Kist) | 1 Pc. | 2 |
| Premium (Nab) | 1 Pc. | 2 |
| Premium (Nabisco) | 1 Pc. | 2 |
| Unsalted Tops | 1 Pc. | 2 |
| Rye (Flavor Kist) | 1 Pc. | 2 |
| Sesame (Flavor Kist) | 1 Pc. | 2 |
| Zesta (Keebler) | 1 Sect. | 2 |
| Sea Toast (Keebler) | 1 Pc. | 11 |
| Sesa Wheat (Austin's) | 1 Pc. | 3 |
| Sesame Bread Wafer: | | |
| (Keebler) | 1 Pc. | 2 |
| (Nabisco) Meal Mates | 1 Pc. | 2 |
| Sip 'N Chips Snacks (Nabisco) | 1 Pc. | 1 |
| Sociables (Nabisco) | 1 Pc. | 1 |
| Soda | 6 | 35 |
| Swedish Rye Wafers (Keebler) | 1 Pc. | 3 |
| Tam Tam (Manischewitz) | 1 Pc. | 1 |
| Toasted Wafers (Sunshine) | 1 Pc. | 1 |
| Tomato Onion (Sunshine) | 1 Pc. | 2 |
| Tortilla Chips (Frito-Lay) Doritos | 1 Oz. | 16 |
| Tortilla Chips (Old London) | 1 Oz. | 16 |
| Town House (Keebler) | 1 Pc. | 2 |
| Triangle Thins (Nabisco) | 1 Pc. | 1 |
| Triscuit Wafers (Nabisco) | 1 Pc. | 3 |
| Uneeda Biscuit, Unsalted Tops (Nabisco) | 1 Pc. | 3 |
| Wafer-ets (Hol-Grain): | | |
| Salted or Unsalted: | | |
| Rice | 1 Pc. | 2 |
| Wheat | 1 Pc. | 1 |
| Waldorf Salt-Free (Keebler) | 1 Sect. | 2 |
| Waverly Wafers (Nabisco) | 1 Pc. | 2 |
| Wheat Skinny Dips (Keebler) | 1 Pc. | T |
| Wheat Thins (Nabisco) | 1 Pc. | 1 |
| Wheat Toast (Keebler) | 1 Pc. | 2 |
| Whistles (General Mills) | 17 Pcs. | 8 |
| White Thins (Pepperidge Farm) | 1 Pc. | 2 |

| FOOD | AMT. | CARB. GRAMS |
|---|---|---|
| Cracker Crumbs: | | |
| Graham (Keebler) | 3 Ozs. | 64 |
| Graham (Nabisco) | 1 Cup | 76 |
| Cracker Meal: | | |
| Salted (Nabisco) | 1 Cup | 68 |
| Unsalted (Nabisco) | 1 Cup | 67 |
| Crax (Keebler) Zesty | 3 Ozs. | 61 |
| Cranberries | 1 Cup | 11 |
| (Ocean Spray) | 1 Oz. | 2 |
| Cranberry Ice Cream | 1 Scp. | 14 |
| Cranberry Jelly | 1 Tbsp. | 9 |
| Cranberry Juice | 1 Cup | 36 |
| Cranberry Juice Cocktail | | |
| (Ocean Spray) | 1 Cup | 39 |
| Cranberry Juice Drink | | |
| (Ocean Spray) | 1 Cup | 46 |
| Cranberry-Orange Relish | | |
| (Ocean Spray) | 4 Ozs. | 52 |
| Cranberry Relish | 1/2 Cup | 26 |
| Cranberry Sauce | 3 Tbsp. | 27 |
| Canned: | | |
| Jellied (Ocean Spray) | 4 Ozs. | 43 |
| Whole Berry (Ocean Spray) | 4 Ozs. | 44 |
| Cranbreaker Mix (Bar-Tender's) | Serv | 17 |
| Cranprune Juice Drink | | |
| (Ocean Spray) | 1 Cup | 40 |
| Crappies, Baked | 1 Serv | 0 |
| Crappies, Fried | 1 Serv | 0 |
| Cream, 1/2 Milk, 1/2 Cream | 4 Oz. | 6 |
| 10.5% Fat (Sealtest) | 1 Cup | 10 |
| 12.0% Fat (Sealtest) | 1 Cup | 10 |
| Cream (20%-A-C) | 3 Tbsp | 2 |
| Cream (Whip A-C) | 1 Tbsp | T |
| Cream Biscuits | 1 Sm | 14 |
| Cream Cheese (A) | 1 Tbsp. | T |
| Cream Cheese & Jelly | | |
| Sandwich | 1 | 50 |
| Cream Cheese & Nut | | |
| Sandwich | 1 | 25 |
| Cream Dressing | 2 Tbsp. | 3 |
| Cream, Heavy | 1 Tbsp | T |
| Cream, Heavy | 1/2 Pt. | 2 |
| Whipping (Sealtest) | 1 Oz. | 1 |
| Cream, Light | 1 Tbsp. | T |
| Cream, Light | 1/2 Pt | 2 |
| 18% Fat (Sealtest) | 1 Tbsp | T |
| 25% Fat (Sealtest) | 1 Tbsp | 1 |
| Whipping (Sealtest) | 1 Oz | 1 |
| Cream, Medium | 1 Tbsp. | 1 |
| Cream Of Crab Soup | 1 Serv | 9 |
| Cream Mint Candies | 2 Sm. | 3 |
| Cream Of Tomato Soup | 1 Cup | 18 |

| FOOD | AMT | CARB. GRAMS |
|---|---|---|
| Cream Of Turkey Soup | 1 Cup | 12 |
| Cream Of Wheat | 3/4 Cup | 23 |
| Instant or Quick, Dry | 1 Cup | 28 |
| Mix'n Eat | 1 Oz. | 21 |
| Regular, Dry | 1 Cup | 29 |
| Cream Pie | 1 Pc. | 42 |
| Cream Pie, Banana | 1 Pc. | 56 |
| Cream Pie, Blueberry | 1 Pc. | 56 |
| Cream Pie, Boston | 1 Pc. | 55 |
| Cream Pie, Coconut Custard | 1 Pc. | 50 |
| Cream Pie, Cherry | 1 Pc. | 55 |
| Cream Pie, Strawberry | 1 Pc. | 50 |
| Cream Puff | 1 Av. | 44 |
| Cream Puff, Choc. | 1 Av. | 20 |
| Cream Sauce, Medium | 2 Tbsp. | 2 |
| Cream Soda | 8 Ozs. | 28 |
| Cream or Creme Soft Drink: | | |
| Sweetened: | | |
| (Canada Dry) | 8 Fl Ozs. | 32 |
| (Dr. Brown's) | 8 Fl Ozs | 27 |
| Fanta | 8 Fl Ozs. | 32 |
| (Hoffman) | 8 Fl. Ozs. | 28 |
| (Key Food) | 8 Fl Ozs | 27 |
| (Kirsch) | 8 Fl. Ozs. | 25 |
| (Shasta) | 8 Fl. Ozs. | 28 |
| (Waldbaum) | 8 Fl Ozs | 27 |
| (Yukon Club) | 8 Fl. Ozs. | 28 |
| Low Calorie: | | |
| (Dr Brown's) | 8 Fl Ozs. | 1 |
| (Hoffman) | 8 Fl. Ozs | 1 |
| (No-Cal) | 8 Fl. Ozs. | T |
| (Shasta) | 8 Fl. Ozs. | T |
| Cream, Sour | 1 Cup | 8 |
| (Borden) | 1 Oz | 1 |
| (Breakstone) | 1 Oz | 1 |
| (Sealtest) | 1 Oz. | 1 |
| Imitation: | | |
| (Borden) Zest 13 5% | | |
| Vegetable Fat | 1 Pt. | 28 |
| (Borden) Zest 13 5% | | |
| Vegetable Fat | 2 Tbsp. | 3 |
| (Breakstone) | 2 Tbsp. | 2 |
| Dressing, Cultured | | |
| (Breakstone) | 2 Tbsp | 1 |
| Cream, Whipped | 1/2 Pt. | 2 |
| Creamed Asparagus | 12 Tips | 7 |
| Creamed Beets | 1/2 Cup | 9 |
| Creamed Carrots | 1/2 Cup | 8 |
| Creamed Cauliflower With | | |
| Sauce | 1 Cup | 9 |
| Creamed Chestnuts | 1 Serv. | 33 |
| Creamed Chicken | 1/2 Cup | 6 |

| FOOD | AMT. | CARB. GRAMS |
|---|---|---|
| Creamed Corn | 1/2 Cup | 19 |
| Creamed Corn Chowder | 1 Serv. | 19 |
| Creamed Finnan Haddie | 2/3 Cup | 12 |
| Creamed Fish | 1/2 Cup | 9 |
| Creamed Lobster | 4 Ozs. | 5 |
| Creamed Mushrooms | 1 Cup | 9 |
| Creamed Mutton | 4 Ozs. | 8 |
| Creamed Onions | 1/2 Cup | 14 |
| Creamed Onion Soup | 1 Serv. | 7 |
| Creamed Oyster Stew With | | |
| 2 Tbsp. Sauce | 1 Cup | 6 |
| Creamed Oyster Stew, 1 Part | | |
| Oysters to 3 Parts Milk | 1/2 Cup | 6 |
| Creamed Peas | 1/2 Cup | 16 |
| Creamed Pink Salmon | 1 Serv. | 0 |
| Creamed Potatoes | 1 Med. | 19 |
| Creamed Salmon on Toast | 1/2 Cup | 16 |
| Creamed Salmon Bisque | 1/2 Cup | 3 |
| Creamed Sweet Breads | Sm. Serv. | 3 |
| Creamed Tomato Soup | 1 Cup | 18 |
| Creamies (Tastykake): | | |
| Banana Cake | 1 Pkg. | 34 |
| Chocolate | 1 Pkg. | 29 |
| Koffee Kake | 1 Pkg. | 47 |
| Vanilla | 1 Pkg. | 32 |
| Creams, Walnut | 1 Av. | 9 |
| Creme D'Amande Liqueur | | |
| (Garnier) | 1 Fl. Oz. | 15 |
| Creme D'Apricot Liqueur | | |
| (Old Mr. Boston) | 1 Fl. Oz. | 6 |
| Creme De Banane Liqueur: | | |
| (Garnier) | 1 Fl. Oz. | 11 |
| (Old Mr. Boston) | 1 Fl. Oz. | 6 |
| Creme De Blackberry Liqueur | | |
| (Old Mr. Boston) | 1 Fl. Oz. | 6 |
| Creme De Cacao Liqueur: | | |
| Brown or White: | | |
| (Bols) | 1 Fl. Oz. | 12 |
| (Garnier) | 1 Fl. Oz. | 13 |
| (Hiram Walker) | 1 Fl. Oz. | 15 |
| (Leroux) Brown | 1 Fl. Oz. | 14 |
| (Leroux) White | 1 Fl. Oz. | 13 |
| (Old Mr. Boston): | | |
| 42 Proof | 1 Fl. Oz. | 7 |
| 54 Proof | 1 Fl. Oz. | 7 |
| Creme De Cafe Liqueur | | |
| (Leroux) | 1 Fl. Oz. | 13 |
| Creme De Cassis Liqueur | | |
| (Garnier) | 1 Fl. Oz. | 13 |
| (Leroux) | 1 Fl. Oz. | 15 |
| Creme De Cherry Liqueur | | |
| Black Cherry (Old Mr. Boston) | 1 Fl. Oz. | 6 |

| FOOD | AMT. | CARB. GRAMS |
|---|---|---|
| Creme de Cocoa | Pony | 7 |
| Creme De Coffee Liqueur | | |
| (Old Mr. Boston) | 1 Fl. Oz. | 6 |
| Creme de Menthe | Pony | 7 |
| Creme De Menthe Liqueur: | | |
| Green or White: | | |
| (Bols) | 1 Fl. Oz. | 13 |
| (Garnier) | 1 Fl. Oz. | 15 |
| (Hiram Walker) | 1 Fl. Oz. | 11 |
| (Leroux) Green | 1 Fl. Oz. | 15 |
| (Leroux) White | 1 Fl. Oz. | 13 |
| (Old Mr. Boston): | | |
| 42 Proof | 1 Fl. Oz. | 6 |
| 60 Proof | 1 Fl. Oz. | 8 |
| Creme de Menthe Frappe | 3 Ozs. | 18 |
| Creme De Noyaux Liqueur: | | |
| (Bols) | 1 Fl. Oz. | 13 |
| (Leroux) | 1 Fl. Oz. | 14 |
| Creme De Peach Liqueur | | |
| (Old Mr. Boston) | 1 Fl. Oz. | 6 |
| Cremora, Non-Dairy (Borden) | 1 Tsp. | 1 |
| Creole Fluff | 1 Serv. | 25 |
| Creole, Gumbo | 4 Ozs. | 9 |
| Creole, Red Snapper | 1 Serv. | 4 |
| Creole Sauce | 1/4 Cup | 8 |
| Creole Sauce, Low Calorie | 1 Tbsp. | T |
| Creole Shrimps | 1 Serv. | 4 |
| Crepe Suzettes | 1 | 22 |
| Cress, Garden, Cooked | 4 Ozs. | 5 |
| Cress, Garden, Fresh | 4 Ozs. | 4 |
| Cress, Water | 10 Sprigs | 3 |
| Crisco, Shortening | | 0 |
| Crisp Relish Salad | 1 Serv. | 2 |
| Crisp Rice (Van Brode): | | |
| Regular | 1 Oz. | 24 |
| Dietetic | 1 Oz. | 25 |
| Crisp, Blueberry | 1 Serv. | 46 |
| Crispy Critters, Cereal | 1 Cup | 23 |
| Croaker, Fresh | 1 Serv. | 0 |
| Croquettes, Beef | 1 Med. | 9 |
| Croquettes, Chicken | 1 Med. | 9 |
| Croquettes, Fish | 1 Med. | 9 |
| Croquettes, Potato | 1 Med. | 17 |
| Croutons | 6 Av. | 3 |
| Croutons, Toasted White | 1 | 3 |
| Crullers | 1 Av. | 19 |
| Cruller, Sugared | 1 | 20 |
| Crumb Cake | 1 Pc. | 20 |
| Crumb Cake, Apple | 1 Pc. | 49 |
| Crumbs, Bread, Dry | 1 Tbsp. | 4 |
| Crushed Pineapple | 1/2 Cup | 15 |
| Crust, Pie (Bottom) | Aver. | 72 |

| FOOD | AMT. | CARB. GRAMS |
|---|---|---|
| Crust, Pie (Double) | Aver. | 142 |
| Crust, Pie, Graham Cracker (Bottom) | | 64 |
| Cuba Libre | 1 Serv. | 19 |
| Cuban Presidente Cktl. | 1 | 1 |
| Cube, Bouillon | 1 | 0 |
| Cube Steak | 1-1/2 Ozs. | 0 |
| Cucumbers | 8 In. | 3 |
| Cucumbers in Consomme | 1 Serv. | 3 |
| Cucumber Pickels | 6 Sl. | 1 |
| Cucumber, Pickels, Bread & Butter | 4 Sl. | 3 |
| Cultured Butter Milk | 8 Ozs. | 12 |
| Cumin | 1/8 Tsp. | 0 |
| Cupcake | 1 | 33 |
| Cupcake, Choc. | 1 | 20 |
| Cupcake, Commercial: | | |
| Chocolate (Hostess) | 1 | 29 |
| Chocolate (Tastykake) | 1 | 33 |
| Chocolate, Chocolate Creme Filled (Tastykake) | 1 | 23 |
| Coconut (Tastykake) | 1 | 16 |
| Creme Filled, Chocolate Butter Cream (Tastykake) | 1 | 23 |
| Lemon Creme Filled (Tastykake) | 1 | 17 |
| Orange (Hostess) | 1 | 26 |
| Orange Creme Filled (Tastykake) | 1 | 17 |
| Vanilla Creme Filled (Tastykake) | 1 | 16 |
| Vanilla Triplets (Tastykake) | 1 | 16 |
| Cupcake, Iced | 1 Sm. | 31 |
| Cup, Lemon Ice | 1 | 28 |
| Cupcake Mix (Flako) | 1 | 16 |
| Cup, Sherry Fruit | 1 | 42 |
| Curacao | 1 Oz. | 6 |
| Curacao Liqueur: | | |
| Curacao-Blue (Bols) | 1 Fl. Oz. | 10 |
| Curacao-Orange (Bols) | 1 Fl. Oz. | 9 |
| (Garnier) | 1 Fl. Oz. | 12 |
| (Hiram Walker) | 1 Fl. Oz. | 12 |
| (Leroux) | 1 Fl. Oz. | 9 |
| Curd, Bean | 1 Serv. | 3 |
| Curd, Boston Pork Butt | 4 Ozs. | 0 |
| Curd, Soybean | 1 Serv. | 3 |
| Currant-Raspberry Danish Dessert (Junket) | 1/2 Cup | 34 |
| Currants, Cooked | 4 Ozs. | 9 |
| Currants, Dried | 4 Ozs. | 74 |
| Currants, Fresh | 4 Ozs. | 10 |
| Currants, Jelly | 1 Tbsp. | 13 |

| FOOD | AMT. | CARB. GRAMS |
|---|---|---|
| Curried Beef | 1 Serv. | 7 |
| Curried Chicken | 1 Serv. | 7 |
| Curried Duck | 1 Serv. | 7 |
| Curried Eggs | 1 Serv. | 7 |
| Curried Fish | 1 Serv. | 7 |
| Curried Lamb | 1 Serv. | 7 |
| Curried Pork | 1 Serv. | 7 |
| Curried Shrimp, Baked | 1 Serv. | 15 |
| Curried Veal | 1 Serv. | 7 |
| Curry Powder | 1 Tsp. | 0 |
| (Crosse & Blackwell) | 1 Tbsp. | 5 |
| Custard | 1/2 Cup | 24 |
| Custard, Banana | 1 Serv. | 24 |
| Custard, Butterscotch | 1 Serv. | 12 |
| Custard (Canned), Instant | 1/2 Cup | 23 |
| Custard, Egg, Baked | 1/2 Cup | 11 |
| Custard, Fig, Baked | 4 Ozs. | 11 |
| Custard, Frozen | 4 Ozs. | 20 |
| Custard Pie | 1 Pc. | 23 |
| Frozen (Banquet) | 5 Ozs. | 41 |
| Frozen Egg Custard (Mrs. Smith's) | 1 Pc. | 14 |
| Custard Pudding | 1/2 Cup | 14 |
| Custard Pudding Mix: | | |
| Prepared With Whole Milk (Jell-O) | 1 Cup | 44 |
| Prepared With Nonfat Milk (Jell-O) | 1 Cup | 44 |
| Real Egg (Lynden) | 4 Ozs. | 71 |
| (Royal) | 1 Cup | 43 |
| Custard, Rice | 1/2 Cup | 38 |
| Custard Sauce | 1 Tbsp. | 2 |
| Custard, Vanilla, Frozen | 4 Ozs. | 20 |
| Cutlets, Veal, Broiled | 1 Serv. | 0 |
| Daiquiri | 1 Serv. | 7 |
| Daiquiri Cocktail: | | |
| (Calvert) | 3 Fl. Ozs. | 9 |
| (Hiram Walker) | 3 Fl. Ozs. | 12 |
| Daiquiri, Frozen | 1 Serv. | 7 |
| Daiquiri Mix (Bar-Tender's) | 1 Serving | 17 |
| Damson Plum Jam | 1 Tbsp. | 14 |
| Damson Plums | 1 | 12 |
| Dandelion Greens, Cooked | 1/2 Cup | 9 |
| Dandelion Greens, Fresh | 1/2 Cup | 9 |
| Danish Pastry | 1 Pc. | 25 |
| Danish Pastry, Cheese | 1 Pc. | 24 |
| Danish-Style Vegetables, Frozen (Birds Eye) | 1 Pkg. | 21 |
| Dark Turkey Meat | 4 Ozs. | 0 |
| Dasheens Cookies | 1 | 6 |
| Date Cookies | 2 | 15 |
| Date Cream Candies | 1 Oz. | 20 |

| FOOD | AMT. | CARB. GRAMS | FOOD | AMT. | CARB. GRAMS |
|---|---|---|---|---|---|
| Date Muffins | 1 Med. | 41 | Devil's Food Cake | 1 Serv. | 32 |
| Date Pudding | 1 Serv. | 16 | Devil's Leap Cktl. | 1 | 0 |
| Date Torte Cake | 1 Serv. | 38 | Dextro-Maltose | 1 Tbsp. | 7 |
| Dates | 4 | 23 | Diamond Wine | | |
| Dates, Dried | 4 | 23 | (Great Western) | 3 Fl. Ozs. | 1 |
| California (Cal-Date) | 1 Oz. | 21 | Diced Fresh Pineapple | 4 Ozs. | 10 |
| California (Cal-Date) | 1 Date | 6 | Diced Mushrooms | | |
| California (Garden of the | | | With Cabbage | 1 Serv. | 2 |
| Setting Sun) | 1 Date | 8 | Diet Dressing, French | 1 Tbsp. | 1 |
| Chopped (Dromedary) | 1 Oz. | 23 | Diet Dressing, Mayonnaise | 1 Tbsp. | T |
| Pitted (Dromedary) | 1 Oz. | 22 | Diet Dressing, Thousand Island | 1 Tbsp. | 1 |
| Imported (Bordo): | | | Dieters Delight Custard | 1 Serv. | 6 |
| Iraq | 1 Oz. | 23 | Dill | 1/8 Tsp. | 0 |
| Iraq | 4 Dates | 5 | Dill Pickles | 1 Aver. | 2 |
| Dehydrated (Vacu-Dry) | 1 Oz. | 26 | Ding Dong (Hostess) | 1 Cake | 21 |
| Date & Nut Bread | 1 Sl. | 21 | Dinkey Twinky (Hostess) | 1 Cake | 22 |
| Dates, Pitted | 1/2 Cup | 67 | Dip: | | |
| Dates, Pitted Candies | 1 | 6 | Bacon-horseradish, neufchatel | | |
| Dates, Stuffed | 2 | 20 | cheese (Kraft) Ready Dip | 1 Oz. | 1 |
| Dates, Unpitted Candies | 1 Bar | 20 | Bacon-horseradish, sour cream | | |
| Deep Dish Huckleberry Pie | 1 Pc. | 44 | (Kraft) Teez | 1 Oz. | 1 |
| Deep Dish Pie, Apple | 1 Pc. | 44 | Blue cheese, neufchatel cheese | | |
| Deep Dish Pie, Blueberry | 1 Serv. | 44 | (Kraft) Ready Dip | 1 Oz. | 1 |
| Deep Dish Pie, Peach | 1 Serv. | 44 | Blue cheese, sour cream (Kraft) | | |
| Dehydrated Apples | 2 Ozs. | 52 | Teez | 1 Oz. | 1 |
| Dehydrated Apples | 1 Lb. | 413 | Clam, neufchatel cheese (Kraft) | | |
| Dehydrated Onions | 2 Tbsp. | 3 | Ready Dip | 1 Oz. | 2 |
| Dehydrated Sweet Potatoes | 3-1/2 Ozs. | 84 | Clam, sour cream (Kraft) Teez | 1 Oz. | 1 |
| Delaware Wine: | | | Dill pickle & neufchatel cheese | | |
| (Gold Seal) | 3 Fl. Ozs. | 2 | (Kraft) Ready Dip | 1 Oz. | 2 |
| (Great Western) | 3 Fl. Ozs. | 3 | Onion: | | |
| Delightful Hamburg Steak | Av. Serv. | 0 | (Borden) | 1 Oz. | 2 |
| Deluxe, Chicken Liver | 1 Serv. | 3 | Neufchatel cheese (Kraft) | | |
| Denver, Western Sand. | 1 | 28 | Ready Dip | 1 Oz. | 2 |
| Dessert, Charlotte Russe | 1 Serv. | 33 | Sour cream (Kraft) Teez | 1 Oz. | 2 |
| Desserts, Gelatin Powdered | 2 Tbsp. | 22 | (Sealtest) | 1 Oz. | 1 |
| Devil Dogs (Drake's) | 1 Cake | 24 | Tasty Tartar (Borden) | 1 Oz. | 2 |
| Devil's Food Cake Mix: | | | Western Bar B-Q (Borden) | 1 Oz. | 2 |
| (Betty Crocker) | 1 Oz. | 23 | Dip Mix (Lawry's): | | |
| Butter Recipe (Betty Crocker) | 1 Oz. | 23 | Caesar | 1 Pkg. | 8 |
| (Duncan Hines) | 1 Pc. | 32 | Fiesta | 1 Pkg. | 10 |
| Red Devil (Pillsbury) | 1 Oz. | 23 | Garlic Sociable | 1 Pkg. | 11 |
| (Swans Down) | 1 Pc. | 36 | Green Onion | 1 Pkg. | 8 |
| Devil Food Sq. Cookie | 1 | 12 | Guacamole | 1 Pkg. | 5 |
| Deviled Crab | 1 Med. | 1 | Toasted Onion | 1 Pkg. | 8 |
| Deviled Crab Meat | 2/3 Cup | 1 | Divinity Candies | 1 Pc. | 23 |
| Deviled Egg | 2 | 2 | Divinity Fudge Candies | 1 Bar | 23 |
| Deviled Ham | 1 Tbsp. | T | Dixie Cup | 1 Cup | 20 |
| Deviled Ham Canape Spread | 1 Serv. | T | Dixie Cup Sundae | 1 Serv. | 53 |
| Deviled Pecans | | | Doctor's Cocktail | 1 | 4 |
| ala General Jackson | 1 Serv. | 8 | Doughnut: | | |
| Deviled Pigeon | 1 Serv. | 4 | Powdered (Morton) | 1 Pc. | 6 |

| FOOD | AMT. | CARB. GRAMS | FOOD | AMT. | CARB. GRAMS |
|---|---|---|---|---|---|
| Sugar & Spice (Morton) | 1 Pc. | 7 | Dried Shark's Fin | 1 Serv. | T |
| Doughnut, Iced | 1 | 37 | Dried Soybeans, Mature | 1/2 Cup | 33 |
| Doughnuts, Plain | 1 | 21 | Drink, Syllabub | 1 Serv. | 61 |
| Doughnuts, French | 1 | 21 | Drops, Orange Candies | 1 Bar | 4 |
| Doughnuts, Jelly | 1 | 37 | Dry Macaroni | 3-1/2 Ozs. | 75 |
| Doughnuts, Sugared | 1 | 16 | Dry Martini | 1 | T |
| Drained Solids Sardines | | | Dry Milk With Cocoa Powder | 3 Tbsp. | 7 |
| With Oil | 3 Ozs. | 0 | Dry Milk & Dextro-Maltose | 2 Tbsp. | 11 |
| Drambuie Liqueur, | | | Dry Mustard | 1 Tsp. | T |
| (Hiram Walker) | 1 Fl. Oz. | 11 | Dry Navy Beans | 1/2 Cup | 62 |
| Dr. Brown's Cel-Ray | | | Dry Nonfat Milk | 1 Cup | 42 |
| Tonic, Soft Drink | 8 Fl. Ozs. | 20 | Dry Noodles (Containing Egg) | 4 Ozs. | 72 |
| Dr. Pepper, Soft Drink: | | | Dry Oat Meal (Rolled Oats) | 4 Ozs. | 68 |
| Regular | 8 Fl. Ozs. | 21 | Dry Precooked Instant Cereals | 1 Oz. | 20 |
| Sugar free | 8 Fl. Ozs. | T | Dry Precooked Oatmeal | 1/2 Cup | 13 |
| Dressing, French | 1 Tbsp. | 4 | Dry Rolled Oats | 1/2 Cup | 17 |
| Dressing, Fruit Gelatin | 2 Tbsp. | T | Dry Sifted Corn Flour | 1/2 Cup | 85 |
| Dressing, Oil & Vinegar | 1 Tbsp. | 0 | Dry Soy Beans | 1/2 Cup | 37 |
| Dressing, Roquefort Cheese | 1 Tbsp. | T | Dry Spaghetti | 1/2 Cup | 22 |
| Dressing, Russian | 1 Tbsp. | T | Dry Uncooked Tapioca | 2 Ozs. | 48 |
| Dressing, Thousand Island | 1 Tbsp. | 2 | Dry White Marrow Beans | 1/2 Cup | 62 |
| Dried Apples | 2 Ozs. | 32 | Dry Whole Milk | 1 Cup | 39 |
| Dried Apricots | 5 Sm. | 13 | Dry Whole Milk Reconstituted | 8 Ozs. | 39 |
| Dried Apricots | 1 Cup | 87 | Dubonnet | 3 Ozs. | 12 |
| Dried Apricots, Cooked | 4 Ozs. | 31 | Duck | 1 Serv. | 0 |
| Dried Beef | 3 Ozs. | 0 | Duck, Gizzard | 4 Ozs. | T |
| Dried Beef, Creamed | 3 Ozs. | 3 | Duck, Raw (Dried & Salted) | 4 Ozs. | 0 |
| Dried Bread Crumbs Grated | 1/2 Cup | 33 | Duck, Roasted | 4 Ozs. | 0 |
| Dried Citron Candied | 1 Oz. | 25 | Duck, Roasted With Dressing | 1 Serv. | 22 |
| Dried Cooked Apples | | | Duck Soup | 1 Cup | 2 |
| Unsweetened | 1 Cup | 51 | Duck Soup, Creamed | 1 Cup | 12 |
| Dried Cooked Peaches | | | Duck, Wild (Raw) | 3-1/2 Ozs. | 0 |
| Sweetened | 1 Cup | 95 | Duck's Eggs | 1 Lg. | 1 |
| Dried Cooked Peaches | | | Dumpling | 1 | 6 |
| Unsweetened | 1 Cup | 58 | Dumplings, Apple | 1 Med. | 63 |
| Dried Currants, Swt. | 4 Ozs. | 74 | Dutch Apple Cake | 1 Pc. | 65 |
| Dried Egg | 1 Tbsp. | 0 | Dutch Cake Mix, | | |
| Dried Eggs | 1 Cup | 3 | Double Dutch (Pillsbury) | 1 Oz. | 21 |
| Dried Eggs (Whites Only) | 1 Tbsp. | 0 | Eclair | 1 Av. | 30 |
| Dried Eggs (Whole) | 1 Tbsp. | T | Eclair, Chocolate | 1 Av. | 30 |
| Dried Eggs (Yolks Only) | 1 Tbsp. | T | Eclair, Choc., (Creamed) | 1 Av. | 15 |
| Dried Figs | 1 Cup | 64 | Eclair, Choc. Custard | 1 | 20 |
| Dried Green Peas | 1/2 Cup | 18 | Edam Cheese | 1-1/2 Ozs. | 2 |
| Dried Lichi Nuts | 1/2 Cup | 34 | Edible Pea Pods | 15 | 6 |
| Dried Lungen | 1/2 Cup | 37 | Eels, Baked | 1 Serv. | 0 |
| Dried Peaches | 1/2 Cup | 55 | Eels, Smoked | 1/2 Cup | 0 |
| Dried Peaches Sulphur | | | Eggs, Boiled (A-B1-B2) | 1 Av | T |
| With Sugar | 1/2 Cup | 41 | Egg Bread | 1 Sl. | 12 |
| Dried Pears | 1/2 Cup | 7 | Egg Butter Spread | 1 Tbsp. | T |
| Dried Peas, Cooked | 1/2 Cup | T | Egg, Coddled | 1 Av. | T |
| Dried Prunes (A) | 4 | 24 | Egg Cream, Chocolate | 1 Cup | 24 |
| Dried Raisins | 1/2 Cup | 62 | Egg Custard | 1/2 Cup | 14 |

| FOOD | AMT. | CARB. GRAMS | FOOD | AMT | CARB. GRAMS |
|------|------|-------------|------|-----|-------------|
| Egg Drop Soup | 1 Cup | 15 | Eggs, Creamed | 2 | 3 |
| Egg, Duck | 1 | 2 | Eggs, Creole | 1 Serv. | 4 |
| Egg Foo Yung, Chicken | 1 Serv. | 4 | Eggs, Deviled | 2 | 2 |
| Egg Foo Yung, | | | Eggs, Dried | 1 Cup | 3 |
| Chicken Sub Gum | 1 Serv. | 1 | Eggs, Dried | 1 Tbsp. | T |
| Egg Foo Yung | 1 Serv. | 0 | Eggs, Duck | 1 Lg. | 2 |
| Egg Foo Yung, Ham | 1 Serv. | 1 | Eggs Florentine | 1 Serv. | 4 |
| Egg Foo Yung, Lobster | 1 Serv. | 1 | Eggs, Fried | 1 Av. | T |
| Egg Foo Yung, Shrimp | 1 Serv. | 1 | Eggs, Italian | 1 Serv. | 8 |
| Egg Sandwich, Fried | 1 | 24 | Eggs, Josette | 1 Serv. | 8 |
| Egg & Fruit Punch | 1 Cup | 26 | Eggs, Raw | 1 Med | T |
| Egg Harbor Punch | 1 Serv. | 29 | Elderberry Cordial | 1 | 7 |
| Egg & Kidney Bake | 1 Serv | 1 | Elderberry Pie | 1 Pc. | 57 |
| Egg Muffins | 1 Med. | 20 | Elderberry Wine | 1 Gl. | 6 |
| Egg Nog | 1 Cup | 25 | Emmenthaler Cheese | 1-1/2 Ozs. | T |
| (Borden) 4.69% fat | 1 Cup | 32 | Enchilades | 1 Av. | 19 |
| (Borden) 6.0% fat | 1 Cup | 32 | Enchilada, Frozen: | | |
| (Borden) 8.0% fat | 1 Cup | 32 | Beef (Banquet) | 5 Pcs. | 92 |
| (Sealtest) 6.8% fat | 1 Cup | 35 | With Sauce (Banquet) | | |
| (Sealtest) 8.8% fat | 1 Cup | 34 | Cookin' Bag | 1 Pc. | 14 |
| With Alcohol | | | Enchilada Dinner, Frozen. | | |
| (Old Mr. Boston) | 1 Fl. Oz. | 4 | Beef (Banquet) | Dinner | 61 |
| Egg Nog Brandy | 1 Cup | 25 | Cheese (Banquet) | Dinner | 58 |
| Egg Nog Cake | 1 Pc. | 29 | Endive | 2 | 4 |
| Egg Nog Ice Cream | 1 Scp. | 14 | Endive (A-C) | Sm. | 2 |
| Egg Nog, Rum | 1 Cup | 25 | Endive (Inner Leaves) | 10 | 1 |
| Egg Nog Sherry | 1 Cup | 25 | Endive & Grape Salad | 4 Ozs. | 8 |
| Egg Nog Whiskey | 1 Cup | 25 | Endive & Grapefruit Salad | 1 Serv. | 16 |
| Egg Plant | 1 Cup | 10 | English Muffins | 1 Av. | 21 |
| Egg Plant, Baked Italian Style | 1 Serv. | 26 | English Tea Cake | 1 Serv. | 53 |
| Egg Plant Parmigan | 1 Serv. | 26 | English Toasted Muffin | 1 | 34 |
| Egg Plant Scalloped | 1 Serv. | 13 | English Toffee | 1 Pc. | 13 |
| Egg Poached (A-B1-B2) | 1 Av. | 1 | Enriched White Bread | 1 Sl. | 12 |
| Egg Poached in Jelly | 1 Med. | 17 | Escalloped Crab & | | |
| Egg Roll, Chinese | 1 Av. | 15 | Lobster Meat | 1 Serv. | 8 |
| Egg Roll, Frozen: | | | Escalloped Potato | 1/2 Cup | 14 |
| Meat (Chun King) | 1 Oz. | 8 | Escarole (A) | 1/2 | 2 |
| Shrimp (Chun King) | 1 Oz. | 7 | Eskimo Pie | Aver. | 32 |
| Shrimp & Meat (Chun King) | 1 Oz. | 5 | Evaporated Milk 1/2 Water | 4 Ozs. | 8 |
| Shrimp (Hung's) | 1 Pc. | 14 | Evaporated Milk (A-B2-D) | | |
| Egg, Scrambled | 1 Av. | T | Sweetened | 1/4 Cup | 21 |
| Egg, Scrambled With Milk | 1 Av. | T | Evaporated Milk, | | |
| Egg Shirred | 1 Av. | 2 | Unsweetened | 1/4 Cup | 8 |
| Egg Sliced Sandwich | | | Extract, Vanilla | 1 Tsp. | 0 |
| With Butter | 1-1/2 Eggs | 25 | Falkland Island Warmer | 1 Gl. | 4 |
| Eggs, Stuffed | 1 Med. | T | Farina | 3/4 Cup | 128 |
| Egg & Tomato Salad | 1 Serv. | 1 | Regular, Dry: | | |
| Egg Whites | 1 | T | Cream, Enriched (H-O) | 1 Cup | 135 |
| Egg Whites, Dried | 2 Ozs. | T | Cream, Enriched (H-O) | 1 Tsp. | 8 |
| Egg Yolk | 1 | T | (Pearls of Wheat) | 1 Cup | 128 |
| Egg Yolks, Dried | 1 Oz. | T | Cooked (Quaker) | 1 Cup | 22 |
| Eggs | 1 Av. | T | Farmers Cheese | 1/2 Cup | 9 |

| FOOD | AMT. | CARB. GRAMS | FOOD | AMT. | CARB. GRAMS |
|---|---|---|---|---|---|
| Fat, Bacon | 1 Tsp. | 0 | Fish, Blue, Fried | 1 Serv. | 0 |
| Fat, Cooking, Vegetable: | | | Fish, Buffalo | 1 Serv. | 0 |
| Snowdrift | 1 Cup | 0 | Fish, Butter Fried | 1 Serv. | 0 |
| Spry | 1 Cup | 0 | Fish Cakes | 1 | 10 |
| Fat, Vegetable | 1 Tsp. | 0 | Frozen (Commodore) | 2 Ozs. | 10 |
| Fats, Chicken | 1 Tsp. | 0 | (Mrs. Paul's) | 2 Ozs. | 10 |
| Fats, Cooking | 1 Tsp. | 0 | Fish Chowder | 1 Serv. | 13 |
| Favorite Crabmeat Salad | 1 Serv. | 15 | Fish, Cod | 1 Serv. | 0 |
| Feet, Pig's | 1 Serv. | 0 | Fish, Cod (Balls) | 1 Av. | 5 |
| Fennel Leaves | 2 | 2 | Fish, Cod (Cakes) | 1 Av. | 10 |
| Fennel Seed | 1/8 Tsp. | 0 | Fish, Cod (Creamed) | 1 Serv. | 8 |
| Festival Main Meal Meat: | | | Fish, Cod (Dried) | 2 Ozs. | T |
| Canned (Wilson Sinclair): | | | Fish, Cod (Steaks) | 1 Serv. | 0 |
| Beef Roast | 4 Ozs. | 0 | Fish, Creamed | ¹/2 Cup | 9 |
| Corned Beef Brisket | 4 Ozs. | 0 | Fish Croquettes | 1 Med. | 9 |
| Ham | 4 Ozs. | 1 | Fish Dinner, Frozen: | | |
| Picnic | 4 Ozs. | 1 | (Morton) | Dinner | 28 |
| Pork Loin, Smoked | 4 Ozs. | 1 | With French Fries | | |
| Pork Roast | 4 Ozs | 0 | (Swanson) | Dinner | 41 |
| Turkey & Dressing | 4 Ozs | 11 | Fish Fillets (Mrs. Paul's) | 2 Ozs. | 4 |
| Turkey Roast | 4 Ozs. | 0 | Fish, Flounder | 1 Serv. | 0 |
| Feta Cheese | 1 Oz | 1 | Fish, Gefilte | 1 Serv. | 0 |
| Fifteen-Minute Meat Loaf | 1 Serv. | 4 | Fish House Punch | 12 Ozs. | 12 |
| Fifth Ave. Candies | 1 Bar | 15 | Fish Mousse | 1 Serv. | 3 |
| Fig Bars | 2 | 22 | Fish, Red | 1 Serv. | 0 |
| Fig Custard | 1 Serv. | 24 | Fish, Smoked | 1/2 | 0 |
| Fig Juice, Real Fig | 1/2 Cup | 15 | Fish Sticks, Frozen | 4 Ozs. | 7 |
| Fig Muffin | 1 | 26 | Cooked (Booth) | 1 Oz. | 2 |
| Fig Newtons | 2 | 22 | (Commodore) | 1 Oz. | 2 |
| Figs (Canned) | 1/2 Cup | 30 | (Mrs. Paul's) | 1 Oz. | 2 |
| Kadota (Diet Delight) | 1/2 Cup | 11 | Fish, Stuffed Carp | 1 Serv. | 2 |
| (S and W) Nutradiet | 6 Figs | 12 | Fish, Sweet & Sour | 1 Serv. | T |
| Dehydrated (Vacu-Dry) | 1 Oz. | 24 | Fish Swirls | 1 Serv. | 8 |
| Figs (Canned), Low-Cal. | 1/2 Cup | 14 | Fish, Tuna (Canned in Oil) | 1/2 Cup | 0 |
| Figs, Dried | 1 | 12 | Fish, Tuna (Cooked) | 3/4 Cup | 0 |
| Figs, Fresh | 4 Sm. | 24 | Fish, White (Broiled) | 1 Serv. | 0 |
| Figs, Stewed | 1/2 Cup | 40 | Fish, White (Fried) | 1 Serv. | 0 |
| Filberts | 6 | 1 | Fish, White (Smoked) | 1 Serv. | 0 |
| Filets of Sole, Broiled | Serv. | 0 | Fish, White (Steamed) | 1 Serv. | 0 |
| Filet Mignon (B2) | 1 Serv. | 0 | Fizz, Rum | 8 Ozs. | 8 |
| Filling, Applebutter | | | Fizz, Sloe Gin | 1 Gl. | 5 |
| Creamy Cake | 1 Serv. | 6 | Flakes, Bran | 3/4 Cup | 21 |
| Filling, Banana | 1/2 Cake | 98 | Flakes, Corn | 1 Cup | 21 |
| Filling, Chocolate | 1 Serv. | 25 | Flakes, Rice | 1 Cup | 26 |
| Fingers, Cocoanut | 1 | 27 | Flakes, Rice (Puffed) | 1 Cup | 10 |
| Fingers, Lady | 1 | 5 | Flakes, Wheat | 1 Cup | 21 |
| Finnan Haddie | 1 Serv. | T | Flakes, Wheat Germ | 1/4 Cup | 13 |
| Finnan Haddie, Creamed | 2/3 Cup | 12 | Flame Tokay Grapes | 1/2 Cup | 8 |
| Finnan Haddies, Smoked | 1 Serv. | 0 | Flamingo Beverage | 12 Ozs. | 21 |
| Fish Balls | 1 Av. | 5 | Flank Beef, Cooked | 4 Ozs. | 0 |
| Fish, Blue | 1 Serv. | 0 | Flick, Instant (Ghirardelli) | 1 Tbsp. | 11 |
| Fish, Blue, Baked | 1 Serv. | 0 | Flip, Port Wine | 1 Serv. | 30 |

| FOOD | AMT. | CARB. GRAMS |
|---|---|---|
| Flip, Sherry Wine | 1 Serv. | 32 |
| Flip, Soft Drink (Dad's) | 6 Fl. Ozs. | 18 |
| Float, Apricot | 1 Sl. | 18 |
| Floating Island | 1 Serv. | 19 |
| Florentine Fillets | 1 Serv. | 3 |
| Florida Avocado | 1/2 Med. | 11 |
| Florida Special Cktl. | 1 Serv. | 5 |
| Flounder | 1 Serv. | 0 |
| Meat Only (Booth) | 4 Ozs. | 0 |
| Flour | 1 Cup | 84 |
| Flour, Arrowroot | 2 Ozs. | 40 |
| Flour, Bisquick | 1/2 Cup | 43 |
| Flour, Buckwheat | 1/2 Cup | 40 |
| Flour, Buckwheat Dark Sifted | 2 Ozs. | 41 |
| Flour, Buckwheat Light Sifted | 2 Ozs. | 45 |
| Flour, Cake | 1 Cup | 85 |
| Flour, Corn Meal | 1/2 Cup | 45 |
| Flour, Gold Medal: | | |
| Regular (Betty Crocker) | 1 Oz. | 21 |
| Self-rising (Betty Crocker) | 1 Oz. | 20 |
| Flour, Red Band: | | |
| Enriched (Betty Crocker) | 1 Oz. | 22 |
| Self-rising (Betty Crocker) | 1 Oz. | 21 |
| Flour, Rice | 1/2 Cup | 50 |
| Flour, Rye | 1 Cup | 62 |
| Flour, Rye, Light | 1/2 Cup | 49 |
| Flour, Softasilk, | | |
| (Betty Crocker) | 1 Oz. | 22 |
| Flour, Soy Bean | 1 Cup | 14 |
| Flour, Soy Bean (Full Fat) | 1/2 Cup | 41 |
| Flour, Soy Bean (Low Fat) | 1/2 Cup | 34 |
| Flour Wheat | 1 Cup | 84 |
| Flour, Wheat Bread | 1 Cup | 79 |
| Flour, Wheat Cake Or Pastry | 1 Pc. | 14 |
| Flour, White | 1 Cup | 84 |
| Flour, Wondra, | | |
| Enriched (Betty Crocker) | 1 Oz. | 21 |
| Fog Cutter Beverage | 14 Ozs. | 7 |
| Folle Blanche Wine, | | |
| (Louis M. Martini) | 3 Fl. Ozs. | T |
| Fondant, Candied | 1 Patty | 10 |
| Fondue, Cheese | 1 Serv. | 9 |
| Fondue, Swiss Cheese | | |
| With Toast | 1 Serv. | 14 |
| Force Cereals | 4 Ozs. | 11 |
| Foundation Cake | 1 Sl. | 30 |
| Fournier Nature (Gold Seal) | 3 Fl. Ozs. | T |
| Frankfurter | 4 Ozs. | T |
| Frankfurter, All Beef | 4 Ozs. | 0 |
| (Vienna) | 1 Frankfurter | 1 |
| All Beef (Wilson) | 4 Ozs. | 1 |
| Skinless (Wilson) | 4 Ozs. | 1 |
| Frankfurter, Barbecued | 1 Av | T |

| FOOD | AMT. | CARB. GRAMS |
|---|---|---|
| Frankfurter & Cabbage | | |
| Casserole | 1 Serv. | 28 |
| Frankfurter, Canned (Hormel) | 4 Ozs. | 1 |
| Frankfurter Rolls | 1 | 12 |
| Frankfurter Sand. | 1 | 12 |
| Frankfurters & Sauerkraut | 1 Serv. | 5 |
| Frankfurters and Potato Salad | 1 Serv. | 17 |
| Frankfurters & Scrambled Egg | 1 Serv. | 2 |
| Franks-N-Blankets, | | |
| Frozen (Durkee) | 1 Pc. | 1 |
| Frappe, Coffee | | |
| (No Whipped Cream) | 1 Cup | 14 |
| Frappe Creme de Menthe | 3 Ozs. | 18 |
| Frappe, Orange | 1 Serv. | 21 |
| French Apple Pie | 1 Pc. | 45 |
| French Apricot Glaze | 1/2 Cup | 87 |
| French Artichokes | 1 Lg. | 14 |
| French Bread | 1 Sl. | 10 |
| French Brioche | 1 | 13 |
| French Diet Dressing | 1 Tbsp. | 1 |
| French Fried Onions | 1 Lg. | 10 |
| French Fried Potatoes | 6 Av. | 12 |
| French Fried Potatoes Frozen | 10 Pcs. | 15 |
| French Garlic Dressing | 1 Tbsp. | 4 |
| French, Homemade Salad | | |
| Dressing | 1 Tbsp. | 2 |
| French Omelet | 1 Serv. | 2 |
| French Onion Soup | 1 Serv. | 5 |
| French Onion Soup | | |
| With Croutons | 1 Cup | 10 |
| French Pancake | 1 | 7 |
| French Pastry | Med. | 40 |
| French Rolls | 1 | 20 |
| French Salad Dressing | 1 Tbsp. | 4 |
| French '75 | 8 Ozs. | 9 |
| French Toast | 1 Sl. | 15 |
| French Toast With Maple Syrup | 1 Pc. | 23 |
| French Toast With Corn Syrup | 1 Pc. | 23 |
| French Vegetable Soup | 1 Serv. | 11 |
| French Vermouth, Dry | 1 Serv. | 0 |
| Fresca, Soft Drink | 8 Fl. Ozs. | T |
| Fresh Apricots | 3 Med | 10 |
| Fresh Bananas | 1 Lg. | 46 |
| Fresh Black Raspberries | 1/2 Cup | 11 |
| Fresh Cherries, Pitted | 1 Cup | 20 |
| Fresh Corn | 1 Ear | 24 |
| Fresh Croaker | 1 | 0 |
| Fresh Currants | 4 Ozs. | 10 |
| Fresh Fruit Flavored | | |
| Ice Cream Soda | 10 Ozs. | 71 |
| Fresh Garden Peas, Cooked | 4 Ozs. | 10 |
| Fresh Grapefruit Sections | 1 Cup | 20 |
| Fresh Kohlrabi | 1/2 Cup | 5 |

| FOOD | AMT. | CARB. GRAMS | FOOD | AMT. | CARB. GRAMS |
|---|---|---|---|---|---|
| Fresh Lobster With Butter | 3/4 Lb. | 1 | Frosting, Butter | 1 Tbsp. | 6 |
| Fresh Matai | 4 Ozs. | 20 | Frosting, Buttermilk | 1 Tbsp. | 13 |
| Fresh Orange | 1 Lg. | 26 | Frosting, Butterscotch | 1 Tbsp. | 6 |
| Fresh Orange | 1 Med. | 17 | Frosting, Candy | 1 Tbsp. | 18 |
| Fresh Orange | 1 Sm. | 11 | Frosting, Choc. Boiled | 1 Tbsp. | 18 |
| Fresh Orange Sections | 1 Cup | 22 | Frosting, Choc. Cheese | 1 Tbsp. | 11 |
| Fresh Ox Tongue, Boiled | 1 Serv. | 2 | Frosting, Choc. Marsh. | 1 Tbsp. | 16 |
| Fresh Peaches | 1 Cup | 18 | Frosting, Choc. Butter | 1 Tbsp. | 6 |
| Fresh Pears | 1 Cup | 32 | Frosting, Fudge | Tbsp. | 6 |
| Fresh Peas, Cooked | 1 Cup | 19 | Frosting, Lemon | 1 Tbsp. | 11 |
| Fresh Peas in Pod | 1 Lb. | 36 | Frosting, Maple | 1 Tbsp. | 6 |
| Fresh Pineapple | 1 Cup | 19 | Frosting, Mocha, Choc. | 1 Tbsp. | 6 |
| Fresh Plums | 1 Med. | 7 | Frosting, Orange | 1 Tbsp. | 6 |
| Fresh Raspberries | 1 Cup | 17 | Frosting, Pineapple | 1 Tbsp. | 6 |
| Fresh Shredded Cocoanut | 1 Cup | 13 | Frosting, Seven Minute | 1 Tbsp. | 6 |
| Fresh Shrimp | 8 Ozs. | 1 | Frozen Apples, Sweetened | 1/2 Cup | 26 |
| Fresh Strawberries | 1 Cup | 12 | Frozen Apricots | 5 Med. | 22 |
| Fresh Sugar Peas | 4 Ozs. | 15 | Frozen Asparagus | 6 | 4 |
| Fresh Tuna | 3 Ozs. | 0 | Frozen Blueberries | 4 Ozs. | 29 |
| Fricassee, Rabbit | 1 Serv. | 0 | Frozen Blueberries, | | |
| Fricasseed, Chicken | 1 Serv. | 6 | Sweetened | 1 Cup | 37 |
| Fried Bacon | 3 Strips | 0 | Frozen Blueberries, | | |
| Fried Bananas | 1 Med. | 35 | Unsweetened | 3 Ozs. | 22 |
| Fried Chicken | 1/2 Serv. | 0 | Frozen Boysenberries, | | |
| Fried Crappies | 1 Serv. | 0 | Sweetened | 1 Cup | 35 |
| Fried Egg (A-B1-B2) | 1 Av. | T | Frozen Boysenberries, | | |
| Fried Frog Legs | 2 | 4 | Unsweetened | 1 Cup | 12 |
| Fried Haddock | 1 Serv. | 6 | Frozen Broccoli | 1 Cup | 8 |
| Fried Ham | 2 Sls. | 0 | Frozen Brussel Sprouts | 3-1/2 Ozs. | 7 |
| Fried Oysters | 6 | 4 | Frozen Carrots | 1/2 Cup | 5 |
| Fried Perch | 1 Serv. | 6 | Frozen Cauliflower | 1 Cup | 8 |
| Fried Potatoes | 1/2 Cup | 20 | Frozen Custard | 1/2 Cup | 20 |
| Fried Rice With Chicken | 1 Serv. | 22 | Frozen Custard Ice Cream | 1/4 Pt. | 26 |
| Fried Rice With Pork | 1 Serv. | 22 | Frozen Dessert, Vegetable | | |
| Fried Rice With Shrimp | 1 Serv. | 22 | Fat Product (Sealtest) | 1 Pt. | 60 |
| Fried Scallops With Batter | 4 Lg. | 15 | Frozen Fish Sticks | 4 Ozs. | 7 |
| Fried Shrimps | 1 Serv. | 0 | Frozen Grapefruit Juice | | |
| Fried Shrimp With Canton | | | Concentrate | 6 Ozs. | 72 |
| Sauce | 1 Serv. | 42 | Frozen Green Beans | 3-1/2 Ozs. | 8 |
| Frijoles (Pinta Beans) | 1/2 Cup | 24 | Frozen Kale | 3-1/2 Ozs. | 5 |
| Fritters, Apple | 1 | 12 | Frozen Kohlrabi | 1 Cup | 10 |
| Fritters, Apricot | 1 Serv. | 28 | Frozen Lemonade Juice | | |
| Fritters, Banana | 1 Av. | 12 | Concentrate | 6 Ozs. | 112 |
| Fritters, Clam | 3-1/2 Ozs. | 31 | Frozen Lima Beans | 3-1/2 Ozs. | 18 |
| Fritters, Corn | 1 Av. | 43 | Frozen Melon Balls | 1 Cup | 12 |
| Frogs Legs | 4 Lg. | 0 | Frozen Mixed Vegetables | 4 Ozs. | 16 |
| Frogs Legs, Fried | 2 | 4 | Frozen Orange Juice | | |
| Froot Loops, Cereal | | | Concentrate | 6 Ozs. | 80 |
| (Kellogg's) | 1 Cup | 24 | Frozen Oyster Stew | 1 Can | 20 |
| Frosted Shake, Any Flavor | | | Frozen Peaches | 12 Ozs. | 69 |
| (Borden) | 1 Can | 45 | Frozen Peas | 1/2 Cup | 11 |
| Frosting (Boiled) | 1 Tbsp. | 6 | Frozen Perch | 1 Serv. | 0 |
| Frosting, Brown Sugar | 1 Tbsp. | 6 | Frozen Pineapple | 1/2 Cup | 26 |

| FOOD | AMT. | CARB. GRAMS |
|------|------|------|
| Frozen Raspberries | 3 Ozs. | 24 |
| Frozen Raspberries | 10 Ozs. | 80 |
| Frozen Rhubarb | 1/2 Cup | 23 |
| Frozen Strawberries With Sugar | 1 Serv. | 27 |
| Frozen Tangerine Juice Concentrate | 6 Ozs. | 80 |
| Frozen Tangerine Juice Diluted | 1 Cup | 27 |
| Fruit, Apricots, Pan Boiled | 1/2 Cup | 10 |
| Fruit, Blueberries (Fresh) | 1/2 Cup | 8 |
| Fruit Bowl Soft Drink: | | |
| (Hires) | 6 Fl. Ozs. | 22 |
| (Nedick's) | 6 Fl. Ozs. | 22 |
| Fruit, Buttermilk Beverage | 1 Serv. | 25 |
| Fruit Cake | 2-1/2 Ozs. | 36 |
| Fruit Cake, Brown Sugar | 1 Sl. | 22 |
| Fruit, Canteloupe | 1/4 Melon | 4 |
| Fruit Cobbler | 1 Serv. | 44 |
| Fruit Cocktail (Canned) | 1 Serv. | 19 |
| (Hunt's) | 4 Ozs. | 22 |
| Unsweetened or Dietetic: | | |
| (Diet Delight) | 1 Oz. | 2 |
| (Libby's) | 1 Oz. | 3 |
| (S and W) Nutradiet | 1 Oz. | 3 |
| Fruit Galaxy (Vacu-Dry) | 1 Oz | 25 |
| Fruit Cocktail, Fresh | 1 Serv. | 12 |
| Fruit Cocktail Whip | 1 Serv. | 4 |
| Fruit Drop Candies | 3 | 10 |
| Fruit & Egg Punch | 8 Ozs. | 26 |
| Fruit, Fresh Apple | 1 Med. | 16 |
| Fruit Gelatin | 1/2 Cup | 27 |
| Fruit Gelatin Dressing | 2 Tbsp. | 4 |
| Fruit Jams | 1 Tbsp. | 14 |
| Fruit Jellies | 1 Tbsp. | 13 |
| Fruit, Mixed, Frozen, Quick-thaw (Birds Eye) | 1 Cup | 72 |
| Fruit Pie (Hostess) | 1 Oz. | 12 |
| Fruit Punch | 6 Ozs. | 33 |
| Fruit Punch Mix (Wyler's) | 6 Fl. Ozs. | 15 |
| Fruit, Fresh Salad | 3 Tbsp. | 21 |
| Canned, Regular (Kraft) | 4 Ozs. | 12 |
| Canned, Dietetic | | |
| (Diet Delight) | 1 Cup | 14 |
| (White Rose) | 4 Ozs. | 10 |
| Fruit Sherbet | 1 Scp. | 29 |
| Fruited Strawberry Mold | 1 Serv. | 4 |
| Fruit Sundae | 1 Serv. | 37 |
| Fruit Syrups | 1 Tbsp. | 14 |
| Fryer, Chicken Raw | 4 Ozs. | 0 |
| Fudge | 1 Sq. | 23 |
| Fudge, Almond | 1 Sq. | 22 |

| FOOD | AMT. | CARB. GRAMS |
|------|------|------|
| Fudge, Brown Sugar | 1 Sq. | 22 |
| Fudge Candies With Nuts | 1 Oz. | 18 |
| Fudge Cake | 1 Serv. | 35 |
| Fudge Cake Mix: | | |
| Butter Recipe (Duncan Hines) | 1 Pc. | 34 |
| Cherry (Betty Crocker) | 1 Oz. | 22 |
| Chocolate (Pillsbury) | 1 Oz. | 22 |
| Dark Chocolate (Betty Crocker) | 1 Oz. | 22 |
| Macaroon (Pillsbury) | 1 Oz. | 21 |
| Marble (Duncan Hines) | 1 Pc. | 36 |
| Sour Cream, Chocolate Flavor (Betty Crocker) | 1 Oz. | 22 |
| Sour Cream Flavor (Pillsbury) | 1 Oz. | 21 |
| Toffee, Batter Cake (Pillsbury) | 1 Oz. | 21 |
| Fudge Choc. Candies | 1 Pc. | 23 |
| Fudge, Choc. Milk | 1 Pc. | 23 |
| Fudge Divinity Candies | 1 Pc. | 23 |
| Fudge Frosting | 1 Tbsp. | 6 |
| Fudge Pop Ice Cream | 1 | 13 |
| Fudge Pudding Mix (Thank You) | 1 Cup | 50 |
| Fudge, Raisin | 1 Sq. | 22 |
| Fudge Sauce | 1 Tbsp. | 18 |
| Fudgsicle, Chocolate (Popsicle Industries) | 2 Fl. Ozs. | 18 |
| Fudge Sundae, Fancy (Hot) | 1 | 53 |
| Gaiety Creme Sand. Cookie | 1 | 14 |
| Garbanzoes (Chick Peas) Dry, Uncooked | 1/4 Cup | 30 |
| Garbanzo Soup, Canned, (Hormel) | 4 Ozs | 8 |
| Garden Cress, Cooked | 1/2 Cup | 5 |
| Garden Peas, Fresh | 4 Ozs. | 14 |
| Garlic Clove | 1 | T |
| Garlic Bread (1 Tsp. Butter) | 1 Sl. | 11 |
| Garlic French Dressing | 1 Tbsp | 4 |
| Garlic Sauce With Butter | 2 Tbsp. | 1 |
| Garlic Sauce With Water | 2 Tbsp. | 1 |
| Gazpacho Spanish Soup | 1 Serv. | 11 |
| Gefilte Fish | 1 Serv. | 13 |
| (Manischewitz) | 4 Ozs. | 4 |
| Jumbo (Manischewitz) | 2 Ozs | 2 |
| Whitefish & Pike (Manischewitz) | 1 Pc | 1 |
| Gelatin | 1 Serv | 18 |
| Unflavored (Knox) | 1 Oz. | 0 |
| Gelatin Desserts, Powder | 2 Tbsp | 22 |
| All Fruit Flavors (Jell-o) | 1 Cup | 36 |
| All Flavors (Jells Best) | 1 Cup | 37 |
| All Flavors (Royal) | 1 Cup | 34 |
| Low Calorie, All Flavors: | | |
| (D-Zerta) | 1 Cup | 0 |
| (Dia-Mel) | 4 Ozs. | 0 |

| FOOD | AMT. | CARB. GRAMS | FOOD | AMT. | CARB. GRAMS |
|---|---|---|---|---|---|
| Gelatin Drink, | | | (Hoffman) | 8 Fl. Ozs. | 20 |
| Any Flavor (Knox) | 1 Envelope | 28 | (Key Food) | 8 Fl. Ozs. | 20 |
| Gelatin Fruit (Ready | | | (Kirsch) | 8 Fl. Ozs. | 20 |
| To Serve) | 1/2 Cup | 27 | (Mission) | 8 Fl. Ozs. | 20 |
| Gelatin Mold, Cherry | 1 Serv. | 19 | (Schweppes) | 8 Fl. Ozs. | 21 |
| Gelatin, Processed & | | | (Shasta) | 8 Fl. Ozs. | 21 |
| Sweetened | 1 Serv. | 15 | (Vernors) | 8 Fl. Ozs. | 23 |
| Gelatin Salad With Fruit | 1 Sq. | 22 | (Waldbaum) | 8 Fl. Ozs. | 20 |
| Gelatin Salad With Vegetables | 1 Sq. | 15 | (Yukon Club) | 8 Fl. Ozs. | 20 |
| German Dinner, Frozen | | | Low Calorie: | | |
| (Swanson) | 11-Oz. Pkg. | 42 | (Dr. Brown's) Slim Ray | 8 Fl. Ozs. | 1 |
| German Pancakes | 1 | 11 | (Hoffman) | 8 Fl. Ozs. | 1 |
| German Veal Balls | 1 Serv. | 3 | (No-Cal) | 8 Fl. Ozs. | T |
| Germ, Wheat | 4 Ozs. | 48 | (Shasta) | 8 Fl. Ozs. | T |
| Gewurztraminer Wine: | | | (Vernors) | 8 Fl. Ozs. | T |
| (Louis M. Martini) | 3 Fl. Ozs. | T | Ginger Beer | 6 Ozs. | 28 |
| (Willm) Alsatian | 3 Fl. Ozs. | 3 | (Canada Dry) | 8 Fl. Ozs. | 24 |
| (Willm) Clos Gaensbronnel | 3 Fl. Ozs. | 3 | (Schweppes) | 8 Fl. Ozs. | 23 |
| Ghee, Fats | 3-1/2 Ozs. | 0 | Ginger Bread | 1 Sq. | 32 |
| Ghee (High Moisture) Fats | 3-1/2 Ozs. | 0 | Gingerbread Cake | 1 Sq. | 21 |
| Ghee (Low Moisture) Fats | 3-1/2 Ozs. | 0 | Gingerbread Mix: | | |
| Giblets, Chicken | 1 Serv. | T | (Betty Crocker) | 1 Oz. | 22 |
| Giblets, Turkey | 1 Serv. | T | (Dromedary) | 1 Oz. | 19 |
| Gilded Lily Cktl. | 1 Gl. | 3 | (Pillsbury) | 1 Oz. | 22 |
| Gin | 2 Ozs. | 0 | Ginger Bread With Hot Water | 1 Serv. | 27 |
| Gin Alexander | 1 Serv. | 1 | Ginger Bread With Sour Milk | 1 Sq. | 27 |
| Gin Buck | 6 Ozs. | 10 | Ginger Cake | 1 Sl. | 26 |
| Gin Collins | 1 Serv. | 14 | Ginger, Candied | 1 Oz. | 21 |
| Gin Collins, Sloe | 1 Oz. | 16 | Ginger Meringues | 1 Serv. | 20 |
| Gin Fizz | 1 Serv. | 4 | Ginger Root Crystalized | 1 Oz. | 25 |
| Gin, Flavored: | | | Ginger Root, Fresh | 4 Ozs. | 8 |
| Lemon (Old Mr Boston) | 1 Fl. Oz. | 1 | Ginger Snaps | 5 | 18 |
| Mint (Leroux) | 1 Fl. Oz. | 3 | Gingersnap Cookie | 1 Lg. | 6 |
| Mint (Old Mr. Boston) | 1 Fl. Oz. | 8 | Ginkgo Seed | 1 | T |
| Orange (Leroux) | 1 Fl. Oz. | 3 | Gizzard, Chicken | 4 Ozs. | 0 |
| Orange (Old Mr Boston) | 1 Fl. Oz. | 1 | Gizzard, Goose | 4 Ozs. | 0 |
| Gin Rickey | 1 Serv. | 4 | Gizzard, Turkey | 4 Ozs. | 0 |
| Gin Sour Cocktail (Calvert) | 3 Fl. Ozs. | 10 | Glazed Carrots | 1 Serv. | 17 |
| Gin, Sloe: | | | Glazed Fruit Candies | 1 Pc. | 8 |
| (Bols) | 1 Fl. Oz. | 4 | Gluten Bread | 1 Sl. | 12 |
| (Garnier) | 1 Fl. Oz. | 8 | Gnocchi (No Sauce) | 1/2 Cup | 8 |
| (Hiram Walker) | 1 Fl. Oz. | 5 | Goat Cheese | 1-1/2 Ozs. | 1 |
| (Leroux) | 1 Fl. Oz. | 6 | Goat Milk | 1 Cup | 10 |
| (Old Mr. Boston) | | | Gold Cake | 1 Sl. | 32 |
| 42 Proof | 1 Fl. Oz. | 2 | Gold Cane | 1 Pc. | 62 |
| 70 Proof | 1 Fl. Oz. | 1 | Gold-O-Mint Liqueur | | |
| Gin and Tonic | 1 Serv. | 11 | (Leroux) | 1 Fl. Oz. | 15 |
| Ginger Ale | 6 Ozs. | 16 | Good Humor | 1 Bar | 32 |
| (Canada Dry) | 8 Fl. Ozs. | 21 | Goose Berries (A-B-C) | 1 Cup | 13 |
| (Clicquot Club) | 8 Fl. Ozs. | 20 | Goose Fat | 1 Tbsp. | 0 |
| (Cott) | 8 Fl. Ozs. | 20 | Goose, Gizzard | 4 Ozs. | 0 |
| (Dr. Brown's) | 8 Fl. Ozs. | 20 | Goose Liver | 1 Serv. | 6 |
| Fanta | 8 Fl. Ozs. | 20 | Goose Liver Paste | 1 Tbsp. | 1 |

| FOOD | AMT. | CARB. GRAMS | FOOD | AMT. | CARB. GRAMS |
|---|---|---|---|---|---|
| Goose, Raw | 4 Ozs. | 0 | (Heinz) | 1 Can | 14 |
| Goose, Roasted | 1 Serv. | 0 | (Stokely-Van Camp) | 1 Cup | 32 |
| Goose, Roasted With Dressing | 1 Serv. | 22 | Grapefruit Juice (Canned), | | |
| Gorgonzola Cheese | 1 Oz. | T | Unsweetened | 6 Ozs. | 16 |
| Gouda Cheese | 1-1/2 Ozs. | T | (Diet Delight) | 1 Cup | 19 |
| Goulash Dinner | | | (Stokely-Van Camp) | 1 Cup | 24 |
| (Chef Boy-Ar-Dee) | 7-1/3 Oz. Pkg. | 32 | Pink (Texsun) | 1 Cup | 32 |
| Goulash, Hungarian | 1 Serv | 4 | Grapefruit Peel, Candied | 1 Oz. | 24 |
| Graacher Himmelreich, German | | | (Liberty) | 1 Oz. | 22 |
| Moselle (Julius Kayser) | 4 Fl. Ozs. | 3 | Grapefruit & Orange Juice | | |
| Graham Bread | 1 Sl. | 14 | (Frozen Concentrate) | 6 Ozs. | 75 |
| Graham Crackers | 3 Med. | 15 | Grapefruit & Orange Sections, | | |
| Graham Crackers, | | | Fresh | 1/2 Cup | 11 |
| Choc. Covered | 1 | 7 | Grapefruit Soft Drink: | | |
| Grandilla (Passion Fruit) | 4 Ozs. | 35 | Sweetened: | | |
| Granulated Sugar | 1 Tsp. | 4 | Golden (Canada Dry) | 8 Fl. Ozs. | 28 |
| Grape Brandy | Shot | 7 | Fanta | 8 Fl Ozs. | 28 |
| Grape, Concord | 1 Cup | 16 | Low Calorie, Pink: | | |
| Grapeade (Sealtest) | 6 Fl. Ozs. | 24 | (Hoffman) | 8 Fl. Ozs | 1 |
| Grape Drink (Hi-C) | 6 Fl. Ozs. | 22 | (No-Cal) | 8 Fl Ozs. | T |
| Grape Drink Mix. | | | (Royal Crown) | 8 Fl Ozs | T |
| (Salada) | 6 Fl. Ozs | 19 | Grape Jam | 1 Tbsp | 14 |
| (Wyler's) | 6 Fl. Ozs | 16 | Dietetic (Dia-Mel) | 1 Oz | 11 |
| Grapefruit | 1/2 Sm | 11 | Grape Jelly, Dietetic | | |
| (Sunkist) | 1/2 | 11 | (Dia-Mel) | 1 Oz. | 11 |
| Grapefruit & Apple | | | Concord (Diet Delight) | 1 Oz | 1 |
| Gelatin Salad | 1 Serv | 26 | (Kraft) | 1 Oz | 3 |
| Grapefruit-Avocado Cktl. | 1 Serv. | 12 | (Slenderella) | 1 Oz | 11 |
| Grapefruit (Broiled With | | | (Tillie Lewis) | 1 Oz. | 4 |
| Tsp. Sugar) | 1/2 | 15 | Grape Juice | 1/2 Cup | 18 |
| Grapefruit Canned (C) | 1/2 Cup | 18 | Canned: | | |
| Grapefruit, Canned Sweetened | 1/2 Cup | 22 | (Heinz) | 1 Can | 27 |
| Grapefruit Drink (Sealtest) | 8 Fl Ozs | 26 | (Seneca) | 1 Cup | 37 |
| Grapefruit & Endive Salad | 1 Serv. | 16 | Sweetened (Seneca) | 1 Cup | 52 |
| Grapefruit, Fresh Sections | 1/2 Cup | 10 | Unsweetened (S and W) | | |
| (Kraft) | 4 Ozs | 12 | Nutradiet | 4 Ozs | 17 |
| Dietetic (Diet Delight) | 1 Cup | 14 | Frozen, Concentrate, Sweetened: | | |
| (Tillie Lewis) | 1 Cup | 20 | (Minute Maid) | 1 Cup | 33 |
| Grapefruit Juice, Frozen | | | (Seneca) | 1 Cup | 31 |
| Concentrate | 6 Ozs | 72 | (Snow Crop) | 1 Cup | 33 |
| Sweetened: | | | Grape Nuts | 2 Ozs | 43 |
| (Minute Maid) | 1 Cup | 28 | Grape Nuts Flakes Cereal | 3/4 Cup | 23 |
| (Snow Crop) | 1 Cup | 28 | Grape Pie (Tastykake) | 4-Oz Pie | 52 |
| Unsweetened: | | | Grape Soda | 8 Ozs. | 28 |
| (Birds Eye) | 1 Cup | 27 | Grape, Soft Drink | 8 Ozs. | 28 |
| (Florida Diet) | 1 Cup | 21 | Sweetened: | | |
| (Minute Maid) | 1 Cup | 24 | (Canada Dry) | 8 Fl. Ozs. | 32 |
| (7L) | 1 Cup | 24 | (Clicquot Club) | 8 Fl. Ozs. | 33 |
| (Snow Crop) | 1 Cup | 24 | (Cott) | 8 Fl. Ozs. | 33 |
| Grapefruit Juice | 6 Ozs. | 15 | (Dr. Brown's) | 8 Fl. Ozs. | 29 |
| (Kraft) | 1 Cup | 22 | (Dr. Pepper) | 8 Fl. Ozs. | 34 |
| Grapefruit Juice (Canned) | | | Fanta | 8 Fl. Ozs. | 32 |
| Sweetened | 1 Cup | 32 | Grapette | 8 Fl. Ozs. | 31 |

| FOOD | AMT. | CARB. GRAMS | FOOD | AMT. | CARB. GRAMS |
|---|---|---|---|---|---|
| (Hires) | 8 Fl. Ozs. | 32 | Gravy Mix: | | |
| (Hoffman) | 8 Fl. Ozs. | 32 | Beef: | | |
| (Key Food) | 8 Fl. Ozs. | 29 | (Swiss) | 1 Oz. | 20 |
| (Mission) | 8 Fl. Ozs. | 33 | (Wyler's) | 1 Oz. | 16 |
| (Nedick's) | 8 Fl. Ozs. | 32 | Brown: | | |
| (Shasta) | 8 Fl. Ozs. | 30 | (Durkee) | 1 Cup | 11 |
| (Waldbaum) | 8 Fl. Ozs. | 29 | (French's) | 1 Pkg. | 9 |
| (Yoo-Hoo) | 8 Fl. Ozs. | 18 | (Kraft) | 1 Oz. | 1 |
| High-protein (Yoo-Hoo) | 8 Fl. Ozs. | 33 | (Lawry's) | 1 Pkg. | 16 |
| (Yukon Club) | 8 Fl. Ozs. | 32 | (McCormick) | 2 Ozs. | 2 |
| Low Calorie: | | | Chicken: | | |
| (Hoffman) | 8 Fl. Ozs. | 1 | (Durkee) | 1 Cup | 11 |
| (No-Cal) | 8 Fl. Ozs. | 0 | (French's) | 1 Pkg. | 14 |
| (Shasta) | 8 Fl. Ozs. | T | (Lawry's) | 1 Oz. | 13 |
| Grape Syrup, Dietetic | | | (McCormick) | 2 Ozs. | 3 |
| (No-Cal) | 1 Tsp. | T | (Swiss) | 1 Pkg. | 22 |
| Grapes (Delaware) | 1 Cup | 16 | (Wyler's) | 1 Oz. | 15 |
| Grapes, Flame Tokay | 4 Ozs. | 16 | Herb (McCormick) | 2 Ozs. | 2 |
| Grapes, Green, Seedless | 1 Cup | 16 | Mushroom: | | |
| Grapes, Malaga | 1 Cup | 17 | (Durkee) | 1 Cup | 13 |
| Grapes, Muscat | 1 Cup | 17 | (French's) | 1 Pkg. | 6 |
| Grapes, Niagara | 1 Cup | 16 | (Lawry's) | 1 Pkg. | 15 |
| Grapes, Scuppernong | 1 Cup | 16 | (McCormick) | 2 Ozs. | 2 |
| Grapes, Thompson Seedless | 4 Ozs. | 17 | (Wyler's) | 1 Pkg. | 8 |
| Grapes, Tokay | 1 Cup | 17 | Onion: | | |
| Grasshopper | 3 Ozs. | 3 | (Durkee) | 1 Cup | 14 |
| Grated Cheese, Dry | 1 Tbsp. | T | (French's) | 1 Oz. | 12 |
| Grated Choc. Candies Bitter | 1 Cup | 42 | (Kraft) | 1 Oz. | 2 |
| Graves Wine | | | (McCormick) | 2 Ozs. | 3 |
| (Barton & Guestier) | 3 Fl. Ozs. | T | (Wyler's) | 1 Pkg. | 11 |
| Gravy, Canned: | | | Gravy, Thick | 1 Tbsp. | 2 |
| Beef (Franco-American) | 4 Ozs. | 7 | Gravy, Thin | 4 Tbsp. | 4 |
| Chicken (Franco-American) | 4 Ozs. | 6 | Greek Herring Salad | 1 Serv. | 6 |
| Chicken Giblet | | | Greek Lemon & Rice Soup | 1 Serv. | 46 |
| (Franco-American) | 4 Ozs. | 5 | Green Beans, Canned | | |
| Giblet (Lynden) | 4 Ozs. | 8 | & Strained | 1 Oz. | 1 |
| Mushroom (Franco-American) | 4 Ozs. | 5 | Green Gage Jam | 1 Tbsp. | 14 |
| Gravy Master | 1 Fl. Oz. | 8 | Green Gage Plums | 1 Cup | 19 |
| Gravy, Chicken | 2 Ozs. | 4 | Green Peas, Canned | 4 Ozs. | 14 |
| Gravy With Meat or Turkey, | | | Green Peas, Dried | 1/2 Cup | 18 |
| Canned or Frozen: | | | Green Peppers, Cooked | 1 Med. | 5 |
| Beef Chunks (Bunker Hill) | 4 Ozs. | 4 | Green Peppers, Stuffed | 1 Med. | 11 |
| Chopped Beef (Bunker Hill) | 4 Ozs. | 4 | Green Olives | 10 Lg. | 1 |
| Sliced Beef (Bunker Hill) | 4 Ozs. | 4 | Green Onions | 6 Sm. | 5 |
| Sliced Beef, Buffet, | | | Green Tea (Japanese) | | |
| Frozen (Banquet) | 4 Ozs. | 3 | No Milk Or Sugar | 1 Cup | T |
| Sliced Beef, Cookin' Bag, | | | Greens, Beet, Cooked | 1 Cup | T |
| Frozen (Banquet) | 4 Ozs. | 3 | Greens, Dandelion | 1/2 Cup | 9 |
| Sliced Beef Liver | | | Greens, Mustard | 1 Lb. | 13 |
| (Bunker Hill) | 4 Ozs. | 8 | Greens, Turnip | 1 Cup | 13 |
| Sliced Turkey, Buffet, | | | Grenadine Syrup | 1 Tsp. | T |
| Frozen (Banquet) | 4 Ozs. | 3 | (Garnier) | 1 Tbsp. | 13 |
| | | | (Giroux) | 1 Tbsp. | 12 |

| FOOD | AMT. | CARB. GRAMS | FOOD | AMT. | CARB. GRAMS |
|---|---|---|---|---|---|
| (Leroux) | 1 Tbsp. | 7 | Halibut | 1 Serv. | 0 |
| Griddle Cakes | 1 | 11 | Halibut, Broiled | 1 Serv. | 0 |
| Griddle Cakes, Blueberry | 1 | 12 | Halibut, Creamed | 1 Serv. | 0 |
| Grilled Ham Slice | 1 | 2 | Halibut Liver Oil | 1 Tbsp. | 0 |
| Grilled Kidneys | 1 Serv. | T | Ham (B1) | 1 Sl. | 0 |
| Grill, Mixed English | 1 Serv. | 0 | Ham, Baked | 1 Sl. | 0 |
| Grilled Mushroom Caps | 1 Serv. | 5 | Ham, Boiled | 1 Sl. | 0 |
| Grits, Corn (Dry) | 1/4 Cup | 28 | Ham Butt, Boiled | 1 Sl. | 0 |
| Grits, Corn (Degermed) | 1/2 Cup | 14 | Ham, Canned Boneless | 3 Ozs. | 0 |
| Grits, Corn Soya | 1/2 Cup | 13 | (Hormel) | 4 Ozs. | 1 |
| Grits, Hominy | 1/2 Cup | 14 | (Wilson) | 4 Ozs. | 1 |
| Grits, Soybean | 4 Ozs. | 13 | (Wilson) Corn King | 4 Ozs. | 1 |
| Grits, Soybean (Med. Fat) | 1 Cup | 14 | Chopped (Armour Star) | 1 Can | 4 |
| Grog, Hot | 6 Ozs. | 0 | (Hormel) | 4 Ozs. | 1 |
| Ground Lamb | 1 Serv. | 0 | Ham, Canned Deviled | 1 Tbsp. | T |
| Gruyere Cheese (A-B1-C) | 2 Ozs. | 1 | (Armour Star) | 4 Ozs. | 0 |
| Guava (B1-B2-C) | 1 Med. | 11 | (Hormel) | 4 Ozs. | 1 |
| Guava Butter | 1 Tbsp. | 10 | (Underwood) | 4 Ozs. | T |
| Guava Jelly | 1 Tbsp. | 13 | Frozen, Sliced With Barbecue | | |
| Guinea Hen, Broiled | 1 Serv. | 0 | Sauce (Banquet) | | |
| Gumbo, Chicken | 1 Cup | 6 | Cookin' Bag | 4 Ozs. | 16 |
| Gumbo Creole | 4 Ozs. | 9 | Ham, Canned Spiced | 2 Ozs. | 0 |
| Gumbo, Seafood | 1 Serv. | 6 | (Hormel) | 4 Ozs. | T |
| Gum Candy, Coated | 1 Lg. | 3 | Ham, Deviled | 1 Tbsp. | T |
| Gum Drops | 3 Lg. | 22 | Ham Dinner, Frozen: | | |
| Gum Drop Candy | 1 Lg. | 9 | (Banquet) | Dinner | 53 |
| Haddock | 1 Serv. | 0 | (Morton) | Dinner | 54 |
| Raw (Booth) | 8 Ozs. | 0 | (Swanson) | Dinner | 42 |
| Haddock, Broiled | 1 Serv. | 0 | Ham Egg Foo Yung | 1 Serv. | 1 |
| Haddock, Creamed | 1 Serv. | 3 | Ham, Fried | 2 Sls. | 0 |
| Haddock Dinner, Frozen: | | | Ham, Fried Sandwich | 1 | 24 |
| (Banquet) | Dinner | 45 | Ham Hock | 3 Ozs. | 0 |
| (Swanson) | Dinner | 36 | Ham Loaf | 4 Ozs. | 7 |
| Haddock, Fried | 1 Serv. | 6 | Ham Pork, Cured | 4 Ozs. | 0 |
| Haddock, Smoked | 1 Serv. | 0 | Ham, Prosciutto | 1-1/2 Ozs. | 0 |
| Hag, Kaffee | 8 Ozs. | 0 | Ham Salad Sandwich | 1 | 26 |
| Hake, Baked | 1 Serv. | 0 | Ham Sandwich, | | |
| Hake, Broiled | 1 Serv. | 0 | Boiled Or Baked | 1 | 24 |
| Halavah | 1 Oz. | 18 | Ham Shank End Pork Cured | 4 | 0 |
| Half & Half (Beer & Stout) | 1 Cup | 13 | Ham, Smoked | 1 Serv. | 0 |
| Half and Half Cream | 2 Tbsp. | 2 | Ham Steak (B1) | 1 Serv. | 0 |
| Half & Half Milk | 1 Cup | 11 | Ham & Swiss Cheese | | |
| Half & Half Soft Drink, Sweetened: | | | Sandwich | 1 | 25 |
| (Canada Dry) | 6 Fl. Ozs. | 21 | Ham, Virginia, Baked | 1 Serv. | 0 |
| (Dr. Brown's) | 6 Fl. Ozs. | 19 | Ham Waffle | 1 | 28 |
| (Hoffman) | 6 Fl. Ozs. | 19 | Hamburger, All Beef | 2 Ozs. | 0 |
| (Kirsch) | 6 Fl. Ozs. | 20 | Hamburger, Broiled | 2 Ozs. | 0 |
| (Yukon Club) | 6 Fl. Ozs. | 22 | Hamburger, Fried | 2 Ozs. | 0 |
| Low Calorie (Hoffman) | 6 Fl. Ozs. | T | Hamburger Rolls | 1 | 21 |
| Half & Half Wine: | | | Hamburger Sandwich | 1 | 21 |
| (Gallo) | 3 Fl. Ozs. | 5 | Hamburger Steak | 1 Serv. | 0 |
| (Lejon) | 3 Fl. Ozs. | 6 | Hamburger Steak Balls | 1 Serv. | 2 |

64

| FOOD | AMT | CARB. GRAMS | FOOD | AMT | CARB. GRAMS |
|---|---|---|---|---|---|
| Hankow Beef & Cabbage Soup | 1 Serv. | 3 | Hershey Kisses | 1 Bar | 6 |
| Haote Pikia Beverage | 10 Ozs. | T | Hershey Milk Choc. Candy | 5c Bar | 16 |
| Hard Candy | 1 Oz. | 28 | Hershey Milk Choc. Candy | | |
| Hard Rolls | 1 Aver | 16 | With Almond | 5c Bar | 16 |
| Hard Salami | 1 Oz. | T | Hibiscus Cocktail | 1 Gl. | 2 |
| Hard Sauce | 1 Tbsp. | 14 | Hickory Nuts | 8 Av. | 2 |
| Harvard Beets | 1 Serv. | 9 | Highball, Apple Jack | 1 Av. | 3 |
| Hasenpfeffer | 1 Serv. | 0 | Highball, Bourbon | 1 Av. | 13 |
| Hash, Corned Beef | 1/2 Cup | 8 | Highball, Canadian Whiskey | 8 Ozs. | 16 |
| Hash, Roast Beef | 1/2 Cup | 8 | Highball, Rye | 1 Av. | 16 |
| Hash, Turkey | 1 Serv. | 8 | Highball, Whiskey | 1 Av. | 16 |
| Hashed Brown Potatoes | 1 Med. | 28 | Hocks, Ham | 1 Serv. | 0 |
| Havana Beach Cocktail | 1 Gl. | 8 | Holiday Duckling | 1 Serv. | 9 |
| Hawaiian Poha | 1 Cup | 11 | Hollandaise Sauce | 1 Tbsp. | T |
| Hawaiian Punch, Soft Drink | 8 Fl. Ozs. | 27 | Hollandaise Sauce, Mock | 1/4 Cup | 6 |
| Hazel Nuts | 10 Aver. | 3 | Holland Rusk Crackers | 1 | 9 |
| Hazel Nut Ice Cream | 1 Scp. | 14 | Home Cooked Salad Dressing | 1 Tbsp | 3 |
| Head Cheese | 1-1/2 Ozs. | T | Honey Cookies | 1 | 23 |
| (Sugardale) | 1 Oz. | T | Homemade Apple Pectine | 1 Lb. | 54 |
| Heart, Beef | 4 Ozs. | T | Hominy | 1/2 Cup | 18 |
| Heart, Beef Braised | 3 Ozs. | 1 | Hominy Grits, Cooked | 1/2 Cup | 14 |
| Heart, Calf, Infant | 4 Ozs. | 1 | Honey | 1 Tbsp. | 17 |
| Heart, Chicken | 3 Ozs. | 1 | Honey Cake | 1 Sl. | 20 |
| Heart, Chicken | 10 | 2 | Honey In Comb | 1 Tbsp. | 17 |
| Heart, Pork | 4 Ozs. | T | Honeydew Melon | 1/4 Aver. | 7 |
| Hearts, Artichoke | 1 Med. | 10 | Honey, Strained | 1 Tbsp. | 16 |
| Hearts, Beef | 3 Ozs. | T | Honi Honi Cocktail | 1 Gl. | 2 |
| Hearts, Calf | 3 Ozs. | 1 | Hors d'Oeuvres, Cold | 4 Ozs. | T |
| Hearts, Chicken | 4 Ozs. | 2 | Hors d'Oeuvres, Hot | 4 Ozs. | T |
| Hearts, Lettuce | 2 | T | Horse Meat | 3-1/2 Ozs. | T |
| Heavy Cream | 1 Tbsp. | T | Horse Radish | 1 Tbsp. | 1 |
| Heavy Cream | 1/2 Pt. | 4 | Horse's Neck | 10 Ozs. | T |
| Hen, Guinea | 1 Serv. | 0 | Hot Anchovy & Mushroom Dip | 1 Serv. | 6 |
| Herbs | 1 Tsp. | 0 | Hot Benefactor Beverage | 1 Serv. | 8 |
| Herb Sauce Casserole Base | | | Hot Biscuits | 1 Lg. | 15 |
| (Pennsylvania Dutch) | 1 Cup | 38 | Hot Breads | 1 Sl. | 12 |
| Hermit Cookies | 1 | 7 | Hot Buttered Rum | | |
| Herring | 1 Serv. | 0 | Batter Beverage | 1 Tsp. | 4 |
| Herring, Atlantic | 4 Ozs. | 0 | Hot Cabbage Slaw | 1 Serv. | 8 |
| Herring, Bismark | 1 Serv. | 0 | Hot Cross Buns | 1 | 18 |
| Herring, Bloasters Smoked | 1/2 Fish | 0 | Hot Dog (No Roll) | 1 | 0 |
| Herring, Cherry | Shot | 7 | Hot Dog Roll | 1 | 19 |
| Herring, Kippered | 1 Serv. | 0 | Hot Dog Bean Soup | | |
| Herring, Lake | 1 Serv. | 0 | Condensed (Campbell) | 4 Ozs. | 20 |
| Herring Marinated | | | Hot Egg Nog Beverage | 1 Serv. | 17 |
| With Cream | Sm. Pc. | 4 | Hot Fudge, Ice Cream Sundae | 1 Serv. | 53 |
| Herring, Pacific | 4 Ozs. | 0 | Hot Grog | 6 Ozs. | 0 |
| Herring, Pickled | 1 Serv. | 0 | Hot Hors d'Oeuvres | 4 Ozs. | T |
| Herring Royal | 1 Serv. | 0 | Hot Milk | 3/4 Cup | 8 |
| Herring Slaw | 1 Serv. | 5 | Hot Milk Punch | 1 Serv. | 16 |
| Herring, Smoked | 1 Serv. | 0 | Hot Pimento | 1 Av. | 8 |
| Herring & Sour Cream | 4 Ozs. | 4 | Hot Rum Cow | 1 Serv. | 16 |

| FOOD | AMT. | CARB. GRAMS | FOOD | AMT. | CARB. GRAMS |
|---|---|---|---|---|---|
| Hot Rum Sling | 1 Serv. | 11 | Ice Cream, Malted Milk | 10 Ozs. | 70 |
| Hot Tamale | 1/2 Cup | 6 | Ice Cream, Maple Nut | 1 Scp. | 14 |
| Huapala Cocktail | 1 Gl. | 2 | Ice Cream, Milk | 1/4 Pt. | 21 |
| Hubbard Squash | 1/2 Cup | 10 | Ice Cream, Nesselrode | 1/4 Pt. | 18 |
| Huckleberries (Canned) | | | Ice Cream Parfait, Coffee | 1 | 20 |
| Sweetened | 1/2 Cup | 19 | Ice Cream Parfait, Maple | 1 | 20 |
| Huckleberries (Canned) Water | 1/2 Cup | 9 | Ice Cream, Peach | 1/2 Cup | 14 |
| Huckleberries (Fresh-C) | 1/2 Cup | 12 | Ice Cream, Pie (On Stick) | 1 | 13 |
| Huckleberry Cream Pie | 1 Sl. | 55 | Ice Cream, Pistachio | 1 Serv. | 17 |
| Huckleberry Jam | 1 Tbsp. | 14 | Ice Cream Pop | 1 | 13 |
| Huckleberry Pie | 1 Sl. | 57 | Ice Cream Pop, Choc. Covered | 1 | 14 |
| Hungarian Goulash | 1 Serv. | 4 | Ice Cream Sandwich | 1 | 45 |
| Hungarian Paprika | 1/8 Tsp. | 0 | (Sealtest) | 1 Sand. | 31 |
| Hungarian Pork Chops | 1 Serv. | 7 | Ice Cream, Sherbet With Milk | 1/4 Pt. | 45 |
| Iceberg Lettuce (A-B2) | 1/2 Head | T | Ice Cream, Sherbet With Water | 1/4 Pt. | 35 |
| Ice Box Cake | 1 Sl. | 26 | Ice Cream Soda | 1 | 71 |
| Ice Box Cookies | 3 Med. | 19 | Ice Cream Sodas, | | |
| Ice, Cherry | 1/4 Pt. | 35 | Artificial Flavors | 10 Ozs. | 71 |
| Ice Cream | 1 Scp. | 14 | Ice Cream Soda, Choc. | 10 Ozs. | 71 |
| Ice Cream, Banana | 1 Scp. | 14 | Ice Cream Soda, | | |
| Ice Cream Bar, Choc Coated, | | | Fresh Fruit Flavor | 10 Ozs. | 50 |
| (Sealtest) | 1 Bar | 14 | Ice Cream Soda, Peach | 10 Ozs. | 71 |
| Ice Cream, Blackberry | 1 Scp. | 14 | Ice Cream Strawberry | 1 Scp. | 14 |
| Ice Cream, Butter Almond | 1/2 Cup | 20 | Ice Cream Sundae | 1 Av. | 50 |
| Ice Cream, Butter Pecan | 1 Scp. | 15 | Ice Cream Sundae, | | |
| Ice Cream, Butterscotch | 1/2 Cup | 15 | Banana Split | 1 Av. | 75 |
| Ice Cream Cake Roll | 1/2 in. Sl. | 30 | Ice Cream Sundae, | | |
| Ice Cream, Caramel | 1/2 Cup | 28 | Butterscotch | 1 Av. | 56 |
| Ice Cream, Cherry | 1 Scp. | 14 | Ice Cream Sundae, Choc. | | |
| Ice Cream, Cherry Vanilla | 1 Scp. | 14 | (Vanilla Ice Cream) | 1 Av. | 53 |
| Ice Cream, Choc. | 1 Scp. | 14 | Ice Cream Sundae, Choc. | | |
| (Sealtest) | 1 Cup | 35 | (Choc. Ice Cream) | 1 Av. | 54 |
| French (Prestige) | 1 Cup | 56 | Ice Cream Sundae (Hot Fudge) | 1 Av. | 53 |
| Ice Cream Mix, Chocolate, | | | Ice Cream, Tutti Fruitti | 1/2 Cup | 14 |
| (Junket) | 1 Oz. | 24 | Ice Cream, Vanilla | 1 Scp. | 14 |
| Ice Cream, Choc., Chip | 1 Scp. | 14 | (Sealtest) | 1 Pt. | 60 |
| Ice Cream, Choc., Cov. Pop | 1 | 14 | (Sealtest) 10.2% fat | 1 Pt. | 61 |
| Ice Cream, Cocoanut | | | (Sealtest) 12.1% fat | 1 Pt. | 61 |
| Covered Pop | 1 | 18 | French (Prestige) | 1 Pt. | 62 |
| Ice Cream, Coffee | 1/4 Pt. | 14 | Fudge Royale (Sealtest) | 1 Pt. | 63 |
| Ice Cream Cone (Cone Alone) | 1 | 7 | Ice Cream Mix, Vanilla, | | |
| (Comet) | 1 Cone | 4 | (Junket) | 4 Ozs. | 110 |
| Assorted Colors (Comet) | 1 Cone | 4 | Ice Cream, Vanilla Fudge | 1 Scp. | 14 |
| Pilot (Comet) | 1 Cone | 4 | Ice Cream, Vanilla Fudge Pop | 1 | 53 |
| Rolled Sugar (Comet) | 1 Cone | 7 | Ice Cream With Vanilla Malted | 1/4 Pt. | 53 |
| Ice Cream Cup | | | Ice Cream, Walnut | 1 Scp. | 14 |
| (Comet) | 1 Cup | 4 | Ice Cup, Lemon | 1 Serv. | 28 |
| Ice Cream, Frozen Custard | 1/4 Pt. | 26 | Iced Coffee (No Sugar | | |
| Deluxe (Carnation) | 1 Cup | 32 | or Cream) | 1 Serv. | 0 |
| Ice Cream, Fudge Pop | 1 | 13 | Iced Butter Cake | 1 Serv. | 46 |
| Ice Cream, Ices | 1/4 Pt. | 35 | Iced Caramel Cake | 1 Sl. | 44 |
| Ice Cream, Lemon | 1/4 Pt. | 14 | Iced Cookie | 1 | 10 |

| FOOD | AMT. | CARB. GRAMS | FOOD | AMT. | CARB. GRAMS |
|---|---|---|---|---|---|
| Iced Doughnut | 1 | 37 | Jambalaya, Crab | 1 Serv. | 16 |
| Iced Tea (No Sugar or Cream) | 1 Serv. | 0 | Jams, Berry | 1 Tbsp. | 14 |
| Ice, Lemon | 1 Scp. | 27 | Jam, Blackberry | 1 Tbsp. | 14 |
| Ice, Lime | 1 Scp. | 27 | Jam, Blackberry & Apricot | 1 Tbsp. | 16 |
| Ice Milk | 1/4 Pt. | 21 | Jam, Blueberry | 1 Tbsp. | 14 |
| Vanilla (Borden) Lite Line | 1 Pt. | 68 | Jam, Cherry | 1 Tbsp. | 14 |
| Ice Milk Bar, Choc. Coated, | | | Jam, Grape | 1 Tbsp. | 14 |
| (Sealtest) | 1 Bar | 16 | Jam, Raspberry | 1 Tbsp. | 14 |
| Ice, Orange | 1 Scp. | 27 | Jam, Strawberry | 1 Tbsp. | 14 |
| Ice, Pineapple | 1 Scp. | 27 | Jams (Most) | 1 Tbsp. | 14 |
| Ice Pop | 1 | 24 | Japanese-Style Vegetables, | | |
| Ice, Raspberry | 1 Scp. | 27 | Frozen (Bird's Eye) | 1 Pkg. | 19 |
| Ices | 1 Av. | 27 | Jasmine Tea (No Sugar | | |
| Ices, Ice Cream | 1/4 Pt. | 35 | or Cream) | 1 Cup | 0 |
| Icing | 1 Tbsp. | 11 | Jellied Chicken | 1 Serv. | 0 |
| Idaho Potato, Baked (B1) | 1 Med. | 28 | Jellied Orange Soup | 1 Serv. | 0 |
| Imported Brandy | 1 Oz. | 0 | Jellies (Most) | 1 Tbsp. | 13 |
| Indian, Baked | 2/3 Cup | 14 | Jello | 1 Serv. | 17 |
| Indian Nuts | 1 Tbsp. | 1 | Jelly, Sweetened: | | |
| Indian Pudding | 2/3 Cup | 23 | (Crosse & Blackwell) | 1 Oz. | 25 |
| (B & M) | 1 Cup | 47 | (Kraft) | 1 Oz. | 18 |
| Infant's Dry Precooked Cereal | 1 Oz. | 20 | (Polaner) | 1 Oz. | 26 |
| Infant Dry Precooked Oatmeal | 1 Oz. | 19 | Jelly Apple | 1 | 40 |
| Infant Food, Chicken | 1/2 Cup | T | Jelly, Apple | 1 Tbsp. | 13 |
| Instant Coffee (No Sugar | | | Jelly Beans | 15 Av. | 24 |
| or Cream) | 1 Cup | T | Jelly, Blackberry | 1 Tbsp. | 13 |
| Instant Tea (No Sugar | | | Jelly, Blintzes | 1 Av. | 35 |
| or Cream) | 1 Cup | T | Jelly, Cherry | 1 Tbsp. | 13 |
| Irish Potatoes, Boiled | 1 Med. | 28 | Jelly, Cranberry | 1 Tbsp. | 9 |
| Irish Stew | 1 Cup | 15 | Jelly, Currant | 1 Tbsp. | 13 |
| Irish Whiskey | Shot | T | Jelly Doughnut | 1 Aver. | 37 |
| Italian Bread | 1 Sl. | 9 | Jelly, Grape | 2 Tbsp. | 13 |
| Italian Bread | 1 Lb. | 243 | Jelly, Guava | 1 Tbsp. | 13 |
| Italian Dinner, Frozen: | | | Jelly, Lemon | 1 Tbsp. | 13 |
| (Banquet) | Dinner | 44 | Jelly, Mint | 1 Tbsp. | 13 |
| (Swanson) | Dinner | 54 | Jelly Omelet | | |
| Italian Minestrone | 1 Serv. | 12 | (With Tbsp. Jelly) | 1 | 13 |
| Italian Salami | 1 Oz. | T | Jelly, Peach | 1 Tbsp. | 13 |
| Italian Spaghetti | | | Jelly Roll | 1 Serv. | 39 |
| With Meat Sauce | 1 Serv | 47 | Jelly, Strawberry | 1 Tbsp. | 13 |
| Italian, White Toasted | 1 Serv. | 8 | Jerusalem Artichokes Raw | 1 Lg. | 17 |
| Italian Vermouth | 2 Ozs. | T | Jewish Rye Bread | 1 Sl. | 12 |
| Jabon Candido Cocktail | 1 Gl. | 5 | Jewish Salami | 1 Oz. | T |
| Jack Cheese | 1-1/2 Ozs. | T | Johannisberger Riesling Wine | | |
| Jack Rose | 3 Ozs. | 4 | (Deinhard) | 3 Fl. Ozs. | 4 |
| Jack Rose Cocktail | 1 Serv. | 17 | (Louis M. Martini) | 3 Fl. Ozs. | T |
| Jack Rose Mix, | | | Judy, Punch and | 1 Serv. | 31 |
| (Bartender's) | 1 Serv. | 17 | Juice Ade, Papaya | 1 Cup | 15 |
| Jalapeno Bean Dip, | | | Juice Ade, Pineapple | 1 Cup | 18 |
| (Frito-Lay) | 1 Oz. | 3 | Juice, Apple | 1 Cup | 28 |
| Jamaica Rum | 1 Oz. | T | Juice, Apple (Canned) | 1/2 Cup | 17 |
| Jam, Apricot | 1 Tbsp. | 14 | Juice, Apricot | 6 Ozs. | 18 |

| FOOD | AMT. | CARB. GRAMS | FOOD | AMT. | CARB. GRAMS |
|---|---|---|---|---|---|
| Juice, Apricot Nectar | 1 Cup | 36 | Juice, Orange & Grapefruit, | | |
| Juice, Black Currant | 1 Cup | 34 | Frozen | 6 Ozs. | 75 |
| Juice, Carrot (A-C) | 1 Cup | 13 | Juice, Orange (Dehydrated) | 3 Ozs. | 75 |
| Juice, Carrot | 1 Cup | 13 | Juice, Papaya | 8 Ozs. | 30 |
| Juice, Clam | 6 Ozs. | 0 | Juice, Passion Fruit | 1/2 Cup | 18 |
| Juice, Cranberry | 1 Cup | 36 | Juice, Peach Nectar (Canned) | 1 Cup | 34 |
| Juice, Grape | 1/2 Cup | 18 | Juice, Pear (Nectar) | 4 Ozs. | 12 |
| Juice, Grapefruit | 6 Ozs. | 15 | Juice, Pineapple | 1 Cup | 30 |
| Juice, Grapefruit | | | Juice, Pineapple | | |
| (Canned, Sweetened) | 6 Ozs. | 24 | (Frozen, Sweetened) | 1 Cup | 31 |
| Juice, Grapefruit | | | Juice, Pomegranate | 1/2 Cup | 9 |
| (Canned, Unsweetened) | 6 Ozs. | 16 | Juice, Prune (Canned) | 1/2 Cup | 23 |
| Juice, Grapefruit | | | Juice, Prune (Canned) | 1 Cup | 46 |
| Frozen Concentrate | 6 Ozs. | 72 | Juice, Raspberry (Red) | 6 Ozs. | 12 |
| Juice, Grapefruit Frozen, | | | Juice, Red Currant | 1 Cup | 25 |
| Diluted | 1 Cup | 28 | Juice, Sauerkraut | 6 Ozs. | 1 |
| Juice, Grapefruit Frozen, | | | Juice, Tangerine (C) | 1/2 Cup | 10 |
| Unsweetened Diluted | 1 Cup | 24 | Juice, Tangerine (Canned), | | |
| Juice, Grapefruit & Orange | | | Unsweetened | 1 Cup | 25 |
| (Canned), Sweetened | 6 Ozs. | 24 | Juice, Tangerine Frozen | 6 Ozs. | 80 |
| Juice, Grapefruit & Orange | | | Juice, Tangerine Frozen, | | |
| (Canned), Unsweetened | 6 Ozs. | 16 | Diluted | 1 Cup | 27 |
| Juice, Lemon (C) | 1/2 Cup | 9 | Juice, Tomato (A-C) | 1 Cup | 10 |
| Juice, Lemon | 1 Tbsp. | 1 | Juice, Vegetable | 6 Ozs. | 7 |
| Juice, Lemon (Canned), | | | Juice, V-8 | 1 Cup | 9 |
| Unsweetened | 1 Cup | 19 | Juicy Meat Loaf | 1 Serv. | 3 |
| Juice, Lemonade, | | | Julep, Mint | 8 Ozs. | 11 |
| Frozen Concentrate | 3 Ozs. | 56 | Julienne Potatoes | 1 Med. | 30 |
| Juice, Lemonade, | | | Juniors (Tastykake): | | |
| Frozen Diluted | 1 Cup | 28 | Chocolate | 1 Pkg. | 71 |
| Juice, Lime | 4 Ozs. | 9 | Chocolate Devil Food | 1 Pkg. | 45 |
| Juice, Lime | 1 Tbsp. | 1 | Coconut | 1 Pkg. | 83 |
| Juice, Limeade, | | | Coconut Devil Food | 1 Pkg. | 60 |
| Frozen Concentrate | 3 Ozs. | 54 | Jelly Square | 1 Pkg. | 91 |
| Juice, Limeade, Frozen Diluted | 1 Cup | 22 | Koffee Kake | 1 Pkg. | 59 |
| Juice, Loganberry | 6 Ozs. | 15 | Lemon | 1 Pkg. | 85 |
| Juice, Nectarine | 6 Ozs. | 19 | Junket | 1 Serv. | 25 |
| Juice, Orange (Calif. Valencia) | 1 Cup | 26 | Kaboom, Cereal | 1.Oz. | 25 |
| Juice, Orange (Canned), | | | Kadota Fig Juice | 1 Tbsp. | 10 |
| Unsweetened | 4 Ozs. | 13 | Kafe Vin (Lejon) | 3 Fl. Ozs. | 23 |
| Juice, Orange, (Canned), | | | Kaffee Hag | 8 Ozs. | 0 |
| Sweetened | 4 Ozs. | 16 | Kailua Cocktail | 1 Gl. | 7 |
| Juice, Orange, Concentrate | 1/2 Cup | 52 | Kaiser Roll | 1 | 21 |
| Juice, Orange (Florida | | | Kale (A-C-B2) | 1 Cup | 7 |
| Early Season) | 1 Cup | 23 | Kale, Frozen | 3-1/2 Ozs. | 5 |
| Juice, Orange (Florida | | | Chopped (Birds Eye) | 1/2 Cup | 4 |
| Late Season) | 1 Cup | 26 | Karo Syrup, Dark Corn, | | |
| Juice, Orange, Fresh (C) | 4 Ozs. | 10 | Light Corn, or Pancake & | | |
| Juice, Orange, Frozen Diluted | 1 Cup | 26 | Waffle Syrup | 1 T. | 14 |
| Juice, Orange, Frozen | 6 Ozs. | 80 | Kebabs, Shish | 1 Serv | 3 |
| Juice, Orange & Grapefruit | | | Kellogg's Concentrate | 1/2 Cup | 7 |
| (Frozen, Diluted) | 1 Cup | 25 | Kellog's Special "K" | 1 Cup | 23 |

| FOOD | AMT. | CARB. GRAMS | FOOD | AMT. | CARB. GRAMS |
|---|---|---|---|---|---|
| Kidney (A-B2) | 1 Serv. | 2 | Lager Beer | 8 Ozs. | 10 |
| Kidney Beans | 1 Cup | 37 | Lake Country Wine (Taylor): | | |
| Kidney, Beef (A-B2) | 1 Serv. | 2 | White Dinner | 3 Fl. Ozs. | 2 |
| Kidney, Beef Broiled | 1/2 Cup | 2 | Red Dinner | 3 Fl. Ozs. | 3 |
| Kidney & Beef Steak Pie | 1 Serv. | 24 | Lake Herring, Raw | 1 Serv. | 0 |
| Kidney, Grilled | 1 Serv. | T | Lake Perch, White, Raw | 1 Serv. | 0 |
| Kippered Herrings | 1/2 | 0 | Lake Perch, Yellow, Raw | 1 Serv. | 0 |
| Kidney, Lamb | 1 Serv. | 2 | Lamb (Canned, Infant) | 4 Ozs. | 0 |
| Kidney Pie | 1 Serv. | 24 | Lamb Chop, Broiled | 1 Serv. | 0 |
| Kidney, Pork (Raw) | 1 Serv. | 2 | Lamb Chop, Fried | 1 Serv. | 0 |
| Kidneys, Sheep | 4 Ozs. | 1 | Lamb Chops, Loin, Fried | 4 Ozs. | 0 |
| Kidney Stew | 1 Serv. | 10 | Lamb Chop, Loin, Broiled | 4 Ozs. | 0 |
| Kidney, Veal | 4 Ozs. | 1 | Lamb Curry | 1/2 Cup | 7 |
| Kielbasa Sausage (Usinger's) | 1 Oz. | T | Lamb, Ground | 1 Serv. | 0 |
| King, Chicken ala | 1/2 Cup | 4 | Lamb Kidney | 1 Serv. | 2 |
| Kingston Cocktail | 1 Gl. | 6 | Lamb, Leg Roast Of | 1 Serv. | 0 |
| Kirsch Liqueur (Garnier) | 1 Fl. Oz. | 9 | Lamb Liver | 1 Serv. | 2 |
| Kirschwasser (Leroux) | 1 Fl. Oz. | 0 | Lamb, Loin Chops | 4 Ozs. | 0 |
| Kisses, Brown Sugar, | | | Lamb Roast | 1 Serv. | 0 |
| Corn Flakes | 1 | 11 | Lamb Shish Kebab | 1 Serv. | 13 |
| Kisses, Molasses | 1 | 10 | Lamb Shoulder Roast | 1 Serv. | 0 |
| Kix Cereal | 1 Cup | 20 | Lamb Stew | 1 Serv. | 15 |
| Knockwurst | 1/4 Lb. | 1 | Lamb Stew (Breast) | 1 Serv. | 15 |
| Kohl-rabi | 2/3 Cup | 7 | Lamb Tongues (Canned) | 3 Sl. | 0 |
| Kohl-rabi | 1 Cup | 10 | Lamb & Vegetable (Infant) | 1 Serv. | 7 |
| Kohl-rabi, Frozen | 1 Cup | 10 | Lard | 1 Tbsp. | 0 |
| Kona Cocktail | 1 Gl. | 5 | Lasagne: | | |
| Kool-Aid (General Foods) | 6 Fl. Ozs. | 19 | Canned (Chef Boy-Ar-Dee) | 4 Ozs. | 15 |
| Kool-Pops (General Foods) | 1 Bar | 7 | Canned (Nalley's) | 4 Ozs. | 13 |
| Kottbullar (Hormel) | 4 Ozs. | 3 | Frozen, With Meat Sauce | | |
| Kraut Juice | 4 Ozs. | 4 | (Buitoni) | 4 Ozs. | 23 |
| Kreplach | 1 Aver. | 7 | Mix, Dinner | | |
| Krimpets (Tastykake): | | | (Chef Boy-Ar-Dee) | 4 Ozs. | 18 |
| Apple Spice | 1 Cake | 25 | Layer Cake | 1 Pc. | 55 |
| Butterscotch | 1 Cake | 23 | Layer, Round With Icing | 1 Pc. | 61 |
| Chocolate | 1 Cake | 21 | Layer, Three With Icing | 1 Pc. | 72 |
| Jelly | 1 Cake | 21 | Layer, Two With Icing | 1 Pc. | 41 |
| Lemon | 1 Cake | 21 | Leak | 1 Pc. | 1 |
| Orange | 1 Cake | 21 | Leaves, Astor | 1 | T |
| Krispies, Cereals | 3/4 Cup | 25 | Leaves, Cedar | 1 | 0 |
| Krumbles, Cereal | 3/4 Cup | 24 | Leaves, Chard, Cooked | 1/2 Cup | 1 |
| Kummel | 1 Oz. | T | Leaves, Fennel | 2 | 2 |
| Kummel Liqueur: | | | Leaves, Mint | 1 | 0 |
| (Garnier) | 1 Fl. Oz. | 4 | Leeks | 1 Pc. | 1 |
| (Hiram Walker) | 1 Fl. Oz. | 3 | Leg Of Lamb | 1 Serv. | 0 |
| (Leroux) | 1 Fl. Oz. | 4 | Lemon Butter Sauce | 1 Tbsp. | 0 |
| (Old Mr. Boston) | 1 Fl. Oz. | 2 | Lemon Juice (Canned), | | |
| Kumquats, Candied | 1 | 6 | Unsweetened | 4 Ozs. | 10 |
| Kumquat & Cheese Salad | 1 Serv. | 41 | Lemon | 1 Med. | 5 |
| Kumquats, Fresh | 5 | 17 | Lemon Cake Mix: | | |
| Lady Fingers | 1 | 5 | (Betty Crocker) Sunkist | 1 Oz. | 21 |
| LaFlorida Rum Daisy Ctl. | 1 Gl. | 13 | (Duncan Hines) | 1 Pc. | 24 |

69

| FOOD | AMT. | CARB. GRAMS | FOOD | AMT. | CARB. GRAMS |
|---|---|---|---|---|---|
| Chiffon (Betty Crocker) | | | Meringue (Jell-O) | 1 Pc. | 35 |
| Sunkist | 1 Oz. | 23 | (My-T-Fine) | 1 Oz. | 26 |
| Coconut (Betty Crocker) | 1 Oz. | 22 | (Royal) | 1 Pc. | 35 |
| Cream Moist Cake | | | Lemon Poached Halibut | 1 Serv. | 1 |
| (Pillsbury) | 1 Oz. | 22 | Lemon Pudding | 1 Serv. | 26 |
| Pudding Cake (Betty Crocker) | | | (Betty Crocker) | 1/2 Cup | 40 |
| Sunkist | 1 Oz. | 24 | Lemon Pudding Mix: | | |
| Lemon & Cheese Tarts | 1 Serv. | 3 | Regular: | | |
| Lemon Chiffon Pie | 1 Pc. | 35 | (Jell-O) | 1 Cup | 52 |
| Lemon Cream Pie | 1 Pc. | 50 | (My-T-Fine) | 1 Oz. | 26 |
| Lemon Drops | 7 | 28 | (Thank-You) | 1 Cup | 72 |
| Lemon Frosting | 1 Tbsp. | 11 | Instant: | | |
| Lemon Ice Cup | 1 Serv. | 28 | (Jell-O) | 1 Cup | 61 |
| Lemon Ice Cream | 1/4 Pt. | 14 | (My-T-Fine) | 1 Oz. | 20 |
| Lemon Jelly | 1 Tbsp. | 13 | (Royal) | 1 Cup | 62 |
| Lemon Juice | 1 Tbsp. | 1 | Dietetic With Skim | | |
| Lemon Juice (Canned) | 1/2 Cup | 7 | Milk (Dia-Mel) | 1 Oz. | 2 |
| Lemon Juice, Fresh | | | Lemon Rennet Custard Mix: | | |
| (Sunkist) | 1 Lemon | 4 | Powder (Junket) | 1 Oz. | 28 |
| Lemon Juice, Frozen: | | | Tablet (Junket) | 1 Tablet | T |
| Unsweetened, Full Strength, | | | Lemon Sauce | 1 Tbsp. | 5 |
| Reconstituted: | | | Lemon Soda | 6 Ozs. | 21 |
| (Minute Maid) | 1 Cup | 17 | Lemon, Soft Drink | 8 Ozs. | 25 |
| (Snow Crop) | 1 Cup | 17 | Sweetened: | | |
| Lemon-Limeade, Sweetened | | | (Canada Dry) | 6 Fl. Ozs. | 18 |
| Concentrate, Frozen: | | | (Dr. Brown's) Tune-Up | 6 Fl. Ozs. | 19 |
| (Minute Maid) | 1 Cup | 26 | (Hoffman) | 6 Fl. Ozs. | 20 |
| (Snow Crop) | 1 Cup | 26 | (Kirsch) | 6 Fl. Ozs. | 16 |
| Lemon-Lime Soft Drink: | | | Low Calorie: | | |
| Sweetened: | | | (Dr. Brown's) Slim-Ray | 6 Fl. Ozs. | 1 |
| Green (Canada Dry) | 8 Fl. Ozs. | 30 | (Hoffman) | 6 Fl. Ozs. | 1 |
| Rickey (Canada Dry) | 8 Fl. Ozs. | 24 | (No-Cal) | 6 Fl. Ozs. | 0 |
| (Dr. Brown's) | 8 Fl. Ozs. | 25 | (Shasta) | 6 Fl. Ozs. | T |
| (Dr. Pepper) | 8 Fl. Ozs. | 24 | Lemon Spice Cookies | 1 Serv. | 7 |
| (Key Food) | 8 Fl. Ozs. | 25 | Lemon Sponge | 1 Serv. | 23 |
| (Kirsch) | 8 Fl. Ozs. | 23 | Lemon Sponge Cake | 1 Pc. | 54 |
| (Shasta) | 8 Fl. Ozs. | 24 | Lemon Sponge Pudding | 1 Serv. | 26 |
| (Waldbaum) | 8 Fl. Ozs. | 25 | Lemon Sponge Pudding | | |
| Low Calorie (Shasta) | 8 Fl. Ozs. | T | With Custard Sauce | 1 Serv. | 41 |
| Lemon Meringue Pie | 1 Pc. | 45 | Lemon Whip | 1 Serv. | 3 |
| Lemon Peel, Candied | 1 Oz. | 24 | Lemonade | 8 Ozs. | 25 |
| (Liberty) | 1 Oz. | 22 | Sweetened (Sealtest) | 1 Cup | 26 |
| Lemon Pie | 1 Pc. | 12 | Frozen Concentrate, Sweetened: | | |
| (Tastykake) | 4 Ozs. | 52 | (Minute Maid) | 1 Cup | 26 |
| Frozen (Mrs. Smith's) | 1 Pc. | 23 | (Seneca) | 1 Cup | 27 |
| Cream, Frozen: | | | (7L) | 1 Cup | 28 |
| (Banquet) | 2 Ozs. | 20 | (Snow Crop) | 1 Cup | 26 |
| (Mrs. Smith's) | 1 Pc. | 11 | Pink (Birds Eye) | 1 Cup | 27 |
| Meringue, Frozen (Mrs. Smith's) | 1 Pc. | 22 | Mix: | | |
| Lemon Pie Filling | | | Twist (General Foods) | 6 Fl. Ozs. | 15 |
| (Lucky Leaf) | 4 Ozs. | 47 | (Salada) | 6 Fl. Ozs. | 19 |
| Lemon Pie Filling Mix: | | | (Wyler's) | 6 Fl. Ozs. | 16 |
| (Jell-O) | 1 Cup | 52 | (Wyler's) Pink | 6 Fl. Ozs. | 16 |

| FOOD | AMT. | CARB. GRAMS | FOOD | AMT. | CARB. GRAMS |
|---|---|---|---|---|---|
| Lemonade, Claret Wine | 1 Serv. | 22 | Plastic Container RealLime | 1 Tbsp. | 1 |
| Lentils | 1/2 Cup | 17 | Lime Pie, Key Lime, Cream, | | |
| (Sinsheimer) | 1 Oz. | 17 | Frozen (Banquet) | 2 Ozs. | 21 |
| Lentils, Dried Cooked | 1/2 Cup | 17 | Lime Pie Filling Mix, | | |
| Lentils Without Seed Coat | 4 Ozs. | 69 | Key Lime (Royal) | 1/8 Pie | 39 |
| Lentil Soup | 1 Cup | 40 | Lime Rickey | 1 Gl. | 23 |
| (Crosse & Blackwell) | 1 Can | 30 | Lime Sherbet or Fruit Ice | | |
| (Manischewitz) | 4 Ozs. | 15 | Mix (Junket) | 1 Oz. | 27 |
| Lentils (Whole Seeds) | 4 Ozs. | 68 | Lime Soda | 6 Ozs. | 19 |
| Lettuce (A-B2) | 1/4 Head | 2 | Lime Soft Drink | | |
| Lettuce Hearts | 4 Ozs. | 3 | (Yukon Club) | 6 Fl. Ozs. | 16 |
| Lettuce With Hot Cream | | | Lime Souffle | 1 Serv. | 3 |
| Dressing | 1 Serv. | 4 | Littleneck Clams | 6 | 5 |
| Lettuce, Romaine | 1/2 Head | 4 | Liver (A-B1-B2-C) | 1 Serv. | 6 |
| Lettuce Salad With | | | Liver, Beef | 1 Serv. | 6 |
| French Dressing | 1 Wedge | 7 | Liver, Calves | 1 Serv. | 4 |
| Lettuce, Shredded | 1 Cup | 2 | Liver, Canned (Infant) | 4 Ozs. | 0 |
| Lettuce & Tomato Salad | 1 Serv. | 6 | Liver, Chicken, Broiled | 1 | T |
| Lichee Nuts, Dried | 3-1/2 Ozs. | 52 | Liver, Chicken, Chopped | 1 Serv. | 2 |
| Licorice Candy | 1 Oz. | 24 | Liver, Chicken, Raw | 4 Ozs. | 3 |
| Licorice Drops | 1 Oz. | 24 | Liver, Goose | 1 Serv. | 6 |
| Licorice Stick | 1 Oz. | 24 | Liver, Lamb | 1 Serv. | 2 |
| Liebfraumilch Wine: | | | Liver, Loaf | 1 Sl. | 9 |
| (Anheuser) | 3 Fl. Ozs. | 1 | Liver Paste | 1 Tbsp. | T |
| (Deinhard) | 3 Fl. Ozs. | 3 | Liver Paste, Goose | 1 Tbsp. | 1 |
| (Deinhard) Hans Christof | 3 Fl. Ozs. | 3 | Liver, Pork | 1 Serv. | 4 |
| (Julius Kayser) Glockenspiel | 3 Fl. Ozs. | 2 | Liver, Sheep (A1-B2-C) | 1 Serv. | 4 |
| Liederkranz Cheese (A) | 1-1/2 Ozs. | T | Liver Spread | 4 Ozs. | 12 |
| Life, Cereal (Quaker) | 1 Cup | 30 | Liver, Steer | 4 Ozs. | 7 |
| Life Savers, All Flavors | 1 Roll | 30 | Liverwurst | 1 Sl. | 2 |
| Light Cream | 1/2 Pt. | 2 | Liverwurst, Canape Spread | 1 Serv. | T |
| Lightening Chicken Fricassee | 1 Serv. | 2 | Liverwurst Sandwich | 1 | 25 |
| Light Rye Flour | 4 Ozs. | 49 | Loaf, Ham | 1 Serv. | 22 |
| Like, Soft Drink, Low | | | Loaf, Liver | 1 Sl. | 9 |
| Calorie (Seven-Up) | 6 Fl. Ozs. | T | Loaf, Meat | 1 Serv. | 3 |
| Lily Cake | 1 Serv. | 22 | Loaf, Salmon | 1 Serv. | 7 |
| Lima Beans (Canned) | 1/2 Cup | 29 | Lobster | 1 Av. | 1 |
| Lima Beans, Dried | 1/2 Cup | 38 | Northern, Meat Only (Booth) | 4 Ozs. | T |
| Lima Beans, Fresh (C) | 1/2 Cup | 29 | Lobster, Baked or Broiled | 1 Av. | 1 |
| Limburger Cheese | 1-1/2 Ozs. | T | Lobster Canapes | 4 | 6 |
| Lime (C) | 1 Med. | 5 | Lobster (Canned) | 1 Serv. | T |
| Limeade Juice, Frozen | | | Lobster Cocktail | 1/2 Cup | T |
| Concentrate | 3 Ozs. | 42 | Lobster Cocktail With Sauce | 1/2 Cup | 8 |
| (Minute Maid) | 1 Cup | 26 | Lobster, Creamed | 1 Serv. | 3 |
| (7L) | 1 Cup | 27 | Lobster Egg Foo Yung | 1 Serv. | 1 |
| (Snow Crop) | 1 Cup | 26 | Lobster, Fresh With | | |
| Limeade Juice, Frozen | | | 2 Tbsp. Butter | 3/4 Lb. | 1 |
| Diluted | 1 Cup | 22 | Lobster Newberg | 1 Serv. | 3 |
| Limeade Mix (Wyler's) | 6 Fl. Ozs. | 15 | Frozen (Stouffer's) | 4 Ozs. | 5 |
| Lime Chiffon Pie | 1 Pc. | 34 | Lobster Paste | 1 Tsp. | 6 |
| Lime Ice | 1 Scp. | 27 | Lobster Salad | 1 Serv. | 9 |
| Lime Juice | 1 Cup | 18 | Lobster Salad Delight | 1 Serv. | 9 |
| Canned (Calavo) | 1 Fl. Oz. | 3 | Lobster Sauce | 1 Tbsp. | 4 |

| FOOD | AMT. | CARB. GRAMS |
|---|---|---|
| Lobster Soup, Canned: | | |
| (Crosse & Blackwell): | | |
| Bisque | 1 Can | 13 |
| Cream of | 1 Can | 13 |
| Lobster Tails | 1 Serv. | T |
| Lobster Thermidor | 1 | 15 |
| Lochon Ora, Scottish Liqueur | | |
| (Leroux) | 1 Fl. Oz. | 1 |
| Loganberries (Canned) | 1/2 Cup | 20 |
| Loganberries, Fresh | 1/2 Cup | 11 |
| Loganberries Juice | 6 Ozs. | 15 |
| Log Cabin, Syrup: | | |
| Buttered | 1 T. | 13 |
| Maple Flavored | 1 T. | 13 |
| Lollipops | 1 Med. | 28 |
| London Broil | 1 Serv. | 0 |
| Look Fit (A & P) | 1 Can | 19 |
| Lorna Doone Cookie | 1 | 5 |
| Lotus Root | 1 Av. | 23 |
| Low Calorie Canned | | |
| Bing Cherries | 1 Cup | 22 |
| Low Calorie Soft Drink | | |
| (Most Flavors) | 8 Ozs. | 0 |
| Lox | 2 Ozs. | 0 |
| Lox, Nova Scotia | 1 Oz. | 0 |
| Lucky Charms, Cereal | 1 Oz. | 23 |
| Lumberjack, Syrup (Nalley's) | 1 Oz. | 19 |
| Luncheon Meat Sand. | 1 | 25 |
| Luncheon Meat: | | |
| (Sugardale) | 1 Oz. | T |
| Old Fashioned Loaf | | |
| (Sugardale) | 1 Oz. | T |
| Pickle & Pimento: | | |
| (Hormel) | 1 Oz. | T |
| (Sugardale) | 1 Oz. | T |
| Spiced (Hormel) | 1 Oz. | T |
| Lyonnaise Potatoes | 1 Med. | 28 |
| Macadonia Nuts | 11 | 1 |
| Macaroni Au Gratin | 1 Serv. | 30 |
| Macaroni & Beef: | | |
| In Tomato Sauce | | |
| (Franco-American) | 4 Ozs. | 12 |
| With Tomatoes, Frozen | | |
| (Stouffer's) | 4 Ozs. | 13 |
| Macaroni & Cheese | 1/2 Cup | 22 |
| Canned: | | |
| (Franco-American) | 4 Ozs. | 12 |
| (Heinz) | 4 Ozs. | 12 |
| (Franco-American) | | |
| MacaroniO's | 4 Ozs. | 11 |
| Frozen: | | |
| (Banquet) | 4 Ozs. | 16 |
| (Banquet) Cookin' Bag | 4 Ozs. | 8 |

| FOOD | AMT. | CARB. GRAMS |
|---|---|---|
| (Kraft) | 4 Ozs. | 17 |
| (Morton) Casserole | 4 Ozs. | 14 |
| (Stouffer's) | 4 Ozs. | 17 |
| (Swanson) | 4 Ozs. | 14 |
| Macaroni & Cheese Mix: | | |
| Cheddar Sauce | | |
| (Betty Crocker) | 4 Ozs. | 18 |
| Mac-A-Roni & Cheddar | | |
| (Golden Grain) | 1 Cup | 36 |
| Stir 'n Serv, Instant | | |
| (Golden Grain) | 1 Cup | 44 |
| Macaroni & Chili Sauce Mix: | | |
| Mac-A-Roni Fiesta | | |
| (Golden Grain) | 1 Cup | 50 |
| Mexi Casserole | | |
| (Betty Crocker) | 6-Oz. Pkg. | 120 |
| Macaroni, Cooked | 1 Cup | 39 |
| Macaroni Creole (Heinz) | 1 Can | 24 |
| Macaroni Dinner: | | |
| & Beef, Frozen: | | |
| (Morton) | Dinner | 58 |
| (Swanson) | Dinner | 35 |
| & Cheese: | | |
| (Chef Boy-Ar-Dee) | 4 Ozs. | 30 |
| (Kraft) | 4 Ozs. | 26 |
| (Kraft) Deluxe | 4 Ozs. | 28 |
| Frozen (Banquet) | Dinner | 47 |
| Frozen (Morton) | Dinner | 66 |
| Frozen (Swanson) | Dinner | 48 |
| Italian-Style (Kraft) | 4 Ozs. | 20 |
| Mexican-Style (Kraft) | 4 Ozs. | 22 |
| Monte Bello With Sauce | | |
| Mix (Betty Crocker) | 4 Ozs. | 85 |
| Macaroni, Dry | 3-1/2 Ozs. | 75 |
| Macaroni Salad | 1 Cup | 26 |
| Macaroni Salad, Canned | | |
| (Nalley's) | 4 Ozs. | 14 |
| Macaroons | 1 Lg. | 18 |
| Macaroons, Almond | 1 | 16 |
| Macaroons, Coconut | 1 | 14 |
| Macaroons, Coca Corn Flake | 1 | 8 |
| Mace | 1/8 Tsp. | 0 |
| Mackerel | 1 Serv. | 0 |
| Mackerel (Canned) | 1 Serv. | 0 |
| Mackerel (Salt) | 1 Serv. | 0 |
| Madeira Wine | 1 Gl. | 5 |
| (Leacock) | 3 Fl. Ozs. | 6 |
| (Leacock) St. John | 3 Fl. Ozs. | 6 |
| Madrilene, Consomme | 1 Cup | 1 |
| Mahukona Beverage | 10 Ozs. | 4 |
| Maison, Pate | 1 Serv. | T |
| Mai Tai Cocktail | | |
| (Lemon Hart) | 3 Fl. Ozs. | 15 |

| FOOD | AMT. | CARB. GRAMS | FOOD | AMT. | CARB. GRAMS |
|---|---|---|---|---|---|
| Mai Tai Mix (Bar-Tender's) | 1 Serv. | 17 | (Fleischmann's) Regular or Soft | 1 Tbsp. | T |
| Malt, Cocoa | 1 Gl. | 22 | (Golden Glow) | 1 Tbsp. | T |
| Malted Choc., Milk Shake | 10 Ozs. | 70 | (Good Luck) | 1 Tbsp. | T |
| Malted Milk | 1 Serv. | 26 | (Good Luck) Soft | 1 Tbsp. | T |
| Malted Milk Mix: | | | (Imperial) | 1 Tbsp. | T |
| Instant (Borden) | 1 Tbsp. | 18 | (Imperial) Soft-Spread | 1 Tbsp. | T |
| (Horlicks) | 1 Oz. | 20 | (Mazola) Polyunsaturated | 1 Tbsp. | T |
| Instant, Chocolate (Borden) | 1 Tbsp. | 21 | (Miracle) Corn Oil | 1 Tbsp. | T |
| Malted Milk, Misc. Float | | | (Nucoa) Polyunsaturated | 1 Tbsp. | T |
| & Ice Cream | 10 Ozs. | 70 | (Nu-Maid) | 1 Oz. | T |
| Malted Milk Powder | 1 Tbsp. | 7 | (Parkay) Regular | 1 Tbsp. | T |
| Maltex Cereal, Cooked | 3/4 Cup | 24 | (Parkay) Soft Cup | 1 Tbsp. | T |
| Malt Liquor, | | | (Parkay) Corn Oil, Deluxe | 1 Tbsp. | T |
| Country Club | 8 Fl. Ozs. | 3 | (Parkay) Corn Oil, Soft | 1 Tbsp. | T |
| Malt-O-Meal, Cereal | 1 Cup | 28 | (Parkay) Safflower Oil, Soft | 1 Tbsp. | T |
| Maltose-Dextro | 1 Tbsp. | 7 | (Saffola) Regular or Soft | 1 Tbsp. | T |
| Mamey Apple | 4 Ozs. | 13 | (Sealtest) | 1 Tbsp. | T |
| Mandarin Orange | 1 Med. | 10 | Margarine, Imitation, Diet: | | |
| Canned (Diet Delight) | 1 Cup | 12 | (Fleischmann's) | 1 Tbsp. | T |
| Mango (A-C) | 1 Av. | 19 | (Imperial) | 1 Tbsp. | 0 |
| Manhattan Cocktail | 1 Gl. | 3 | (Mazola) | 1 Tbsp. | T |
| (Calvert) | 3 Fl. Ozs. | 2 | (Nucoa) | 1 Tbsp. | T |
| (Hiram Walker) | 3 Fl. Ozs. | 3 | (Parkay) Soft | 1 Tbsp. | 0 |
| Manhattan Mix | | | Margarine, Whipped: | | |
| (Bar-Tender's) | 1 Serv. | 5 | (Blue Bonnet) | 1 Tbsp. | T |
| Manhattan Scotch | 3 Ozs. | 3 | (Imperial) | 1 Tbsp. | T |
| Manicotti, Without Sauce, | | | (Miracle) Cottonseed-Soybean | 1 Tbsp. | T |
| Frozen (Buitoni) | 1 Pc. | 10 | (Miracle) Sticks | 1 Tbsp. | T |
| Maple Ice Cream Parfait | 1 | 20 | (Nucoa) | 1 Tbsp. | T |
| Maple Mousse Sundae | 1 Av. | 25 | (Parkay) Cup | 1 Tbsp. | T |
| Maple Nut Ice Cream | 1 Scp. | 14 | Margarita Cocktail (Calvert) | 3 Fl. Ozs. | 9 |
| Maple Nut Sundae | 1 Av. | 27 | Margarita Mix (Bar-Tender's) | 1 Serv. | 17 |
| Maple Rennet Custard Mix: | | | Margaux, French Red Bordeaux | | |
| Powder (Junket) | 1 Oz. | 28 | (Barton & Guestier) | 3 Fl. Ozs. | 3 |
| Tablet (Junket) | 1 Tablet | T | Marinade Mix: | | |
| Maple Sugar | 1 Tsp. | 4 | (Adolph's) Instant | 1 Pkg. | 6 |
| Maple Syrup | 1 Tbsp. | 13 | (Lawry's) Lemon Pepper | 1 Pkg. | 29 |
| Imitation (Karo) | 1 Tbsp. | 14 | Marinated With Cream, | | |
| Dietetic (Dia-Mel) | 1 Tbsp. | 5 | Herring | 1 Sm. Pc. | 4 |
| Maple Walnut Sundae Fancy | 2 Scps. | 30 | Marjoram | 1/8 Tsp. | T |
| Maple Walnut Sundae Plain | 2 Scps. | 28 | Marmalade | 1 Tbsp. | 14 |
| Maraschino Cherries | 2 Aver. | 2 | Sweetened: | | |
| Maraschino Liqueur: | | | (Crosse & Blackwell) | 1 Tbsp. | 15 |
| (Garnier) | 1 Fl. Oz. | 11 | (Kraft) | 1 Tbsp. | 9 |
| (Leroux) | 1 Fl. Oz. | 9 | Low Calorie: | | |
| Marble Cake | 1 Pc. | 30 | (Dia-Mel) | 1 Tbsp. | 5 |
| Marble Cake Mix | | | (Louis Sherry) | 1 Tbsp. | 1 |
| (Betty Crocker) | 1 Pc. | 37 | (Polaner) | 1 Tbsp. | 1 |
| Margarine | 1 Tbsp. | 0 | (Slenderella) | 1 Tbsp. | 5 |
| (Blue Bonnet) Regular | | | Marmalade, Cherry | 1 Tbsp. | 14 |
| or Soft | 1 Tbsp. | T | Marmalade, Orange | 1 Tbsp. | 14 |
| (Borden) Danish Flavor | 1 Tbsp. | T | Marmalade, Pineapple | 1 Tbsp. | 14 |

| FOOD | AMT. | CARB. GRAMS | FOOD | AMT. | CARB. GRAMS |
|---|---|---|---|---|---|
| Marrons, Roasted | 15 | 26 | Mayonnaise, Diet Dressing | 1 Tbsp. | T |
| Marsala Wine (Italian Swiss | | | Maypo Oat Cereal, Cooked | 3/4 Cup | 21 |
| Colony-Private Stock) | 3 Fl. Ozs. | 7 | Maypo Cereal, Dry, Any Flavor: | | |
| Marshmallow Candy | 1 Oz. | 23 | Instant | 1 Oz. | 20 |
| Marshmallow Choc. Candy | 1 Oz. | 9 | 1-Minute | 1 Oz. | 20 |
| Marshmallow Sauce | 1 Tbsp. | 6 | May Wine (Deinhard) | 3 Fl. Ozs. | 1 |
| Marshmallow Sundae, Plain | 2 Scps. | 41 | Mazola Oil | 1 Tbsp. | 0 |
| Marshmallow Sundae Fancy | 2 Scps. | 44 | Meal, Cracker | 1 Tbsp. | 7 |
| Marshmallows | 1 Av. | 6 | Meal, Wheat Cereal | 1/2 Cup | 20 |
| Mars Bar Candy | 1 Bar | 22 | Meal, Whole Cooked | 1 Cup | 22 |
| Mars Forever Yours | 1 Bar | 25 | Meal, Whole Wheat Germ, | | |
| Mars Milky Way Candy | 1 Bar | 58 | Cooked | 1 Cup | 27 |
| Mars Snickers | 1 Bar | 25 | Meat Balls | 2 Ozs. | 2 |
| Mars Three Musketeers | 1 Bar | 35 | Dinner, With Kluski Noodles, | | |
| Martini | 3 Ozs. | T | Frozen (Tom Thumb) | 8 Ozs. | 20 |
| Martini Cocktail: | | | In Sauce, Canned | | |
| Gin (Calvert) | 3 Fl. Ozs. | T | (Prince) | 8 Ozs. | 18 |
| Gin (Hiram Walker) | 3 Fl. Ozs. | T | Stew, Canned | | |
| Vodka (Hiram Walker) | 3 Fl. Ozs. | T | (Chef Boy-Ar-Dee) | 8 Ozs. | 14 |
| Martini, Dry | 3 Ozs. | T | (Chef Boy-Ar-Dee) | 4 Ozs. | 10 |
| Martini, Sweet | 3 Ozs. | 9 | Meat Balls and Spaghetti | 4 Ozs. | 45 |
| Martinique Swizzle Bev. | 14 Ozs. | 5 | Meat Ball Soup (Costa Rica) | 1 Serv. | 12 |
| Masa Harina (Quaker) Dry | 1 Cup | 78 | Meat, Bologna Cups | 1 Serv. | 2 |
| Mashed Potatoes | 1/2 Cup | 16 | Meat, Buffalo | 4 Ozs. | 0 |
| Mashed Turnips | 1 Cup | 10 | Meat Gravy, Med. | 1 Tbsp. | 5 |
| Matai, Fresh | 4 Ozs. | 20 | Meat, Horse | 3-1/2 Ozs. | 1 |
| Matzoth | 1 | 17 | Meat, Italian Sauce | 1 Cup | 21 |
| Regular, Daily & Passover | | | Meat Loaf | 1 Serv. | 3 |
| (Manischewitz) | 1 | 26 | Meat Loaf Dinner: | | |
| Diet-10's (Goodman's) | 1 | 23 | (Banquet) | Dinner | 29 |
| Diet Thins (Manischewitz) | 1 | 23 | (Morton) | Dinner | 23 |
| Egg 'n Onion (Manischewitz) | 1 | 23 | (Swanson) | Dinner | 42 |
| Egg, Passover (Manischewitz) | 1 | 26 | (Swanson) 3-Course | Dinner | 51 |
| Midgetea (Goodman's) | 1 | 8 | Meat Loaf Sand. | 1 | 30 |
| Round Tea (Goodman's) | 1 | 14 | Meat Loaf Seasoning Mix | | |
| Tasteas (Manischewitz) | 1 | 20 | (Lawry's) | 1 Pkg. | 65 |
| Thin Tea (Manischewitz) | 1 | 24 | Meat Or Poultry Stuffing | 4 Ozs. | 28 |
| Unsalted (Goodman's) | 1 | 23 | Meat, Potted: | | |
| Unsalted (Horowitz-Margareten) | 1 | 28 | (Armour Star) | 1 Can | 0 |
| Whole Wheat, Passover | | | (Hormel) | 1 Can | 1 |
| (Manischewitz) | 1 | 24 | Meat Tenderizer (Adolph's): | | |
| Matzoth & 2 Eggs | 1 Serv. | 18 | Unseasoned | 1 T. | T |
| Matzoth Balls | 1 Av. | 17 | Seasoned | 1 T. | T |
| Matzoth Meal (Manischewitz) | 1 Cup | 94 | Mediterranean Mackerel | 1 Serv. | 0 |
| Mayonnaise | 1 Tbsp. | T | Medium Cream | 1 Tbsp. | 1 |
| (Best Foods) Real | 1 Pt. | 7 | Medium Fat, Pork Carcass | 4 Ozs. | 0 |
| (Hellman's) Real | 1 Oz. | T | Melba Crackers | 1 | 3 |
| (Kraft) | 1 Oz. | T | Melba Toast | 1 Sl. | 6 |
| (Kraft) Salad Bowl | 1 Oz. | T | Garlic (Keebler) | 1 Pc. | 1 |
| (Nalley's) | 1 Oz. | 1 | Garlic (Old London) | 1 Pc. | 1 |
| (Saffola) | 1 Oz. | 4 | Onion (Old London) | 1 Pc. | 1 |
| (Wesson) | 1 Oz. | T | Plain (Keebler) | 1 Pc. | 1 |

| FOOD | AMT. | CARB. GRAMS | FOOD | AMT. | CARB. GRAMS |
|---|---|---|---|---|---|
| Pumpernickel (Old London) | 1 Pc. | 3 | (Sealtest) | 1 Cup | 25 |
| Rye: | | | With Skim Milk: | | |
| (Keebler) | 1 Pc. | 1 | (Sealtest) | 1 Cup | 25 |
| (Old London) | 1 Pc. | 3 | Milk, Choc. Skimmed | 8 Ozs. | 26 |
| Unsalted (Old London) | 1 Pc. | 3 | Milk, Choc., 1/2 Water, | | |
| Sesame (Keebler) | 1 Pc. | 1 | 1/2 Milk | 8 Ozs. | 11 |
| Sesame, Rounds | | | Milk, Choc. All Milk | 8 Ozs. | 25 |
| (Old London) | 1 Pc. | 1 | Milk Choc. With Almonds | 1 Bar | 17 |
| Wheat (Old London) | 1 Pc. | 3 | Milk Choc. Crunch, Nestles | 1 Bar | 15 |
| Wheat, Unsalted | | | Milk, Coconut | 1 Cup | 10 |
| (Old London) | 1 Pc. | 3 | Milk Condensed (B1-C) | 1 Tbsp. | 8 |
| White: | | | Sweetened, Canned: | | |
| (Keebler) | 1 Pc. | 3 | (Dime) | 1 Oz. | 21 |
| (Old London) | 1 Pc. | 3 | (Eagle) | 1 Oz. | 20 |
| Rounds (Old London) | 1 Pc. | 1 | (Magnolia) | 1 Oz. | 21 |
| Unsalted (Old London) | 1 Pc. | 3 | (Nestle's) Lion Brand | 1 Oz. | 13 |
| Melon Balls, Frozen | 1 Cup | 12 | (Sealtest) | 1 Oz. | 22 |
| Mixed (Birds Eye) | 4 Ozs. | 12 | Milk, Dried, Skimmed | 1 Tbsp. | 3 |
| Melon Ball Crisps | | | Milk, Dried, Whole | 1 Tbsp. | 2 |
| (Epicure) | 1 Oz. | 22 | (Sealtest) | 2 Tbsps. | 5 |
| Melon & Berry Salad | 1 Serv. | 9 | Milk, Dry, Nonfat | 1 Tbsp. | 2 |
| Melon, Casaba | 1/8 Av. | 7 | (Carnation) | 1 Cup | 11 |
| Melon, Honeydew | 1/4 Av. | 7 | (Pet) | 1 Cup | 12 |
| Menthe, Creme de | Pony | 7 | (Sanalac) | 1 Cup | 11 |
| Meringue | 1/4 Cup | 8 | (Sealtest) | 2 Tbsps. | 7 |
| Meringued Pears | 1 Serv. | 24 | Milk, Dry, Whole | 1 Cup | 39 |
| Metrecal Dinner | 9 Ozs. | 23 | Milk, Evaporated, | | |
| Mexican Dinner: | | | Sweetened (A-B2-D) | 2 Tbsp. | 21 |
| (Banquet) | Dinner | 74 | Milk, Evaporated, | | |
| (Swanson) | Dinner | 67 | Unsweetened (A-B2-D) | 1/4 Cup | 8 |
| Mexican El Diablo Bev. | 10 Ozs. | 13 | Milk, Evaporated, 1/2 Water | 4 Ozs. | 12 |
| Mexican-Style Vegetables, | | | Milk Evaporated, Canned: | | |
| Frozen (Birds Eye) | 1 Pkg. | 82 | Regular: | | |
| Mexican Tomato & | | | (Carnation) | 1 Cup | 24 |
| Cheese Dip | 1 Serv. | 3 | (Pet) | 1 Cup | 24 |
| Middle East Turkey | 1 Serv. | 8 | (Sealtest) | 1 Cup | 24 |
| Miguel Ligero Cktl. | 1 Gl. | 4 | Skimmed: | | |
| Milk (A-B2-C) | 3/4 Cup | 8 | (Pet) | 1 Cup | 26 |
| Milk, Acidophilus | 3/4 Cup | 6 | (Sunshine) | 1 Cup | 25 |
| Milk Amplifier, Syrup | | | Milk, Fresh: | | |
| (Hershey's) | 1 Oz. | 18 | Whole: | | |
| Milk, 1/2 Milk, 1/2 Cream | 4 Ozs. | 6 | 3.5% Fat (Borden) | 1 Cup | 12 |
| Milk, Butter | 8 Ozs. | 12 | 3.5% Fat (Sealtest) | 1 Cup | 11 |
| Milk, Butter-Cultured | 8 Ozs. | 12 | 3.7% Fat (Sealtest) | 1 Cup | 11 |
| 0.1% Fat (Borden) | 1 Cup | 12 | Multivitamin (Sealtest) | 1 Cup | 11 |
| 1.0% Fat (Borden) | 1 Cup | 12 | Skim: | | |
| 3.5% Fat (Borden) | 1 Cup | 12 | (Sealtest) | 1 Cup | 11 |
| (Sealtest) | 1 Cup | 9 | Diet (Sealtest) | 1 Cup | 13 |
| Milk, Buttermilk (B1-B2) | 1 Cup | 12 | Light 'n Lively | | |
| Milk, Choc. Flavored | 1 Cup | 25 | (Sealtest) | 1 Cup | 13 |
| With Whole Milk: | | | Lite Line (Borden) | 1 Cup | 14 |
| Dutch Chocolate (Borden) | 1 Cup | 26 | n-r-g (Sealtest) | 1 Cup | 13 |

| FOOD | AMT. | CARB. GRAMS | FOOD | AMT. | CARB. GRAMS |
|---|---|---|---|---|---|
| Vita Lure (Sealtest) | 1 Cup | 13 | Mixed Cereal, Corn & Soy Grits | 1/2 Cup | 13 |
| Milk, Goat | 1 Cup | 10 | Mixed Cereal, Wheat & Barley | 1/2 Cup | 24 |
| Milk, Grade A, Whole (A-B2-C) | 3/4 Cup | 8 | Mixed Cheese Ball Garnish | 1 Ball | T |
| Milk, Ice | 1/4 Pt. | 21 | Mixed Corn-Soy Grits, Breakfast Food | 1/2 Cup | 13 |
| Milk, Ice Cream | 1/4 Pt. | 21 | Mixed Green Salad | | |
| Milk, Malted | 1 | 26 | With French Dressing | 1/2 Cup | 5 |
| Milk Punch, Hot | 4 Ozs. | 16 | Mixed Peppers With Olives | 1 Serv. | 5 |
| Milk, Reindeer | 1/2 Cup | 4 | Mixed Sweet Pickles | 2 Med. | 5 |
| Milk Shake | 1 | 30 | Mixed Vegetables (Canned) | 4 Ozs. | 15 |
| Milk Shake Mix: | | | Mixed Vegetables, Frozen | 4 Ozs. | 16 |
| Great Shakes: | | | Mocha Custard | 1 Serv. | 5 |
| With Whole Milk | 1 Cup | 37 | Mocha Frosting | 1 Tbsp. | 6 |
| With Nonfat Milk | 1 Cup | 38 | Mocha Nut Pudding Mix | | |
| Milkshake, Choc. | 10 Ozs. | 57 | Instant (Royal) | 1 Cup | 60 |
| Milkshake, Choc. Malted | 10 Ozs. | 70 | Mock Turtle Soup | 1 Cup | 0 |
| Milk, Sheep's | 1 Cup | 11 | Mofuco Cocktail | 1 Gl. | 7 |
| Milk, Skimmed (B) | 1 Cup | 13 | Mojito Beverage | 10 Ozs. | 7 |
| Milk, Skimmed Choc. | 1 Gl. | 10 | Mojito Criollo Bev. | 8 Ozs. | 11 |
| Milk, Soy Bean | 8 Ozs. | 5 | Molasses | 1 Tbsp. | 13 |
| Milk, Sweet Choc. | 1 Bar | 16 | (Brer Rabbit): | | |
| Milk, Sweetened Condensed | 4 Ozs. | 60 | Gold Label | 1 Tbsp. | 13 |
| Milk Toast | 1 Sl. | 14 | Green Label | 1 Tbsp. | 12 |
| Milk, Top | 1/2 Cup | 1 | Unsulphured (Grandma's) | 1 Tbsp. | 15 |
| Milk, Unsweetened Condensed | 1 Cup | 20 | Molasses, Cane (Barbados) | 1 Tbsp. | 11 |
| Milk, Whole | 1 Cup | 12 | Molasses, Blackstrap | 1 Tbsp. | 11 |
| Milk, Whole Dry Reconstituted | 8 Ozs. | 39 | Molasses, Cane-Black Strap | 1 Tbsp. | 11 |
| Mincemeat: | | | Molasses, Cane, Light | 1 Tbsp. | 13 |
| (Crosse & Blackwell) | 1 Tbsp. | 14 | Molasses, Cane Syrup Light | 1 Tbsp. | 13 |
| Condensed (None-Such) | 3 Ozs. | 70 | Molasses, Cane Syrup, Medium | 1 Tbsp. | 13 |
| Ready-to-Use (None-Such) | 6 Ozs. | 88 | Molasses, Cane Syrup, Blackstrap | 1 Tbsp. | 11 |
| Mince Pie | 1 Pc. | 52 | Molasses Cookie | 1 | 5 |
| Frozen: | | | Molasses Kisses | 1 | 10 |
| (Banquet) | 1 Oz. | 13 | Molasses Taffy | 1 | 10 |
| (Marvin) | 1 Pc. | 23 | Mor (Wilson) Canned Luncheon Meat | 3 Ozs. | 1 |
| (Mrs. Smith's) | 1 Pc. | 24 | Moselmaid, German Moselle Wine (Deinhard) | 3 Fl. Ozs. | 1 |
| Mineral Oil | 1 Tbsp. | 0 | Mounds Candy | 10¢ Bar | 32 |
| Minestrone | 1 Serv. | 10 | Mountain Wine | | |
| Minestone Soup: | | | (Louis M. Martini) | 3 Fl. Ozs | T |
| Condensed (Campbell) | 4 Ozs. | 10 | Mousse, Pineapple | 1 Serv. | 35 |
| (Crosse & Blackwell) | 1 Can | 28 | Mousse, Strawberry | 1 Serv. | 17 |
| Mix (Golden Grain) | 1 Cup | 11 | Moxie, Soft Drink | 6 Fl. Ozs. | 22 |
| Mint, Chopped | 1 Tsp. | 0 | Mrs. Butterworth's Syrup | 1 Tbsp. | 13 |
| Mints, After Dinner Chocolate | 1 Bar | 23 | Muenster Cheese | 1-1/2 Ozs. | T |
| Mints, After Dinner, Plain | 1 Pc. Sm. | 7 | Muffet Cereal | 1 | 39 |
| Mints, After Dinner | 5 | 14 | Muffins | 1 Av. | 19 |
| Mints, Chocolate | 8 Sm. | 21 | | | |
| Mint Jelly | 1 Tbsp. | 13 | | | |
| Mint Julep | 8 Ozs. | 11 | | | |
| Mint Leaves | 1 Tbsp. | 0 | | | |
| Mint Sauce (Powd. Sug.) | 1 Tbsp. | 10 | | | |
| Miracle Whip | 1 Tbsp. | T | | | |

76

| FOOD | AMT. | CARB. GRAMS | FOOD | AMT. | CARB. GRAMS |
|---|---|---|---|---|---|
| Muffins, Blueberry | 1 Av. | 23 | (Gold Seal) | 3 Fl. Ozs. | 9 |
| Muffins, Boston Brown | 1 Av. | 20 | (Italian Swiss Colony- | | |
| Muffins, Bran | 1 Av. | 24 | Gold Medal) | 3 Fl. Ozs. | 9 |
| Muffins, Cinnamon | 1 Av. | 23 | (Italian Swiss Colony-Private | | |
| Muffins, Corn (Thomas') | 1 Av. | 26 | Stock) Golden | 3 Fl. Ozs. | 11 |
| Muffins, Date | 1 Med. | 41 | (Taylor) | 3 Fl. Ozs. | 11 |
| Muffins, Egg | 1 Med. | 20 | Mushrooms | 1/2 Cup | 3 |
| Muffins, English | 1 Av. | 21 | Mushrooms ala Cossack | 1 Serv. | 5 |
| (Cain's) | 1 | 28 | Mushroom & Barley Soup | 1 Cup | 13 |
| (Di Carlo) | 1 | 28 | Mushrooms, Broiled | | |
| (Hostess) | 1 | 28 | (With Tsp. Butter) | 1 Cup | 6 |
| (Newly Weds): | | | Mushrooms, Button | 1/2 Cup | 3 |
| King Size | 1 | 35 | Mushrooms, Canned | 1/2 Cup | 3 |
| Queen Size | 1 | 20 | (B in B) | 4 Ozs. | 4 |
| (Thomas') | 1 | 28 | (Oxford Royal) | 4 Ozs. | 2 |
| (Wonder) | 1 | 28 | Mushrooms, Cooked Fresh | 1/2 Cup | 3 |
| Muffins, (Golden Egg) | | | Mushrooms, Creamed | 1 Cup | 5 |
| (Arnold) | 1 | 24 | Mushrooms, Frozen: | | |
| Muffin Mix: | | | (Birds Eye) | 1 Pkg. | 6 |
| Apple Cinnamon | | | (Green Giant) | 4 Ozs. | 9 |
| (Betty Crocker) | 4 Ozs. | 88 | Mushroom Pizza | 1 Sl. | 23 |
| Banana Nut (Betty Crocker) | | | Mushrooms, Sauteed | 1/2 Cup | 2 |
| Chiquita | 4 Ozs. | 81 | Mushroom & Shrimp Borghese | 1 Serv. | 8 |
| Blueberry: | | | Mushroom Soup, Creamed | 1 Cup | 13 |
| Wild (Betty Crocker) | 4 Ozs. | 68 | Mushroom Soup: | | |
| (Duncan Hines) | 1/4 Pkg. | 51 | Barley (Manischewitz) | 8 Ozs. | 12 |
| (Duncan Hines) | 1 | 17 | Bisque (Crosse & Blackwell) | 1 Can | 16 |
| Coffee Nut (Betty Crocker) | 4 Ozs. | 76 | Cream of: | | |
| Corn: | | | Condensed (Campbell) | 8 Ozs. | 17 |
| (Betty Crocker) | 4 Ozs. | 82 | (Heinz) Great American | 1 Cup | 11 |
| (Dromedary) | 1 | 27 | (Heinz) | 1 Cup | 10 |
| (Flako) | 1 | 21 | Dietetic (Claybourne) | 8 Ozs. | 10 |
| (Pillsbury) Golden | 4 Ozs. | 76 | Low Sodium (Campbell) | 8 Ozs. | 8 |
| Date (Betty Crocker) | 4 Ozs. | 87 | Golden, Condensed (Campbell) | 8 Ozs. | 16 |
| Honey Bran | | | Mushroom Soup Mix: | | |
| (Betty Crocker) | 4 Ozs | 86 | (Golden Grain) | 1 Cup | 16 |
| Oatmeal (Betty Crocker) | 4 Ozs. | 77 | (Lipton) | 1 Pkg. | 24 |
| Orange (Betty Crocker) | | | (Wyler's) | 8 Fl. Ozs. | 9 |
| Sunkist | 4 Ozs. | 88 | Muskellunge | 3-1/2 Ozs. | 0 |
| Muffins, Raisin | 1 Med. | 27 | Muskmelon | 1/2 Med. | 5 |
| Muffins Soy | 1 Med. | 17 | Mussels | 12 | 0 |
| Muffins, White | 1 Med. | 21 | Mustard | 1 Tbsp. | T |
| Muffins, Whole Wheat | 1 Av. | 19 | Mustard Broiled Mackerel | 1 Serv. | T |
| Mulled Cider | 1/2 Cup | 18 | Mustard, Dry | 1 Tsp. | T |
| Mulligatawny | 1 Cup | 20 | Mustard Greens (A-B2-C) | 1 Cup | 5 |
| Mung Bean Sprouts | 1 Cup | 4 | Frozen, Chopped | | |
| Mung Beans, Dried | 4 Ozs. | 68 | (Birds Eye) | 1 Cup | 4 |
| Muscatel Wine | 1 Gl. | 4 | Mustard Pickle Relish | 1 Tbsp. | 4 |
| (Gallo): | | | Mustard, Prepared | 1 Tbsp. | T |
| 14% Alcohol | 3 Fl. Ozs. | 8 | Brown: | | |
| 16% Alcohol | 3 Fl. Ozs. | 7 | (Gulden's) | 1 Tbsp. | 1 |
| 20% Alcohol | 3 Fl. Ozs. | 8 | (Heinz) | 1 Tbsp. | 2 |

| FOOD | AMT. | CARB. GRAMS | FOOD | AMT. | CARB. GRAMS |
|---|---|---|---|---|---|
| Dusseldorf (Kraft) | 1 Tbsp. | 1 | Noodle Dinner: | | |
| Horseradish (Kraft) | 1 Tbsp. | 1 | Cantong Dinner Mix | | |
| Salad (Kraft) | 1 Tbsp. | 1 | (Betty Crocker) | 5-Oz. Pkg. | 88 |
| Yellow: | | | With Chicken, Canned | | |
| (Gulden's) | 1 Tbsp. | 1 | (Lynden) | 4 Ozs. | 33 |
| (Heinz) | 1 Tbsp. | T | With Chicken & Vegetables, | | |
| (Kraft) | 1 Tbsp. | 1 | Canned (Lynden) | 4 Ozs. | 50 |
| Mustard Sauce | 1/4 Cup | 6 | With Chicken, Frozen | | |
| Mutton, Boiled | 1 Serv. | 0 | (Swanson) | Dinner | 46 |
| Mutton Chop | 1 Serv. | 0 | Romanoff Dinner Mix | | |
| Mutton, Chops or Roast | 4 Ozs. | 0 | (Kraft) | 4 Ozs. | 19 |
| Mutton, Creamed | 4 Ozs. | 9 | Stroganoff Dinner Mix | | |
| Mutton, Leg Roast | 1 Serv. | 0 | (Betty Crocker) | Pkg. | 100 |
| Myrtle Bank Punch | 10 Ozs. | 7 | With Turkey, Canned | | |
| Nabisco Cookies | 1 | 12 | (Lynden) | 4 Ozs. | 28 |
| Nabisco Devil Cookies | 1 | 12 | Noodle Mix: | | |
| Napoleons | 1 Serv. | 17 | Almondine (Betty Crocker) | 4 Ozs. | 68 |
| Nassau Dry Wine (Gallo) | 3 Fl. Ozs. | 7 | Almondine Noodle-Roni | 1 Cup | 38 |
| Natural Pack Sardines | 3 Ozs. | 0 | Casserole Noodle-Roni | 1 Cup | 29 |
| Navy Bean, Dehydrated | 1/2 Cup | 62 | Italiano (Betty Crocker) | 4 Ozs. | 70 |
| Navy Beans (B1-B2) | 1 Cup | 25 | Parmesano Noodle-Roni | 1 Cup | 30 |
| Navy Beans (Canned) | 8 Ozs. | 38 | Romanoff (Betty Crocker) | Pkg. | 95 |
| Navy Beans, Dried | 1/2 Cup | 48 | Romanoff Noodle-Roni | 1 Cup | 39 |
| Navy Bean Soup | 1 Cup | 27 | Scallop-A-Roni | 1 Cup | 26 |
| Neapolitan Cream Pie  Frozen: | | | Twist-A-Roni | 1 Cup | 36 |
| (Banquet) | 4 Ozs. | 43 | Noodle Soup | 1 Cup | 7 |
| (Mrs. Smith's) | 1 Pc. | 13 | With Ground Beef, Condensed, | | |
| Nectarine (A) | 1 Med. | 12 | Canned (Campbell) | 4 Ozs. | 9 |
| Nectarine Juice | 6 Ozs. | 19 | Noodles | 3/4 Cup | 22 |
| Nesselrode Pie | 1 Pc. | 47 | Noodles & Beef, Canned: | | |
| Nesselrode Ice Cream | 1/4 Pt. | 18 | (Heinz) | 4 Ozs. | 9 |
| Nestle's Milk Choc. Plain | 1 Bar | 15 | (Nalley's) | 4 Ozs. | 6 |
| Nestle's Milk Choc. | | | With Gravy (College Inn) | 4 Ozs. | 59 |
| With Almonds | 1 Bar | 15 | With Tomato Sauce | | |
| Nestle's Milk Choc. Crunch | 1 Bar | 15 | (College Inn) | 4 Ozs. | 47 |
| Nestles Semi-Sweet Bits | 1 Oz. | 15 | Noodles & Chicken: | | |
| Neufchatel Cheese | 1-1/2 Ozs. | 1 | Canned (College Inn) | 4 Ozs. | 53 |
| Newberg, Lobster | 1 Serv. | 3 | Mix (Kraft) | 4 Ozs. | 19 |
| New England Boiled Dinner, | | | Noodles, Butter Cheese | 1 Serv. | 10 |
| With 4 Ozs. Corned Beef | 1 Serv. | 28 | Noodles, Dry Containing Egg | 4 Ozs. | 72 |
| New England Clam Chowder | 1 Serv. | 6 | Noodles, Fried (Canned) | 1 Oz. | 17 |
| New England Spice Cake | 1 Sl. | 27 | Norwegian Chowder | 1 Serv. | 5 |
| New Orleans Praline | 1 | 56 | Northern Style Chili Con Carne | 1 Serv. | 20 |
| New Orleans Sword Fish | 1 Serv. | 4 | Northern Beef & Southern | | |
| New Orleans Anchovy- | | | Cucumber Soup | 1 Serv. | 5 |
| Cream Cheese Spread | 1 Serv. | 1 | Northside Special Bev. | 12 Ozs. | 28 |
| Niersteiner, German Rhine | | | Northern Pike | 1 Serv. | 0 |
| Wine (Julius Kayser) | 3 Fl Ozs. | 1 | Nougats | 1 Aver. | 20 |
| Noodle, Chow Mein, Canned: | | | Nougats With Nuts | 1 Bar | 22 |
| (Chun King) | 4 Ozs. | 64 | Nourmahal Punch | 10 Ozs. | 3 |
| (Hung's) | 4 Ozs. | 64 | Nova Scotia Salmon | 1 Serv. | 0 |

| FOOD | AMT. | CARB. GRAMS |
|---|---|---|
| Nuits St. George, French Red Burgundy. | | |
| (Barton & Guestier) | 3 Fl Ozs. | T |
| Nut Bread, Date & | 1 Sl | 21 |
| Nut Bread, Brown | 1 Sl | 27 |
| Nut Brittle | 1 Pc. | 21 |
| Nut Cake, Rich Sherry | 1 Serv | 51 |
| Nutmeg | 1/8 Tsp. | 0 |
| Nut Mixed: | | |
| Dry Roasted: | | |
| (Skippy) | 1 Oz. | 7 |
| Oil Roasted: | | |
| With or Without Peanuts | | |
| (Planters) | 1 Oz. | 6 |
| (Skippy) | 1 Oz. | 4 |
| Nut Spice Cake | 1 Serv | 32 |
| Nutrament (Drackett). | | |
| Liquid: | | |
| Cherry | 1 Can | 56 |
| Chocolate or Chocolate Marshmallow | 1 Can | 50 |
| Dutch Chocolate | 1 Can | 56 |
| Strawberry | 1 Can | 44 |
| Vanilla | 1 Can | 47 |
| Powder: | | |
| Chocolate or Chocolate Malt | 1 Pkt. | 37 |
| Strawberry or Vanilla | 1 Pkt. | 38 |
| Nuts, Brazil Shelled | 4 Ozs. | 11 |
| Nuts, Butter | 5 Av. | 1 |
| Nuts, Cashew | 1 Oz. | 8 |
| Nuts, Cashew Roasted | 1 Cup | 35 |
| Nuts, Hazel | 10 Av. | 3 |
| Nuts, Hickory | 8 Av. | 2 |
| Nuts, Indian | 1 Tbsp. | 1 |
| Nuts, Lichi | 6 Av. | 1 |
| Nuts, Lichi Dried | 3-1/2 Ozs. | 52 |
| Nuts, Macadamia | 11 | 1 |
| Nuts, Pine | 1 Tsp. | 1 |
| Nuts, Pistachio | 16 | 2 |
| Nuts, Sugared | 1/2 Cup | 48 |
| Oat Flakes, Cereal (Post) Fortified | 1 Cup | 28 |
| Oatmeal: | | |
| Instant, Dry: | | |
| (H-O) | 1 Cup | 42 |
| (Quaker) | 1 Cup | 25 |
| (3 Minute) | 1 Cup | 25 |
| With Apple & Cinnamon (Quaker) | 1 Cup | 32 |

| FOOD | AMT. | CARB. GRAMS |
|---|---|---|
| With Maple & Brown Sugar (Quaker) | 1 Cup | 48 |
| With Raisins & Spice (Quaker) | 3/4 Cup | 32 |
| Quick, Dry: | | |
| (H-O) | 1 Cup | 42 |
| (Ralston Oats) | 1 Oz. | 18 |
| Quick, Cooked: | | |
| (Albers) | 1 Cup | 26 |
| (Quaker) | 1 Cup | 28 |
| (Ralston Oats) | 1 Cup | 27 |
| Regular, Dry: | | |
| Old Fashioned (H-O) | 1 Cup | 42 |
| (Ralston Oats) | 5 Tbsps. | 18 |
| Regular, Cooked: | | |
| Old Fashioned (Albers) | 1 Cup | 26 |
| Old Fashioned (Quaker) | 1 Cup | 28 |
| (Ralston Oats) | 1 Cup | 27 |
| Oatmeal, Cooked | 1/2 Cup | 14 |
| Oatmeal Cookies | 1 Lg. | 15 |
| Oatmeal Crackers | 3 | 15 |
| Oats, Rolled Dry | 4 Ozs. | 17 |
| Oats, Rolled-Cooked Meal | 4 Ozs. | 11 |
| Oatmeal, Dry (Rolled Oats) | 4 Ozs. | 68 |
| Oatmeal (Infant), Dry, Precooked | 1 Oz. | 19 |
| Oat Cereal, Ready-To Eat | 1/2 Cup | 13 |
| Ocean Perch Dinner (Banquet) | Dinner | 49 |
| Oestrichler Lenchen Riesling, German Rhine Wine (Deinhard) | 3 Fl. Ozs. | 4 |
| OH Henry Candy | 1 Bar | 40 |
| Oil, Buttery Flavor (Wesson) | 1 T. | 0 |
| Oil, Cod Liver (A) | 1 Tbsp. | 0 |
| Oil, Corn | 1 Tbsp. | 0 |
| (Mazola) | 1 Tbsp. | 0 |
| Oil, Cotton Seed | 1 Tbsp. | 0 |
| Winterized (Kraft) | 1 Tbsp. | 0 |
| Oil, Hailbut Liver | 1 Tbsp. | 0 |
| Oil, Mazola | 1 Tbsp. | 0 |
| Oils, Palm, Red Unrefined | 1 Tbsp. | 0 |
| Oil, Peanut | 1 Tbsp. | 0 |
| (Planters) | 1 Tbsp. | 0 |
| Oil, Safflower (Kraft) | 1 Tbsp. | 0 |
| Oil, Safflower (Saff-O-Life) | 1 Tbsp. | 0 |
| Oil (Saffola) | 1 Tbsp. | 0 |
| Oil, Salad | 1 Tbsp. | 0 |
| Oil (Wesson) | 1 Tbsp. | 0 |
| Oil & Vinegar Dressing, 1/2 Oil, 1/2 Vinegar | 1 Tbsp. | 0 |
| Okra (B2-C) | 1 Cup | 10 |
| Okra (Canned), Cooked | 1/2 Cup | 5 |

| FOOD | AMT | CARB. GRAMS | FOOD | AMT | CARB. GRAMS |
|---|---|---|---|---|---|
| With Tomatoes (King Pharr) | 1 Cup | 10 | Frozen (Commodore) | 2 Ozs. | 8 |
| Okra Chowder | 1 Serv | 10 | Onions, Fried | 1 Lg. | 10 |
| OKs, Cereal (Kellogg's) | 1 Cup | 15 | Onions, Frozen: | | |
| Olafsson's Punch | 12 Ozs. | 24 | Chopped (Birds Eye) | 4 Ozs. | 10 |
| Old English Cheese Spread | 1 Oz. | 2 | Whole, Small (Birds Eye) | 3 Ozs. | 9 |
| Old Fashioned | 1 Serv | 5 | Onions, Green | 6 Sm. | 5 |
| Old Fashioned Cocktail | | | Onions, Pickled: | | |
| (Hiram Walker) | 3 Fl Ozs. | 3 | Cocktail (Crosse & Blackwell) | 1 Tbsp. | T |
| Old Fashioned Mix | | | Sweet Dutch (Smucker's) | 1 | 1 |
| (Bar-Tender's) | 1 Serv | 4 | Onions, Raw Chopped | 1 Tbsp. | 1 |
| Old Fashioned, Scotch | 1 Serv | 5 | Onions, Raw | 1 Lg. | 11 |
| Old Fashioned Sherry | 1 Serv. | 10 | Onions, Raw (Bermuda) | 1 Med | 10 |
| Olives | 6 Sm. | T | Onions, Raw (Mature) | 1 Tbsp. | 1 |
| Olives & Celery | 1 Serv | 2 | Onion Roll | 1 | 23 |
| Olives, Green | 4 Ozs. | 0 | Onions, Scalloped | 1/2 Cup | 15 |
| Olive & Nut Gelatin Salad | 1 Serv | 9 | Onion Soup (Clear) | 1 Cup | 4 |
| Olive Oil | 1 Tbsp. | 0 | Condensed (Campbell) | 8 Ozs. | 6 |
| Olive Pimento Cheese Spread | 1 Oz. | 2 | (Crosse & Blackwell) | 1 Can | 9 |
| Olive Pimento Spread | 1 Oz. | 2 | (Hormel) | 1 Can | 5 |
| Olives, Ripe Or Black | 10 Lg. | 1 | Onion Soup, Creamed | 4 Ozs. | 7 |
| By Size: | | | Onion Soup, French | 4 Ozs. | 5 |
| Select (Lindsay) | 1 | T | Onion Soup Mix: | | |
| Medium (Lindsay) | 1 | T | French (Croyden House) | 1 Tbsp. | 7 |
| Large (Lindsay) | 1 | T | (Golden Grain) | 1 Cup | 7 |
| Extra Large (Lindsay) | 1 | T | (Lipton) | 1 Pkg. | 22 |
| Mammoth (Lindsay) | 1 | T | (Wyler's) | 8 Fl. Ozs. | 7 |
| Giant (Lindsay) | 1 | T | Onions, Stewed | 1/2 Cup | 9 |
| Jumbo (Lindsay) | 1 | T | Oolong Tea, Plain | 1 Cup | 0 |
| Colossal (Lindsay) | 1 | T | Orange | 1 Med. | 17 |
| Supercolossal (Lindsay) | 1 | T | Orange Ambrosia | 1 Serv | 28 |
| Super Supreme (Lindsay) | 1 | T | Orange Blossom Cktl. | 1 Serv. | 8 |
| Oleomargarine | 1 Tbsp. | 0 | Orange Cake Mix: | | |
| Omelet (2 Eggs) | 1 Serv | 1 | (Betty Crocker) Sunkist | 1 Oz. | 23 |
| Omelet, Asparagus | 1 Serv. | 1 | Chiffon (Betty Crocker) | | |
| Omelet, Cheese | 1 Serv. | 1 | Sunkist | 1 Oz. | 23 |
| Omelet, Jelly | 1 Serv | 13 | (Duncan Hines) | 1 Pc. | 48 |
| Omelet, Mushroom | 1 Serv. | 2 | (Pillsbury) | 1 Oz. | 22 |
| Omelet, Onion | 1 Serv. | 1 | Orange Cooled | 1 Serv. | 20 |
| Omelet, Plain (1 Egg) | 1 Serv. | T | Orange Drink: | | |
| Omelet, Spanish | 1 Serv. | 8 | Canned (Hi-C) | 8 Fl. Ozs. | 29 |
| Omelet, Western | 1 Serv | 1 | Canned (Sealtest) | 8 Fl. Ozs. | 27 |
| Onions, Boiled | 1 Lg. | 11 | Mix (Wyler's) | 8 Fl. Ozs. | 21 |
| Onion Bouillon: | | | Orange Drops Candy | 1 | 4 |
| Cube (Herb-Ox) | 1 Cube | 1 | Oranges, Fresh | 1 Cup | 22 |
| Cube (Wyler's) | 1 Cube | 1 | Orange, Fresh | 1 Lg. | 26 |
| Instant (Herb-Ox) | 1 Pkt. | 1 | Oranges, Fresh | 1 Sm. | 11 |
| Onions, Creamed | 1/2 Cup | 14 | Oranges, Fresh | 1 Med. | 17 |
| Canned (Durkee) O & C | 1 Can | 36 | Sections (Kraft) | 4 Ozs. | 12 |
| Frozen (Birds Eye) | 3 Ozs. | 12 | Unpeeled (Sunkist) | 1 Orange | 24 |
| Onions, Dehydrated | 2 Tbsp. | 8 | Cut (Sunkist) | 1 Cup | 32 |
| Onions, French Fried | 1 Lg. | 10 | Orange-Grapefruit Sections, | | |
| (Durkee) O & C | 1 Cup | 22 | Frozen | 4 Ozs. | 52 |
| Frozen (Birds Eye) | 2 Ozs. | 17 | | | |

80

| FOOD | AMT. | CARB. GRAMS | FOOD | AMT | CARB. GRAMS |
|------|------|-------------|------|-----|-------------|
| Orange-Grapefruit Juice, Frozen | 6 Ozs. | 75 | Orange Sherbet | 1 Scp. | 29 |
| (Birds Eye) | 1 Cup | 25 | Orange Soda | 8 Ozs. | 28 |
| (7L) | 1 Cup | 26 | Orange Soft Drink. Sweetened: | | |
| Unsweetened (Minute Maid) | 1 Cup | 25 | (Canada Dry) | 8 Fl. Ozs. | 33 |
| Unsweetened (Snow Crop) | 1 Cup | 25 | (Clicquot Club) | 8 Fl. Ozs. | 33 |
| Orange-Grapefruit Salad With Dressing | 1 Serv | 9 | (Cott) | 8 Fl. Ozs. | 33 |
| Orange & Grapefruit Sections, Fresh | 1/2 Cup | 11 | (Dr. Brown's) | 8 Fl. Ozs. | 29 |
| Orange Ice | 1/2 Cup | 14 | (Dr. Pepper) | 8 Fl. Ozs. | 33 |
| (Sealtest) | 1 Pt. | 130 | Fanta | 8 Fl. Ozs. | 32 |
| Orange Juice, Calif. Valencia | 1 Cup | 26 | (Hires) | 8 Fl. Ozs. | 29 |
| (Sunkist) | 1 Cup | 26 | (Hoffman) | 8 Fl. Ozs. | 32 |
| Orange Juice (Canned), Unsweetened | 4 Ozs. | 13 | (Key Food) | 8 Fl. Ozs. | 29 |
| Chilled (Kraft) | 1 Cup | 22 | (Kirsch) | 8 Fl. Ozs. | 29 |
| (Sealtest) | 1 Cup | 29 | (Mission) | 8 Fl. Ozs. | 33 |
| (Stokely-Van Camp) | 1 Cup | 28 | (Nedick's) | 8 Fl. Ozs. | 22 |
| Orange Juice (Canned), Sweetened | 4 Ozs. | 16 | Orangette | 8 Fl. Ozs. | 32 |
| (Heinz) | 1 Can | 15 | (Shasta) | 8 Fl. Ozs. | 32 |
| (Stokely-Van Camp) | 1 Cup | 31 | (Waldbaum) | 8 Fl. Ozs. | 22 |
| (Treesweet) | 1 Cup | 31 | (Yoo-Hoo) | 8 Fl. Ozs. | 24 |
| Orange Juice, Conc. | 1/2 Cup | 40 | High Protein (Yoo-Hoo) | 8 Fl. Ozs. | 33 |
| Orange Juice, Conc. Diluted | 4 Ozs | 13 | (Yukon Club) | 8 Fl. Ozs. | 29 |
| Orange Juice, Conc., Frozen, Undiluted | 4 Ozs. | 52 | Low Calorie: | | |
| Orange Juice Dehydrated | 2 Ozs. | 50 | (Dr. Brown's) Slim-Ray | 8 Fl. Ozs. | 1 |
| Orange Juice, Florida, Early Season | 1 Cup | 23 | (Hoffman) | 8 Fl. Ozs. | 1 |
| Orange Juice, Florida, Late Season | 1 Cup | 26 | (No-Cal) | 8 Fl. Ozs. | 0 |
| Orange Juice Frozen | 6 Ozs. | 80 | (Shasta) | 8 Fl. Ozs. | T |
| (Birds Eye) | 1 Cup | 25 | Orange Sponge Cake | 1 Serv | 12 |
| Imitation (Birds Eye) | 1 Cup | 33 | Orangeade: | | |
| (Lake Hamilton) | 1 Cup | 26 | (Sealtest) Container | 1 Cup | 31 |
| (Minute Maid) | 1 Cup | 28 | Frozen, Sweetened: | | |
| (Seald-Sweet) | 1 Cup | 26 | (Minute Maid) | 1 Cup | 30 |
| (7L) | 1 Cup | 27 | (Snow Crop) | 1 Cup | 30 |
| (Snow Crop) | 1 Cup | 28 | Mix (General Foods) Twist | 1 Cup | 21 |
| Orange, Mandarine | 1 Med. | 10 | Mix (Salada) | 6 Fl. Ozs. | 19 |
| Orange, Marmalade | 1 Tbsp. | 14 | Orangeade, Burgundy | 1 Serv. | 12 |
| Orange Peel, Candied | 1 Oz. | 24 | Orangeade Juice | 1/2 Cup | 19 |
| (Liberty) | 1 Oz. | 22 | Oregano | 1/8 Tsp. | 0 |
| Orange-Pineapple Drink, Canned (Hi-C) | 6 Fl. Ozs. | 22 | Oreo Cream Sand. Cookie | 1 | 8 |
| Orange-Pineapple Pie (Tastykake) | 4-Oz. Pie | 56 | Orgeat Syrup (Julius Wile) | 1 Tbsp. | 13 |
| Orange Rennet Custard Mix: | | | Oriental Beef | 1 Serv. | 12 |
| Powder (Junket) | 1 Oz. | 27 | Orvieto Wine, Italian White: | | |
| Tablet (Junket) | 1 Tablet | T | (Antinori) | 3 Fl. Ozs. | 6 |
| Orange Sections | 1/2 Cup | 11 | (Antinori) Castello La Scala | 3 Fl. Ozs. | 6 |
| | | | Ovaltine, Skim Milk | 1 Cup | 22 |
| | | | Ovaltine, Whole Milk | 1 Cup | 22 |
| | | | Ovaltine, 1/2 Water, 1/2 Milk | 1 Cup | 18 |
| | | | Oxtails, Broiled | 1 Serv. | 0 |
| | | | Oxtail Soup Canned | 1 Cup | 0 |
| | | | (Crosse & Blackwell) | 1 Can | 15 |
| | | | Oyster Cocktail, Raw | 6 Med. | 6 |
| | | | Oyster Crackers | 1/2 Cup | 10 |
| | | | Oyster Plant | 1/2 Cup | 17 |

81

| FOOD | AMT. | CARB. GRAMS |
|---|---|---|
| Oyster, Fried Sandwich | 1 | 41 |
| Oyster Stew, Canned, Condensed (Campbell) | 4 Ozs. | 6 |
| Oyster Stew, Creamed | 1/2 Cup | 6 |
| Oyster Stew With Milk | 1 Cup | 21 |
| Oyster Stew, Skimmed Milk | 1 Cup | 12 |
| Oyster Stew, Frozen Condensed (Campbell) | 1 Can | 20 |
| | 4 Ozs. | 7 |
| Oysters, Baked | 1 Doz. | 8 |
| Oysters, Blue Point | 12 | 7 |
| Oysters, Cape Cod | 6 Med. | 5 |
| Oysters, Fried With Batter | 6 | 19 |
| Oysters On The Half Shell | 6 Med. | 6 |
| Oysters, Raw | 12 Med. | 8 |
| Oysters, Raw Blue Point | 1 Cup | 7 |
| Oysters, Rockefeller | 6 | 4 |
| Oysters, Scalloped | 6 | 6 |
| Pablum, Cereal | 2 Tbsp. | 4 |
| Pabst-ett Cheese | 1 Oz. | 2 |
| Pacific Herring | 1 Serv. | 0 |
| Packaged Candies | 2 Rolls | 60 |
| Pagan Pink Wine (Gallo) | 3 Fl. Ozs. | 6 |
| Paisano Wine (Gallo) | 3 Fl. Ozs. | 1 |
| Parkerhouse Roll | 1 Aver. | 15 |
| Palm, Red Unrefined Oil | 1 Tsp. | 0 |
| Pan Broiled Apricots | 1/2 Cup | 10 |
| Pancakes (With 2 Tbsp. Butter, 2 Tbsp. Syrup) | 3 | 30 |
| Pancake Batter (Perx) | 1 Pancake | 9 |
| Pancakes, Blueberry | 1 4-In. | 12 |
| Pancakes, Buckwheat | 1 4-In. | 21 |
| Pancakes, Choc. | 1 Serv. | 26 |
| Pancakes, French | 4 Ozs. | 7 |
| Pancakes, German | 1 4-In. | 11 |
| Pancakes (Griddle) | 1 4-In. | 11 |
| Pancake Mix, Wheat Flour (Mixture For 1 Cake) | | 7 |
| Pancakes, Wheat | 1 4-In. | 11 |
| Pancakes, Wheat (Enriched Flour) | 4 Ozs. | 86 |
| Pancake & Waffle Mix: | | |
| Blueberry (Pillsbury) | 1 Oz. | 20 |
| Buckwheat: | | |
| (Aunt Jemima) | 1 Oz. | 8 |
| Hungry Jack (Pillsbury) | 1 Oz. | 20 |
| Buttermilk: | | |
| (Aunt Jemima) | 1 Oz. | 9 |
| (Betty Crocker) | 1 Oz. | 21 |
| Complete (Betty Crocker) | 1 Oz. | 21 |
| (Duncan Hines) | 1 Oz. | 14 |
| Hungry Jack (Pillsbury) | 1 Oz. | 20 |
| Plain: | | |
| (Aunt Jemima) | 1 Oz. | 8 |

| FOOD | AMT. | CARB. GRAMS |
|---|---|---|
| (Aunt Jemima) Deluxe Easy Pour | 1 Oz. | 11 |
| (Albers) | 1 Cup | 99 |
| (Golden Mix) | 1 Cup | 80 |
| Hungry Jack (Pillsbury) | 1 Oz. | 20 |
| Hungry Jack, Extra Light (Pillsbury) | 1 Oz. | 20 |
| Sweet Cream (Pillsbury) | 1 Oz. | 20 |
| Pancake & Waffle Mix, Dietetic | | |
| Buttermilk (Tillie Lewis) | 1 Oz. | 18 |
| Plain (Tillie Lewis) | 1 Oz. | 18 |
| Pancake & Waffle Syrup: | | |
| Sweetened (Polaner) | 1 Tbsp. | 13 |
| Low Calorie: | | |
| (Dia-Mel) | 1 Tbsp. | 5 |
| (Diet Delight) | 1 Tbsp. | 1 |
| (Tillie Lewis) | 1 Tbsp. | 3 |
| Papaya Juice | 1 Cup | 30 |
| Papaya Juice Ade | 1 Cup | 15 |
| Papaya Marmalade | 1 Tbsp. | 15 |
| Parfait, Coffee | 1 Av. | 14 |
| Parfait, Maple | 1 Av. | 14 |
| Parfait, Peach | 1 Av. | 14 |
| Parisian Eggs | 1 Serv. | 5 |
| Parmesan Cheese | 1 Tsp. | T |
| Parmesan Cheese, Dry Grated | 4 Ozs. | 2 |
| Parmesan Cheese, Grated | 1 Tbsp. | T |
| Parmesan Cheese, Fresh Grated | 4 Ozs. | 2 |
| Parsley | 1 Tbsp. | T |
| Parsnips, Cooked (B1) | 1 Lg. | 16 |
| Parsnips, Raw | 4 Ozs. | 17 |
| Party Fruit, Soft Drink (Kirsch) | 6 Fl. Ozs. | 22 |
| Party Herring Mold | 1 Serv. | 4 |
| Party Punch, Undiluted (Mogen David) | 3 Fl. Ozs. | 21 |
| Party Sliced Rye Bread | 1 Sl. | 8 |
| Pasha Turkish Coffee, Turkish Liqueur (Leroux) | 1 Fl. Oz. | 13 |
| Passion Fruit Grandilla | 4 Ozs. | 35 |
| Passion Fruit Juice | 1/2 Cup | 18 |
| Paste, Anchovy | 1 Tbsp. | 1 |
| Paste, Crab | 1 Tsp. | T |
| Paste, Liver | 1 Tbsp. | T |
| Paste, Lobster | 1 Tsp. | 0 |
| Pastrami | 4 Ozs. | 0 |
| (Vienna) | 1 Oz. | T |
| Pastrami Sand. | 1 | 24 |
| Pastry, Cream Puff | 1 Av. | 16 |
| Pastry, Danish | 1 Pc. | 25 |
| Pastry, Eclair Choc. Cream | 1 Av. | 15 |
| Pastry, Eclair Choc. Custard | 1 | 20 |

| FOOD | AMT. | CARB. GRAMS |
|---|---|---|
| Pastry, French | 1 Med. | 40 |
| Pastry, Petite Fours | 1 | 25 |
| Pastry Shell: | | |
| Frozen (Pepperidge Farm) | 1 Shell | 15 |
| (Stella D'oro) | 1 Shell | 16 |
| Pot Pie (Keebler) | 4" Shell | 29 |
| Tart, Sweet (Keebler) | 3" Shell | 16 |
| Pate, Canned: | | |
| Liver (Hormel) | 1 Oz. | 1 |
| (Sell's) | 1 Oz. | 20 |
| Pate de Fois Gras | 1 Tbsp. | 1 |
| Pate Maison | 4 Ozs. | T |
| Patty Choc. Covered Peppermint | 1 Sm. | 7 |
| Peach Brandy | Shot | 7 |
| Peach Ice Cream | 1/2 Cup | 14 |
| Peach Ice Cream Soda | 10 Ozs. | 71 |
| Peach Jelly | 1 Tbsp. | 13 |
| Peach Liqueur: | | |
| (Bois) | 1 Fl. Oz. | 9 |
| (Hiram Walker) | 1 Fl. Oz. | 8 |
| (Leroux) | 1 Fl. Oz. | 9 |
| Peach Mousse | 1 Serv. | 17 |
| Peach Parfait | 1 Aver. | 14 |
| Peach Pie | 1 Pc. | 70 |
| (Tastykake) | 4 Ozs. | 52 |
| Frozen (Banquet) | 4 Ozs. | 36 |
| Frozen (Mrs. Smith's) | 1 Pc. | 21 |
| Peach Pie Filling: | | |
| (Lucky Leaf) | 4 Ozs. | 37 |
| Peach Preserve, Low Calorie: | | |
| (Dia-Mel) | 1 Oz. | 10 |
| (Kraft) | 1 Oz. | 11 |
| (Tillie Lewis) | 1 Oz. | 4 |
| Peach Short Cake | 1 Serv. | 41 |
| Peaches (Canned) | 2 Halves | 11 |
| Heavy Syrup: | | |
| Halves (Hunt's) | 4 Ozs. | 19 |
| Spiced (Hunt's) | 4 Ozs. | 28 |
| (Stokely-Van Camp) | 2 Halves | 23 |
| (White House) | 1 Cup | 51 |
| Peaches (Canned In Water) | 2 Halves | 4 |
| (Blue Boy) Sliced | 4 Ozs. | 7 |
| (Diet Delight): | | |
| Cling, Halves | 1 Cup | 12 |
| Cling, Slices | 1 Cup | 12 |
| Freestone, Halves | 1 Cup | 11 |
| Freestone, Slices | 1 Cup | 11 |
| (Libby's) | 4 Ozs. | 9 |
| (Naturmade) | 4 Ozs. | 8 |
| (S and W) Nutradiet, Cling: | | |
| Halves, Unsweetened | 2 Halves | 5 |
| Slices, Unsweetened | 4 Ozs. | 5 |
| (Yes Madame) Elberta, Halves & Slices | 4 Ozs. | 8 |
| Peaches (Canned), Strained | 1 Oz. | 5 |
| Peach Crisps (Epicure) | 1 Oz. | 22 |
| Peaches, Dried | 1/2 Cup | 55 |
| Slices (Vacu-Dry) | 1 Oz. | 24 |
| Peaches, Dried, Cooked, Sweetened | 1 Cup | 95 |
| Peaches, Dried, Cooked, Unsweetened | 1 Cup | 58 |
| Peaches, Dried Sulphured With Sugar | 4 Ozs. | 21 |
| Peaches, Fresh | 1 Cup | 18 |
| Peaches, Fresh (A) | 1 Med. | 11 |
| (Kraft) | 4 Ozs. | 17 |
| Peaches, Frozen | 12 Ozs. | 69 |
| Quick Thaw (Birds Eye) | 1 Cup | 44 |
| (Spiegl) | 1 Cup | 44 |
| With Whole Strawberries, Quick Thaw (Birds Eye) | 1 Cup | 40 |
| Peaches, Spiced | 2 Halves | 28 |
| Peanut & Banana Salad | 1 Serv. | 34 |
| Peanut Bar Candy | 2 Ozs. | 17 |
| Peanut Brittle | 1 Pc. Sm. | 10 |
| Peanut Butter: | | |
| (The Peanut Kids) | 1 Tbsp. | 5 |
| (Peter Pan) | 1 Tbsp. | 4 |
| (Planters) | 1 Tbsp. | 4 |
| (Skippy) | 1 Tbsp. | 2 |
| Diet Spread (Peter Pan) | 1 Tbsp. | 2 |
| Peanut Butter Sand. | 1 | 29 |
| Peanut Butter & Jelly Sandwich | 1 | 35 |
| Peanut Butter Spread | 1 Tbsp. | 3 |
| Peanut Cookie | 1 | 9 |
| Peanut Oil | 1 Tbsp. | 0 |
| Peanuts (B1-B2) | 10 | 3 |
| Peanuts | 1 Cup | 34 |
| Roasted: | | |
| Dry (Franklin) | 1 Oz. | 5 |
| Dry (Frito-Lay) | 1 Oz. | 2 |
| Dry (Planters) | 1 Oz. | 5 |
| Dry (Planters) Peanut Crisps | 1 Oz. | 6 |
| Dry (Skippy) | 1 Oz. | 6 |
| Oil (Planters) Cocktail | Bag | 3 |
| Oil (Planters) Cocktail | 1 Oz. | 5 |
| Oil (Skippy) | 1 Oz. | 3 |
| (Nab) | 1 Oz. | 6 |
| Spanish, Dry (Planters) | 1 Oz. | 3 |
| Spanish, Oil (Planters) | 1 Oz. | 3 |
| Pear, Alligator (A-C) | 1/2 Sm. | 3 |
| Pear Cheese | 1-1/2 Ozs. | T |
| Pear Juice Nectar | 4 Ozs. | 12 |
| Pearled Barley, Light, Dry | 1/2 Cup | 80 |

| FOOD | AMT. | CARB. GRAMS | FOOD | AMT. | CARB. GRAMS |
|---|---|---|---|---|---|
| Pear, Prickley | 1 Med. | 12 | Pea Soup, Split | 1 Cup | 17 |
| Pear & Roquefort Cheese | | | With Ham, Condensed | | |
| Salad | 1 Serv. | 8 | (Campbell) | 4 Ozs. | 21 |
| Pears, Canned (2 Halves | | | (Manischewitz) | 4 Ozs. | 11 |
| With 2 Tbsp. Syrup) | | 17 | With Ham (Heinz) | 1 Cup | 21 |
| Pears, Canned (Water-Pack) | 1 Cup | 20 | With Smoked Ham (Heinz) | | |
| Pears (Canned), Low Calorie | 1 Cup | 14 | Great American | 1 Cup | 21 |
| Pears (Canned), Strained | 1 Oz. | 4 | Canned, Dietetic: | | |
| Pears (Canned), Water Pack | 4 Ozs. | 20 | Condensed (Claybourne) | 1 Cup | 19 |
| Pears (Canned), Cooked | 2 Halves | 12 | (Tillie Lewis) | 1 Cup | 26 |
| Unsweetened: | | | Pea With Sauteed Mushrooms | | |
| (Blue Boy) Bartlett | 4 Ozs. | 9 | Frozen (Birds Eye) | 1 Cup | 23 |
| (Diet Delight) | 1 Cup | 15 | Peas, Black-Eyed (Canned), | | |
| (Libby's) Halves | 4 Ozs. | 9 | Drained | 1/2 Cup | 17 |
| (S and W) Nutradiet, | | | Peas (Canned), Cooked | | |
| Quartered | 4 Ozs. | 7 | (A-B1-C) | 1 Cup | 19 |
| (Yes Madame) Bartlett, | | | Peas (Canned), Strained | 1 Oz. | 2 |
| Halves | 1 Cup | 17 | Peas, Chick (Garbanzos Dry) | 1/2 Cup | 60 |
| Heavy Syrup: | | | Peas, Chick, Dry | 1/2 Cup | 64 |
| (Hunt's) Bartlett | 4 Ozs. | 13 | Peas, Cow, Boiled, Drained | 4 Ozs. | 13 |
| (Stokely-Van Camp) | 2 Halves | 23 | Peas, Cow (Blackeyed Dry) | 1/2 Cup | 22 |
| Pears, Dried | 1/2 | 12 | Peas, Cow (Dry, Raw) | 1/2 Cup | 14 |
| Pears, Fresh | 1 Med. | 18 | Peas, Dried, Cooked | 1/2 Cup | 18 |
| Pears, Fresh (Quartered) | 1 Cup | 32 | Peas, Edible Pods | 15 | 6 |
| Pears, Spiced | 2 Halves | 26 | Peas, Fresh In Pod | 1 Lb. | 36 |
| Pears, Spiced With Syrup | 1/2 Cup | 25 | Peas, Fresh, Cooked | 1 Cup | 19 |
| Pea Beans, Dried, Cooked | 4 Ozs. | 18 | Peas, Fresh (Garden) | 1/2 Cup | 10 |
| Pea & Carrot: | | | Peas, Fresh, Sugar | 3-1/2 Ozs. | 15 |
| Canned: | | | Peas, Frozen | 1/2 Cup | 11 |
| (Blue Boy) | 4 Ozs. | 5 | Peas, Glazed With Carrots | 1 Serv. | 12 |
| (Diet Delight) | 1 Cup | 13 | Peas, Green (Canned) | 4 Ozs. | 14 |
| (S and W) Nutradiet | 4 Ozs. | 6 | Alaska (Butter Kernel) | 1 Cup | 25 |
| Frozen: | | | Alaska or Early | | |
| (Birds Eye) | 1 Cup | 21 | (Stokely-Van Camp) | 1 Cup | 31 |
| (Blue Goose) | 4 Ozs. | 10 | Early June (Cannon) | 4 Ozs. | 19 |
| Pea & Celery, Frozen | | | Early June (Fall River) | 1 Cup | 25 |
| (Birds Eye) | 1 Cup | 21 | Sweet (Butter Kernel) | 1 Cup | 20 |
| Pea & Onion, Frozen | | | Sweet (Cannon) | 4 Ozs. | 17 |
| (Birds Eye) | 1 Cup | 25 | Sweet (Fall River) | 1 Cup | 20 |
| Pea & Potato, With Cream Sauce | | | (Green Giant) | 1 Cup | 25 |
| Frozen (Birds Eye) | 1 Cup | 28 | (King Pharr) | 1 Cup | 34 |
| Pea Soup | 1 Cup | 16 | Dietetic: | | |
| Pea Soup, Condensed | 4 Ozs. | 20 | (Blue Boy) | 4 Ozs. | 7 |
| Pea Soup, Creamed | 1 Cup | 23 | (Diet Delight) | 1 Cup | 15 |
| Pea Soup, Dehydrated | 4 Ozs | 64 | (S and W) Nutradiet | 4 Ozs. | 7 |
| Pea Soup, Green: | | | (Tillie Lewis) | 1 Cup | 17 |
| Canned (Campbell) | 4 Ozs. | 12 | Peas, Green (Canned, Infant) | 1 Oz. | 2 |
| Condensed (Campbell) | 4 Ozs. | 21 | Peas, Green, Dried | 1/2 Cup | 18 |
| Dry Mix (Golden Grain) | 1 Cup | 14 | Peas, Green, Frozen: | | |
| Dry Mix (Lipton) | 4 Ozs | 67 | (Blue Goose) | 4 Ozs. | 12 |
| Frozen With Ham (Campbell) | 4 Ozs. | 16 | (Stokely-Van Camp) | 4 Ozs. | 14 |

84

| FOOD | AMT. | CARB. GRAMS | FOOD | AMT. | CARB. GRAMS |
|------|------|------|------|------|------|
| Sweet or Tender Tiny | | | Perch, Lake, White, Raw | 1 Serv. | 0 |
| (Birds Eye) | 1 Cup | 24 | Perch, Lake, Yellow, Raw | 1 Serv. | 0 |
| In Butter Sauce: | | | Pernod (Julius Wile) | 1 Fl. Oz. | 1 |
| (Birds Eye) | 1 Cup | 21 | Persian Melons | 1/8 Av. | 15 |
| Baby Peas (Green Giant) | 4 Ozs. | 12 | Persian Walnuts | 4 Ozs. | 8 |
| Sweet (Green Giant) | 4 Ozs. | 13 | Persimmons | 1 Med. | 24 |
| With Cream Sauce: | | | Persimmons, Seeded Type | 1 Med. | 20 |
| (Birds Eye) | 1 Cup | 26 | Petite Fours | 1 | 25 |
| (Green Giant) Boil-in-the-Bag | 4 Ozs. | 10 | Petite Marmite Soup, Canned | | |
| Peas, Mature Seed (Sinsheimer) | 1 Oz. | 17 | (Crosse & Blackwell) | 1 Can | 7 |
| Peas, Pigeonpeas, Mature | 1/2 Cup | 19 | Pettijohns (Quaker) Rolled | | |
| Pecan Buns | 1 | 37 | Whole Wheat, Cooked | 1 Cup | 32 |
| Pecan Pie | 1 Pc. | 58 | Pheasant, Roasted | 1 Serv. | 0 |
| Frozen (Mrs. Smith's) | 1 Pc. | 26 | Philadelphia Pepper Pot Soup | 1 Serv. | 15 |
| Pecans | 3 | 1 | Philadelphia Scrapple | 1 Serv. | 26 |
| Shelled, Dry Roasted | | | Picalilli | 1 Tbsp. | 2 |
| (Planters) | 1 Oz. | 3 | Picalilli Beets | 1 Serv. | 12 |
| Pecans (Halves) | 1 Cup | 14 | Pickerel | 1 Serv. | 0 |
| Pecans, Chopped | 1 Tbsp. | 1 | Pickle Relish, Mustard | 1 Tbsp. | 4 |
| Pectin, Homemade Apple | 1 Lb. | 54 | Pickled Beets | 1/2 Cup | 10 |
| Peking Cocktail | 1 Gl. | 2 | Pickled Cucumber | 6 Sls. | 1 |
| Penny Candy | 2 Ozs. | 28 | Pickled Herring | 1 Serv | 0 |
| Pep Cereal | 1 Cup | 23 | Pickled Pigs Feet | 4 Ozs. | T |
| Pepper | 1/8 Tsp. | T | Pickled Tripe | 4 Ozs. | 0 |
| Pepper, Black: | | | Pickles, Bread & Butter | 4 Sls. | 5 |
| (Lawry's) Seasoned | 1 Tsp. | 1 | Pickles, Chow-Chow | 4 Pcs. | 1 |
| Pepper, Cayenne | 1/8 Tsp. | 0 | Pickles, Chow-Chow, Sour | 2 Ozs. | 2 |
| Peppermint Candy Choc. | | | Pickles, Chow-Chow (Sweet) | 2 Ozs. | 13 |
| Covered | 1 Oz. | 21 | Pickles, Cucumber | | |
| Peppermint Ice Cream | 1 Scp. | 14 | (Bread & Butter) | 4 Sls. | 5 |
| Peppermint Patties | 1 Sm. | 14 | (Heinz) | 1 Sl. | 1 |
| Peppermint Patty Choc. | | | Pickles, Dill or Sour | 1 Lg. | 3 |
| Covered | 1 Sm. | 7 | Dill: | | |
| Peppermint Stick Candies | 1 Oz. | 26 | (Albro) | 2 Ozs. | 1 |
| Peppermint Taffy | 1 Sm. | 10 | (Heinz) | 1 Pickle | 2 |
| Pepper Pot Soup | 1 Cup | 15 | Processed (Heinz) | 1 Pickle | T |
| Condensed (Campbell) | 8 Ozs. | 17 | (Smucker's) | 1 Oz. | 1 |
| Pepper Steak | 1 Serv. | 5 | Candied Sticks (Smucker's) | 1 Pickle | 9 |
| Pepper Steak (Chinese) | 1 Serv | T | Hamburger (Heinz) | 3 Sls. | T |
| Peppers, Green-Bell | 1 Med. | 3 | Hamburger (Smucker's) | 1 Oz. | 1 |
| Peppers Green Cooked | 1 Lg. | 5 | Kosher Dill (Smucker's) | 1 Oz. | 1 |
| Peppers, Green, Fresh | 1 Lg. | 5 | Sour: | | |
| Peppers, Red, Fresh | 1 Med. | 5 | (Albro) | 2 Ozs. | 1 |
| Peppers, Red Hot, Dried | 1 Tbsp. | 9 | (Heinz) | 1 Pickle | 1 |
| Peppers, Stuffed | 1 | 11 | Pickles, Sweet | 1 Sm. | 5 |
| (Holloway House) | 7 Ozs. | 58 | (Albro) | 1 Oz. | 6 |
| Pepsi-Cola | 8 Ozs. | 27 | (Smucker's) | 1 Pickle | 6 |
| Perch | 1 Serv. | 0 | Candied, Midgets | 1 Pickle | 2 |
| Perch, Fried | 3 Ozs. | 6 | Chips, Fresh Pack | 1 Pickle | 2 |
| Perch, Sea | 1 Serv. | 0 | Gherkin (Heinz) | 1 Pickle | 7 |
| Perch, Lake, Raw | 1 Serv. | 0 | Mixed (Heinz) | 3 Sls. | 5 |

| FOOD | AMT. | CARB. GRAMS | FOOD | AMT. | CARB. GRAMS |
|---|---|---|---|---|---|
| Mixed (Smucker's) | 1 Pickle | 6 | Pie, Mince | 1 Pc. | 52 |
| Mustard (Heinz) | 1 T. | 7 | Pie, Nesselrode | 1 Pc. | 47 |
| Sticks, Fresh Pack | | | Pie, Peach | 1 Pc. | 70 |
| (Smucker's) | 1 Pickle | 4 | Pie, Peach Cream | 1 Pc. | 55 |
| Pickles, Sweet Mixed | 2 Med. | 5 | Pie, Pineapple | 1 Pc. | 53 |
| Pie, Apple | 1 Pc. | 42 | Pie, Pineapple Cheese | 1 Pc. | 57 |
| Pie, Apple, Deep Dish | 1 Serv. | 44 | Pie, Pineapple Cream | 1 Pc. | 57 |
| Pie, Apricot | 1 Pc. | 31 | Pie, Pumpkin | 1 Pc. | 34 |
| Pie, Apricot-Prune | 1 Serv. | 31 | Pie, Raisin | 1 Pc. | 65 |
| Pie, Banana Cream | 1 Serv. | 56 | Pie, Rhubarb | 1 Pc. | 78 |
| Pie, Beef | 1 Serv. | 32 | Pie (On Stick), Ice Cream | 1 | 13 |
| Pie, Berry | 1 Pc. | 57 | Pie, Prune With Whipped Cream | 1 Pc. | 54 |
| Pie, Blackberry | 1 Pc. | 38 | Pie, Pizza With Cheese | 1 Pc. | 25 |
| Pie, Blueberry | 1 Pc. | 38 | Pie, Shoofly | 1 Pc. | 48 |
| Pie, Blueberry Cream | 1 Pc. | 55 | Piesporter Reisling, German | | |
| Pie, Boston Cream | 1 Pc. | 55 | Moselle Wine | | |
| Pie, Boysenberry | 1 Pc. | 0 | (Julius Kayser) | 3 Fl. Ozs. | 1 |
| Pie, Butterscotch | 1 Pc. | 57 | Pie, Strawberry | 1 Pc. | 56 |
| Pie, Cheese | 1 Pc. | 57 | Pie, Strawberry Cream | 1 Pc. | 55 |
| Pie, Cherry | 1 Pc. | 55 | Pie, Sweet Potato | 1 Pc. | 52 |
| Pie, Cherry Chiffon | 1 Pc. | 46 | Pie, Youngberry | 1 Pc. | 2 |
| Pie, Chocolate Chiffon | | | Pig Brains, Raw | 1 Serv. | 2 |
| With Whipped Cream | 1 Pc. | 33 | Pig Liver | 1 Serv. | 2 |
| Pie, Chocolate Chip | 1 Pc. | 30 | Pigeonpeas, Mature | 1/2 Cup | 13 |
| Pie, Chocolate Cream | 1 Pc. | 47 | Pignolias | 1/2 Cup | 6 |
| Pie, Chocolate Meringue | 1 Pc. | 32 | Pig's Feet, Boiled | 4 Ozs. | 0 |
| Pie, Chiffon Chocolate | | | Pig's Feet, Pickled | 4 Ozs. | T |
| With Whipped Cream | 1 Pc. | 33 | (Hormel) | 1 Can | T |
| Pie, Clam | 1 Serv. | 12 | Pigweed Or Lambsquarter | 1/2 Cup | 8 |
| Pie, Coconut Cream | 1 Pc. | 50 | Pikaki Cocktail | 1 Serv. | 12 |
| Pie, Coconut Custard | 1 Pc. | 50 | Pike | 1 Serv. | 0 |
| Pie, Cream | 1 Pc. | 42 | Pillsbury Instant Breakfast: | | |
| Pie Crust (Bottom) | Av. | 72 | Chocolate | 1 Oz. | 19 |
| Pie Crust (Double) | Av. | 142 | Chocolate Malt | 1 Oz. | 19 |
| Pie Crust, Graham Cracker | | | Strawberry | 1 Oz. | 19 |
| (Bottom) | Av. | 64 | Vanilla | 1 Oz. | 18 |
| Pie, Custard | 1 Pc. | 23 | Pimentoes (A) | 1 Av. | 6 |
| Pie, Custard Cream | 1 Pc. | 55 | Canned (Cannon) | 4 Ozs. | 6 |
| Pie, Deep Dish Apple | 1 Serv. | 44 | Pieces, Pods, Slices | | |
| Pie, Deep Dish Blueberry | 1 Serv. | 44 | (Dromedary) | 4 Ozs. | 4 |
| Pie, Deep Dish Huckleberry | 1 Serv. | 44 | Pimento Cheese | 1-1/2 Ozs. | 0 |
| Pie, Deep Dish Peach | 1 Serv. | 44 | Pimento Cheese Spread | 1 Oz. | 2 |
| Pie, Elderberry | 1 Pc. | 57 | Pimento, Hot | 1 Av. | 6 |
| Pie, Gooseberry | 1 Pc. | 57 | Pimm's Cup (Julius Wile): | | |
| Pie, Huckleberry | 1 Pc. | 57 | #1-#3 | 1 Fl. Oz. | 3 |
| Pie, Huckleberry Cream | 1 Pc. | 55 | #4 | 1 Fl. Oz. | 1 |
| Pie, Kidney | 1 Serv. | 24 | #5 | 1 Fl. Oz. | 1 |
| Pie, Lemon Chiffon | 1 Pc. | 35 | #6 | 1 Fl. Oz. | 2 |
| Pie, Lemon Cream | 1 Pc. | 50 | Pineapple, Canned | 1 Sl. | 12 |
| Pie, Lemon Meringue | 1 Pc. | 45 | Diced (Calavo) | 1 Cup | 19 |
| Pie, Lime Chiffon | 1 Pc. | 34 | Crushed (Stokely-Van Camp) | 1 Cup | 50 |
| Pie, Loganberry | 1 Pc. | 57 | Slices (Stokely-Van Camp) | 2 Sls. | 24 |

| FOOD | AMT. | CARB. GRAMS |
|---|---|---|
| Pineapple, Candied | 1 Sl. | 30 |
| (Liberty) | 1 Oz. | 22 |
| Pineapple Canned | | |
| Low Calorie | 1/2 Cup | 11 |
| Chunks (Diet Delight) | 1 Cup | 22 |
| Crushed (Diet Delight) | 1 Cup | 26 |
| Slices: | | |
| (Diet Delight) | 1 Cup | 17 |
| (Libby's) | 4 Ozs. | 11 |
| (S and W) Nutradiet | 2 Sls. | 11 |
| (White Rose) | 4 Ozs. | 16 |
| Tidbits (S and W) | | |
| Nutradiet | 4 Ozs. | 19 |
| Pineapple Cake Mix: | | |
| (Betty Crocker) Dole | 1 Oz. | 23 |
| Chiffon (Betty Crocker) | | |
| Dole | 1 Oz. | 22 |
| Upside Down (Betty Crocker) | | |
| Dole | 1 Oz. | 19 |
| (Duncan Hines) | 1 Pc. | 36 |
| (Pillsbury) | 1 Oz. | 22 |
| Pineapple Crisps (Epicure) | 1 Oz. | 22 |
| Pineapple Cheesecake | 1 Pc. | 34 |
| Pineapple Cheese Pie | 1 Pc. | 57 |
| Pineapple Cream Pie | 1 Pc. | 57 |
| Pineapple Crushed (Canned) | 1/2 Cup | 15 |
| Pineapple Fluff | 1 Serv. | 7 |
| Pineapple, Fresh | 1 Cup | 16 |
| Pineapple, Fresh Sliced | 2 | 23 |
| Pineapple Frosting | 1 Tbsp. | 6 |
| Pineapple, Frozen | 1/2 Cup | 26 |
| Pineapple & Grapefruit Drink, | | |
| Canned (Hi-C) | 1/2 Cup | 16 |
| Pineapple Ice Cream | 1 Scp. | 14 |
| Pineapple Ice Cream Soda | 1 Av. | 50 |
| Pineapple Ice Cream Sundae | 1 Av. | 39 |
| Pineapple Ices | 1 Scp. | 27 |
| Pineapple Juice | 1 Cup | 30 |
| Canned, Unsweetened: | | |
| (Heinz) | 1 Can | 20 |
| (S and W) Nutradiet | 4 Ozs. | 16 |
| (Stokely-Van Camp) | 1 Cup | 34 |
| Pineapple Juice Ade | 4 Ozs. | 18 |
| Pineapple Juice, Frozen, | | |
| Sweetened | 1 Cup | 31 |
| Pineapple & Orange Juice | | |
| (Kraft) | 1 Cup | 25 |
| Pineapple Pie: | | |
| (Tastykake) | 4 Ozs. | 58 |
| With Cheese (Tastykake) | 4 Ozs. | 59 |
| Frozen (Banquet) | 4 Ozs. | 44 |
| Frozen (Mrs. Smith's) | 1 Pc. | 22 |
| Pineapple Pie Filling | | |
| (Lucky Leaf) | 4 Ozs. | 29 |
| Pineapple Preserve, Low Calorie: | | |
| (Dia-Mel) | 1 Tbsp. | 5 |
| (Tillie Lewis) | 1 Tbsp. | 2 |
| Pineapple Sherbet | 1 Scp. | 29 |
| Pineapple Snow | 1 Serv. | 4 |
| Pineapple Soft Drink: | | |
| (Hires) | 8 Fl. Ozs. | 30 |
| (Kirsch) | 8 Fl. Ozs. | 29 |
| (Nedick's) | 8 Fl. Ozs. | 30 |
| (Yoo-Hoo) | 8 Fl. Ozs. | 24 |
| High-Protein (Yoo-Hoo) | 8 Fl. Ozs. | 32 |
| Pineapple Sundae, Fancy | 2 Scps. | 45 |
| Pineapple Upside Down Cake | 1 Serv. | 38 |
| Pine Nuts | 1 Tsp. | 1 |
| Pink Lady | 1 Serv. | T |
| Pino Frio Beverage | 14 Ozs. | 4 |
| Pinot Chardonnay Wine | | |
| (Louis M. Martini) | 3 Fl. Ozs. | T |
| Pinot Noir Wine | | |
| (Louis M. Martini) | 3 Fl. Ozs. | T |
| Pinto Beans, Dry | 1/2 Cup | 63 |
| Pinto Bean Soup | 8 Ozs. | 17 |
| Pike, Northern, Raw | 1 Serv. | 0 |
| Pike, Wall Eyed | 1 Serv. | 0 |
| Piquant Pot Roast | 1 Serv. | 1 |
| Piquant Pollack | 1 Serv. | 2 |
| Pistachio Ice Cream | 1 Scp. | 17 |
| Pistachio Nuts | 16 | 2 |
| Pistachio Nuts, Chopped | 1 Tbsp. | 1 |
| Pistachio Nuts, Shelled | 1 Cup | 24 |
| Pistachio Nut Pudding, | | |
| Instant (Royal) | 1 Cup | 61 |
| Pistachio Pop Ice Cream | 1 Serv. | 17 |
| Pitanga | 4 Ozs. | 14 |
| Pitted Date Candies | 1 | 6 |
| Pizza | 4 Ozs. | 29 |
| Frozen: | | |
| Instant (Buitoni) | 1 Pc. | 21 |
| Little, With Cheese | | |
| (Chef Boy-Ar-Dee) | 2 Ozs. | 18 |
| With Cheese | | |
| (Chef Boy-Ar-Dee) | 2 Ozs. | 18 |
| With Pepperoni | | |
| (Chef Boy-Ar-Dee) | 2 Ozs. | 17 |
| Little, With Sausage | | |
| (Chef Boy-Ar-Dee) | 2 Ozs. | 18 |
| With Sausage | | |
| (Chef Boy-Ar-Dee) | 2 Ozs. | 18 |
| Pizza, Anchovy With Cheese | 1 Pc. | 23 |
| Pizza, Mushroom | 1 Pc. | 23 |

| FOOD | AMT. | CARB. GRAMS | FOOD | AMT. | CARB. GRAMS |
|---|---|---|---|---|---|
| Pizza Pie Mix: | | | Polish Sausage | 4 Ozs. | 1 |
| With Cheese | | | (Wilson) | 4 Ozs. | 1 |
| (Chef Boy-Ar-Dee) | 3 Ozs. | 26 | Pollack, Broiled | 1 Serv. | 0 |
| With Cheese (Kraft) | 4 Ozs. | 26 | Pomegranate | 1 Aver. | 24 |
| With Sausage | | | Pomegranate Juice | 1 Cup | 18 |
| (Chef Boy-Ar-Dee) | 4 Ozs. | 26 | Pomegranate Juice | 4 Ozs. | 9 |
| Pizza Pie With Cheese | 1 Pc. | 25 | Pommard Wine, French Red Burgundy: | | |
| Pizza, Sausage | 1 Pc. | 23 | (Barton & Guestier) | 3 Fl. Ozs. | T |
| Pizza Sauce, Canned: | | | (Chanson) St. Vincent | 3 Fl. Ozs. | 6 |
| (Buitoni) | 1 Cup | 21 | Pompano | 1 Serv. | 0 |
| (Chef Boy-Ar-Dee) | 1 Can | 14 | Pondo Punch | 14 Ozs. | 11 |
| (Contadina) | 1 Cup | 21 | Popcorn Balls with Syrup | 1 Av. | 13 |
| Pizza, Shrimp | 1 Pc. | 23 | Popcorn, Caramel-Coated: | | |
| Pizza, Tomato | 1 Pc. | 23 | Peanut (Wise) | 1 Cup | 27 |
| Plain Cake | 1 Pc. | 23 | Pixies With Peanuts (Wise) | 1 Oz. | 23 |
| Plain Cookie | 1 | 7 | (Old London) | 1 Oz. | 22 |
| Plain Cup Cake | 1 | 33 | (Wise) | 1 Cup | 29 |
| Plain Delicious Broccoli | 1 Serv. | 6 | Popcorn, Cheese-Flavored: | | |
| Plain Milk Choc. | 1 Oz. | 16 | (Old London) | 1 Oz. | 22 |
| Plain Omelet | 1 Egg | T | (Wise) | 1 Cup | 5 |
| Plain Short Cake | 1 Serv. | 31 | Popcorn Crackerjack | 1 Box | 48 |
| Plantain | 1 | 44 | Regular-Size Pack | 1 Cup | 32 |
| Plantation Cocktail | 1 Gl. | 5 | Pass Around Pack | 1 Cup | 32 |
| Plate, Beef | 4 Sls. | 0 | Popcorn, Fiddle Faddle | | |
| Planter's Punch | 1 | 10 | (Ovaltine) | 1 Oz. | 23 |
| Planter's Punch | | | Popcorn, No Butter | 1 Cup | 11 |
| (Sloppy Joe's) | 1 Av. Gl. | 3 | (Jiffy Pop) | 1 Pkg. | 59 |
| Planter's Punch | | | Popcorn With 1 Tbsp. Butter | 1 Cup | 11 |
| (Trader Vic's) | 12 Ozs. | 6 | Buttered (Wise) | 1 Cup | 6 |
| Planter's Punch (Trinidad) | 12 Ozs. | 3 | Butter Flavor (Jiffy Pop) | 1 Pkg. | 58 |
| Plums (Canned), With 2 Tbsp. | | | Popcorn, Sugar Coated | 1 Box | 48 |
| Syrup | 6 Halves | 25 | Pop Ice | 4 Ozs. | 24 |
| Plums (Canned) | 2 Med. | 18 | Pop, Ice Cream | 1 | 13 |
| Plums (Canned), | | | Popovers | 1 Av. | 11 |
| Low Calorie | 1/2 Cup | 10 | Popover Mix (Flako) | 2 Ozs. | 20 |
| (Diet Delight) | 1 Cup | 25 | Popsicle (Popsicle Industries) | | |
| Whole (Yes Madame) | 1 Cup | 25 | Non-Chocolate Flavors | 3 Fl. Ozs. | 17 |
| Plums, Fresh | 1 Med. | 7 | Poppyseeds | 1/8 Tsp. | T |
| Plum Jam | 1 Tbsp. | 14 | Porgy | 1 Serv. | 0 |
| Plum Pie (Tastykake) | 4 Ozs. | 54 | Pork, Boston Butt, Cured | 4 Ozs. | 0 |
| Plum Preserve, Damson, | | | Pork, Canned, Chopped | | |
| Low Calorie (Polaner) | 1 Tbsp. | T | (Hormel) | 1 Oz. | T |
| Plum Pudding | 1 Serv. | 41 | Pork, Canned (Infant) | 4 Ozs. | 0 |
| (Crosse & Blackwell) | 4 Ozs. | 62 | Pork (Canned), Spiced | 4 Ozs. | 0 |
| Plum Pudding Sauce | 1 Tbsp. | 5 | Pork Chops, Baked | 1 Med. | 0 |
| Poached Eggs & Chicken | | | Pork Chops, Broiled | 1 Med. | 0 |
| Livers | 1 Serv. | 2 | Pork Chops, Fried | 1 Med. | 0 |
| Poached Egg in Jelly | 1 Serv. | 17 | Pork Chops, Loin, Center Cut | 4 Ozs. | 0 |
| Poached Fish Fillets | 1 Serv. | 0 | Pork Chop Suey | 1/2 Cup | 4 |
| Poached Peaches | 1 Serv. | 10 | Pork, Cured Bacon | 4 Ozs. | 0 |
| Poached Turkey | 1 Serv. | 0 | Pork, Cured Ham | 4 Ozs. | 0 |
| Poha Hawaiian | 1 Cup | 11 | Parti-Style (Armour Star) | 3 Ozs. | T |
| Polish Borsch | 1 Serv. | 12 | (Wilson) | 3 Ozs. | 0 |

| FOOD | AMT. | CARB. GRAMS | FOOD | AMT. | CARB. GRAMS |
|---|---|---|---|---|---|
| Pork Cured Ham, Shank End | 4 Ozs. | 0 | (Taylor) | 3 Fl. Ozs. | 11 |
| Pork Dinner, Loin of Pork, | | | (Taylor) Tawny | 3 Fl. Ozs. | 10 |
| Frozen (Swanson) | Dinner | 40 | Port Wine Flip | 1 Serv. | 30 |
| Pork Egg Foo Yung | 1 Serv. | 1 | Port Wine Punch | 1 Serv. | 22 |
| Pork, Heart | 3 Ozs. | T | Post Toasties Cereal | 4 Ozs. | 12 |
| Pork, Picnic (Wilson) | 3 Ozs. | 0 | Postum (No Milk) | 1 Cup | 3 |
| Pork, Kidney | 1 Serv. | 2 | Pot Cheese | 1/2 Cup | 9 |
| Pork, Leg Roast | 4 Ozs. | 0 | Potato, American, Fried | 1 Med. Sl. | 7 |
| Pork Liver | 1 Serv. | 4 | Potato Au Gratin | 1 Serv. | 16 |
| Pork, Loin Of, Roasted | 1 Sl. | 0 | Potato, Baked (B1) | 1 Med. | 28 |
| Pork, Medium Fat | 4 Ozs. | 0 | Potato, Boiled | 1 Med. | 28 |
| Pork, Roast | 1 Serv. | 0 | Potato, Boiled, Peeled | 1 Med. | 23 |
| Pork, Salt | 4 Ozs. | 0 | Potato, Browned | 1 Med. | 28 |
| Pork Sausage | Two 3 Ins. | 0 | Potato & Cheese Casserole | 1 Serv. | 24 |
| Pork Sausage (Canned) | 4 Ozs. | 2 | Potato Chips | 1/2 Cup | 7 |
| Pork Sausage, Dried | 4 Ozs. | 0 | (Lay's) | 1 Oz. | 14 |
| Pork Sausage Patty | 1 Av. | 0 | (Nalley's) | 1 Oz. | 14 |
| Pork Sausage Sandwich | 1 | 24 | (Ruffles) | 1 Oz. | 14 |
| Pork Shoulder | 1 Serv. | 0 | (Wise) | 1 Oz. | 14 |
| Pork Sirloin | 1 Serv. | 0 | Barbecue Flavored (Wise) | 1 Oz. | 14 |
| Pork Spareribs | 4 Ozs. | 0 | Onion-Garlic Chips (Wise) | 1 Oz. | 14 |
| Pork, Sweet & Sour | | | Ridgies (Wise) | 1 Oz. | 14 |
| With 2 Tbsp. Sauce | 1 Serv. | 3 | Potato, Creamed, | | |
| Pork Tenderloin | 4 Ozs. | 0 | 2 Tbsp. Sauce | 1 Med. | 19 |
| Pork, Tongue | 4 Ozs. | 1 | Potato Croquettes | 1 Med. | 17 |
| Port | 4 Ozs. | 16 | Potato, French Fried | 6 Aver. | 12 |
| Port Wine: | | | Potatoes, Hashed Brown | 1 Med. | 28 |
| (Gallo) | 3 Fl. Ozs. | 8 | Potato, Idaho, Baked (B1) | 1 Med. | 28 |
| (Gallo) Ruby | 3 Fl. Ozs. | 8 | Potato, Irish, Boiled | 1 Med. | 28 |
| (Gallo) Tawny, Old Decanter | 3 Fl. Ozs. | 8 | Potato, Julienne | 1 Med. | 30 |
| (Gallo) White | 3 Fl. Ozs. | 8 | Potato Leek Soup | 1 Serv. | 21 |
| (Gold Seal) | 3 Fl. Ozs. | 9 | Potato, Lyonnaise | 1 Med. | 28 |
| (Great Western) Solera | 3 Fl. Ozs. | 11 | Potato, Mashed (With 1 Tsp. | | |
| (Great Western) Solera, | | | Butter & 2 Tbsp. Milk) | 1 Med. | 28 |
| Tawny | 3 Fl. Ozs. | 11 | Potato, Pan Browned | 1 Med. | 33 |
| (Great Western) White | 3 Fl. Ozs. | 12 | Potato Pancake | 1 Serv. | 39 |
| (Italian Swiss Colony- | | | Potato Salad | 1/2 Cup | 16 |
| Gold Medal) | 3 Fl. Ozs. | 8 | Canned (Nalley's) | 4 Ozs. | 20 |
| (Italian Swiss Colony- | | | Potato Soup, Cream Of | 1 Cup | 15 |
| Gold Medal) White | 3 Fl. Ozs. | 9 | Canned, Condensed | | |
| (Italian Swiss Colony- | | | (Campbell) | 8 Ozs. | 20 |
| Private Stock) | 3 Fl. Ozs. | 11 | Frozen, Condensed | | |
| (Italian Swiss Colony- | | | (Campbell) | 8 Ozs. | 23 |
| Private Stock) Tawny | 3 Fl. Ozs. | 10 | Potato Soup Mix: | | |
| (Louis M. Martini) | 3 Fl. Ozs. | 2 | (Lipton) | 1 Pkg. | 57 |
| (Louis M. Martini) Tawny | 3 Fl. Ozs. | 2 | With Leek (Wyler's) | 8 Fl. Ozs. | 9 |
| (Robertson's) Ruby | 3 Fl. Ozs. | 10 | Potato Stick: | | |
| (Robertson's) Tawny, Dry | | | O & C (Durkee) | 1 Cup | 16 |
| Humour | 3 Fl. Ozs. | 10 | O & C (Durkee) | 1 Oz. | 14 |
| (Robertson's) Tawny, | | | Julienne (Wise) | 1 Oz. | 15 |
| Game Bird | 3 Fl. Ozs. | 10 | Potato, Sweet, Baked | 1 Med. | 45 |
| (Robertson's) Rebello | | | Potato, Sweet, Boiled | 1 Med. | 45 |
| Valente | 3 Fl. Ozs. | 10 | Potato, Sweet, Candied | 6 Ozs. | 60 |

| FOOD | AMT. | CARB. GRAMS | FOOD | AMT. | CARB. GRAMS |
|---|---|---|---|---|---|
| Potato, Sweet (Canned) | 1 Cup | 45 | Pouilly-Fuisse Wine, French | | |
| Potato, Sweet Pie | 1 Sl. | 52 | White Burgundy: | | |
| Potatoes | 4 Ozs. | 21 | (Barton & Guestler) | 3 Fl. Ozs. | T |
| Potatoes (Canned), Drained | 3-4 Sm. | 19 | (Chanson) St. Vincent | 3 Fl. Ozs. | 6 |
| White (Butter Kernel) | 3 | 22 | Pouilly-Fume, French White Loire | | |
| Whole, New (Hunt's) | 4 Ozs. | 11 | Valley (Barton & Guestier) | 3 Fl. Ozs. | T |
| Potatoes (Canned With | | | Poultry Stuffing | 1/2 Cup | 28 |
| Liquid) | 4 Ozs. | 10 | Pound Cake | 1 Sl. | 35 |
| Potatoes, Escalloped | 1/2 Cup | 14 | Marble (Drake's) | 1 Sl. | 31 |
| Potatoes, French Fried | 10 Pcs. | 15 | Plain (Drake's) | 1 Sl. | 40 |
| (Birds Eye) | 3 Ozs. | 22 | Raisin (Drake's) | 1 Sl. | 40 |
| Crinkle-Cut (Birds Eye) | 3 Ozs. | 22 | Pound Cake Mix: | | |
| Fanci-Fries (Birds Eye) | 3 Ozs. | 21 | (Betty Crocker) | 1 Oz. | 20 |
| (Mrs. Paul's) | 4 Ozs. | 38 | (Dromedary) | 1 Sl. | 36 |
| Potato Puffs (Birds Eye) | 3 Ozs. | 15 | Powder, Chili | 1 Tbsp. | T |
| Potatoes, Fried | 1/2 Cup | 12 | Powdered Milk, Malted | 1 Tbsp. | 7 |
| Potatoes, Frozen: | | | Powdered Cocoa, Milk & | | |
| Au Gratin (Stouffer's) | 1 Pkg. | 35 | Sugar | 3 Tbsp. Each | 52 |
| Au Gratin (Swanson) | 1 Pkg. | 16 | Powdered Sugar | 1 Tbsp. | 24 |
| Potatoes, Mashed | 4 Ozs. | 16 | Power House Candy | 1 Bar | 9 |
| Potato Mix: | | | Praline | 1 | 56 |
| Au Gratin (French's) | 1 Cup | 16 | Pream, Cream Substitute | 1 Tsp. | 1 |
| Buds, Instant (Betty | | | Prepared Mustard | 1 Tbsp. | T |
| Crocker) | 5 Ozs. | 114 | Preserve: | | |
| Escalloped, With Sauce | | | Sweetened: | | |
| (Betty Crocker) | 5 Ozs. | 105 | (Crosse & Blackwell) | 1 Tbsp. | 15 |
| Mashed, Country Style | | | (Kraft) | 1 Tbsp. | 9 |
| (French's) | 1 Cup | 33 | (Polaner) | 1 Tbsp. | 13 |
| Mashed, Instant (French's) | 1 Cup | 32 | Low Calorie (Kraft) | 1 Tbsp. | 2 |
| Scalloped (French's) | 1 Cup | 40 | Preserves, Apricot | 2 Tbsp. | 28 |
| Scalloped (Pillsbury) | 1 Oz. | 20 | Preserves, Blackberry | 1 Tbsp. | 14 |
| Potato Pancake Mix | | | Preserves, Cherry | 2 Tbsp. | 28 |
| (French's) | 1 Pancake | 6 | Preserves, Raspberry | 2 Tbsp. | 28 |
| Potatoes, Pressure Cooked | 4 Ozs. | 21 | Preserves, Strawberry | 2 Tbsp. | 28 |
| Potatoes, Scalloped | 1/2 Cup | 14 | Pressure Cooked Potatoes | 4 Ozs. | 21 |
| (Swanson) | 1 Pkg. | 13 | Pretzel: | | |
| Potatoes, Shredded for Hash- | | | (Keebler): | | |
| Browns (Birds Eye) | 3 Ozs. | 14 | Log | 1 Pc. | 3 |
| Potatoes, Stuffed: | | | Stix | 1 Pc. | 1 |
| (Holloway House) | 1 Potato | 28 | Twist | 1 Pc. | 4 |
| Baked, With Sour Cream & | | | (Nab): | | |
| Chives (Holloway House) | 1 Potato | 27 | Pretzelette | 1 Pkt. | 21 |
| Potatoes, Sweet, Dehydrated | 4 Ozs. | 84 | Very-Thin Sticks | 1 Pkt. | 16 |
| Potatoes, Sweet, Raw | 3-1/2 Ozs. | 28 | (Nabisco): | | |
| Potatoes, Sweet, Yam | 1 Cup | 48 | Pretzelette | 1 Pc. | 1 |
| Potatoes, Sweet Yam With | | | Mister Salty Dutch | 1 Pc. | 11 |
| Marshmallow Topping | 1 Cup | 61 | Mister Salty 3-Ring | 1 Pc. | 2 |
| Pot-Pie, Apple | 1 Serv. | 46 | Mister Salty Veri-Thin | 1 Pc. | 4 |
| Pot-Pie, Beef | 1 Serv. | 37 | Mister Salty Veri-Thin Stick | 1 Pc. | T |
| Pot-Pie, Chicken | 1 Serv. | 20 | (Old London) Chick-a-Dees | 1 Oz. | 22 |
| Pot Roast | 1 Serv. | 0 | (Rold Gold) Stix | 1 Pkg. | 24 |

| FOOD | AMT. | CARB. GRAMS | FOOD | AMT. | CARB. GRAMS |
|------|------|-------------|------|------|-------------|
| (Sunshine) Extra Thin | 1 Pc. | 4 | Pudding, Butterscotch | | |
| Pretzel Cracker | 1 Lg. | 13 | Sugar-Free | 1/2 Cup | 9 |
| Pretzel, 3 Ring | 1 | 2 | Pudding Caramel | 1/2 Cup | 29 |
| Pretzel Sticks | 3 Med. | 4 | Pudding, Chocolate | 1/2 Cup | 31 |
| Prickly Pear | 1 Med. | 12 | Pudding, Chocolate | | |
| Prince Blanc Wine, French | | | (Skim Milk) | 1/2 Cup | 30 |
| White Bordeaux (Barton | | | Pudding, Chocolate | | |
| & Guestier) | 3 Fl. Ozs. | T | Blanc Mange | 1/2 Cup | 23 |
| Prince Noir Wine, French Red | | | Pudding, Chocolate- | | |
| Bordeaux (Barton | | | Marshmallow | 1 Serv. | 37 |
| & Guestier) | 3 Fl. Ozs. | T | Pudding Cottage | 1 Pc. | 44 |
| Product 19, Cereal | | | Pudding, Cottage With 2 Tbsp. | | |
| (Kellogg's) | 1 Cup | 22 | Lemon Sauce | 1 Pc. | 61 |
| Protein Bread | 1 Sl. | 5 | Pudding, Cornstarch, | | |
| Provolone Cheese | 1-1/2 Ozs. | T | Chocolate | 1/2 Cup | 37 |
| Prune & Cheese Salad | 1 Serv. | 19 | Pudding, Cornstarch, | | |
| Prune Juice | 1/2 Cup | 23 | Butterscotch | 1/2 Cup | 37 |
| Canned (Heinz) | 1 Cup | 48 | Pudding, Cornstarch, Vanilla | 1/2 Cup | 20 |
| Canned (Santa Clara) | 8 Ozs. | 48 | Pudding, Custard | 1/2 Cup | 14 |
| Prune Nut Cake | 1 Serv. | 9 | Pudding, Indian | 2/3 Cup | 23 |
| Prune Pie, With | | | Pudding, Lemon | 1 Serv. | 26 |
| Whipped Cream | 1 Pc. | 54 | Pudding, Lemon Sponge | 1 Serv. | 26 |
| Prune Struedel | 1 Pc. | 14 | Pudding Lemon Sponge | | |
| Prune Whip | 1 Cup | 24 | With Custard Sauce | 1 Serv. | 41 |
| Prune Whipped Cream Pie | 1 Pc. | 54 | Pudding, Plum | 1 Serv. | 41 |
| Prune Whip Pudding | 1/2 Cup | 25 | Pudding, Prune Whip | 1/2 Cup | 25 |
| Prunes, Canned & Strained | 1 Oz. | 7 | Pudding, Rice | 1/2 Cup | 32 |
| Diet (Dia-Mel) | 1 Prune | 3 | Pudding, Snow | 1 Serv. | 21 |
| Prunes, Cooked (A) | 3 | 24 | Pudding, Tapioca | 1/2 Cup | 24 |
| Prunes, Cooked (Sugar Added) | 4-5 | 31 | Pudding, Tapioca, Apricot | 1/2 Cup | 41 |
| Prunes, Dried (A) | 4 | 24 | Pudding, Vanilla | | |
| Prunes, Stewed (No Sugar) | 4 Ozs. | 40 | Blanc Mange | 1/2 Cup | 20 |
| Prunes, Stuffed With | | | Pudding, Yorkshire | | |
| Cottage Cheese | 4 | 28 | (No Meat) | 1 Serv. | 28 |
| Prosciutto Ham | 1-1/2 Ozs. | 0 | Puddings, Junket | 1/2 Cup | 5 |
| Pudding, Apple Snow | 1/2 Cup | 25 | Puerto Rico Swizzle | 14 Ozs. | 10 |
| Pudding Bread | 1/2 Cup | 32 | Puerto Rican Cocktail | 1 Serv. | 4 |
| Pudding, Butterscotch | 1/2 Cup | 23 | Puff Balls, Cheese | 1 Serv. | 2 |
| Pudding, Cornstarch | 1/2 Cup | 24 | Puffa Puffa Rice, Cereal | | |
| Pudding, Date | 1 Serv. | 16 | (Kellogg's) | 1 Cup | 24 |
| Pudding, Peach | 1 Serv. | 24 | Puffed Oats | 1/2 Cup | 10 |
| Pudding, American Steamed | 1 Serv. | 25 | Puffed Wheat | 3/4 Cup | 10 |
| Pudding, Apple Brown Betty | 1/2 Cup | 35 | Puffed Wheat Cereal, | | |
| Pudding, Apple Dumpling | 1 Serv. | 54 | Sweetened | 1 Oz. | 18 |
| Pudding, Apple Snow | 1/2 Cup | 25 | Puligny Montrachet Wine, | | |
| Pudding, Banana Custard | | | French White Burgundy: | | |
| With Meringue | 1/2 Cup | 19 | (Barton & Guestier) | 3 Fl. Ozs. | T |
| Pudding, Banana Whip | 1/2 Cup | 15 | (Chanson) | 3 Fl. Ozs. | 6 |
| Pudding, Bavarian Orange | 1 Serv. | 40 | Pumpernickel Bread | 1 Sl. | 16 |
| Pudding, Blanc Mange | 1/2 Cup | 20 | Pumpernickel Bread | 1 Lb. | 238 |
| Pudding, Bread & Butter | 1 Pc. | 28 | Pumpkin | 1 Cup | 19 |

| FOOD | AMT. | CARB. GRAMS | FOOD | AMT. | CARB. GRAMS |
|---|---|---|---|---|---|
| Pumpkin, Canned | 1 Cup | 18 | (Schweppes) | 8 Fl. Ozs. | 22 |
| (Stokely-Van Camp) | 1 Cup | 19 | (Shasta) | 8 Fl. Ozs. | 19 |
| Pumpkin Pie | 1 Pc. | 34 | (Yukon Club) | 8 Fl. Ozs. | 22 |
| (Tastykake) | 4 Ozs. | 50 | Low Calorie: | | |
| Frozen (Banquet) | 5 Ozs. | 46 | (Hoffman) | 8 Fl. Ozs. | T |
| Frozen (Mrs. Smith's) | 1 Pc. | 17 | (No-Cal) | 8 Fl. Ozs. | 0 |
| Pumpkin Seeds | 4 Ozs. | 15 | Quisp, Cereal (Quaker) | 1 Cup | 19 |
| Punch, Brandy | 1 Cup | 22 | | | |
| Punch, Burgundy | 1 Serv. | 62 | | | |
| Punch, Burgundy Pineapple | 1 Serv. | 55 | Rabbit | Av. Serv. | 0 |
| Punch, Claret | 1 | 31 | Rabbit Baked | Av. Serv. | 0 |
| Punch, Coopers Ranch | 12 Ozs. | 60 | Rabbit Fricasse | Av. Serv. | 0 |
| Punch Drink Mix (Salada) | 6 Fl. Ozs. | 19 | Rabbit Fried | Av. Serv. | 0 |
| Punch, Egg & Fruit | 8 Ozs. | 26 | Rabbit Stew | Av. Serv. | 15 |
| Punch, Egg Harbor | 1 Serv. | 29 | Radishes | 4 Sm. | 2 |
| Punch, Fish House | 12 Ozs. | 12 | Radishes, Chinese | 3-1/2 Ozs. | T |
| Punch, Fruit | 6 Ozs. | 33 | Raisins | 4 | 3 |
| Punch & Judy | 1 Serv. | 31 | Raisins | 1/2 Cup | 62 |
| Punch, Myrtle Bank | 10 Ozs. | 7 | Seedless, California | | |
| Punch, Nourmahal | 10 Ozs. | 3 | Thompson (Sun Maid) | 1/2 Cup | 16 |
| Punch, Olaffson's | 12 Ozs. | 24 | Raisin & Apple Salad | 1/2 Cup | 25 |
| Punch, Planter's | | | Raisin Bran | 1 Cup | 33 |
| (Sloppy Joe's) | 1 Gl. | 3 | Raisin Bran Cereal | 1 Cup | 33 |
| Punch, Planter's | | | Raisin Bread | 1 Sl. | 12 |
| (Trader Vic's) | 12 Ozs. | 6 | Raisin Bread | 1/4 Lb. | 67 |
| Punch, Planter's (Trinidad) | 12 Ozs. | 3 | Raisin Bread (Toast) | 1 Sl. | 12 |
| Punch, Pondo | 14 Ozs. | 11 | Raisins, Cooked, Sweetened | 1/2 Cup | 36 |
| Punch, Port Wine | 1 Serv. | 22 | Raisin Cookies | 1/4 Lb. | 90 |
| Punch, Roman | 12 Ozs. | 6 | Raisin Dried, Cooked | 4 Ozs. | 62 |
| Punch, Ruby Rum | 1 Serv. | 8 | Raisin Fudge | 1 In. Sq. | 22 |
| Punch, Rum | 8 Ozs. | 8 | Raisin, Muffins | 1 Med. | 27 |
| Punch, Sauterne | 1 Serv. | 37 | Raisin Pie | 1 Pc. | 65 |
| Punch, Tahitian Rum | 10 Ozs. | 7 | (Tastykake) | 4-Oz. Pie | 61 |
| Punch, West Indies | 1/2 Cup | 22 | Frozen (Mrs. Smith's) | 1/6 Pie | 31 |
| Pureed Apricot | 1 Serv. | 33 | Raisin Pie Filling | | |
| Puree, Tomato | 1 Cup | 16 | (Lucky Leaf) | 8 Ozs. | 68 |
| Puree, Mongole | 1 Serv. | 7 | Raisin Sauce | 1/4 Cup | 26 |
| Pure Starch | 4 Ozs. | 99 | Raisins, Seeded | 1/2 Cup | 56 |
| Purple Passion, Soft Drink | | | Raisins, Sugar Added | 4 Ozs. | 36 |
| (Canada Dry) | 6 Fl. Ozs. | 22 | Raisin Toast | 1 Sl. | 12 |
| Pussycat Mix (Bar-Tender's) | 1 Serv. | 18 | Raised Or Yeast | 1 Sl. | 14 |
| Quail, Broiled | Av. Serv. | 0 | Ralston Cereal, Cooked | 2/3 Cup | 20 |
| Quake, Cereal (Quaker) | 1 Cup | 23 | Ralston Cereal, Dry: | | |
| Queen's Park Swizzle Bev. | 14 Ozs. | 11 | Instant | 1 Oz. | 20 |
| Quince, Fresh | 1 | 12 | Regular | 1 Oz. | 20 |
| Quinine Water | 8 Ozs. | 12 | Ralston Health Cereal, | | |
| Quinine Soft Drink or Tonic Water: | | | Cooked | 2/3 Cup | 20 |
| Sweetened: | | | Ralston Hot Or Instant, | | |
| (Canada Dry) | 8 Fl. Ozs. | 24 | Uncooked | 3/4 Cup | 22 |
| (Dr. Brown's) | 8 Fl. Ozs. | 22 | Ralston Wheat Cereal | 1/2 Cup | 23 |
| Fanta | 8 Fl. Ozs. | 20 | Rarebit, Welsh | 1/2 Cup | 22 |
| (Hoffman) | 8 Fl. Ozs. | 22 | Raspberries, Black | 1 Cup | 16 |

| FOOD | AMT. | CARB. GRAMS | FOOD | AMT. | CARB. GRAMS |
|---|---|---|---|---|---|
| Raspberries (Canned) | 1/2 Cup | 18 | (Chef Boy-Ar-Dee) | 8 Ozs. | 31 |
| Raspberries (Canned) Water Pack | 1 Cup | 6 | (Prince) | 8 Ozs. | 29 |
| Raspberries, Fresh | 1/2 Cup | 8 | Canned, Chicken (Nalley's) | 8 Ozs. | 82 |
| Raspberries, Frozen | 3 Ozs. | 24 | Frozen: | | |
| Raspberries, Red | 1 Cup | 17 | Beef (Kraft) | 8 Ozs. | 31 |
| Frozen, Quick Thaw (Birds Eye) | 1/2 Cup | 32 | Cheese, Without Sauce (Buitoni) | 1 Cup | 16 |
| Raspberries Icy | Av. Scp. | 27 | Cheese (Kraft) | 8 Ozs. | 30 |
| Raspberry Drink Mix (Wyler's) | 6 Fl. Ozs. | 15 | Meat, Without Sauce (Buitoni) Raviolettes | 1 Cup | 16 |
| Raspberry Jam | 1 Tbsp. | 14 | Ravioli, Cheese Filling | 4 Sq. | 24 |
| Dietetic. Black (Slenderella) | 1 Oz. | 12 | Raw Apples | 1 Lg. | 25 |
| Raspberry Juicy Red | 6 Ozs. | 12 | Raw Apples | 1 Med. | 17 |
| Raspberry Liqueur (Leroux) | 1 Fl. Oz. | 8 | Raw Apples | 1 Sm. | 11 |
| Raspberry Pie | Av. Sl. | 57 | Raw Apples | 1 Cup | 19 |
| Raspberry Preserve, Dietetic· | | | Raw Beets | 2 | 10 |
| Red (Polaner) | 1 Tbsp. | 1 | Raw Carrots, Grated | 1 Cup | 10 |
| Black Seedless (Dia-Mel) | 1 Tbsp. | 5 | Raw Carrot Sticks | 3 | 3 |
| Black (Kraft) | 1 Tbsp. | 2 | Raw Chicken Liver | 4 Ozs. | 3 |
| Raspberry, Red, Pie Filling (Lucky Leaf) | 4 Ozs. | 40 | Raw Clams, Meat Only | 5-10 Ozs. | 3 |
| Raspberry Rennet Custard Mix· | | | Raw Converted Rice | 2 Ozs. | 44 |
| Powder (Junket) | 1 Tbsp. | 28 | Raw Duck, Dried & Salted | 4 Ozs. | 0 |
| Tablet (Junket) | 1 Tablet | T | Raw Eggs | 1 Med. | T |
| Raspberry Sherbet | Av Scp | 29 | Raw Goose | 4 Ozs. | 0 |
| Raspberry Shortcake | Med. Serv. | 47 | Raw Onions | 1 Tbsp. | 1 |
| Raspberry Soft Drink: | | | Raw Onions | 1 Lg. | 11 |
| Sweetened: | | | Raw Onions (Mature) | 1 Med. | 10 |
| (Canada Dry) | 6 Fl. Ozs | 26 | Raw Oysters | 12 Med. | 8 |
| (Hoffman) | 6 Fl. Ozs | 22 | Raw Parsnips | 4 Ozs. | 17 |
| (Yukon Club) | 6 Fl. Ozs | 22 | Raw Rhubarb | 1 Cup | 5 |
| Black· | | | Raw Sweet Potato | 3-1/2 Ozs | 28 |
| (Dr. Brown's) | 6 Fl. Ozs | 22 | Raw Spinach | 1/2 Lb. | 6 |
| (Key Food) | 6 Fl. Ozs | 22 | Raw Turkey | 4 Ozs. | 0 |
| (Kirsch) | 6 Fl. Ozs | 22 | Raw Water Cress | 1 Bunch | 3 |
| (Waldbaum) | 6 Fl. Ozs | 22 | Raw White Rice | 4 Ozs. | 91 |
| Low Calorie: | | | Raw Wild Rice | 4 Ozs. | 38 |
| (Hoffman) | 6 Fl. Ozs | 1 | Red Cabbage, Boiled | 1 Cup | 4 |
| (No-Cal) | 6 Fl. Ozs | T | Red Cabbage, Raw | 3/4 Cup | 7 |
| Raspberry Syrup, Dietetic· | | | Red Cabbage & Chestnut | 1 Serv. | 30 |
| (Dia-Mel) | 1 Tbsp. | 5 | Red Currant Juice | 1 Cup | 25 |
| (No-Cal) | 1 Tsp. | T | Red Fish | Av. Serv. | 0 |
| Ravioli | 1 Serv. | 7 | Red Horse Raddish | 1 Tbsp. | 1 |
| Canned, Beef or Meat: | | | Red, Hot Dried Peppers | 1 Tbsp. | 9 |
| (Buitoni) | 1 Cup | 28 | Red Mexican Dry Beans | 1/2 Cup | 64 |
| (Chef Boy-Ar-Dee) | 8 Ozs. | 30 | Red Peppers, Fresh | 1 Med. | 5 |
| (Nalley's) | 8 Ozs. | 62 | Red Raspberries | 1 Cup | 17 |
| (Prince) | 8 Ozs. | 38 | Red Rum Swizzle Barbados | 10 Ozs. | 5 |
| Canned, Cheese: | | | Red Salmon (Canned) | Av. Serv. | 0 |
| (Buitoni) | 1 Cup | 31 | Red Snapper | Av. Serv. | 0 |
| | | | Meat Only (Booth) | 6 Ozs. | 0 |
| | | | Red Snapper a la Creole | Av. Serv. | 4 |

| FOOD | AMT. | CARB. GRAMS | FOOD | AMT. | CARB. GRAMS |
|---|---|---|---|---|---|
| Red Snapper, Baked | Av. Serv. | 0 | Sweetened (Birds Eye) | 1/4 Pkg. | 35 |
| Red Wine | 1 Gl. | 4 | Rhubarb, Raw | 1 Cup Diced | 5 |
| Reggiano Cheese | 1-1/2 Ozs. | T | Rib Roast Beef | 1 Serv. | 0 |
| Reindeer Milk | 1/2 Cup | 4 | Rib Roast (Standing) | Av. Serv. | 0 |
| Relish: | | | Rib Steak | Av. Serv. | 0 |
| Barbecue (Crosse & | | | Rice Boiled (White) | 3/4 Cup | 22 |
| Blackwell) | 1 Tbsp. | 5 | Rice Brown | 3/4 Cup | 22 |
| Barbecue (Heinz) | 1 Tbsp. | 3 | (Carolina) | 4 Ozs. | 29 |
| Corn (Crosse & Blackwell) | 1 Tbsp. | 3 | (River Brand) | 4 Ozs. | 29 |
| Hamburger (Crosse & | | | Rice Cakes | 2 Ozs. | 25 |
| Blackwell) | 1 Tbsp. | 4 | Rice & Cheese | Av. Serv. | 20 |
| Hamburger (Heinz) | 1 Tbsp. | 4 | Rice Chex, Cereal | | |
| Hot Dog (Crosse & Blackwell) | 1 Tbsp. | 5 | (Ralston Purina) | 1 Oz. | 25 |
| Hot Dog (Heinz) | 1 Tbsp. | 5 | Rice & Chicken, | | |
| Hot Pepper (Crosse & | | | Puerto Rican | 6 Serv. | 31 |
| Blackwell) | 1 Tbsp. | 5 | Rice, Converted, Cooked | 3/4 Cup | 24 |
| India (Crosse & Blackwell) | 1 Tbsp. | 6 | Rice, Converted, Raw | 4 Ozs. | 88 |
| India (Heinz) | 1 Tbsp. | 6 | Rice Crispies | 1 Cup | 26 |
| Onion, Spicy (Crosse & | | | Rice Custard | 1/2 Cup | 38 |
| Blackwell) | 1 Tbsp. | 5 | Rice Flakes Cereal | 1 Cup | 27 |
| Piccalilli (Crosse & Blackwell) | 1 Tbsp | 6 | Dietetic (Van Brode) | 1 Oz. | 25 |
| Piccalilli (Heinz) | 1 Tbsp. | 4 | Rice Flakes, Puffed | 1 Cup | 26 |
| Picnic, Tangy (Crosse & | | | Rice, Puffed, Cereal: | | |
| Blackwell) | 1 Tbsp. | 6 | (Checker) | 1 Oz. | 28 |
| Sweet: | | | (Kellogg's) | 1 Cup | 13 |
| (Crosse & Blackwell) | 1 Tbsp. | 6 | (Quaker) | 1 Cup | 16 |
| (Heinz) | 1 Tbsp. | 5 | (Van Brode) Dietetic | 1 Oz. | 25 |
| (Smucker's) | 1 Tbsp. | 5 | Rice Flour | 1/2 Cup | 50 |
| Relish, Beet & Cabbage | 1 Serv. | 6 | Rice, Fried (Chinese) | 1 Cup | 22 |
| Relish Cranberry With | | | Rice, Fried, Frozen | | |
| Orange | 1/2 Cup | 26 | (Chun King) | 4 Ozs. | 28 |
| Relish Pickle | 1 Tbsp. | 3 | Rice, Fried With Chicken | 1 Cup | 22 |
| Relish Salad Mold | Av. Serv. | 4 | Rice, Fried With Pork | 1 Cup | 22 |
| Renault Am. Champagne | 1 Gl. | 30 | Rice Honeys, Cereal | | |
| Rhineskeller Wine (Italian | | | (Nabisco) | 1 Cup | 32 |
| Swiss Colony-Gold Medal) | 3 Fl. Ozs. | 3 | Rice Krispies, Cereal | | |
| Rhine Wine | 1 Gl. | 4 | (Kellogg's) | 1 Cup | 24 |
| (Deinhard) Rheinritter | 3 Fl. Ozs. | 3 | Rice, Mexican | 1 Cup | 20 |
| (Gallo) | 3 Fl. Ozs. | 1 | Rice Mix: | | |
| (Gallo) Rhine Garten | 3 Fl. Ozs. | 3 | Beef: | | |
| (Great Western) Dutchess | 3 Fl. Ozs. | 2 | Rice-A-Roni | 1 Cup | 26 |
| (Gold Seal) | 3 Fl Ozs. | T | (Uncle Ben's) | 1 Cup | 21 |
| (Italian Swiss Colony- | | | (Village Inn) | 1 Cup | 24 |
| Gold Medal) | 3 Fl. Ozs. | T | Cheese Rice-A-Roni | 1 Cup | 20 |
| (Italian Swiss Colony- | | | Chicken: | | |
| Private Stock) | 3 Fl. Ozs. | T | Rice-A-Roni | 1 Cup | 51 |
| (Louis M. Martini) | 3 Fl. Ozs. | T | (Uncle Ben's) | 1 Cup | 42 |
| (Taylor) | 3 Fl Ozs. | T | (Village Inn) | 1 Cup | 48 |
| Rhine Wine Sour | 1 Gl. | 19 | Chinese, Fried, Rice-A-Roni | 1 Cup | 48 |
| Rhubarb (Canned, Low | | | Curry (Uncle Ben's) | 1 Cup | 48 |
| Calorie) | 1 Cup | 5 | Curry (Village Inn) | 1 Cup | 48 |
| Rhubarb, Frozen | 1/2 Cup | 23 | Drumstick (Minute Rice) | 1 Cup | 48 |

| FOOD | AMT. | CARB. GRAMS | FOOD | AMT. | CARB. GRAMS |
|---|---|---|---|---|---|
| Ham Rice-A-Roni | 1 Cup | 28 | Rice & Peas With Mushrooms, | | |
| Herb (Village Inn) | 1 Cup | 48 | Frozen (Birds Eye) | 1 Cup | 15 |
| Keriyaki Dinner | | | Rich Cake with Icing | Av. Serv. | 62 |
| (Betty Crocker) | 1 Pkg. | 106 | Rich Sherry Nut Cake | 1 Serv. | 51 |
| Long & Wild Grain: | | | Riesling | 1 Gl. | 4 |
| (Uncle Ben's) | 1 Cup | 42 | Riesling Wine, Alsatian: | | |
| (Village Inn) | 1 Cup | 48 | (Willm) | 3 Fl. Ozs. | 3 |
| Milanese (Betty Crocker) | 1 Pkg. | 90 | (Willm) Grand Reserve | | |
| Provence (Betty Crocker) | 1 Pkg. | 109 | Exceptionelle | 3 Fl. Ozs. | 3 |
| Rib Roast (Minute Rice) | 1 Cup | 48 | Ripe or Black Olives | 10 Lg. | 1 |
| Spanish: | | | Ripple Wine (Gallo): | | |
| Rice-A-Roni | 1 Cup | 36 | Red | 3 Fl. Ozs. | 3 |
| (Minute Rice) | 1 Cup | 50 | White | 3 Fl. Ozs. | 3 |
| (Uncle Ben's) | 1 Cup | 48 | Rinds, Watermelon (Pickled) | 1/4 Lb. | 25 |
| (Village Inn) | 1 Cup | 48 | Rind, Watermelon (Relish) | 1/4 Lb. | 25 |
| Turkey Rice-A-Roni | 1 Cup | 50 | Ritz Crackers | 1 | 2 |
| Wild Rice-A-Roni | 1 Cup | 42 | Roast Beef | Av. Serv. | 0 |
| Yellow (Village Inn) | 1 Cup | 48 | Roast Beef (Canned) | 4 Ozs. | 0 |
| Rice Pudding | 1/2 Cup | 30 | Roast Beef Hash | 1/2 Cup | 8 |
| Rice Pudding With Cinnamon | | | Roast Beef Sandwich | 1 | 24 |
| Canned (Bounty) | 4 Ozs. | 29 | Roast Beef Sandwich | | |
| Rice Pudding With Eggs | 1/2 Cup | 17 | With Gravy | 1 | 27 |
| Rice Pudding With Raisins | 1/2 Cup | 32 | Roast Capon | Av. Serv. | 0 |
| Rice With Raisin Pudding | 1/2 Cup | 32 | Roast Chestnut | 1 Serv. | 13 |
| Rice Soup | 1 Serv. | 7 | Roast Chicken | Av. Serv. | 0 |
| Rice, Spanish | Av. Serv. | 20 | Roast Duck With Dressing | Av. Serv. | 22 |
| Canned: | | | Roast Goose | Av. Serv. | 0 |
| (College Inn) | 4 Ozs. | 48 | Roast Guinea Hens | Av. Serv. | 5 |
| (Heinz) | 4 Ozs. | 10 | Roast Lamb | Av. Serv. | 0 |
| (Nalley's) | 4 Ozs. | 32 | Roast Leg of Lamb | Av. Serv. | 0 |
| Rice, Spanish, Seasoning Mix | | | Roast Mutton Leg | 1 Sl. | 0 |
| (Lawry's) | 1-1/2 Ozs. | 20 | Roast Pork | Av. Serv. | 0 |
| Rice, Steamed | 1/2 Cup | 22 | Roast Pork (Chinese) | Av. Serv. | 0 |
| Rice, White & Raw | 4 Ozs. | 91 | Roast Pork Egg | | |
| Instant or Precooked: | | | Foo Yung | 2 Cups | 4 |
| (Carolina) | 4 Ozs. | 27 | Roast Pork Leg | 4 Ozs. | 0 |
| (Minute Rice) | 1 Cup | 20 | Roast Pork Sandwich | 1 Oz. | 24 |
| Long Grain (Uncle Ben's | | | Roast Pork Sandwich | | |
| Quick) | 1 Cup | 22 | With Gravy | 1 | 27 |
| Parboiled: | | | Roast Squab | 1/2 Med. | 0 |
| (Aunt Caroline) | 4 Ozs. | 26 | Roast Veal | Av. Serv. | 0 |
| Long Grain (Uncle Ben's | | | Roasted Chicken | 1 Serv. | 0 |
| Converted) | 1 Cup | 38 | Roasted Clams | 6 | 5 |
| Regular, Cooked: | | | Roasted Duck | 4 Ozs. | 0 |
| Extra Long-Grain | | | Roasted Turkey | 1 Serv. | 0 |
| (Carolina) | 4 Ozs. | 27 | Roasters, Chicken Raw | 4 Ozs. | 0 |
| (Mahatma) | 4 Ozs. | 27 | Rob, Roy | 3 Ozs. | T |
| (River Brand) | 4 Ozs. | 27 | Rock Cornish Game Hens | | |
| (Water Maid) | 4 Ozs. | 27 | In Marinade | Av. Serv. | 0 |
| Rice Wild | 3/4 Cup | 128 | Rock Rye | 1 | 15 |
| Rice, Wild & Cooked | 4 Ozs. | 15 | Rock & Rye Liqueur: | | |
| Rice Wild, Shoots | 4 Ozs. | 20 | (Garnier) | 1 Fl. Oz. | 6 |

| FOOD | AMT. | CARB. GRAMS | FOOD | AMT | CARB. GRAMS |
|---|---|---|---|---|---|
| (Hiram Walker) | 1 Fl. Oz. | 9 | Roll Mix (Pillsbury) | 1 Oz. | 19 |
| (Leroux) | 1 Fl. Oz. | 8 | Roll, Onions | 1 | 23 |
| (Leroux) Irish Moss | 1 Fl. Oz. | 13 | Roll, Parkerhouse | 1 | 15 |
| (Old Mr. Boston) 48 Proof | 1 Fl. Oz. | 6 | Roll, Plain | 1 | 21 |
| (Old Mr. Boston) 60 Proof | 1 Fl. Oz. | 6 | Roll, Sweet | 1 | 21 |
| Rock Shad | Av Serv. | 0 | Roll, Whole Wheat | 1 | 14 |
| Roka Bleu Cheese Spread | 1 Oz. | 2 | Rolled Chipped Beef | | |
| Rolaids (Warner-Lambert) | 1 Pc. | 1 | Canapes | Av Serv | 2 |
| Rolls, Asparagus Toasted | 1 | 15 | Rolled Oatmeal, Cooked | 1/2 Cup | 11 |
| Roll & Bun: | | | Rolled Oatmeal (Infant | | |
| Barbeque (Arnold) | 1 Pc. | 19 | Dry Precd.) | 1 Oz. | 19 |
| Brown & Serve (Wonder) | 1 Roll | 12 | Rolled Oats, Cooked | 1/2 Cup | 13 |
| Cinnamon, Iced | | | Rolled Oats, Cooked Meal | 4 Ozs. | 13 |
| (Pepperidge Farm) | 1 Roll | 20 | Rolled Oats, Dry, | | |
| Deli Twists (Arnold) | 1 Roll | 17 | Precooked | 4 Ozs. | 9 |
| Dinner (Arnold) | 1 Roll | 9 | Rolled Wheat Cereal, | | |
| Dinner, Fully Baked | | | Cooked | 1/2 Cup | 20 |
| (Pepperidge Farm) | 1 Roll | 9 | Rolled Wheat, Cooked | 4 Ozs. | 20 |
| Dutch Egg Sandwich | | | Romaine | 1 Leaf | 0 |
| Buns (Arnold) | 1 Bun | 16 | Romaine Lettuce | 1/2 Head | 4 |
| Finger (Arnold) | 1 Roll | 9 | Roman Meal | 1/2 Cup | 24 |
| Frankfurter: | | | Roman Meal Bread | 1 Sl. | 14 |
| (Arnold) | 1 Bun | 18 | Roman Punch | 12 Ozs. | 8 |
| New England (Arnold) | 1 Roll | 18 | Romano Cheese | 1-1/2 Ozs. | T |
| French, Brown & Serve | | | Ron-Cacao Cocktail | 1 Gl. | 5 |
| (Pepperidge Farm) | 1 Roll | 75 | Root Beer | 6 Ozs. | 18 |
| Giraffe Sandwich Buns | | | Root Beer Drink Mix | | |
| (Arnold) | 1 Bun | 22 | (Wyler's) | 8 Fl. Ozs. | 30 |
| Golden Twist, Brown & Serve | | | Root Beer Soft Drink. | | |
| (Pepperidge Farm) | 1 Roll | 13 | Sweetened: | | |
| Hard (Levy's) | 1 Roll | 37 | (Canada Dry) | 8 Fl. Ozs. | 27 |
| Hearth, Brown & Serve | | | (Clicquot Club) | 8 Fl. Ozs. | 26 |
| (Pepperidge Farm) | 1 Roll | 10 | (Cott) | 8 Fl. Ozs. | 26 |
| Parker (Arnold) | 1 Roll | 9 | (Dad's) | 8 Fl. Ozs. | 26 |
| Poppy Finger (Arnold) | 1 Roll | 9 | (Dr. Brown's) | 8 Fl. Ozs. | 27 |
| Sesame Crisp, Brown & Serve | | | (Dr. Pepper) | 8 Fl. Ozs. | 30 |
| (Pepperidge Farm) | 1 Roll | 11 | Fanta | 8 Fl. Ozs. | 32 |
| Tea (Arnold) | 1 Roll | 5 | (Hires) | 8 Fl. Ozs. | 26 |
| Roll, Braids | 1 | 13 | (Hoffman) | 8 Fl. Ozs. | 27 |
| Roll Caraway | 1 Av. | 15 | (Key Food) | 8 Fl. Ozs. | 27 |
| Roll, Chocolate | 1 Sl. | 13 | (Kirsch) | 8 Fl. Ozs. | 23 |
| Roll, Clover Leaf | 1 | 20 | (Mason's) | 8 Fl. Ozs. | 20 |
| Roll Dough, Refrigerated: | | | (Mission) | 8 Fl. Ozs. | 26 |
| Cinnamon With Icing | | | (Shasta) | 8 Fl. Ozs. | 28 |
| (Pillsbury) | 1 Oz. | 14 | (Waldbaum) | 8 Fl. Ozs. | 27 |
| Dinner (Pillsbury): | | | (Yukon Club) | 8 Fl. Ozs. | 27 |
| Butterflake | 1 Oz. | 12 | Low Calorie: | | |
| Crescent | 1 Oz. | 11 | (Dad's) | 8 Fl. Ozs. | T |
| Parkerhouse | 1 Oz. | 12 | (Hoffman) | 8 Fl. Ozs. | 1 |
| Snowflake | 1 Oz. | 12 | (No-Cal) | 8 Fl. Ozs. | T |
| Roll, Frankfurter | 1 | 12 | Draft (Shasta) | 8 Fl. Ozs. | T |
| Roll, Hamburger | 1 | 21 | Root Beer With 1 Scp. | | |
| Roll, Kaiser | 1 | 21 | Ice Cream | 1 Serv. | 22 |

| FOOD | AMT. | CARB. GRAMS | FOOD | AMT. | CARB. GRAMS |
|---|---|---|---|---|---|
| Root, Ginger Fresh | 3-1/2 Ozs. | 7 | Rum Float Bev. | 6 Ozs. | 7 |
| Root Lotus | 2/3 Av Seg. | 16 | Rum, Hot Buttered | 1 Gl. | 0 |
| Roquefort Cheese (A) | 1-1/2 Ozs. | T | Rum Jamaica | 1 Oz. | T |
| Roquefort Cheese & Pear Salad | Av. Serv. | 8 | Rum Man. Cocktail | 1 Gl. | 3 |
| Roquefort Cream Spread | 1 Oz. | T | Rum, Mocha Bev. | 14 Ozs. | 28 |
| Roquefort Dressing | 1 Tbsp. | T | Rum Old-Fashioned Cktl. | 1 Gl. | 7 |
| Roquefort Spread Sandwich | 1 | 26 | Rum Pickup Bev. | 10 Ozs. | 2 |
| Roseapple | 4 Ozs. | 11 | Rum Punch | 1 Oz. | 1 |
| Rosemary | 1/8 Tbsp. | 0 | Rum Ramsey Cocktail | 1 Gl. | 3 |
| Rose Wine: | | | Rum Sling, Hot | 1 Serv. | 11 |
| (Antinori) | 3 Fl. Ozs. | 6 | Rumba Cocktail | 1 Gl. | 2 |
| Chateau Ste. Roseline | 3 Fl. Ozs. | 6 | Rump Roast (Beef) | 4 Ozs. | 0 |
| (Chanson) Rose des Anges | 3 Fl. Ozs. | 6 | Rusk Holland | 1 | 9 |
| (Gallo) | 3 Fl. Ozs. | 2 | (Nabisco) | 1 Pc. | 6 |
| (Gallo) Gypsy | 3 Fl. Ozs. | 12 | Dutch (Sunshine) | 1 Pc. | 10 |
| (Great Western) | 3 Fl. Ozs. | 4 | Russian Dressing | 1 Tsp. | T |
| (Great Western) Isabella | 3 Fl. Ozs. | 4 | Rutabaga | 1/2 Cup | 9 |
| (Italian Swiss Colony-Gold Medal) Grenache | 3 Fl. Ozs. | 2 | Rye Bread | 1 Sl. | 12 |
| (Italian Swiss Colony-Private Stock) Grenache | 3 Fl. Ozs. | T | Rye Bread (Jewish) | 1 Sl. | 12 |
| (Italian Swiss Colony-Gold Medal) Napa-Sonoma-Mendocino | 3 Fl. Ozs. | 2 | Rye Bread, Light | 1/4 Lb. | 60 |
| | | | Rye Bread, Partly Sliced | 1 Sl. | 8 |
| (Louis M. Martini) Gamay | 3 Fl. Ozs. | T | Rye Bread (Russian) | 1 Sl. | 14 |
| (Mogen David) | 3 Fl. Ozs. | 9 | Rye Bread Toast | 1 Sl. | 12 |
| Nectarose, Vin Rose d'Anjou | 3 Fl. Ozs. | 2 | Rye Flakes Cereals | 1/2 Cup | 13 |
| (Taylor) | 3 Fl. Ozs. | T | Rye Flour | 1 Cup | 62 |
| Rose Wine, Sparkling | | | Rye Flour, Light | 1/2 Cup | 49 |
| (Chanson) | 3 Fl. Ozs. | 3 | Rye Highball | 8 Ozs. | 3 |
| Round Steak | Av. Serv. | 0 | Ry-King (Wasa): | | |
| Round Steak, Beef Bottom Cooked | 4 Ozs. | 0 | Brown Rye | 1 Sl. | 8 |
| | | | Golden Rye | 1 Sl. | 7 |
| Royal Anne Low Cal. Cherries (Canned) | 1 Cup | 21 | Lite Rye | 1 Sl. | 6 |
| | | | Seasoned Rye | 1 Sl. | 7 |
| Ruby Rum Punch | 1 Serv. | 8 | Ry-Krisp | 3 | 10 |
| Rudesheimer Schlossberg, German Rhine Wine | | | Rye Light Flour | 1 Cup | 98 |
| (Deinhard) | 3 Fl. Ozs. | 4 | Rye Muffin | 1 | 21 |
| Rum Bacardi | 1 Shot | 0 | Rye Wafer Crackers | 1 | 2 |
| Rum, Bishop Cooler | 10 Ozs. | 15 | Rye & Wheat Bread | 1 Sl. | 12 |
| Rum, Carioca | 1 Gl. | 0 | Rye Whiskey | 1 Shot | T |
| Rum & Cola | 1 Gl. | 21 | Sabra, Israeli Liqueur | | |
| Rum Collins | 1 Oz. | 9 | (Leroux) | 1 Fl. Oz. | 10 |
| Rum Cooler | 1 Gl. | 19 | Saccharine | 1/8 Tsp. | 0 |
| Rum Cow, Hot | 1 Gl. | 16 | (Dia-Mel) | 1 Tablet | 0 |
| Rum Daisy Cocktail | 1 Gl. | 3 | Sage | 1/8 Tsp. | 0 |
| Rum Egg Nog | 1 Cup | 25 | Ssint-Emilion Wine, French Bordeaux: | | |
| Rum Fizz | 1 Oz. | 3 | (Barton & Guestier) | 3 Fl. Ozs. | 1 |
| Rum Fizz, Cherry | 12 Ozs. | 5 | Salads, Apple Carrot | 1/2 Cup | 11 |
| | | | Salad, Apple & Raisin | 1/2 Cup | 25 |
| | | | Salad, Apricot W/Lettuce & French Dressing | 1 Serv. | 7 |
| | | | Salad, Artichoke | 1 Serv. | 14 |
| | | | Salad, Asparagus | 5 Spears | 4 |
| | | | Salad, Aspic Tomato | 1/2 Cup | 4 |

| FOOD | AMT. | CARB. GRAMS | FOOD | AMT. | CARB. GRAMS |
|---|---|---|---|---|---|
| Salads, Avocado W/Dressing | 1/2 Cup | 5 | (Wish-Bone) Classic | 1 Tbsp. | 2 |
| Salad, Avocado & Lime | | | (Wish-Bone) Deluxe | 1 Tbsp. | 2 |
| Gelatin | 1 Serv. | 6 | French Homemade | 1 Tbsp. | 2 |
| Salads, Avocado-Tomato | | | Garlic: | | |
| Cheese | 1 Serv. | 9 | (Best Foods) | | |
| Salad, Banana | 1/2 Ban. | 15 | Old Homestead | 1 Tbsp. | 3 |
| Salad, Banana & Nut | 1/2 Ban. | 15 | (Hellmann's) | | |
| Salad, Banana & Orange | 1/2 Ea. | 23 | Old Homestead | 1 Tbsp. | 3 |
| Salad, Banana & Peanut | 1 Serv. | 34 | (Kraft) Salad Bowl | 1 Tbsp. | 2 |
| Salad, Cabbage & Raisin | 4 Ozs. | 20 | (Lawry's) San Francisco | 1 Tbsp. | T |
| Salad, Cabbage Slaw | 1/2 Cup | 5 | (Wish-Bone) | 1 Tbsp. | 3 |
| Salad, California | 1 Serv. | 10 | (Wish-Bone) Monaco | 1 Tbsp. | 3 |
| Salad, Cantaloupe, Pineapple | | | Green Goddess: | | |
| & Cherry | 1 Serv. | 13 | (Kraft) | 1 Tbsp. | T |
| Salad, Carrot-Raisin | 3 Tbsp. | 28 | (Lawry's) | 1 Tbsp. | T |
| Salad, Celery & Meat | 1 Serv. | 9 | (Wish-Bone) | 1 Tbsp. | 1 |
| Salad, Cheese & Olive | 1 Serv. | 4 | Hawaiian (Lawry's) | 1 Tbsp. | 6 |
| Salad, Chef's Bowl | 1 Serv. | 24 | Heinz Salad Dressing | 1 Tbsp. | 2 |
| Salad, Cherry & Cheese | 1 Serv. | 17 | Herb & Garlic (Kraft) | 1 Tbsp. | T |
| Salad, Chicken | 4 Ozs. | 3 | Hickory Bits (Wish-Bone) | 1 Tbsp. | T |
| Salad, Chicken With Celery | 1/2 Cup | 2 | Home Cooked | 1 Tbsp. | 3 |
| Salad, Combination Vegetable | 1/2 Cup | 16 | Italian: | | |
| Salad, Crab With Celery | 1/2 Cup | 3 | (Hellmann's) True | 1 Tbsp. | 1 |
| Salad Dressing: | | | (Kraft) | 1 Tbsp. | T |
| Avocado | 2 Tbsp. | 1 | (Kraft) Salad Bowl | 1 Tbsp. | T |
| Bacon Vinegar | 1 Tbsp. | 1 | (Lawry's) With Cheese | 1 Tbsp. | 4 |
| Blue Cheese | 1 Tbsp. | 1 | (Wish-Bone) Golden | 1 Tbsp. | 1 |
| (Kraft) | 1 Tbsp. | T | (Wish-Bone) Low Oil | 1 Tbsp. | 1 |
| (Lawry's) | 1 Tbsp. | 1 | (Wish-Bone) Rose | 1 Tbsp. | T |
| Roka (Kraft) | 1 Tbsp. | T | Mayonnaise | 1 Tbsp. | T |
| Boiled | 1/4 Cup | 12 | Oil & Vinegar | 1/2 Cup | 0 |
| Caesar: | | | (Kraft) | 1 Tbsp. | T |
| (Lawry's) | 1 Tbsp. | T | Onion, Creamy (Wish-Bone) | 1 Tbsp. | 1 |
| (Wish-Bone) | 1 Tbsp. | T | Orleans (Wish-Bone) | 1 Tbsp. | 1 |
| Canadian (Lawry's) | 1 Tbsp. | T | Roquefort Cheese | 1 Tbsp. | T |
| Cheese (Wish-Bone) | 1 Tbsp. | 1 | (Kraft) Refrigerated | 1 Tbsp. | 1 |
| Chef Style, Salad Bowl (Kraft) | 1 Tbsp. | 2 | Russian | 1 Tbsp. | T |
| Chiffonade | 1 Tbsp. | 1 | (Kraft) Pourable | 1 Tbsp. | 4 |
| Coleslaw (Kraft) | 1 Tbsp. | 3 | (Wish-Bone) | 1 Tbsp. | 7 |
| Commercial, Mayonnaise Type | 1 Tbsp. | T | Salad Bowl (Kraft) | 1 Tbsp. | 2 |
| Miracle Whip (Kraft) | 1 Tbsp. | 1 | Salad Secret (Kraft) | 1 Tbsp. | 2 |
| Cuisine (Kraft) | 1 Tbsp. | 2 | Sherry (Lawry's) | 1 Tbsp. | 1 |
| French | 1 Tbsp. | 4 | Spin Blend (Hellmann's) | 1 Tbsp. | 2 |
| (Best Foods) Family | 1 Tbsp. | 3 | Sweet & Sour (Kraft) | 1 Tbsp. | 7 |
| (Hellmann's) Family | 1 Tbsp. | 3 | Tahitian Isle (Wish-Bone) | 1 Tbsp. | 7 |
| (Heinz) | 1 Tbsp. | 2 | Tang (Nalley's) | 1 Tbsp. | 2 |
| (Kraft) | 1 Tbsp. | 2 | Thousand Island: | | |
| (Kraft) Casino | 1 Tbsp. | 3 | (Best Foods) Pourable | 1 Tbsp. | 3 |
| (Kraft) Catalina | 1 Tbsp. | 3 | (Hellmann's) Pourable | 1 Tbsp. | 3 |
| (Kraft) Miracle | 1 Tbsp. | 2 | (Kraft) | 1 Tbsp. | 2 |
| (Lawry's) California | 1 Tbsp. | 1 | (Kraft) Pourable | 1 Tbsp. | 3 |
| (Nalley's) | 1 Tbsp. | 2 | (Kraft) Refrigerated | 1 Tbsp. | 2 |

| FOOD | AMT. | CARB. GRAMS | FOOD | AMT. | CARB. GRAMS |
|---|---|---|---|---|---|
| (Kraft) Salad Bowl | 1 Tbsp. | 1 | Coleslaw (Good Seasons) | | |
| (Wish-Bone) | 1 Tbsp. | 2 | Thick, Creamy | 1 Tbsp. | 2 |
| Wine Vinegar & Oil | | | French, Old Fashioned: | | |
| (James H. Black) | 1 Tbsp. | 2 | (Good Seasons) | 1 Tbsp. | T |
| Salad Dressing, Low Calorie: | | | (Lawry's) | 1 Tbsp. | 10 |
| Blue: | | | Garlic (Good Seasons) | 1 Tbsp. | T |
| (Dia-Mel) | 1 Tbsp. | T | Green Goddess: | | |
| (Kraft) | 1 Tbsp. | T | (Good Seasons) | | |
| (Tillie Lewis) | 1 Tbsp. | T | Thick, Creamy | 1 Tbsp. | T |
| Caesar (Tillie Lewis) | 1 Tbsp. | T | (Lawry's) | 1 Tbsp. | 7 |
| Chef Style (Kraft) | 1 Tbsp. | 2 | Italian: | | |
| Chefs (Tillie Lewis) | 1 Tbsp. | T | (Good Seasons) | 1 Tbsp. | T |
| Cole Slaw (Kraft) | 1 Tbsp. | T | (Lawry's) | 1 Tbsp. | 7 |
| Diet Whip (Dia-Mel) | 1 Tbsp. | T | (Lawry's) With Cheese | 1 Tbsp. | 5 |
| French: | | | Onion (Good Seasons) | 1 Tbsp. | T |
| (Dia-Mel) | 1 Tbsp. | T | Parmesan (Good Seasons) | 1 Tbsp. | T |
| Green Garlic | 1 Tbsp. | T | Thousand Island (Good Seasons) | | |
| (Frenchette) | 1 Tbsp. | 2 | Thick, Creamy | 1 Tbsp. | T |
| (Kraft) | 1 Tbsp. | 2 | Salad, Egg & Tomato | 1/2 of Ea. | 4 |
| (Kraft) Fruit 'n Slaw | 1 Tbsp. | 3 | Salad, Endive & Grapefruit | 4 Ozs. | 8 |
| (Marzetti's) | 1 Tbsp. | 3 | Salad, Endive & Grapefruit | 1 Serv. | 16 |
| (Tillie Lewis) | 1 Tbsp. | 1 | Salad, Frozen Cheese | 1 Serv. | T |
| (Wish-Bone) | 1 Tbsp. | 3 | Salad, Fruit Fresh | 3 Tbsp. | 21 |
| (Wish-Bone) Garlic | 1 Tbsp. | 2 | Salad, Gelatin With Fruit | 1 Sq. | 22 |
| Italian: | | | Salad, Gelatin With Vegetables | 1 Sq. | 15 |
| (Dia-Mel) | 1 Tbsp. | T | Salad, Grapefruit & | | |
| Italianette (Frenchette) | 1 Tbsp. | T | Apple Gelatin | 1 Serv. | 26 |
| (Kraft) | 1 Tbsp. | T | Salad, Lettuce With | | |
| (Marzetti's) | 1 Tbsp. | 1 | French Dressing | 1 Wedge | 7 |
| (Tillie Lewis) | 1 Tbsp. | T | Salad, Lettuce & Tomato | 1 Serv. | 6 |
| (Wish-Bone) | 1 Tbsp. | 1 | Salad Lobster | 1 Serv. | 5 |
| May-Lo-Naise (Tillie Lewis) | 1 Tbsp. | T | Salad, Macaroni | 1 Cup | 26 |
| Russian (Dia-Mel) | 1 Tbsp. | 1 | Salad, Melon & Berry | 1 Serv. | 9 |
| Russian (Wish-Bone) | 1 Tbsp. | 5 | Salad, Mixed Greens With | | |
| Slaw (Marzetti's) | 1 Tbsp. | 3 | French Dressing | 1/2 Cup | 5 |
| Supreme (McCormick) | 1 Tbsp. | 2 | Salad Oil | 1 Tbsp. | 0 |
| Thousand Island: | | | Salad, Orange-Grapefruit | | |
| (Kraft) | 1 Tbsp. | T | With Dressing | 1 Serv. | 9 |
| (Marzetti's) | 1 Tbsp. | 3 | Salad, Pear & Roquefort | | |
| (Tillie Lewis) | 1 Tbsp. | T | Cheese | 1 Serv. | 8 |
| Whipped (Tillie Lewis) | 1 Tbsp. | T | Salad, Potato With Onions | 1/2 Cup | 13 |
| Salad Dressing Mix: | | | Salad, Prunes, Stuffed With | | |
| Bacon (Lawry's) | 1 Tbsp. | 9 | Cottage Cheese | 4 | 28 |
| Bleu or Blue Cheese: | | | Salad, Salmon With Celery | 1/2 Cup | 2 |
| (Good Seasons) | 1 Tbsp. | T | Salad Seasoning: | | |
| (Good Seasons) | | | (Durkee) | 1 Tsp. | T |
| Thick, Creamy | 1 Tbsp. | T | With Cheese (Durkee) | 1 Tsp. | T |
| (Lawry's) | 1 Tbsp. | 3 | Salad, Shrimp with Celery | 1 Serv. | 5 |
| Caesar Garlic Cheese | | | Salad, Tomato Aspic | 1/2 Cup | 4 |
| (Lawry's) | 1 Tbsp. | 7 | Salad, Tomato & Cucumber | 1 of Ea. | 7 |
| Cheese Garlic | | | Salad, Tuna | 1/2 Cup | 2 |
| (Good Seasons) | 1 Tbsp. | T | Salad, Waldorf | 1/2 Cup | 10 |

| FOOD | AMT. | CARB. GRAMS | FOOD | AMT. | CARB. GRAMS |
|------|------|------|------|------|------|
| Salad, Waldorf | 4 Ozs. | 12 | Salmon-Scramble Eggs | | |
| Salami | 8 Ozs. | 3 | With Ringed Onions | 4 | 2 |
| (Vienna) | 1 Oz. | T | Salmon Smoked | 2 Ozs. | 0 |
| Beef (Sugardale) | 1 Sl. | T | Salt | 1/8 Tsp. | 0 |
| Cotto (Wilson) | 1 Oz. | T | Garlic (Lawry's) | 1 Tsp. | 1 |
| Salami, Hard | 1 Oz. | T | Imitation, Butter Flavored | | |
| Salami, Italian | 1 Oz. | T | (Durkee) | 1 Tsp. | T |
| Salami, Jewish | 1 Oz. | T | Seasoned (Lawry's) | 1 Tsp. | T |
| Salami Sandwich | 1 | 24 | Substitute (Adolph's) | 1 Dash | T |
| Salami Sausage | 8 Ozs. | 3 | Substitute, Seasoned | | |
| Salisbury Steak | Av. Serv. | T | (Adolph's) | 1 Dash | T |
| Frozen: | | | Salt Butter | 1 Tbsp. | T |
| (Banquet) Buffet | 1 Lb. | 23 | Salt Butter, Patty | 1 Patty | T |
| (Banquet) Cookin' Bag | 1 Lb. | 23 | Salt Celery | 1/8 Tsp. | 0 |
| (Holloway House) | 1 Steak | 50 | Salt Mackerel | Av. Serv. | 0 |
| (Swanson) | 1 Pkg. | 35 | Salt Pork Fat | 2 Ozs. | 0 |
| Dinner, Frozen: | | | Salt Pork | Av. Serv. | 0 |
| (Banquet) | Dinner | 21 | Salt Water Taffy | 1 In. Cube | 10 |
| (Morton) | Dinner | 16 | Salted Almonds | 12 Med. | 3 |
| (Swanson) 3-Course | Dinner | 50 | Saltine Crackers | 6 | 36 |
| Sally Lunn Bread | 1 Sq. | 22 | Sancerre Wine, French White, | | |
| Salmon, Baked | 1 Serv. | 0 | Loire Valley: | | |
| Salmon, Broiled | 4 Ozs. | 0 | (Barton & Guestier) | 3 Fl. Ozs. | T |
| Salmon (Canned, A-C-D) | 1/2 Cup | 0 | (Chanson) | 3 Fl. Ozs. | 6 |
| Chinook or King: | | | Sandwiches, Bacon-Egg | 1 | 24 |
| (Icy Point) | 1 Can | 0 | Sandwich, Bacon, Tomato, Lettuce | 1 | 29 |
| (Pillar Rock) | 1 Can | 0 | Sandwich, Barbecue Beef | 1 | 24 |
| Pink or Humpback: | | | Sandwich, Barbecue Pork | 1 | 24 |
| (Icy Point) | 1 Can | 0 | Sandwich, Bologna | 1 | 26 |
| (Del Monte) | 1 Can | 0 | Sandwich, Cervelat | 1 | 24 |
| (Pink Beauty) | 1 Can | 0 | Sandwich, Cheeseburger | 1 | 22 |
| Sockeye, Red or Blueback: | | | Sandwich, Cheese, Camembert | 1 | 24 |
| (Icy Point) | 1 Can | 0 | Sandwich, Cheese, Cheddar | 1 | 26 |
| (Pillar Rock) | 1 Can | 0 | Sandwich, Cheese & Olive | 1 | 25 |
| Unseasoned (S and W) | | | Sandwich, Cheese, Swiss | 1 | 24 |
| Nutradiet | 1 Can | 1 | Sandwich, Chicken Liver | 1 | 26 |
| Salmon (Canned), | | | Sandwich, Chicken Salad | 1 | 25 |
| Humpback | Av. Serv. | 0 | Sandwich, Club | 1 | 39 |
| Salmon Chowder | 1 Cup | 7 | Sandwich, Club—3 Decker | 1 | 42 |
| Salmon (Canned), Chum | Av. Serv. | 0 | Sandwich, Corned Beef | 1 | 24 |
| Salmon, Creamed | 1/2 Cup | 4 | Sandwich, Crabmeat | 1 | 25 |
| Salmon, Creamed On Toast | 1/2 Cup | 16 | Sandwich, Cream Cheese & Jelly | 1 | 50 |
| Salmon Delights | Av. Serv. | 0 | Sandwich, Cream Cheese & Nut | 1 | 25 |
| Salmon, King | 1 Serv. | 0 | Sandwich, Denver, Western | 1 | 28 |
| Salmon Loaf | Av. Serv. | 7 | Sandwich, Egg, Fried | 1 | 24 |
| Salmon, Nova Scotia | 2 Ozs. | 0 | Sandwich, Frankfurter | 1 | 12 |
| Salmon Pink Canned | Av. Serv. | 0 | Sandwich, Ham, Boiled or Baked | 1 | 24 |
| Salmon Red & Sockeye, | | | Sandwich, Hamburger | 1 | 21 |
| Canned | Av. Serv. | 0 | Sandwich, Ham, Fried | 1 | 24 |
| Salmon, Salad With Celery | 1/2 Cup | 2 | Sandwich, Ham Salad | 1 | 26 |
| Salmon Salad Sandwich | 1 | 25 | Sandwich, Ham & Swiss Cheese | 1 | 25 |
| Salmon Sandwich | 1 | 24 | Sandwich, Ice Cream | 1 | 45 |

| FOOD | AMT. | CARB. GRAMS |
|---|---|---|
| Sandwich, Liverwurst | 1 | 25 |
| Sandwich, Luncheon Meat | 1 | 25 |
| Sandwich, Meat Loaf | 1 | 30 |
| Sandwich, Oyster, Fried | 1 | 41 |
| Sandwich, Pastrami | 1 | 24 |
| Sandwich, Peanut Butter | 1 | 29 |
| Sandwich, Peanut Butter & Jelly | 1 | 35 |
| Sandwich, Pork Sausage | 1 | 24 |
| Sandwich, Roast Beef | 1 | 24 |
| Sandwich, Roast Beef With Gravy | 1 | 27 |
| Sandwich, Roast Pork | 1 | 24 |
| Sandwich, Roast Pork With Gravy | 1 | 27 |
| Sandwich, Roquefort Spread | 1 | 26 |
| Sandwich, Salami | 1 | 24 |
| Sandwich, Salmon | 1 | 24 |
| Sandwich, Salmon Salad | 1 | 25 |
| Sandwich, Sardine | 1 | 24 |
| Sandwich, Shrimp Fried (6 Small) | 1 | 32 |
| Sandwich, Shrimp Salad | 1 | 26 |
| Sandwich, Sole, Fried | 1 | 36 |
| Sandwich Spread: | | |
| (Best Foods) | 1 Tbsp. | 2 |
| (Hellmann's) | 1 Tbsp. | 2 |
| Miracle (Kraft) | 1 Tbsp. | 3 |
| (Nalley's) | 1 Tbsp. | 3 |
| (Tillie Lewis) Dietetic | 1 Tbsp. | T |
| Sandwich, Steak | 1 | 24 |
| Sandwich, Tomato & Lettuce | 1 | 26 |
| Sandwich, Tongue | 1 | 24 |
| Sandwich, Tuna | 1 | 24 |
| Sandwich, Tuna Salad | 1 | 26 |
| Sandwich, Turkey | 1 | 24 |
| Sandwich, Turkey With Gravy | 1 | 28 |
| Sandwich, Vienna Sausage | 1 | 24 |
| Santiago Cocktail | 1 Gl. | 3 |
| Sepodilla, Raw | 4 Ozs. | 22 |
| Sepote, Marmalade Plums, Raw | 4 Ozs. | 32 |
| Sardines (Canned) | Av Serv | T |
| Norwegian (Underwood) | 3 Ozs. | 1 |
| In Oil, Drained Solids | 3 Ozs. | 0 |
| In Tomato Sauce | 3 Ozs. | 1 |
| Sardines (Canned With Tomato Sauce) | 1 | T |
| Sardine, Natural Pack | 3 Ozs. | 0 |
| Sardines, W/Oil Drained | 2 Ozs. | 0 |
| Sardines W/Oil & Solids | 3 Ozs. | 1 |
| Sardine Sandwich | 1 | 24 |
| Sarsaparilla, Soft Drink | 8 Ozs. | 28 |
| (Hoffman) | 8 Fl. Ozs. | 28 |
| (Yukon Club) | 8 Fl. Ozs. | 29 |
| Sauce, A-1 | 1 Tsp. | 0 |

| FOOD | AMT. | CARB. GRAMS |
|---|---|---|
| Sauce, Anchovy | 3/4 Cup | 2 |
| Sauce, Apple Canned (Infant) | 1 Oz. | 5 |
| Sauce, Apple Canned-Strained | 1/2 Cup | 22 |
| Sauce, Apple With Sugar | 1/2 Cup | 23 |
| Sauce, Barbecue | 1 Tbsp. | T |
| (Good Seasons) Open Pit | 1 Tbsp. | 6 |
| (Heinz) With Onions | 1 Tbsp. | 4 |
| (Kraft) | 1 Tbsp. | 4 |
| (Kraft) Garlic | 1 Tbsp. | 3 |
| (Kraft) Hot | 1 Tbsp. | 3 |
| (Kraft) Smoked | 1 Tbsp. | 4 |
| Sauce, Bechamel | 1/2 Cup | 7 |
| Sauce, Bolognaise (Crosse & Blackwell) | 1 Tbsp. | 1 |
| Sauce, Bordelaise (Crosse & Blackwell) | 1 Tbsp. | 1 |
| Sauce, Brittany | 1 Tbsp. | 2 |
| Sauce, Brown | 1 Tbsp. | 1 |
| Sauce, Butterscotch | 1 Tbsp. | 5 |
| Sauce, Caper | 1 Tbsp. | T |
| Sauce, Caramel | 1 Tbsp. | 46 |
| Sauce, Champignon (Crosse & Blackwell) | 1 Tbsp. | 1 |
| Sauce, Cheese (Kraft) Deluxe Dinner | 1 Tbsp. | 1 |
| Sauce, Cheese | 1/2 Cup | 5 |
| Sauce, Cherry | 2 Tbsp. | 19 |
| Sauce, Chili | 1 Tbsp. | 4 |
| Sauce, Chocolate | 1 Tbsp. | 5 |
| Sauce, Chocolate Custard | 1 Tbsp. | 2 |
| Sauce, Chocolate-Mint | 1 Serv. | 53 |
| Sauce, Cocktail Refrigerated (Kraft) | 1 Tbsp. | 3 |
| Sauce, Cranberry | 3 Tbsp. | 27 |
| Sauce, Cream | 2 Tbsp. | 2 |
| Sauce, Creole | 1/4 Cup | 8 |
| Sauce, Custard | 1 Tbsp. | 2 |
| Sauce, Enchilada (Rosarita) | 1 Tbsp. | T |
| Sauce, Famous (Durkee) | 1 Tbsp. | 1 |
| Sauce, 57 (Heinz) | 1 Tbsp. | 3 |
| Sauce, Fudge | 1 Tbsp. | 18 |
| Sauce, Garlic | 1 Tbsp. | 3 |
| Sauce, Garlic w/Butter | 2 Tbsp. | 1 |
| Sauce, Garlic w/Water | 2 Tbsp. | T |
| Sauce, Hard | 1 Tbsp. | 14 |
| (Crosse & Blackwell) | 1 Tbsp. | 8 |
| Sauce, Hollandaise | 1 Tbsp. | 1 |
| Sauce, Hollandaise, Mock | 1/4 Cup | 6 |
| Sauce, Horseradish (Kraft) | 1 Tbsp. | 1 |
| Sauce, H.P. (Lea & Perrins) | 1 Tbsp. | T |
| Sauce, Hot Tomato (Rosarita) | 1 Tbsp. | T |

101

| FOOD | AMT. | CARB. GRAMS |
|---|---|---|
| Sauce, Lemon | 1 Tbsp. | 5 |
| Sauce, Lobster | 1 Tbsp. | 4 |
| Sauce, Marinara: | | |
| (Buitoni) | 1 Tbsp. | 1 |
| (Chef Boy-Ar-Dee) | 1 Can | 40 |
| Sauce, Marshmallow | 1 Tbsp. | 6 |
| Sauce, Meat, Italian | 1 Cup | 21 |
| Sauce, Mint (Crosse & Blackwell) | 1 Tbsp. | 4 |
| Sauce, Mustard | 1/4 Cup | 6 |
| Sauce, Newburg | | |
| (Crosse & Blackwell) | 1 Tbsp. | 1 |
| Sauce, Plum Pudding | 1 Tbsp. | 5 |
| Sauce, Polynesian | | |
| (Crosse & Blackwell) | 1 Tbsp. | 3 |
| Sauce, Raisin | 1/4 Cup | 26 |
| Sauce, Remoulade, Dietetic | | |
| (Tillie Lewis) | 1 Tbsp. | T |
| Sauce, Savory (Heinz) | 1 Tbsp. | 1 |
| Sauce, Seafood Cocktail | | |
| (Crosse & Blackwell) | 1 Tbsp. | 5 |
| Sauce, Shrimp Cocktail | | |
| (Crosse & Blackwell) | 1 Tbsp. | 5 |
| Sauce, Simple Syrup | 1 Tbsp. | 9 |
| Sauce, Sour Cream | 1 Tbsp. | 3 |
| Sauce, Soybean | 1 Tbsp. | 0 |
| Sauce, Steak | | |
| (Crosse & Blackwell) | 1 Tbsp. | 5 |
| Sauce, Sweet & Sour (Kraft) | 1 Tbsp. | 2 |
| Sauce, Tartar | 1 Tbsp. | T |
| (Best Foods) | 1 Tbsp. | T |
| (Kraft) | 1 Oz. | T |
| (Kraft) Spice Blend | 1 Oz. | T |
| Sauce, Tomato | 1/4 Cup | 4 |
| Sauce, White Medium | 1 Tbsp. | 1 |
| Sauce, Wine | 1 Tbsp. | 2 |
| Sauce, Worcestershire | 1 Tbsp. | 2 |
| (Crosse & Blackwell) | 1 Tbsp. | 3 |
| (Heinz) | 1 Tbsp. | 1 |
| (Lea & Perrins) | 1 Tbsp. | T |
| Sauce Mix: | | |
| A la King, Without Chicken | | |
| (Durkee) | 1 Oz. | 19 |
| Barbecue (Kraft) | 1 Oz. | 6 |
| Cheese: | | |
| (Durkee) | 1 Oz. | 10 |
| (French's) | 1 Oz. | 5 |
| (Kraft) | 1 Oz. | 2 |
| (McCormick) | 1 Oz. | 2 |
| Chicken (Kraft) | 1 Oz. | 2 |
| Cream (Kraft) | 1 Oz. | 2 |
| Enchilada (Lawry's) | 1 Oz. | 16 |
| Hollandaise: | | |
| (Durkee) | 1 Oz. | 5 |

| FOOD | AMT. | CARB. GRAMS |
|---|---|---|
| (French's) | 1 Oz. | 6 |
| (Kraft) | 1 Oz. | 4 |
| (McCormick) | 1 Oz. | 4 |
| Newburg (French's) | 1 Oz. | 8 |
| Seafood Cocktail (Lawry's) | 1 Oz. | 17 |
| Sour Cream: | | |
| (French's) | 1 Oz. | 4 |
| (Kraft) | 1 Oz. | 4 |
| (McCormick) | 1 Oz. | 1 |
| With Skim Milk | | |
| (Durkee) | 1 Oz. | 8 |
| With Whole Milk | | |
| (Durkee) | 1 Oz. | 8 |
| Stroganoff (French's) | 1 Oz. | 13 |
| White Sauce Supreme | | |
| (McCormick) | 1 Oz. | 2 |
| Sauerbraten | Av. Serv. | 0 |
| Sauerkraut | 1/2 Cup | 5 |
| Canned (Steinfield's) | 1 Cup | 6 |
| Sauerkraut Juice | 6 Ozs. | 1 |
| Sausage, Bologna | 2 Ozs. | 2 |
| Sausage, Breakfast (Hormel) | 1 Oz. | T |
| Sausage, Brown & Serve | | |
| Canned (Hormel) | 1 Oz. | T |
| Sausage (Canned) Pork | 4 Ozs. | 2 |
| Sausage, Cervelat | 4 Ozs. | 1 |
| Sausage With Chicken | Av. Serv. | 3 |
| Sausage, Frankfurter, Cooked | 1 | 1 |
| Sausage, Frankfurter | 1 Av. | T |
| Sausage In Sauce (Prince) | 1 Av. | 1 |
| Sausage, Knockwurst | 1 Av. | 1 |
| Sausage, Liver | 1 Slice | T |
| Sausage, New England Brand | | |
| (Wilson) | 1 Oz. | T |
| Sausage, Pizza | 1 Slice | 23 |
| Sausage, Polish | 4 Ozs. | 1 |
| Sausage, Pork | Two 3" | 0 |
| Sausage, Pork Dried | 4 Ozs. | 0 |
| Sausage, Pork Patty | 1/2 Av. | 0 |
| Sausage, Salami | 8 Ozs. | 3 |
| Sausage, Vienna Canned | 8 Ozs. | 1 |
| Saute Chasseur, Chicken | 1 Serv. | 7 |
| Sauteed Mushrooms With | | |
| 2 Tbsp. Butter | 1/2 Cup | 4 |
| Sauteed Chicken | 1 Serv. | 5 |
| Sauteed Okra And | | |
| Tomatoes | 1 Av. Serv. | 9 |
| Sauterne Punch | 1 Av. Serv. | 37 |
| Sauterne Wine, Dry | 1 Gl. | 1 |
| Sauterne Wine, Sweet | 1 Gl. | 4 |
| Sauternes: | | |
| (Barton & Guestier) French | | |
| White Bordeaux | 3 Fl. Ozs. | 7 |

| FOOD | AMT. | CARB. GRAMS | FOOD | AMT. | CARB. GRAMS |
|---|---|---|---|---|---|
| (Barton & Guestier) Haut, French White Bordeaux | 3 Fl. Ozs. | 8 | Sea Bass | 4 Ozs. | 0 |
| (Gallo) | 3 Fl. Ozs. | 1 | Seafood Aspic | 1 Serv. | 2 |
| (Gallo) Haut | 3 Fl. Ozs. | 2 | Seafood Au Gratin | 1/2 Cup | 12 |
| (Gold Seal) Dry | 3 Fl. Ozs. | T | Seafood Cocktail | 1 Serv. | 1 |
| (Gold Seal) Semi-Soft | 3 Fl. Ozs. | 2 | Seafood Cocktail Sauce | 1 Tbsp. | T |
| (Great Western) Aurora | 3 Fl. Ozs. | 4 | Seafood-Stuffed Avocados | 1 Serv. | 7 |
| (Italian Swiss Colony-Gold Medal) | 3 Fl. Ozs. | T | Sea Perch, Yellow, Raw | 1 Serv. | 0 |
| (Louis M. Martini) Dry | 3 Fl. Ozs. | T | Sea Perch, White, Raw | 1 Serv. | 0 |
| (Mogen David) Cream | 3 Fl. Ozs. | 6 | Sectioned Orange | 1 Cup | 11 |
| (Mogen David) Dry, American | 3 Fl. Ozs. | 2 | Seed, Lotus Root | 2/3 Av. Seg. | 16 |
| (Taylor) | 3 Fl. Ozs. | 3 | Seed, Pumpkin, Dry | 4 Ozs. | 15 |
| Savory | 1/8 Tsp. | 0 | Seeded Persimmons | 1 Med. | 20 |
| Savory Lamb Patties | 1 Av. Serv. | 0 | Seedless Grape, Thompson | 1/2 Cup | 17 |
| Sazerac | 3 Ozs. | T | Seeds, Caraway | 1/8 Tsp. | 0 |
| Scallions | 5 | 5 | Seeds, Fennel | 1/8 Tsp. | 0 |
| Scallops Royale | Av. Serv. | | Seeds, Sesame Whole | 1 Oz. | 6 |
| Scalloped Cod & Clams | 1 Serv. | 8 | Seeds, Sesame | 1 Oz. | 0 |
| Scalloped Onions | 1/2 Cup | 15 | Seeds, Soybean, Immature | 4 Ozs. | 37 |
| Scalloped Oysters | 6 | 6 | Sego, Diet Food: | | |
| Scalloped Potatoes | 1/2 Cup | 14 | Instant Mix With Whole Milk | 1 Cup | 17 |
| Scallops | Av. Serv. | 2 | Liquid Diet | 1 Cup | 28 |
| Breaded, Fried: | | | Sekt Sparkling Wine | | |
| Reheated (Booth) | 4 Ozs. | 12 | (Deinhard) | 3 Fl. Ozs. | 3 |
| (Mrs. Paul's) | 4 Ozs. | 12 | Self Rising Wheat Flour | 1 Cup | 85 |
| Scallops, Banana | 1 Serv. | 31 | Seltzer (Carbonated Water) | 4 Ozs. | 0 |
| Scallops, Broiled | 1 Serv. | 2 | Seltzer Water | 8 Ozs. | 0 |
| Scallops, Fried W/Batter | 3-4 Lg. | 15 | Semi-Sweet Chocolate | 1 Oz. | 17 |
| Scamorze Cheese | 1-1/2 Ozs. | T | Senegalese Soup | | |
| Scampi Shrimp | 6 In Garlic Butter | T | (Crosse & Blackwell) | 1 Can | 13 |
| Scarlett O'Hara Cocktail | 1 Gl. | 4 | Sesame Seeds | 1 Oz. | 0 |
| Schnapps, Peppermint: | | | Sesame Seeds, Whole | 1 Oz. | 6 |
| (Garnier) | 1 Fl. Oz. | 8 | Seven Minute Frosting | 1 Tbsp. | 6 |
| (Hiram Walker) | 1 Fl. Oz. | 7 | Seven-Up, Soft Drink | 8 Fl. Ozs. | 24 |
| (Leroux) | 1 Fl. Oz. | 9 | Shad, Baked | Av. Serv. | 0 |
| (Old Mr. Boston): | | | Shad, Broiled | Av. Serv. | 0 |
| 42 Proof | 1 Fl. Oz. | 4 | Shad Roe | Av. Serv. | 0 |
| 60 Proof | 1 Fl. Oz. | 4 | Shake 'N Bake (Good Seasons) Seasoned: | | |
| Scone (Hostess) | 1 Pkg. | 34 | Chicken-Coating Mix | 1 Pkg. | 30 |
| Scotch | Shot | 0 | Fish-Coating Mix | 1 Pkg. | 25 |
| Scotch Broth | Av. Serv. | 0 | Pork-Coating Mix | 1 Pkg. | 45 |
| Condensed (Campbell) | 4 Ozs. | 9 | Shake, Milk | 1 Aver. | 49 |
| Scotch Mist | 6 Ozs. | 0 | Shakes, Malted Milk, Misc. Flavor | 8 Ozs. | 56 |
| Scotch Oatmeal Cooked | 4 Ozs. | 10 | Shalots | 1 Clove | 0 |
| Scotch Shortbread Cookie | 1 | 5 | Shape (Drackett): | | |
| Scotch & Soda | 1 Drink | 0 | Liquid, Any Flavor | 8 Fl. Ozs. | 33 |
| Scotch Whiskey | 1 Oz. | 0 | Powder: | | |
| Scrambled Eggs | Av. Serv. | T | Chocolate | 1 Oz. | 19 |
| Scrapple, Philadelphia | Av. Serv. | 26 | Strawberry or Vanilla | 1 Oz. | 20 |
| Screwdriver Mixer, Soft Drink | | | Shark's Fin, Dried | Av. Serv. | T |
| (Canada Dry) | 6 Fl. Ozs. | 19 | Sheep Liver | Av. Serv. | 4 |

103

| FOOD | AMT. | CARB. GRAMS |
|---|---|---|
| Sheep's Kidney | 1 Serv. | 1 |
| Sheep's Milk | 1/2 Cup | 6 |
| Shelled Brazil Nuts | 4 Ozs. | 11 |
| Shepherd's Eggs | Av. Serv. | 2 |
| Sherbet | Av. Scp. | 29 |
| Sherbet, Orange | Av. Scp. | 29 |
| (Sealtest) | 1 Cup | 53 |
| Sherbet, Pineapple | Av. Scp. | 29 |
| Sherbet, Raspberry | Av. Scp. | 29 |
| Sherbet Or Ice, Avocado | 1 Serv. | 8 |
| Sherbet Ice Cream, With Milk | 1/4 Pt. | 45 |
| Sherbet Ice Cream, With Water | 1/4 Pt. | 35 |
| Sherried Consomme | Av. Serv. | 0 |
| Sherry: | | |
| (Gallo) 20% Alcohol | 3 Fl. Ozs. | 2 |
| (Gallo) 16% Alcohol | 3 Fl. Ozs. | 3 |
| (Gold Seal) | 3 Fl. Ozs. | 4 |
| (Great Western) Solera | 3 Fl. Ozs. | 8 |
| (Taylor) | 3 Fl. Ozs. | 7 |
| Cocktail (Gold Seal) | 3 Fl. Ozs. | 1 |
| Cream: | | |
| (Gallo) | 3 Fl. Ozs. | 8 |
| (Gallo) Old Decanter, Livingston | 3 Fl. Ozs. | 12 |
| (Gold Seal) | 3 Fl. Ozs. | 9 |
| (Great Western) Solera | 3 Fl. Ozs. | 11 |
| (Italian Swiss Colony-Private Stock) | 3 Fl. Ozs. | 8 |
| (Louis M. Martini) | 3 Fl. Ozs. | 1 |
| (Taylor) | 3 Fl. Ozs. | 11 |
| (Williams & Humbert) Canasta | 3 Fl. Ozs. | 5 |
| Dry: | | |
| (Gallo) | 3 Fl. Ozs. | 1 |
| (Gallo) Old Decanter, Very Dry | 3 Fl. Ozs. | 2 |
| (Great Western) Solera | 3 Fl. Ozs. | 4 |
| (Italian Swiss Colony-Gold Medal) | 3 Fl. Ozs. | 4 |
| (Italian Swiss Colony-Private Stock) | 3 Fl. Ozs. | 1 |
| (Louis M. Martini) | 3 Fl. Ozs. | 1 |
| (Williams & Humbert) Carlito Amontillado | 3 Fl. Ozs. | 4 |
| (Williams & Humbert) Cedro | 3 Fl. Ozs. | 4 |
| (Williams & Humbert) Dos Cortados | 3 Fl. Ozs. | 4 |
| (Williams & Humbert) Pando | 3 Fl. Ozs. | 4 |
| Dry Sack (Williams & Humbert) | 3 Fl. Ozs. | 4 |
| Hartley (Italian Swiss Colony-Private Blend) | 3 Fl. Ozs. | 2 |
| Medium: | | |
| (Great Western) Cooking | 3 Fl. Ozs. | 7 |
| (Italian Swiss Colony-Gold Medal) | 3 Fl. Ozs. | 2 |
| (Italian Swiss Colony-Private Stock) | 3 Fl. Ozs. | 3 |
| Sherry Wine | 1 Glass | 5 |
| Sherry Wine Flip | 1 Glass | 32 |
| Sherry Cobbler | 1 Av. | 44 |
| Sherry Fruit Cup | 1 Serv. | 42 |
| Sherry Old-Fashioned | 1 Glass | 10 |
| Sherried Mushroom & Chicken | 1 Serv. | 16 |
| Sherried Mushroom Consomme | 1 Serv. | 3 |
| Sherried Veal Scallops | 1 Serv. | 2 |
| Shingle Stain Beverage | 12 Ozs. | 3 |
| Shirred Egg | 1 Av. Serv. | 2 |
| Shish Kebab | Av. Serv. | 3 |
| Shish Kebab, Lamb | Av. Serv. | 13 |
| Shish Kebab Sauce | 1 Tbsp. | T |
| Shoofly Pie | 1 Piece | 48 |
| Shoots Bamboo | 2/3 Cup | 5 |
| Short Bread | 1 Slice | 19 |
| Short Cake, Plain | 1 Serv. | 31 |
| Short Cake, Banana | Av. Serv. | 44 |
| Short Cake, Biscuit | 1 | 27 |
| Short Cake, Peach | Av. Serv. | 41 |
| Short Cake, Raspberry | Med. Serv. | 47 |
| Short Cake, Strawberry | Av. Serv. | 43 |
| Shortening, Crisco | 1 Tbsp. | 0 |
| Short Ribs of Beef, Braised | Av. Serv. | 0 |
| Shoulder Pork | Av. Serv. | 0 |
| Shredded Cabbage | 1 Cup | 5 |
| Shredded Dried Coconut Sweetened | 1 Cup | 33 |
| Shredded Wheat | 1 | 18 |
| (Kellogg's) | 1 Biscuit | 15 |
| (Nabisco) | 1 Biscuit | 19 |
| (Nabisco) Spoon Size | 1 Biscuit | 1 |
| (Quaker) | 1 Biscuit | 15 |
| (Sunshine) | 1 Biscuit | 22 |
| Shredded Wheat, Ralston Bite Size | 1 Oz. | 23 |
| Shredded Wheat Malt Sugar & Salt | 4 Ozs. | 81 |
| Shredded Wheat Biscuit | 1 | 18 |
| Shredded Fresh Coconut | 1/2 Cup | 11 |

| FOOD | AMT. | CARB. GRAMS | FOOD | AMT. | CARB. GRAMS |
|---|---|---|---|---|---|
| Shrimp | 10 Av. | T | Sirloin Chops, Lamb | 4 Ozs. | 0 |
| Shrimp And Lobster Aspic | 1 Serv. | 22 | Sirloin Steak | Av. Serv. | 0 |
| Shrimp, Boiled | 4 Ozs. | 2 | Sirloin Tips, Beef | Av. Serv. | 0 |
| Shrimp, Canned Drained | 3 Ozs. | T | Skimmed Chocolate Milk | 8 Ozs. | 26 |
| (Pink Beauty) | 4 Ozs. | 27 | Skimmed Milk | 1 Cup | 13 |
| Shrimp, Canned, Dry Packed | 3 Ozs. | T | Skimmed Milk Cocoa | 3/4 Cup | 9 |
| Dry Packed | 3 Ozs. | T | Skimmed Milk Cocoa | 8 Ozs. | 12 |
| Shrimp, Canned, Wet Pack | 3 Ozs. | T | Skimmed Milk Oyster Stew | 1 Cup | 12 |
| Shrimp Cocktail | 6 Med. Size | 1 | Slender (Carnation) | 1 Envelope | 7 |
| (Sau-Sea) | 4 Ozs. | 18 | Slender | 1 Large | 30 |
| (Sea Snack) | 4 Ozs. | 15 | Sliced Bananas | 1 Large | 30 |
| Shrimp Creole | Av. Serv. | 4 | Sliced Pineapple, Fresh | 2 Slices | 23 |
| Shrimp Dinner, Frozen: | | | Slimming Roast Chicken | Av. Serv. | 0 |
| (Morton) | Dinner | 33 | Sling, Singapore | 8 Ozs. | 9 |
| Fried (Swanson) | Dinner | 41 | Sloe Gin | 1 Oz. | 3 |
| Shrimp Egg Foo Yung | Av. Portion | 8 | Sloe Gin Cocktail | 1 Oz. | 3 |
| Shrimp French Fried | 10 Av. | 11 | Sloe Gin Collins | 10 Ozs. | 16 |
| Shrimp, Fried | 3 Jumbo | 8 | Sloe Gin Fizz | 1 Glass | 5 |
| Shrimp, Fried, Sandwich | 1 W/6 Small | 32 | Sloppy Joe, Frozen | | |
| Shrimp, Fried | | | (Banquet) Cookin' Bag | 5 Ozs. | 11 |
| w/Canton Sauce | 1 Serv. | 42 | Sloppy Joe Mix: | | |
| Shrimp, Frozen: | | | Sauce (French's) | Pkg. | 26 |
| Breaded (Booth) | 4 Ozs. | 22 | With Meat & Tomato Paste | | |
| Breaded (Chicken of the Sea) | 4 Ozs. | 22 | (Durkee) | 1 Cup | 33 |
| Breaded, Fried | | | Seasoning (Lawry's) | 1 Pkg. | 27 |
| (Mrs. Paul's) | 4 Ozs. | 23 | Seasoning (Wyler's) | 1 Pkg. | 20 |
| Shrimp Oslo | 1 Serv. | 15 | Small Dinger Cocktail | 1 Cktl. Gl. | 0 |
| Shrimp Pizza | 1/6 12" Dia. | 23 | Smelts | 7 Med. | 0 |
| Shrimp Roll, Frozen (Temple) | 1 Roll | 20 | Smelts, Broiled | 7 Med. | 0 |
| Shrimp Salad With Celery | 1 Serv. | 5 | Smelts, Fried | 7 Med. | 7 |
| Shrimp Salad With | | | Smoked Brook Trout | 3 Ozs. | 0 |
| Bean Sprouts | 1 Serv. | 9 | Smoked Eels | 4 Ozs. | 0 |
| Shrimp Soup, Cream Of: | | | Smoked Finnan Haddie | 1 | 0 |
| Canned (Crosse & Blackwell) | 4 Ozs. | 4 | Smoked Haddock | 1 Serv. | 0 |
| Frozen, Condensed | | | Smoked Herring | 1/2 Fish | 0 |
| (Campbell) | 4 Ozs. | 7 | Smoked Lake Trout | 3 Ozs. | 0 |
| Shrimp Salad Sandwich | 1 | 26 | Smoked Lox Nova Scotia | 1 Serv. | 0 |
| Shrimp Salad Oriental | 1 Serv. | 4 | Smoked Salmon | 2 Ozs. | 0 |
| Shrimp Scampi | 6 In Garlic Butter | T | Smoked Sturgeon | 1 Serv. | 0 |
| Shrimp-Stuffed Mackerel | 1 Serv. | 8 | Smoked Tuna | 3 Ozs. | 0 |
| Sidecar | 3 Ozs. | 12 | Smoked Whitefish | 1/2 Med. | 0 |
| Silhouette Salmon Salad | 1 Serv. | 9 | Smokie Sausage (Wilson) | 4 Ozs. | 2 |
| Silver Cake, 3 Layer | 1 Piece | 73 | Smorgasbord Caviar | | |
| Silver Satin Wine (Italian | | | And Eggs | 1 Serv. | 24 |
| Swiss Colony-Gold Medal): | | | Snails, Bourguignonne | 6 Med. | 2 |
| With Bitter Lemon | 3 Fl. Ozs. | 9 | Snails, Raw | 4 Ozs. | 2 |
| Simba, Soft Drink | 6 Fl. Ozs. | 21 | Snap Beans, Green, Canned | 8 Ozs. | 6 |
| Simmered Chicken | 1 Serv. | 3 | Snap Beans, Green, Fresh | 1 Serv. | 5 |
| Simmered Celery | 1 Serv. | 9 | Snickers Candy | 1 Bar | 25 |
| Simple Syrup Sauce | 1 Tbsp. | 9 | Sno Ball (Hostess) | 1 Cake | 28 |
| Singapore Sling | 8 Ozs. | 9 | Snow-Capped Oranges | 1 | 16 |
| Sirloin Pork | 1 Serv. | 0 | Snow Pudding | 1 Serv. | 21 |
| | | | Social Tea Cookie | 1 | 4 |

105

| FOOD | AMT. | CARB. GRAMS |
|---|---|---|
| Soda, Black & White | 10 Ozs. | 73 |
| Soda Crackers | 6 | 35 |
| Soda, Chocolate | 1 Serv. | 15 |
| Soda, Cream | 8 Ozs. | 28 |
| Soda, Grape | 8 Ozs. | 28 |
| Soda, Ice Cream, Fresh Fruit Flavor | 10 Ozs. | 71 |
| Soda, Orange | 8 Ozs. | 28 |
| Soda, Lemon | 6 Ozs. | 21 |
| Soda, Lime | 6 Ozs. | 19 |
| Soda, Vanilla | 10 Ozs. | 71 |
| Soda, Ice Cream, Artif. Flavors | 1 Serv. | 71 |
| Soda, Ice Cream, Choc. | 1 Serv. | 71 |
| Soft Drinks: | | |
| Banana (Yoo-Hoo): | | |
| Regular | 8 Fl. Ozs. | 29 |
| High-Protein | 8 Fl. Ozs. | 33 |
| Birch Beer: | | |
| (Canada Dry) | 8 Fl. Ozs. | 28 |
| (Yukon Club) | 8 Fl. Ozs. | 28 |
| Bitter Lemon: | | |
| (Canada Dry) | 8 Fl. Ozs. | 28 |
| (Hoffmann) | 8 Fl. Ozs. | 28 |
| (Schweppes) | 8 Fl. Ozs. | 31 |
| Bitter Orange: | | |
| (Schweppes) | 8 Fl. Ozs. | 30 |
| Cactus Cooler: | | |
| (Canada Dry) | 8 Fl. Ozs. | 29 |
| Cherry, Black: | | |
| Sweetened: | | |
| (Canada Dry) | 8 Fl. Ozs. | 32 |
| (Dr. Brown's) | 8 Fl. Ozs. | 27 |
| (Hoffman) | 8 Fl. Ozs. | 30 |
| (Key Food) | 8 Fl. Ozs. | 27 |
| (Kirsch) | 8 Fl. Ozs. | 29 |
| (Shasta) | 8 Fl. Ozs. | 29 |
| (Waldbaum) | 8 Fl. Ozs. | 27 |
| Unsweetened or Low Calorie: | | |
| (Dr. Brown's) Slim-Ray | 8 Fl. Ozs. | 1 |
| (Hoffman) | 8 Fl. Ozs. | 1 |
| (No-Cal) | 8 Fl. Ozs. | 0 |
| (Shasta) | 8 Fl. Ozs. | T |
| Cherry, Sweetened: | | |
| (Canada Dry) | 8 Fl. Ozs. | 29 |
| Fanta | 8 Fl. Ozs. | 28 |
| (Hires) | 8 Fl. Ozs. | 27 |
| (Nedick's) | 8 Fl. Ozs. | 27 |
| (Yoo-Hoo) | 8 Fl. Ozs. | 24 |
| High-Protein (Yoo-Hoo) | 8 Fl. Ozs. | 32 |
| (Yukon Club) | 8 Fl. Ozs. | 29 |
| Chocolate: | | |
| (Yoo-Hoo) | 8 Fl. Ozs. | 24 |

| FOOD | AMT. | CARB. GRAMS |
|---|---|---|
| High-Protein (Yoo-Hoo) | 8 Fl. Ozs. | 32 |
| Club Soda, Any Brand: | | |
| Regular | 8 Fl. Ozs. | 0 |
| Dietetic | 8 Fl. Ozs. | 0 |
| Cocoa-Cream: | | |
| (Hoffman) | 8 Fl. Ozs. | 27 |
| (Yukon Club) | 8 Fl. Ozs. | 27 |
| Coconut (Yoo-Hoo): | | |
| Regular | 8 Fl. Ozs. | 24 |
| High-Protein | 8 Fl. Ozs. | 32 |
| Cola: | | |
| Sweetened: | | |
| (Canada Dry) | 8 Fl. Ozs. | 27 |
| (Clicquot Club) | 8 Fl. Ozs. | 27 |
| Coca-Cola | 8 Fl. Ozs. | 24 |
| (Cott) | 8 Fl. Ozs. | 27 |
| (Dr. Brown's) | 8 Fl. Ozs. | 27 |
| (Hoffman) | 8 Fl. Ozs. | 27 |
| (Key Food) | 8 Fl. Ozs. | 27 |
| (Kirsch) | 8 Fl. Ozs. | 27 |
| (Mission) | 8 Fl. Ozs. | 27 |
| Mr. Cola | 8 Fl. Ozs. | 27 |
| Pepsi-Cola | 8 Fl. Ozs. | 26 |
| (Shasta) | 8 Fl. Ozs. | 26 |
| (Waldbaum) | 8 Fl. Ozs. | 27 |
| Cherry (Shasta) | 8 Fl. Ozs. | 26 |
| Low Calorie: | | |
| Diet Pepsi-Cola | 8 Fl. Ozs. | 1 |
| (Dr. Brown's) Slim-Ray | 8 Fl. Ozs. | 2 |
| (Hoffman) | 8 Fl. Ozs. | 2 |
| (No-Cal) | 8 Fl. Ozs. | T |
| (Shasta) | 8 Fl. Ozs. | T |
| Cherry (Shasta) | 8 Fl. Ozs. | T |
| Tab | 8 Fl. Ozs. | T |
| Cream: | | |
| Sweetened: | | |
| (Canada Dry) | 8 Fl. Ozs. | 32 |
| (Dr. Brown's) | 8 Fl. Ozs. | 27 |
| Fanta | 8 Fl. Ozs. | 32 |
| (Hoffman) | 8 Fl. Ozs. | 18 |
| (Key Food) | 8 Fl. Ozs. | 27 |
| (Kirsch) | 8 Fl. Ozs. | 25 |
| (Shasta) | 8 Fl. Ozs. | 28 |
| (Waldbaum) | 8 Fl. Ozs. | 27 |
| (Yukon Club) | 8 Fl. Ozs. | 28 |
| Low Calorie: | | |
| (Dr. Brown's) | 8 Fl. Ozs. | 1 |
| (Hoffman) | 8 Fl. Ozs. | 1 |
| (No-Cal) | 8 Fl. Ozs. | T |
| (Shasta) | 8 Fl. Ozs. | T |
| Dr. Brown's Cel-Ray Tonic | 8 Fl. Ozs. | 20 |
| Dr. Pepper: | | |
| Regular | 8 Fl. Ozs. | 21 |

| FOOD | AMT. | CARB. GRAMS | FOOD | AMT. | CARB. GRAMS |
|------|------|------|------|------|------|
| Sugar-Free | 8 Fl. Ozs. | T | Grapefruit: | | |
| Coffee, Low Calorie: | | | Sweetened: | | |
| (No-Cal) | 8 Fl. Ozs. | T | Golden (Canada Dry) | 8 Fl. Ozs. | 28 |
| Flip (Dad's) | 8 Fl. Ozs. | 23 | Fanta | 8 Fl. Ozs. | 28 |
| Fresca | 8 Fl. Ozs. | T | Low Calorie, Pink: | | |
| Ginger Ale: | | | (Hoffman) | 8 Fl. Ozs. | 1 |
| Sweetened: | | | (No-Cal) | 8 Fl. Ozs. | T |
| (Canada Dry) | 8 Fl. Ozs. | 21 | (Royal Crown) | 8 Fl. Ozs. | T |
| (Clicquot Club) | 8 Fl. Ozs. | 20 | Half & Half: | | |
| (Cott) | 8 Fl. Ozs. | 20 | Sweetened: | | |
| (Dr. Brown's) | 8 Fl. Ozs. | 20 | (Canada Dry) | 8 Fl. Ozs. | 28 |
| Fanta | 8 Fl. Ozs. | 20 | (Dr. Brown's) | 8 Fl. Ozs. | 24 |
| (Hoffman) | 8 Fl. Ozs. | 20 | (Hoffman) | 8 Fl. Ozs. | 27 |
| (Key Food) | 8 Fl. Ozs. | 20 | (Kirsch) | 8 Fl. Ozs. | 27 |
| (Kirsch) | 8 Fl. Ozs. | 20 | (Yukon Club) | 8 Fl. Ozs. | 28 |
| (Mission) | 8 Fl. Ozs. | 20 | Low Calorie (Hoffman) | 8 Fl. Ozs. | 2 |
| (Schweppes) | 8 Fl. Ozs. | 21 | Hawaiian Punch | 8 Fl. Ozs. | 27 |
| (Shasta) | 8 Fl. Ozs. | 21 | Hi-Spot (Canada Dry) | 8 Fl. Ozs. | 26 |
| (Vernors) | 8 Fl. Ozs. | 23 | Lemon-Lime: | | |
| (Waldbaum) | 8 Fl. Ozs. | 20 | Sweetened: | | |
| (Yukon Club) | 8 Fl. Ozs. | 20 | Green (Canada Dry) | 8 Fl. Ozs. | 30 |
| Low Calorie: | | | Rickey (Canada Dry) | 8 Fl. Ozs. | 24 |
| (Dr. Brown's) Slim Ray | 8 Fl. Ozs. | 1 | (Dr. Brown's) | 8 Fl. Ozs. | 25 |
| (Hoffman) | 8 Fl. Ozs. | 1 | (Dr. Pepper) | 8 Fl. Ozs. | 24 |
| (No-Cal) | 8 Fl. Ozs. | T | (Key Food) | 8 Fl. Ozs. | 25 |
| (Shasta) | 8 Fl. Ozs. | T | (Kirsch) | 8 Fl. Ozs. | 23 |
| (Vernors) | 8 Fl. Ozs. | 0 | (Shasta) | 8 Fl. Ozs. | 24 |
| Ginger Beer: | | | (Waldbaum) | 8 Fl. Ozs. | 25 |
| (Canada Dry) | 8 Fl. Ozs. | 23 | Low Calorie (Shasta) | 8 Fl. Ozs. | T |
| (Schweppes) | 8 Fl. Ozs. | 22 | Lemon: | | |
| Grape: | | | Sweetened: | | |
| Sweetened: | | | (Canada Dry) | 8 Fl. Ozs. | 23 |
| (Canada Dry) | 8 Fl. Ozs. | 32 | (Dr. Brown's) Tune-Up | 8 Fl. Ozs. | 24 |
| (Clicquot Club) | 8 Fl. Ozs. | 33 | (Hoffman) | 8 Fl. Ozs. | 27 |
| (Cott) | 8 Fl. Ozs. | 33 | (Kirsch) | 8 Fl. Ozs. | 21 |
| (Dr. Brown's) | 8 Fl. Ozs. | 29 | Low Calorie: | | |
| (Dr. Pepper) | 8 Fl. Ozs. | 34 | (Dr. Brown's) Slim-Ray | 8 Fl. Ozs. | 2 |
| Fanta | 8 Fl. Ozs. | 32 | (Hoffman) | 8 Fl. Ozs. | 2 |
| Grapette | 8 Fl. Ozs. | 31 | (No-Cal) | 8 Fl. Ozs. | 0 |
| (Hires) | 8 Fl. Ozs. | 32 | (Shasta) | 8 Fl. Ozs. | T |
| (Hoffman) | 8 Fl. Ozs. | 32 | Like, Low Calorie | | |
| (Key Food) | 8 Fl. Ozs. | 29 | (Seven-Up) | 8 Fl. Ozs. | 1 |
| (Mission) | 8 Fl. Ozs. | 33 | Moxie | 8 Fl. Ozs. | 28 |
| (Nedick's) | 8 Fl. Ozs. | 32 | Orange: | | |
| (Shasta) | 8 Fl. Ozs. | 30 | Sweetened: | | |
| (Waldbaum) | 8 Fl. Ozs. | 29 | (Canada Dry) | 8 Fl. Ozs. | 33 |
| (Yoo-Hoo) | 8 Fl. Ozs. | 24 | (Clicquot Club) | 8 Fl. Ozs. | 33 |
| High-Protein (Yoo-Hoo) | 8 Fl. Ozs. | 33 | (Cott) | 8 Fl. Ozs. | 33 |
| (Yukon Club) | 8 Fl. Ozs. | 32 | (Dr. Brown's) | 8 Fl. Ozs. | 29 |
| Low Calorie: | | | (Dr. Pepper) | 8 Fl. Ozs. | 33 |
| (Hoffman) | 8 Fl. Ozs. | 1 | Fanta | 8 Fl. Ozs. | 32 |
| (No-Cal) | 8 Fl. Ozs. | 0 | (Hires) | 8 Fl. Ozs. | 29 |
| (Shasta) | 8 Fl. Ozs. | T | (Hoffman) | 8 Fl. Ozs. | 32 |

| FOOD | AMT. | CARB. GRAMS |
|---|---|---|
| (Key Food) | 8 Fl. Ozs. | 29 |
| (Kirsch) | 8 Fl. Ozs. | 29 |
| (Mission) | 8 Fl. Ozs. | 33 |
| (Nedick's) | 8 Fl. Ozs. | 22 |
| Orangette | 8 Fl. Ozs. | 32 |
| (Shasta) | 8 Fl. Ozs. | 32 |
| (Waldbaum) | 8 Fl. Ozs. | 22 |
| (Yoo-Hoo) | 8 Fl. Ozs. | 24 |
| High-protein (Yoo-Hoo) | 8 Fl. Ozs. | 33 |
| (Yukon Club) | 8 Fl. Ozs. | 29 |
| Low Calorie: | | |
| (Dr. Brown's) Slim-Ray | 8 Fl. Ozs. | 1 |
| (Hoffman) | 8 Fl. Ozs. | 1 |
| (No-Cal) | 8 Fl. Ozs. | 0 |
| (Shasta) | 8 Fl. Ozs. | T |
| Pineapple: | | |
| (Hires) | 8 Fl. Ozs. | 30 |
| (Kirsch) | 8 Fl. Ozs. | 29 |
| (Nedick's) | 8 Fl. Ozs. | 30 |
| (Yoo-Hoo) | 8 Fl. Ozs. | 24 |
| High-Protein (Yoo-Hoo) | 8 Fl. Ozs. | 32 |
| Quinine Soft Drink or Tonic Water: | | |
| Sweetened: | | |
| (Canada Dry) | 8 Fl Ozs | 24 |
| (Dr. Brown's) | 8 Fl. Ozs. | 22 |
| Fanta | 8 Fl. Ozs. | 20 |
| (Hoffman) | 8 Fl. Ozs. | 22 |
| (Schweppes) | 8 Fl. Ozs. | 22 |
| (Shasta) | 8 Fl. Ozs. | 19 |
| (Yukon Club) | 8 Fl Ozs | 22 |
| Low Calorie: | | |
| (Hoffman) | 8 Fl. Ozs. | T |
| (No-Cal) | 8 Fl Ozs | 0 |
| Raspberry: | | |
| Sweetened: | | |
| (Canada Dry) | 8 Fl Ozs | 33 |
| (Hoffman) | 8 Fl Ozs | 28 |
| (Yukon Club) | 8 Fl. Ozs. | 28 |
| Black: | | |
| (Dr. Brown's) | 8 Fl Ozs | 28 |
| (Key Food) | 8 Fl Ozs | 28 |
| (Kirsch) | 8 Fl Ozs | 28 |
| (Waldbaum) | 8 Fl Ozs | 28 |
| Low Calorie (Hoffman) | 8 Fl Ozs | 2 |
| Low Calorie (No-Cal) | 8 Fl. Ozs | T |
| Root Beer Drink Mix | | |
| (Wyler's) | 8 Fl. Ozs. | 30 |
| Root Beer: | | |
| Sweetened: | | |
| (Canada Dry) | 8 Fl. Ozs. | 27 |
| (Clicquot Club) | 8 Fl. Ozs. | 26 |
| (Cott) | 8 Fl. Ozs. | 26 |
| (Dad's) | 8 Fl. Ozs. | 26 |
| (Dr. Brown's) | 8 Fl. Ozs. | 27 |
| (Dr. Pepper) | 8 Fl. Ozs. | 30 |
| Fanta | 8 Fl. Ozs. | 32 |
| (Hires) | 8 Fl. Ozs. | 26 |
| (Hoffman) | 8 Fl. Ozs. | 27 |
| (Key Food) | 8 Fl. Ozs. | 27 |
| (Kirsch) | 8 Fl. Ozs. | 23 |
| (Mason's) | 8 Fl. Ozs. | 20 |
| (Mission) | 8 Fl. Ozs. | 26 |
| (Shasta) | 8 Fl. Ozs. | 28 |
| (Waldbaum) | 8 Fl. Ozs. | 27 |
| (Yukon Club) | 8 Fl. Ozs. | 27 |
| Low Calorie: | | |
| (Dad's) | 8 Fl. Ozs. | T |
| (Hoffman) | 8 Fl. Ozs. | 1 |
| (No-Cal) | 8 Fl. Ozs. | T |
| Draft (Shasta) | 8 Fl. Ozs. | T |
| Sarsaparilla: | | |
| (Hoffman) | 8 Fl. Ozs. | 28 |
| (Yukon Club) | 8 Fl. Ozs. | 29 |
| Seven-Up | 8 Fl. Ozs. | 24 |
| Sour Mixer (Canada Dry) | 8 Fl. Ozs. | 24 |
| Sport Cola (Canada Dry) | 8 Fl. Ozs. | 25 |
| Sprite | 6 Fl. Ozs. | 18 |
| Strawberry: | | |
| Sweetened: | | |
| (Canada Dry) | 8 Fl. Ozs. | 29 |
| Fanta | 8 Fl. Ozs. | 32 |
| (Shasta) | 8 Fl. Ozs. | 27 |
| (Yoo-Hoo) | 8 Fl. Ozs. | 24 |
| High-protein (Yoo-Hoo) | 8 Fl. Ozs. | 30 |
| Low Calorie (Shasta) | 8 Fl. Ozs. | T |
| Tahitian Treat | | |
| (Canada Dry) | 8 Fl. Ozs. | 35 |
| Tee Up (Kirsch) | 8 Fl. Ozs. | 21 |
| Tiki (Shasta): | | |
| Regular | 8 Fl. Ozs. | 28 |
| Diet | 8 Fl. Ozs | T |
| Tom Collins or Collins Mixer | | |
| (Dr. Brown's) | 8 Fl. Ozs. | 22 |
| (Hoffman) | 8 Fl Ozs | 22 |
| (Key Food) | 8 Fl. Ozs. | 22 |
| (Kirsch) | 8 Fl. Ozs. | 20 |
| (Waldbaum) | 8 Fl. Ozs. | 22 |
| (Yukon Club) | 8 Fl. Ozs. | 20 |
| Tropical Punch | | |
| (Yukon Club) | 8 Fl Ozs | 28 |
| Vanilla: | | |
| (Yoo-Hoo) | 8 Fl. Ozs. | 24 |
| High-Protein (Yoo-Hoo) | 8 Fl. Ozs | 32 |
| Wild Berry: | | |
| Fruit Drink (Hi-C) | 8 Fl Ozs | 28 |
| Wink (Canada Dry) | 8 Fl. Ozs | 28 |

| FOOD | AMT. | CARB. GRAMS | FOOD | AMT. | CARB. GRAMS |
|---|---|---|---|---|---|
| Soft Drink, Cherry | 8 Ozs. | 28 | Soup, Green Pea, Condensed | 4 Ozs. | 18 |
| Soft Drink, Cream Soda | 8 Ozs. | 28 | Soup, Lamb & Vegetable | 4 Ozs. | 6 |
| Soft Drink, Ginger Ale | 8 Ozs. | 21 | Soup, Lamb & Vegetable | | |
| Soft Drink, Grape | 8 Ozs. | 28 | Stew | Av. Serv. | 6 |
| Soft Drink, Lemon | 8 Ozs. | 28 | Soup, Lentil | 1 Cup | 40 |
| Soft Drink, Low Calorie, | | | Soup, Mock Turtle | 1 Cup | 0 |
| Most Flavors | 8 Ozs. | 0 | Soup, Mulligatawny | 1 Cup | 20 |
| Soft Drinks, Sarsaparilla | 8 Ozs. | 28 | Soup, Mushroom & Barley | 1 Cup | 13 |
| Sole | Av. Serv. | 0 | Soup, Mushroom, Creamed | 1 Cup | 13 |
| Sole, Filet of, Broiled | Av. Serv. | 0 | Soup, Noodle | 1 Cup | 7 |
| Sole, Filet of, Fried | Av. Serv. | 0 | Soup, Onion, Clear | 1 Cup | 4 |
| Sole, Fried Sandwich | 1 | 36 | Soup, Onion, Creamed | 1 Serv. | 7 |
| Solid Sardines w/Oil | 3 Ozs. | T | Soup, Onion, French | 1 Serv. | 5 |
| Sorghum Syrup | 3 Ozs. | 58 | Soup, Oxtail | 1 Cup | 0 |
| Souffle, Almond | 1 Serv. | 40 | Soup, Pea, Creamed | 1 Cup | 23 |
| Souffle, Cheese | 1/2 Cup | 6 | Soup, Pea Dehydrated | 4 Ozs. | 70 |
| Souffle, Chestnut | 1 Serv. | 15 | Soup, Pea Split | 3/4 Cup | 13 |
| Soup, Apple | 1 Serv. | 18 | Soup, Pea Split, Creamed | 8 Ozs. | 22 |
| Soup, Asparagus, Creamed | 1 Cup | 13 | Soup, Pepperpot | 1 Cup | 15 |
| Soup, Barley | 1 Cup | 13 | Soup, Philadelphia Pepperpot | 1 Serv. | 15 |
| Soup, Barley, Cr. | 1 Cup | 13 | Soup, Pinto Bean | 8 Ozs. | 17 |
| Soup, Barley & Mushroom | 1 Cup | 13 | Soup, Potato | 1 Cup | 15 |
| Soup, Bean | 1 Cup | 17 | Soup, Potato, Creamed | 1 Cup | 15 |
| Soup, Beef, Cold | 1 Cup | 2 | Soup, Potato Leek | Serv. | 21 |
| Soup, Beef Broth | 1 Cup | 2 | Soup, Rice, As Served | 4 Ozs. | 7 |
| Soup, Black Bean | 1 Cup | 17 | Soup, Spinach, Creamed | 8 Ozs. | 8 |
| Soup, Buttermilk | 1 Serv. | 10 | Soup, Split Pea, Condensed | 4 Ozs. | 17 |
| Soup, Cabbage | Av. Serv. | 0 | Soup, Tomato | 1 Cup | 13 |
| Soup, Casserole | 1 Serv. | 18 | Soup, Tomato Clear | 1 Serv. | 4 |
| Soup, Celery, Clear | 1 Cup | 7 | Soup, Tomato, Creamed | 1 Cup | 18 |
| Soup, Celery, Creamed | 2/3 Cup | 8 | Soup, Tomato Skimmed Milk | 1 Cup | 15 |
| Soup, Cheese | 1 Serv. | 8 | Soup, Turkey | Serv. | 13 |
| Soup, Chicken | 1 Cup | 2 | Soup, Vegetable | 1 Cup | 11 |
| Soup, Chicken Condensed, | | | Soup, Water Cress | Av. Serv. | 5 |
| Regular | 4 Ozs. | 5 | Soup, Wine | Av. Serv. | 15 |
| Soup, Chicken, Creamed | 1 Cup | 12 | Soup, Won Ton | Av. Serv. | 7 |
| Soup, Chicken Gumbo | 1 Cup | 6 | Sour Balls | 6 or 1 Oz. | 28 |
| Soup, Chicken & Matzoth Balls | 1 Cup | 34 | Sour Brandy | 6 Ozs. | 10 |
| Soup, Chicken Noodle | 1 Cup | 8 | Sour Cream | 5 | 8 |
| Soup, Chicken Rice | 1 Cup | 5 | Sour Cream | 1/4 Cup | 2 |
| Soup, Chilled Cucumber | 1 Serv. | 16 | Sour Cream, Clam Dip | 3 Tsp. | T |
| Soup, Clam & Tomato | Av. Serv. | 9 | Sour Cream & Herring | 4 Ozs. | 4 |
| Soup, Clear | Av. Serv. | 3 | Sour Cream Sauce | 1 Tbsp. | 3 |
| Soup, Corn, Creamed | 1 Cup | 9 | Sour Milk Biscuits | 1 Sm. | 14 |
| Soup, Cream of Crab | 1 Serv. | 9 | Sour Mixer, Soft Drink | | |
| Soup, Cream of Turkey | 1 Cup | 12 | (Canada Dry) | 8 Fl. Ozs. | 24 |
| Soup, Duck | 1 Cup | 12 | Sour Rhine Wine | 1 Gl. | 19 |
| Soup, Duck, Creamed | 1 Cup | 12 | South Sea Cocktail | 1 Gl. | 6 |
| Soup, Egg Drop | 1 Cup | 15 | Southern Beaten Biscuits | 1 Med. | 20 |
| Soup, French Onion | | | Southern Belles | Av. Serv. | 79 |
| With Croutons | 1 Cup | 10 | Southern Comfort, Mint Julep | | |
| Soup, Greek Lemon & Rice | Av. Serv. | 46 | Beverage | 1 Gl. | 0 |

| FOOD | AMT. | CARB. GRAMS |
|---|---|---|
| Southern Corn Pudding | 1/2 Cup | 13 |
| Southern Cross Cocktail | 1 Gl. | 8 |
| Southern Fried Apple | Av. Serv. | 16 |
| Southern Style Corn Bread | 2 In. Sq. | 22 |
| Soy Beans | 1/2 Cup | 6 |
| Soy Muffins | 1 Med. | 17 |
| Soy Sauce | 1 Tsp. | 1 |
| Soybean Curd | 1 Cake | 3 |
| Soybean Flour, Full Fat | 4 Ozs. | 24 |
| Soybean Flour, Med. Fat | 1 Cup | 32 |
| Soybean, Grits Med. Fat | 1 Cup | 7 |
| Soybean Grits, 1/2 Corn | 4 Ozs. | 13 |
| Soybeans, (Immature) Raw | 4 Ozs. | 13 |
| Soybeans, Immature Seeds | 4 Ozs. | 16 |
| Soybean, Mature-Dried | 4 Ozs. | 33 |
| Soybean, Milk | 8 Ozs. | 5 |
| Soybean, Soup | Av. Serv. | 18 |
| Soybean, Sprouts, Raw | 1/2 Cup | 3 |
| Space Food: | | |
| Applesauce Mix (Epicure) | 1 Oz. | 26 |
| Banana Pudding Powder | | |
| (Epicure) | 1 Oz. | 10 |
| Beef Bites (Epicure) | 1 Oz. | T |
| Beef Pot Roast Bars | | |
| (Epicure) | 1 Oz. | 0 |
| Beef Sandwiches Bites | | |
| (Epicure) | 1 Oz. | 10 |
| Beef & Vegetable Bar | | |
| (Epicure) | 1 Oz. | 7 |
| Brownie Bites (Epicure) | 1 Oz. | 21 |
| Butterscotch Pudding Powder | | |
| (Epicure) | 1 Oz. | 10 |
| Caramel Stick (Pillsbury) | 1 Oz. | 19 |
| Caramel Stick (Pillsbury) | 1 Pc. | 6 |
| Cheese Sandwich Bites | | |
| (Epicure) | 1 Oz. | 4 |
| Chicken Bites (Epicure) | 1 Oz. | 0 |
| Chicken Sandwich Bites | | |
| (Epicure) | 1 Oz. | 9 |
| Chicken & Vegetable Bar | | |
| (Epicure) | 1 Oz. | 8 |
| Chocolate Malt Stick | | |
| (Epicure) | 1 Oz. | 20 |
| Chocolate Pudding Powder | | |
| (Epicure) | 1 Oz. | 10 |
| Chocolate Stick (Pillsbury) | 1 Oz. | 20 |
| Chocolate Stick (Pillsbury) | 1 Pc. | 6 |
| Cinnamon Toast Bites | | |
| (Epicure) | 1 Oz. | 18 |
| Cocoa Beverage Powder | | |
| (Epicure) | 1 Oz. | 12 |
| Corn Bar (Epicure) | 1 Oz. | 23 |
| Corn Flake Mix (Epicure) | 1 Oz. | 22 |

| FOOD | AMT. | CARB. GRAMS |
|---|---|---|
| Fruit Cocktail Bar | | |
| (Epicure) | 1 Oz. | 25 |
| Mushroom Soup Powder | | |
| (Epicure) | 1 Oz. | 11 |
| Orange Beverage Powder | | |
| (Epicure) | 1 Oz. | 25 |
| Pea Bar (Epicure) | 1 Oz. | 19 |
| Peach Bar (Epicure) | 1 Oz. | 21 |
| Peanut Butter Sandwich | | |
| Bite (Epicure) | 1 Oz. | 11 |
| Peanut Butter Stick | | |
| (Pillsbury) | 1 Oz. | 20 |
| Peanut Butter Stick | | |
| (Pillsbury) | 1 Pc. | 6 |
| Pea Soup Powder | | |
| (Epicure) | 1 Oz. | 18 |
| Pineapple Beverage Powder | | |
| (Epicure) | 1 Oz. | 25 |
| Potato Salad Bar | | |
| (Epicure) | 1 Oz. | 11 |
| Shrimp Cocktail Bar | | |
| (Epicure) | 1 Oz. | 13 |
| Spaghetti & Sauce | | |
| (Epicure) | 1 Oz. | 10 |
| Tea (Epicure) | 1 Oz. | 23 |
| Toast Bites (Epicure) | 1 Oz. | 13 |
| Spaghetti | 5/8 Cup | 20 |
| Spaghetti With Butter | 1/4 Lb. | 20 |
| Spaghetti, Cooked | 4 Ozs. | 23 |
| Spaghetti With Cheese | 1/4 Lb. | 20 |
| Spaghetti & Chicken | 1 Serv. | 16 |
| Spaghetti With Clam Sauce | 1/4 Lb. | 43 |
| Spaghetti With Clams, Baked | 1 Serv. | 17 |
| Spaghetti Dinner: | | |
| With Meat Balls: | | |
| (Chef Boy-Ar-Dee) | 1 Pkg. | 62 |
| Frozen (Banquet) | Dinner | 57 |
| Frozen (Morton) | Dinner | 86 |
| Frozen (Swanson) | Dinner | 44 |
| With Meat Sauce: | | |
| (Chef Boy-Ar-Dee) | 1 Pkg. | 50 |
| (Kraft) Deluxe Dinner | 4 Ozs. | 23 |
| With Mushroom Sauce: | | |
| (Chef Boy-Ar-Dee) | 1 Pkg. | 51 |
| Spaghetti, Dry | 4 Ozs. | 85 |
| Spaghetti & Frankfurters In | | |
| Tomato Sauce, Canned: | | |
| SpaghettiO's | | |
| (Franco-American) | 4 Ozs. | 12 |
| (Heinz) | 4 Ozs. | 12 |
| Spaghetti & Ground Beef In | | |
| Tomato Sauce, Canned: | | |
| (Chef Boy-Ar-Dee) | 1 Can | 52 |

| FOOD | AMT. | CARB. GRAMS | FOOD | AMT. | CARB. GRAMS |
|---|---|---|---|---|---|
| (Franco-American) | 8 Ozs. | 25 | Tomato Paste (Durkee) | 1 Oz. | 70 |
| (Nalley's) | 8 Ozs. | 28 | Without Meat (Durkee) | 1 Oz. | 14 |
| Spaghetti With 2 Meatballs | 1/4 Lb. | 45 | Spaghetti With Tomato Sauce | 1 Serv. | 47 |
| Canned: | | | Twists (Buitoni) | 1 Cup | 32 |
| (Austex) | 4 Ozs. | 12 | (Franco-American) | 4 Ozs. | 17 |
| (Buitoni) | 1 Cup | 24 | SpaghettiO's | | |
| (Chef Boy-Ar-Dee) | 4 Ozs. | 13 | (Franco-American) | 4 Ozs. | 17 |
| (Franco-American) | 4 Ozs. | 12 | With Cheese: | | |
| SpaghettiO's | | | (Chef Boy-Ar-Dee) | 4 Ozs. | 16 |
| (Franco-American) | 4 Ozs. | 11 | Italian Style | | |
| (Hormel) | 4 Ozs. | 5 | (Franco-American) | 4 Ozs. | 15 |
| Frozen (Banquet) Buffet | 4 Ozs. | 13 | (Heinz) | 4 Ozs. | 17 |
| Spaghetti With Meat Sauce | 1/4 Lb | 47 | Spam (Hormel): | | |
| Canned (Heinz) | 8 Ozs. | 20 | Regular | 12-Oz. Can | 5 |
| Frozen: | | | Spread | 3-Oz. Can | 3 |
| (Banquet) Cookin' Bag | 8 Ozs. | 34 | Spanish Omelet | 2 Eggs | 8 |
| (Kraft) | 8 Ozs. | 30 | Spanish Rice | Av. Serv. | 20 |
| (Swanson) | 8 Ozs. | 28 | Spanish Rice & Meat | Av. Serv. | 17 |
| Spaghetti Mix: | | | Spanish Sherried Olives | Av. Serv. | 7 |
| American Style (Kraft) | 4 Ozs. | 22 | Spanish-Style Vegetables, | | |
| Italiano (Golden Grain) | 4 Ozs. | 26 | Frozen (Birds Eye) | 1 Pkg. | 20 |
| Italian Style (Kraft) | 4 Ozs. | 20 | Spanish Vegetable Soup | Av. Serv. | 5 |
| Spaghetti Sauce: | | | Spareribs, Barbecued | 6 Av. | 1 |
| Clam, Red (Buitoni) | 1 Cup | 21 | Spareribs, Pork | 4 Ozs. | 0 |
| Clam, White (Buitoni) | 1 Cup | 20 | Spareribs, Pork, Med. Fat | 4 Ozs. | 0 |
| Meat: | | | Spareribs 'n' Sauerkraut | Av. Serv. | 6 |
| (Buitoni) | 1 Cup | 21 | Sparkling Burgundy | 1 Serv. | 4 |
| (Chef Boy-Ar-Dee) | 4 Ozs. | 9 | Special K, Cereal | | |
| With Ground Meat | | | (Kellogg's) | 1 Cup | 14 |
| (Chef Boy-Ar-Dee) | 4 Ozs. | 9 | Special Spinach Salad | 1 Serv. | 5 |
| (Franco-American) | 4 Ozs. | 9 | Spencer Steak | Av. Serv. | 0 |
| (Prince) | 1/2 Cup | 10 | Spice Cake Mix: | | |
| Meatball (Chef Boy-Ar-Dee) | 4 Ozs. | 17 | & Apple (Betty Crocker) | 4 Ozs. | 88. |
| Meatless or Plain: | | | Chocolate Flavor, | | |
| (Buitoni) | 1/2 Cup | 11 | New Orleans Style | | |
| (Chef Boy-Ar-Dee) | 4 Ozs. | 12 | (Betty Crocker) | 4 Ozs. | 88 |
| (Prince) | 1 Cup | 26 | Honey (Betty Crocker) | 4 Ozs. | 88 |
| Mushroom: | | | (Duncan Hines) | 1 Pc. | 36 |
| (Buitoni) | 1/2 Cup | 12 | Spiced Apricots | 4 Med. | 26 |
| (Chef Boy-Ar-Dee) | 4 Ozs. | 12 | Spiced Canned Pork | 4 Ozs. | 0 |
| (Franco-American) | 4 Ozs. | 12 | Spiced Green Olives | Av. Serv. | T |
| Spaghetti Sauce Mix: | | | Spiced Hard Candy | 1 Oz. | 28 |
| (Kraft) | 1 Oz. | 2 | Spiced Peaches | 2 Halves | 28 |
| (McCormick) | 1 Oz. | 3 | Spiced Pears | 2 Halves | 26 |
| (Wyler's) | 1 Oz. | 25 | Spiced Pears W/Syrup | 1/2 Cup | 25 |
| Italian (French's) | 1 Oz. | 15 | Spiced Vegetables Milanese | Av. Serv. | 10 |
| Prepared Without Oil | | | Spicy Jellied Chicken | | |
| (Spatini) | 1 Oz. | 2 | Consomme | Av. Serv. | 2 |
| Prepared With Oil | | | Split Peas, Cooked | 1 Cup | 37 |
| (Spatini) | 1 Oz. | 1 | Split Pea Soup | 3/4 Cup | 7 |
| With Mushrooms: | | | Spinach (A-B2-C) | 1/2 Cup | 3 |
| (French's) | 1 Oz. | 8 | Spinach (Canned) | 1 Cup | 6 |
| (Lawry's) | 1 Oz. | 14 | (Stokely-Van Camp) | 1 Cup | 8 |

| FOOD | AMT. | CARB. GRAMS | FOOD | AMT. | CARB. GRAMS |
|---|---|---|---|---|---|
| (Hunt's) | 4 Ozs. | 3 | Start, Instant Breakfast | | |
| Dietetic: | | | Drink | 1/2 Cup | 15 |
| (Blue Boy) | 4 Ozs. | 2 | Stax, Cereal (General Mills) | 1 Cup | 22 |
| Spinach (Canned, Infant) | 1 Oz. | 2 | Steak, Barbecued | 1 Serv. | T |
| Spinach, Cream Of, Soup | 8 Ozs. | 8 | Steak, Beef | Av. Serv. | 0 |
| Spinach, Frozen | 8 Ozs. | 6 | Steak, Chopped (B2) | 1/4 Lb. | 0 |
| Chopped: | | | Steak, Chuck With Bone | Av. Serv. | 0 |
| (Birds Eye) | 4 Ozs. | 3 | Steak, Cube | 1-1/2 Ozs. | 0 |
| (Stokely-Van Camp) | 4 Ozs. | 4 | Steak, Flank | Av. Serv. | 0 |
| Leaf: | | | Steak, Ham (B1) | Av. Serv. | 0 |
| (Birds Eye) | 4 Ozs. | 4 | Steak With Onions | | |
| (Stokely-Van Camp) | 4 Ozs. | 5 | And Peppers | Av. Serv. | 5 |
| In Butter Sauce: | | | Steak, Pepper | Av. Serv. | 5 |
| (Birds Eye) | 4 Ozs. | 4 | Steak, Porterhouse | Av. Serv. | 0 |
| (Green Giant) | 4 Ozs. | 2 | Steak, Rib | Av. Serv. | 0 |
| In Cream Sauce | | | Steak, Round | Av. Serv. | 0 |
| (Green Giant) | 4 Ozs. | 7 | Steak, Sandwich | 1 | 24 |
| Spinach, Raw | 1/2 Lb. | 6 | Steak, Salisbury (B2) | Av. Serv. | T |
| Spinach Souffle | Av. Serv. | 8 | Steak, Sirloin | Av. Serv. | 0 |
| Frozen (Stouffer's) | 4 Ozs. | 10 | Steak, Spencer | Av. Serv. | 0 |
| Frozen (Swanson) | 4 Ozs. | 8 | Steak, Swiss | Av. Serv. | 15 |
| Sponge Cake | Av. Pc. | 22 | Steak, T-Bone | Av. Serv. | 0 |
| Sponge Cake, Prepared Mix | Av. Pc. | 22 | Steak, Tenderloin | Av. Serv. | 0 |
| Sport Cola, Soft Drink | | | Steak, Veal | Av. Serv. | 0 |
| (Canada Dry) | 8 Fl. Ozs. | 27 | Steer Liver | 3-1/2 Ozs. | 7 |
| Sprite, Soft Drink | 8 Fl. Ozs. | 24 | Stew, Beef | 1 Cup | 15 |
| Sprats, Salted | Av Serv. | 0 | Stew, Beef & Vegetable | 1 Cup | 15 |
| Spread, Avocado Puree | 1 Tbsp. | 1 | Stew Chicken | 1/2 Med. | 15 |
| Spread, Liver | 2 Tbsp. | 3 | Stew, Irish | 1 Cup | 15 |
| Spread, Olive Pimento | 1 Oz. | 2 | Stew, Lamb | 1 Serv. | 15 |
| Spread, Peanut Butter | 1 Tbsp. | 3 | Stew, Lamb Breast | Av. Serv. | 15 |
| Spread, Roquefort Cream | 1 Oz. | 2 | Stew, Oyster With Milk | Av. Serv. | 21 |
| Springtime Cottage Cheese | | | Stew, Rabbit | Av. Serv. | 15 |
| Salad | Av. Serv. | 6 | Stew, Veal Breast | Av. Serv. | 15 |
| Springtime Turkey, Mold | Av. Serv. | 1 | Stewed Apples | Av. Serv. | 29 |
| Sprouts, Bean, Mung | 1 Cup | 14 | Stewed Apricots | 1/2 Cup | 31 |
| Sprouts, Bean, Soy | 1 Cup | 16 | Stewed Figs | 1/2 Cup | 40 |
| Sprouts, Brussel (A-C) | 1 Cup | 12 | Stewed Onions | 1/2 Cup | 9 |
| Sprouts, Soybean (Raw) | 1/2 Cup | 3 | Stewed Prunes, No Sugar | 1/2 Cup | 40 |
| Squab | 1 | 0 | Stewed Prunes, With Sugar | 4-5 | 40 |
| Squab, Broiled | 1 | 0 | Stewed Rhubarb, No Sugar | 1 Cup | 8 |
| Squab, Roasted | 1 | 0 | Stewed Rhubarb, With Sugar | 1/2 Cup | 41 |
| Squash, Acorn | 1/2 Cup | 12 | Stewed Tomatoes | 1 Cup | 10 |
| Squash, Butternut | 1 Cup | 24 | Stewing Hen | 4 Ozs. | 0 |
| Squash, Hubbard | 1/2 Cup | 10 | Stilton Cheese | 1-1/2 Ozs. | 1 |
| Squash, Summer (A) | 1 Cup | 8 | Stinger | 1 | 9 |
| Slices (Birds Eye) | 1 Cup | 7 | Stock, Brown | 1 Serv. | 3 |
| Cooked (Birds Eye) | 1 Cup | 18 | Stout | 8 Ozs. | 11 |
| Squash, Winter, Boiled | 8 Ozs. | 20 | Strained Honey | 1 Tbsp. | 16 |
| Squid | Av. Serv. | 2 | Strawberry Cheese Cake | Av. Pc. | 17 |
| Starch, Pure | 4 Ozs. | 99 | Strawberry Chiffon Pie | | |
| Stars, Cereal (Kellogg's) | 1 Cup | 25 | (Crumb Crust) | 1 Sl. | 34 |

| FOOD | AMT | CARB. GRAMS |
|------|-----|-------------|
| Strawberry Cream Pie | Av Serv. | 55 |
| Strawberry Crisps (Epicure) | 1 Oz. | 19 |
| Strawberry Danish Dessert (Junket) | 1 Cup | 67 |
| Strawberry Drink Mix: | | |
| Quik | 1 Tbsp. | 22 |
| (Wyler's) | 3 Fl. Ozs. | 8 |
| Strawberry Flavoring, Imitation, (No-Cal) | 1 Tsp. | T |
| Strawberry Ice Cream | Av Scp. | 14 |
| (Sealtest) | 1 Pt. | 74 |
| Strawberry Ice Cream Mix (Junket) | 1 Oz. | 18 |
| Strawberry Jam | 1 Tbsp. | 14 |
| Dietetic: | | |
| (Diet Delight) | 1 Tbsp. | 1 |
| (Slenderella) | 1 Tbsp. | 5 |
| Strawberry Mousse | Av. Serv. | 17 |
| Strawberry Pie | Av. Serv. | 56 |
| Creme (Tastykake) | 4 Ozs. | 50 |
| Frozen: | | |
| (Mrs. Smith's) | 1 Pc. | 23 |
| Cream (Banquet) | 1 Oz. | 11 |
| Cream (Morton) | 1 Pc. | 8 |
| Cream (Mrs Smith's) | 1 Pc. | 12 |
| Strawberry Pie Filling (Lucky Leaf) | 4 Ozs. | 30 |
| Strawberry Preserve, Dietetic: | | |
| (Dia-Mel) | 1 Tbsp. | 5 |
| Wild (Louis Sherry) | 1 Tbsp. | 6 |
| (Tillie Lewis) | 1 Tbsp. | 2 |
| Strawberry Pudding Mix (Royal) Shake-A-Pudd'n | 1 Cup | 64 |
| Strawberry Rennet Custard Mix. | | |
| Powder (Junket) | 1 Oz. | 28 |
| Tablet (Junket) | 1 Tablet | T |
| Strawberry-Rhubarb Pie: | | |
| (Tastykake) | 4 Ozs. | 63 |
| Frozen (Mrs. Smith's) | 1 Pc. | 23 |
| Strawberry-Rhubarb Pie Filling (Lucky Leaf) | 4 Ozs. | 31 |
| Strawberry Sherbet | Av. Serv. | 29 |
| Strawberry Shortcake | Av. Serv. | 43 |
| Strawberry Soda, Ice Cream | 1 Av. | 71 |
| Strawberry Soft Drink: | | |
| Sweetened: | | |
| (Canada Dry) | 8 Fl. Ozs. | 29 |
| Fanta | 8 Fl. Ozs. | 32 |
| (Shasta) | 8 Fl. Ozs. | 27 |
| (Yoo-Hoo) | 8 Fl. Ozs. | 24 |
| High-Protein (Yoo-Hoo) | 8 Fl. Ozs. | 32 |
| Low Calorie (Shasta) | 8 Fl. Ozs. | T |

| FOOD | AMT | CARB. GRAMS |
|------|-----|-------------|
| Strawberry Sponge Short Cake | Med. Serv. | 60 |
| Strawberry Sundae | 1 Av. | 32 |
| Strawberry Syrup, Dietetic. | | |
| (Dia-Mel) | 1 Tbsp. | 5 |
| (No-Cal) | 1 Tbsp. | T |
| Strawberry Tart, Deep | 1 Av. | 21 |
| Strawberries (C) | 1 Cup | 12 |
| Strawberries, Cooked or Canned | 1 Cup | 12 |
| Strawberries, Fresh | 1/2 Cup | 6 |
| Strawberries, Frozen | 1/2 Cup | 27 |
| Whole (Birds Eye) | 4 Ozs. | 26 |
| Halves (Birds Eye) | 4 Ozs. | 48 |
| Quick Thaw (Birds Eye) | 4 Ozs. | 36 |
| Straws, Cheese | 3 | 3 |
| Streamlined Scrambled Eggs | 1 Serv. | 2 |
| Striped Bass Creole Style | Av. Serv. | 51 |
| Strogonoff, Beef | Av. Serv. | 7 |
| Canned (Hormel) | 8 Ozs. | 9 |
| Frozen (Swanson) | 1 Pkg. | 6 |
| Dinner (Chef Boy-Ar-Dee) | 1 Pkg. | 30 |
| Mix (Lipton) | 1 Pkg. | 97 |
| Noodle-Roni | 1 Cup | 32 |
| Sauce Casserole Base (Pennsylvania Dutch) | 1 Cup | 42 |
| Seasoning Mix (Lawry's) | 1 Pkg. | 23 |
| Strudel, Apple | Av. Serv. | 34 |
| Strudel, Cheese | Av. Serv. | 14 |
| Strudel, Prune | Av. Serv. | 14 |
| Stuffed Artichoke With Mushrooms | 1 | 11 |
| Stuffed Cabbage | Av. Serv. | 7 |
| Stuffed Celery | 2 Med. | 1 |
| Stuffed Baked Clams | 2 | 10 |
| Stuffed Cucumber Appetizers | 1 | 3 |
| Stuffed Dates | 2 | 20 |
| Stuffed Egg | 1 Med. | T |
| Stuffed Mushrooms With Peppers Genovese | 1 Serv. | 10 |
| Stuffed Peppers | 1 | 11 |
| Stuffing, Apricot | 1/2 Cup | 34 |
| Stuffing, Bread | 1/2 Cup | 28 |
| Stuffing, Chestnut | 1/2 Cup | 26 |
| Stuffing, Meat | 1/2 Cup | 28 |
| Stuffing, Poultry | 1/2 Cup | 28 |
| Sturgeon, Smoked | 2 Ozs. | 0 |
| Sturgeon, Smoked | 3 Ozs. | 0 |
| Succotash, Canned | 1/2 Cup | 21 |
| Succotash, Fresh | 1/2 Cup | 21 |
| Succotash, Frozen (Birds Eye) | 1 Cup | 36 |

| FOOD | AMT. | CARB. GRAMS | FOOD | AMT. | CARB. GRAMS |
|---|---|---|---|---|---|
| Suet, Beef | 3-1/2 Ozs. | 0 | Swedish Fruit Soup | 1 Serv. | 40 |
| Sugar, Beet | 1 Tsp. | 4 | Swedish Pickled Herring | 1 Serv. | 0 |
| Sugar, Brown | 1 Tsp. | 4 | Swedish Health Bread | 1 Sl. | 16 |
| Sugar, Cane | 1 Tsp. | 4 | Swedish Rye Bread | 1 Sl. | 12 |
| Sugar Cane, Juice Only | 5 Tbsp. | 73 | Sweet Apple Cider | 6 Ozs. | 18 |
| Sugar Coated Popcorn | 1 Box | 48 | Sweet Breads (C) | Sm. Av. Serv. | 0 |
| Sugar Cookie | 1 | 7 | Sweet Breads Broiled | Sm. Serv. | 0 |
| Sugar Frosted Flakes Cereal | 1 Cup | 34 | Sweet Breads, Creamed, | | |
| Sugar, Granulated | 1 Tsp. | 4 | 2 Tbsp. Sauce | Sm Serv. | 3 |
| Sugar Krisps Cereal | 1 Cup | 26 | Sweet Butter (A-D) | 1 Tbsp. | T |
| Sugar, Maple | 1 Tsp. | 4 | Sweet Carbonated Soda | 8 Ozs. | 28 |
| Sugar Peas, Fresh | 3-1/2 Ozs. | 15 | Sweet Cider | 1 Cup | 24 |
| Sugar, Powdered | 1 Tbsp. | 24 | Sweet Pickles, Mixed | 2 Med. | 5 |
| Sugar Substitute: | | | Sweet Potatoes, Baked | 5 Ozs. | 45 |
| (Adolph's) | 1 Tsp. | 0 | Sweet Potatoes, Boiled | 5 Ozs. | 45 |
| Sweetness & Light | 1 Tsp. | 1 | Sweet Potatoes, Candied | 6 Ozs. | 60 |
| Sweetin (Tillie Lewis) | 1 Tsp. | 0 | Frozen: | | |
| Sweet'n It (Dia-Mel): | | | (Mrs. Paul's) | 4 Ozs. | 39 |
| Liquid | 1 Tsp. | 0 | Yams (Birds Eye) | 4 Ozs. | 53 |
| Powdered | 1 Packet | 1 | Sweet Potatoes, Canned | 1 Cup | 45 |
| Sugar Wafer Cookie | 1 | 2 | (King Pharr) | 1 Cup | 45 |
| Sugar, White | 1 Tsp. | 4 | Yam (King Pharr) | 1 Cup | 54 |
| Sugared Cruller | 1 | 20 | Vacuum Pack (Taylor's) | 1 Cup | 64 |
| Sugared Nuts | 1/2 Cup | 48 | Sweet Potato Pie | Av. Pc. | 52 |
| Sukiyaki | Av. Serv. | 4 | (Tastykake) | 4 Ozs. | 50 |
| Sultana Grapes | 1/2 Cup | 13 | Sweet Potatoes, Raw | 3-1/2 Ozs. | 28 |
| Summer Squash (A) | 1 Cup | 8 | Sweet Rolls | Aver. | 21 |
| Summer Surprise Soup | Av. Serv. | 3 | Sweet & Sour Cabbage | | |
| Sundae, Butterscotch | 1 Av. | 24 | With 2 Tbsp. Sauce | Av. Serv. | 7 |
| Sundae, Carmel | 1 Av. | 46 | Sweet Wine | 3-1/2 Ozs. | 4 |
| Sundae, Chocolate | 1 Av. | 29 | Sweetened Condensed Milk | 1/2 Cup | 60 |
| Sundae, Chocolate | | | Swing (Shasta): | | |
| With Nuts | 1/2 Cup | 33 | Sweetened | 6 Fl. Ozs. | 20 |
| Sundae, Fudge | 1 Av. | 42 | Low Calorie | 6 Fl. Ozs. | T |
| Sundae, Fudge, Hot | 1 Av. | 42 | Swiss Chard, Cooked | 1 Cup | 9 |
| Sundae, Maple Mousse | 1 Av. | 25 | Swiss Cheese | 1 Oz. | T |
| Sundae, Maplenut | 1 Av. | 27 | Swiss Cheese Fondue | | |
| Sundae, Maple Walnut, | | | With Toast | 1 Serv. | 14 |
| Fancy | 2 Scps. | 30 | Swiss Cheese, Grueyere | | |
| Sundae, Maple Walnut, | | | (A-B1-B2) | 2 Ozs. | 1 |
| Plain | 2 Scps. | 28 | Swiss Cheese, Processed | 4 Ozs. | 1 |
| Sundae, Marshmallow | 1 Aver. | 41 | Swiss Grueyere Cheese | 4 Ozs. | 2 |
| Sundae, Marshmallow | | | Swiss Steak | Av. Serv. | 15 |
| With Nuts | 2 Scps. | 44 | Frozen: | | |
| Sundae, Pineapple, Fancy | 2 Scps. | 45 | (Stouffer's) | 1 Pkg. | 14 |
| Sundae, Walnut | 1 Av. | 50 | Dinner (Swanson) | Dinner | 17 |
| Sundae, Walnut, Fancy | 1 Av. | 57 | With Gravy (Holloway | | |
| Sunshine Cake | 1 Pc. | 36 | House) | 1 Steak | 32 |
| Suzettes, Crepe | 1 | 22 | Sword Fish | Av. Serv. | 0 |
| Suzy Q (Hostess) | 1 Cake | 39 | Syllabub Drink | 1 Av. | 61 |
| Swamp Cabbage | 4 Ozs. | 5 | Sylvaner Wine | | |
| Swedish Anchovy Eyes | Av. Serv. | 6 | (Louis M. Martini) | 3 Fl. Ozs. | T |
| Swedish Caviar Timbales | Av. Serv. | 7 | Syrup, Brown Sugar | 1 Tbsp. | 15 |

| FOOD | AMT. | CARB. GRAMS |
|---|---|---|
| Syrup, Caramel | 1 Tbsp. | 16 |
| Syrup, Cocoa | 1 Tbsp. | 12 |
| Syrup, Corn | 2 Tbsp. | 24 |
| Syrup, Chocolate | 1 Tbsp. | 10 |
| Syrup, Grenadine | 1 Tbsp. | T |
| Syrup, Molasses, Cane Barbados | 1 Tbsp. | 11 |
| Syrup, Molasses, Cane Blackstrap | 1 Tbsp. | 11 |
| Syrup, Molasses, Cane, Light | 1 Tbsp. | 13 |
| Syrup, Molasses, Cane, Med. | 1 Tbsp. | 13 |
| Syrup, Maple | 1 Tbsp. | 13 |
| Syrup, Sorghum | 3 Ozs. | 58 |
| Table Top, Bouillabaisse | 1 Serv. | 6 |
| Tabu Cocktail | 1 Serv. | 19 |
| Taco, Beef, Frozen (Banquet) | 1 Taco | 14 |
| Taffy, Maple | 1 In. Sq. | 10 |
| Taffy, Molasses | 1 In. Sq. | 10 |
| Taffy, Peppermint | 1 In. Sq. | 10 |
| Taffy, Saltwater | 1 In. Cube | 10 |
| Taffy, Turkish | 1 Box | 92 |
| Taffy Vanilla | 1 In. Cube | 10 |
| Tahitian Honey Bee Cocktail | 1 Cktl. Gl. | 6 |
| Tahitian Rum Punch | 10 Ozs. | 7 |
| Tahitian Treat, Soft Drink (Canada Dry) | 8 Fl. Ozs. | 35 |
| Tamale: Canned: | | |
| (Hormel) | 15-Oz. Can | 41 |
| (Wilson) | 4 Ozs. | 16 |
| Frozen: | | |
| (Banquet) Cookin' Bag | 1 Tamale | 8 |
| Tank Bark Candy | 1 Pc. | 14 |
| Tangerine (C) (Sunkist) | 1 Lg. | 8 |
| Tangerine (C) (Sunkist) | 1 Lg. | 8 |
| Tangerine Juice, Fresh (C) | 1/2 Cup | 10 |
| Frozen, Concentrate, Sweetened: | | |
| (Minute Maid) | 1 Cup | 27 |
| (Snow Crop) | 1 Cup | 27 |
| Tangy Onions | 1 | 13 |
| Tapioca, Apple | 4 Ozs. | 26 |
| Tapioca, Apricot Pudding | 1/2 Cup | 41 |
| Tapioca, Cherry (Minute Tapioca) | 1 Serv. | 47 |
| Tapioca, Cherry (Minute Tapioca) | 1 Cup | 50 |
| Tapioca, Pudding | 1/2 Cup | 24 |
| All Flavors (Jell-O) | 1 Cup | 54 |
| Chocolate (Royal) | 1 Cup | 59 |
| Vanilla (Royal) | 1 Cup | 58 |
| Tapioca, Ready-To-Serve | 1/2 Cup | 19 |
| Tapioca, Uncooked-Dry | 2 Ozs. | 49 |
| Taro, Corms and Tubers | 4 Ozs. | 23 |

| FOOD | AMT. | CARB. GRAMS |
|---|---|---|
| Tarragon | 1/8 Tsp. | 0 |
| Tarter Sauce | 1 Tbsp. | T |
| Tarts, Apple | 1 Med. | 21 |
| Tarts, Blueberry | 1 Med. | 21 |
| Tart With Filling | 1 Med. | 21 |
| T-Bone Steak | Av. Serv. | 0 |
| Tea, Black | 1 Cup | T |
| Instant: | | |
| (Lipton) | 1 Cup | T |
| (Tender Leaf) | 1 Tsp. | T |
| Tea, Iced, No Sugar Or Cream | Gl. | T |
| Tea, Japanese Green, Plain | 1 Cup | T |
| Tea Mix, Iced: | | |
| All Flavors, Nestea | 1 T. | 15 |
| All Flavors (Salada) | 1 Cup | 13 |
| (Tender Leaf) | 1 Cup | 3 |
| (Wyler's) | 1 Cup | 14 |
| Lemon Flavored: | | |
| (Lipton) | 1 Tbsp. | T |
| Low Calorie (Lipton) | 8 Fl. Ozs. | T |
| Nestea | 1 Tbsp. | 1 |
| Low Calorie (Tender Leaf) | 1 Cup | T |
| Tea, With Lemon | 1 Cup | 1 |
| Tea, Oolong, Plain | 1 Cup | T |
| Team Flakes, Cereal (Nabisco) | 1 Cup | 18 |
| Temptys (Tastykake): | | |
| Butter Creme | 1 Cake | 13 |
| Chocolate | 1 Cake | 17 |
| Lemon | 1 Cake | 17 |
| Tenderloin Pork | 4 Ozs. | 0 |
| Tenderloin Steak | Av. Serv. | 0 |
| Tender Made Main Meal Meat, Canned (Wilson): | | |
| Beef Roast | 4 Ozs. | 0 |
| Corned Beef Brisket | 4 Ozs. | 1 |
| Ham | 4 Ozs. | 1 |
| Picnic | 4 Ozs. | 1 |
| Pork Roast | 4 Ozs. | 0 |
| Pork Loin, Smoked | 4 Ozs. | 1 |
| Turkey & Dressing | 4 Ozs. | 12 |
| Turkey Roast | 4 Ozs. | 0 |
| Tequila Sour (Calvert) | 3 Fl. Ozs. | 11 |
| Terrapin | Av. Serv. | 0 |
| Tetrazzini, Chicken | 1 Serv. | 16 |
| Thanksgiving Punch Bev. | 4 Ozs. | 26 |
| Thermidor, Lobster | 1 | 15 |
| Thin Gravy | 4 Tbsp. | 4 |
| Thompson Seedless Grapes | 4 Ozs. | 17 |
| Thousand Island Diet Dressing | 1 Tbsp. | 1 |
| Thousand Island Dressing | 1 Tbsp. | 2 |

| FOOD | AMT. | CARB. GRAMS | FOOD | AMT. | CARB. GRAMS |
|------|------|-------------|------|------|-------------|
| Three Musketeers Mars | 1 Bar | 35 | Toll House Cookie | 1 | 7 |
| Three-Ring Pretzel | 1 | 2 | Tomato Aspic | Av. Serv. | 9 |
| Thunderbird Wine (Gallo): | | | Tomato Aspic Salad | 1/2 Cup | 4 |
| 14% Alcohol | 3 Fl. Ozs. | 8 | Tomato Avocado Appetizer | 1 Serv. | 5 |
| 20% Alcohol | 3 Fl. Ozs. | 7 | Tomato, Canned: | | |
| Thyme | 1/8 Tsp. | 0 | Baby, Sliced (Contadina) | 1 Cup | 16 |
| Tia Maria, Liqueur | | | Diced, in Puree | | |
| (Hiram Walker) | 1 Fl. Oz. | 10 | (Contadina) | 1 Cup | 16 |
| Tiki, Soft Drink (Shasta): | | | Italian Style (Hunt's) | 4 Ozs. | 5 |
| Regular | 8 Fl. Ozs. | 28 | Pear-Shaped (Contadina) | 1 Cup | 8 |
| Diet | 8 Fl. Ozs. | T | Round, Peeled | | |
| Timbales, Chicken | 1 Serv. | 6 | (Contadina) | 1 Cup | 12 |
| Toast, Cinnamon | 1 Sl. | 29 | Stewed (Contadina) | 1 Cup | 23 |
| Toast, French, 1 Tbsp. | | | Whole, Peeled (Hunt's) | 4 Ozs. | 5 |
| Corn Syrup | 1 Pc. | 23 | Tomato Catsup | 1 Tbsp. | 4 |
| Toast, French, 1 Tbsp. | | | Tomato Chutney | 5 Tbsp. | 40 |
| Maple Syrup | 1 Pc. | 23 | Tomato Cocktail | | |
| Toast, French Without Syrup | 1 Pc. | 15 | (College Inn) | 4 Ozs. | 6 |
| Toast, Melba | 1 Sl. | 6 | Tomato Consomme | 1 Serv. | 6 |
| Toast, Milk | 1 Sl. | 14 | Tomato & Cucumber Salad | 1 Ea. | 7 |
| Toast, Raisin | 1 Sl. | 12 | Tomato, Dietetic, Canned: | | |
| Toast, Rye | 1 Sl. | 12 | (Blue Boy) | 4 Ozs. | 4 |
| Toast, White | 1 Sl. | 12 | Whole, Peeled | | |
| Toast, Whole Wheat | 1 Sl. | 11 | (Diet Delight) | 4 Ozs. | 4 |
| Toasted, Cracked Wheat | 1 Sl. | 12 | Whole, Unseasoned (S and W) | | |
| Toasted Italian Bread, White | 1 Sl. | 11 | Nutradiet | 4 Ozs. | 4 |
| Toasted, White Croutons | 1 | 3 | (Tillie Lewis) | 4 Ozs. | 4 |
| Toasted Whole Wheat | | | Tomato-Egg Scramble | 1 Serv. | 5 |
| Raisin Bread | 1 Sl. | 15 | Tomato, Fresh (C) | Med. | 4 |
| Toaster Cake: | | | Tomato Juice (A-C) | 1 Cup | 10 |
| Toast 'Em (General Foods): | | | (Campbell) | 4 Ozs. | 4 |
| Animal | 1 Pc. | 33 | (Green Giant) | 4 Ozs. | 4 |
| Frosted | 1 Pc. | 37 | (Heinz) | 4 Ozs. | 6 |
| Fruit Flavors | 1 Pc. | 32 | (Hunt's) | 4 Ozs. | 5 |
| Toastette (Nabisco): | | | Dietetic: | | |
| Apple | 1 Pc. | 34 | (Blue Boy) | 4 Ozs. | 4 |
| Blueberry | 1 Pc. | 34 | (Diet Delight) | 4 Ozs. | 4 |
| Brown Sugar, | | | (Stokely-Van Camp) | 4 Ozs. | 5 |
| Cinnamon | 1 Pc. | 34 | Unseasoned (S and W) | | |
| Cherry | 1 Pc. | 35 | Nutradiet | 4 Ozs. | 4 |
| Strawberry | 1 Pc. | 34 | Tomato & Lettuce Salad | 1 Serv. | 6 |
| Toast-r-Cake: | | | Tomato & Lettuce Sandwich | 1 | 26 |
| Bran (Thomas') | 1 Pc. | 17 | Tomato and Mushrooms | | |
| Corn (Thomas') | 1 Pc. | 20 | With Anchovies | 1 Serv. | 8 |
| Toddy, Hot | 1 Cup | 24 | Tomato Paste, Canned: | | |
| Toffee Coffee | 1 Med. | 8 | (Contadina) | 4 Ozs. | 20 |
| Toffee, English | Av. Pc. | 13 | (Hunt's) | 4 Ozs. | 21 |
| Tokay Wine | Serv. | 6 | Tomato Pizza | 1 | 23 |
| (Gallo) | 3 Fl. Ozs. | 7 | Tomato Puree | 1 Cup | 16 |
| (Gallo) | 3 Fl. Ozs. | 8 | Tomato, Puree (Canned) | 4 Ozs. | 9 |
| (Italian Swiss Colony- | | | (Contadina) | 1 Oz. | 2 |
| Gold Medal) | 3 Fl. Ozs. | 8 | (Hunt's) | 1 Oz. | 2 |
| (Taylor) White | 3 Fl. Ozs. | 11 | Tomato Rabbit, Cheese | 1 Serv. | 20 |

| FOOD | AMT. | CARB. GRAMS | FOOD | AMT. | CARB. GRAMS |
|---|---|---|---|---|---|
| Tomato Salad, Jellied (Contadina) | 4 Ozs. | 11 | (Smucker's) | 1 Tbsp. | 15 |
| Tomato Sauce: | | | Caramel: | | |
| (Contadina) | 8 Ozs. | 17 | (Kraft) | 1 Tbsp. | 9 |
| (Hunt's) All Varieties | 8 Ozs. | 13 | Chocolate (Kraft) | 1 Tbsp. | 9 |
| Tomato Sauced Round Steak | 1 Serv. | 5 | Chocolate or Chocolate Flavored: | | |
| Tomato, Skimmed Milk Soup | 4 Ozs. | 15 | (Kraft) | 1 Tbsp. | 9 |
| Tomato Soup | 1 Cup | 13 | Fudge (Hershey's) | 1 Tbsp. | 8 |
| Condensed (Campbell) | 8 Ozs. | 28 | Fudge, Regular (Smucker's) | 1 Tbsp. | 12 |
| (Heinz) | 1 Cup | 16 | Mint (Hershey's) | 1 Tbsp. | 9 |
| (Manischewitz) | 8 Ozs. | 9 | Peanut Butter (Hershey's) | 1 Tbsp. | 7 |
| Beef (Campbell) | | | Marshmallow | 2 Tbsp. | 13 |
| Noodle-O's | 8 Ozs. | 31 | Marshmallow Creme (Kraft) | 1 Tbsp. | 11 |
| Bisque (Campbell) | 8 Ozs. | 19 | Pineapple (Kraft) | 1 Tbsp. | 10 |
| Rice, Old Fashioned (Campbell) | 8 Ozs. | 15 | Strawberry (Kraft) | 1 Tbsp. | 10 |
| Rice (Manischewitz) | 8 Ozs. | 13 | Walnut (Kraft) | 1 Tbsp. | 7 |
| With Vegetable (Heinz) | | | Dietetic, Chocolate: | | |
| Great American | 1 Cup | 15 | (Diet Delight) | 1 Tbsp. | 1 |
| Canned, Dietetic: | | | (Tillie Lewis) | 1 Tbsp. | 1 |
| Low Sodium (Campbell) | 8 Ozs. | 17 | Topping, Whipped: | | |
| With Rice (Claybourne) | 8 Ozs. | 14 | (Birds Eye) Cool Whip | 1 Tbsp. | 1 |
| (Tillie Lewis) | 8 Ozs. | 14 | (Kraft) | 1 Tbsp. | 2 |
| Tomato Soup, Clear | 1 Serv. | 4 | (Lucky Whip) | 1 Tbsp. | T |
| Tomato Soup, Creamed | 1 Serv. | 18 | Topping, Whipped, Mix: | | |
| Tomatoes, Stewed or Canned | 1 Cup | 10 | (D-Zerta) | 1 Tbsp. | T |
| Tomato Vegetable Soup Mix: | | | (Dream Whip) | 1 Tbsp. | 1 |
| (Golden Grain) | 1 Cup | 13 | (Lucky Whip) | 1 Tbsp. | 1 |
| (Lipton) | 1 Pkg. | 48 | Tortilla | 1 | 10 |
| Tom Collins | Tall | 16 | Tortoni, Biscuit | 1 Sm. | 14 |
| Tom Collins or Collins Mixer | | | Tortuga Beverage | 14 Ozs. | 3 |
| Soft Drink: | | | Trader Vic Punch | 14 Ozs. | 19 |
| (Dr. Brown's) | 8 Fl. Ozs. | 22 | Trader Vic's White Wine Cup | 1 Cup | 8 |
| (Hoffman) | 8 Fl. Ozs. | 22 | Treet (Armour) | 4 Ozs. | 1 |
| (Key Food) | 8 Fl. Ozs. | 22 | Tripe (Canned) | 4 Ozs. | 0 |
| (Kirsch) | 8 Fl. Ozs. | 20 | Tripe (Pickled) | 4 Ozs. | 0 |
| (Waldbaum) | 8 Fl. Ozs. | 22 | Triple Jack Wine (Gallo) | 3 Fl. Oz. | 6 |
| (Yukon Club) | 8 Fl. Ozs. | 20 | Triple Sec Liqueur: | | |
| Tongue, Beef-Potted, Deviled | 1 Tbsp. | T | (Bols) | 1 Fl. Oz. | 9 |
| Tongue, Boiled, Beef | 3 Ozs. | T | (Garnier) | 1 Fl. Oz. | 8 |
| Tongue Canape Spread | 1 Serv. | T | (Hiram Walker) | 1 Fl. Oz. | 10 |
| Tongue (Canned) | 2 Av. Sl. | 0 | (Leroux) | 1 Fl. Oz. | 9 |
| (Hormel) | 4 Ozs. | T | (Old Mr. Boston) | 1 Fl. Oz. | 10 |
| Tongue (Pickled) | 2 Av. Sl. | T | Trix, Cereal (General Mills) | 1 Cup | 25 |
| Tongue, Pork | 4 Ozs. | 1 | Tropical Punch Soft Drink | | |
| Tongue Sandwich | 1 | 24 | (Yukon Club) | 8 Fl. Ozs. | 28 |
| Tootsie Roll | 1 Roll | 22 | Trout | 1/2 Lb. | 0 |
| Top Milk | 1/2 Cup | 1 | Trout, Brook, Smoked | 3 Ozs. | 0 |
| Topping: | | | Trout, Fried | 1 | T |
| Butterscotch: | | | Trout In Aspic | 1 | 4 |
| (Hershey's) | 1 Tbsp. | 7 | Trout, l ake, Smoked | 3 Ozs. | 0 |
| (Kraft) | 1 Tbsp. | 9 | Tumeric | 1/8 Tsp. | 0 |
| | | | Tuna, Canned, Drained | 3 Ozs. | 0 |
| | | | Tuna, Canned In Oil | 1/4 Cup | 0 |

| FOOD | AMT. | CARB. GRAMS |
|---|---|---|
| Solids & Liquid: | | |
| (Breast O'Chicken) | 8 Ozs. | 0 |
| (Star-Kist) | 8 Ozs. | 0 |
| Chunk (Star-Kist) | 8 Ozs. | 0 |
| Chunk, Light: | | |
| (Chicken of the Sea) | 8 Ozs. | 0 |
| (Icy Point) | 8 Ozs. | 0 |
| (Pillar Rock) | 8 Ozs. | 0 |
| White (Icy Point) | 8 Ozs. | 0 |
| White (Pillar Rock) | 8 Ozs. | 0 |
| Drained Solids: | | |
| (Del Monte) | 8 Ozs. | 0 |
| Chunk, Light | | |
| (Chicken of the Sea) | 8 Ozs. | 0 |
| Chunk, White | | |
| (Bumble Bee) | 8 Ozs. | 0 |
| White (Icy Point) | 8 Ozs. | 0 |
| White (Pillar Rock) | 8 Ozs. | 0 |
| Tuna, Canned In Water: | | |
| (Breast O'Chicken) | 8 Ozs. | 0 |
| (Deep Blue) | 8 Ozs. | 0 |
| (Star-Kist) | 8 Ozs. | 0 |
| Dietetic: | | |
| (Chicken of the Sea) | 8 Ozs. | 0 |
| (Star-Kist) | 8 Ozs. | 0 |
| Tuna, Cooked | 3/4 Cup | 0 |
| Tuna, Creamed | Av. Serv. | T |
| Tuna, Fresh | 3 Ozs. | 0 |
| Tuna Pie, Frozen: | | |
| (Banquet) | 8-Oz. Pie | 40 |
| (Swanson) | 8-Oz. Pie | 38 |
| Tuna Salad | 1/2 Cup | 2 |
| Tuna Salad Sandwich | 1 | 26 |
| Tuna Sandwich | 1 | 24 |
| Tuna Smoked | 3 Ozs. | 0 |
| Tuna Soup, Creole, Canned | | |
| (Crosse & Blackwell) | 1 Cup | 6 |
| Turkey | Av. Serv. | 0 |
| Turkey, All Dark | 4 Ozs. | 0 |
| Turkey, All White | 4 Ozs. | 0 |
| Turkey (Canned, Boned) | 4 Ozs. | 0 |
| (Lynden) | 5 Ozs. | 0 |
| Turkey, Cream of, Soup | 1 Cup | 12 |
| Turkey Dinner, Frozen: | | |
| (Banquet) | Dinner | 28 |
| (Morton) | Dinner | 25 |
| (Swanson) | Dinner | 43 |
| Turkey, Frozen: | | |
| (Banquet) Cookin' Bag | 5 Ozs. | 6 |
| (Swanson) | 1 Pkg. | 33 |
| Turkey Gizzard | 4 Ozs. | 0 |
| Turkey Hash | Av. Serv. | 8 |

| FOOD | AMT. | CARB. GRAMS |
|---|---|---|
| Turkey Pie, Frozen: | | |
| (Banquet) | 8 Ozs. | 45 |
| (Morton) | 8 Ozs. | 39 |
| (Swanson) | 8 Ozs. | 40 |
| (Swanson) Deep Dish | 8 Ozs. | 26 |
| Turkey Primavera, Dinner | | |
| (Lipton) | 1 Pkg. | 86 |
| Turkey, Raw | 4 Ozs. | 0 |
| Turkey, Roasted | 4 Ozs. | 0 |
| Turkey Sandwich | 1 | 24 |
| Turkey Sandwich With Gravy | 1 | 28 |
| Turkey Soup | 1 Serv. | 13 |
| Turkey Soup: | | |
| Noodle: | | |
| Condensed (Campbell) | 8 Ozs. | 15 |
| (Heinz) | 1 Cup | 8 |
| (Heinz) Great American | 1 Cup | 11 |
| Low Sodium (Campbell) | 1 Cup | 9 |
| Vegetable, Condensed | | |
| (Campbell) | 8 Ozs. | 16 |
| Turkish Delight | 1 Pc. | 85 |
| Turkish Taffy | 1 Bar | 92 |
| Turnip Greens (Canned) | 1 Cup | 11 |
| Turnip Greens, Cooked | 1 Cup | 8 |
| Frozen (Birds Eye) | 4 Ozs. | 3 |
| Turnips, Cooked | 1 Cup | 12 |
| Turnips, Mashed | 1 Cup | 10 |
| Turnovers, Apple | 1 Med. | 37 |
| Turtle, Mock, Soup | 1 Cup | 0 |
| Tutti Fruitti Ice Cream | 1/2 Cup | 14 |
| T.V. Dinner, Chicken | 1 | 42 |
| 20-20 Wine (Mogen David) | 3 Fl. Ozs. | 10 |
| Twinkie (Hostess) | 1 Cake | 26 |
| Twinkles, Cereal | | |
| (General Mills) | 1 Cup | 27 |
| Twister, Wine (Gallo) | 3 Fl. Ozs. | 8 |
| Two Layer Cake | 1 Pc. | 61 |
| Upside Down Cake, Apricot | 1 Pc. | 38 |
| Upside Down Cake, Blueberry | 1 Pc. | 38 |
| Upside Down Cake, Cherry | Av. Pc. | 38 |
| Upside Down Cake, Pineapple | Av. Pc. | 38 |
| Uneeda Cracker | 1 | 4 |
| Unpitted Dates Candies | 1 Bar | 13 |
| Unsweetened Chocolate Candies | 1 Bar | 8 |
| Unusual Hamburgers | 1 | 4 |
| V-8 Juice | 1 Cup | 9 |
| Valpolicella Wine | | |
| Italian Red (Antinori) | 3 Fl. Ozs. | 6 |
| Vandermint, Dutch Liqueur | | |
| (Leroux) | 1 Fl. Oz. | 10 |
| Vanilla Cake, No Icing | 1 Serv. | 31 |
| Vanilla Cake, With Icing | 1 Sl. | 41 |

| FOOD | AMT. | CARB. GRAMS | FOOD | AMT. | CARB. GRAMS |
|---|---|---|---|---|---|
| Vanilla Cake Mix, | | | Vanilla Taffy | 1 In. Sq. | 10 |
| French (Betty Crocker) | 1 Oz. | 23 | Vanilla Wafer Cookie | 1 | 4 |
| Vanilla Custard | 1/2 Cup | 20 | Vanilla Wafers | Av. Size | 4 |
| Vanilla Drink Mix, Quik | 2 Tsp. | 15 | Veal Birds | 2 Av. | 22 |
| Vanilla Extract | 1 Tsp. | 0 | Veal (Canned, Infant) | 4 Ozs. | 0 |
| Vanilla Fudge Ice Cream | 1 Serv. | 14 | Veal Chop | 1 Med. | 0 |
| Vanilla Fudge Pop Ice Cream | 1 Serv. | 53 | Veal Cutlet, Breaded | 4 Ozs. | 8 |
| Vanilla Ice Cream | 1 Scp. | 14 | Veal Cutlet, Broiled | Av. Serv. | 0 |
| (Sealtest) | 1 Pt. | 60 | Veal in Aspic | Serv. | 0 |
| (Sealtest) 10.2% Fat | 1 Pt. | 61 | Veal Kidneys | 1/2 Cup | 1 |
| (Sealtest) 12.1% Fat | 1 Pt. | 61 | Veal Loaf | Av. Serv. | 3 |
| French (Prestige) | 1 Pt. | 62 | Veal Marsala | Av. Serv. | T |
| Fudge Royale (Sealtest) | 1 Pt. | 63 | Veal Parmigiana Dinner, | | |
| Vanilla Ice Cream Mix | | | Frozen (Swanson) | Dinner | 47 |
| (Junket) | 4 Ozs. | 110 | Veal & Peppers | Av. Serv. | 0 |
| Vanilla Ice Cream Soda, With | | | Veal Roast | Av. Serv. | 0 |
| Chocolate Top Cream | 10 Ozs. | 60 | Veal Scallopini | Av. Serv. | T |
| Vanilla Ice Milk (Sealtest) | 1/6 Qt. | 23 | Veal Steak | Av. Serv. | 0 |
| Vanilla Malted w/Ice Cream | 1/4 Pt. | 53 | Veal Stew | Av. Serv. | 15 |
| Vanilla Pie Filling Mix: | | | Veal Stew Meat, Breast | 4 Ozs. | 15 |
| (Jell-O) | 1/2 Cup | 31 | Vegetable, Beet Cups | 1/2 Cup | 8 |
| (My-T-Fine) | 1 Oz. | 27 | Vegetable Bouillon Cube: | | |
| (D-Zerta): | | | (Herb-Ox) | 1 Cube | T |
| With Whole Milk | 1/2 Cup | 12 | (Wyler's) | 1 Cube | T |
| With Nonfat Milk | 1/2 Cup | 12 | Vegetables, California Celery | 1 Serv. | 11 |
| Vanilla Pudding, Canned: | | | Vegetables, Celery Au Gratin | 1 Serv. | 6 |
| (Betty Crocker) | 4 Ozs. | 26 | Vegetable Fat | 1 Tbsp. | 0 |
| French Vanilla (Bounty) | 4 Ozs. | 21 | Vegetable, Glazed Carrots | | |
| Vanilla Pudding Mix: | | | With Peas | 1 Serv. | 12 |
| Sweetened: | | | Vegetable Juice | 6 Ozs. | 7 |
| (Jell-O) | 1 Cup | 62 | Vegetable Juice Cocktail, Canned: | | |
| Instant (Jell-O) | 1 Cup | 61 | Unseasoned (S and W) | | |
| French, Instant (Jell-O) | 1 Cup | 61 | Nutradiet | 4 Ozs. | 5 |
| (My-T-Fine) | 1 Oz. | 27 | V-8 (Campbell) | 4 Ozs. | 4 |
| Instant (My-T-Fine) | 1 Oz. | 20 | Vegemato (College Inn) | 4 Ozs. | 4 |
| (Royal) | 1 Cup | 53 | Vegetable & Lamb, Infant Soup | 1 Cup | 11 |
| Instant (Royal) | 1 Cup | 60 | Vegetables, Mixed: | | |
| Shake-A-Pudd'n (Royal) | 1 Cup | 64 | Canned (Veg-All) | 4 Ozs. | 8 |
| (Thank You) | 1 Cup | 58 | Frozen: | | |
| Low Calorie (Dia-Mel): | | | (Birds Eye) | 1 Cup | 23 |
| With Whole Milk | 4 Ozs. | 8 | Jubilee (Birds Eye) | 1 Cup | 37 |
| With Nonfat Milk | 4 Ozs. | 8 | (Blue Goose) | 1 Cup | 30 |
| Low Calorie (D-Zerta): | | | In Butter Sauce | | |
| With Whole Milk | 1/2 Cup | 10 | (Birds Eye) | 1 Cup | 22 |
| With Nonfat Milk | 1/2 Cup | 10 | With Onion Sauce | | |
| Vanilla Rennet Custard Mix: | | | (Birds Eye) | 1 Cup | 22 |
| Powder (Junket) | 1 Oz. | 28 | Vegetable Soup | 1 Cup | 11 |
| Tablet (Junket) | 1 Tablet | T | Canned: | | |
| Vanilla Soda With Ice Cream | 10 Ozs. | 71 | Condensed (Campbell) | 8 Ozs. | 25 |
| Vanilla Soft Drink: | | | Condensed (Campbell) | | |
| (Yoo-Hoo) | 8 Fl. Ozs. | 24 | Old Fashioned | 8 Ozs. | 16 |
| High-Protein (Yoo-Hoo) | 8 Fl. Ozs. | 32 | Beef, Condensed (Campbell) | 8 Ozs. | 14 |

| FOOD | AMT. | CARB. GRAMS |
|---|---|---|
| & Beef Stockpot (Campbell) | 8 Ozs. | 17 |
| & Noodles (Campbell) Noodle-O's | 8 Ozs. | 19 |
| Beef (Heinz) | 1 Cup | 11 |
| Beef (Heinz) Great American | 1 Cup | 11 |
| With Beef Broth (Heinz) Great American | 1 Cup | 17 |
| With Beef Stock (Heinz) | 1 Cup | 13 |
| With Ground Beef (Heinz) Great American | 1 Cup | 11 |
| Vegetarian: | | |
| Condensed (Campbell) | 8 Ozs. | 23 |
| (Heinz) | 1 Cup | 12 |
| (Heinz) Great American | 1 Cup | 17 |
| (Manischewitz) | 8 Ozs. | 10 |
| Canned, Dietetic: | | |
| Low Sodium (Campbell) | 8 Ozs. | 11 |
| Beef, Low Sodium (Campbell) | 8 Ozs. | 7 |
| Condensed (Claybourne) | 1 Cup | 21 |
| (Tillie Lewis) | 1 Cup | 13 |
| Frozen, With Beef, Condensed, Old Fashioned (Campbell) | 8 Ozs. | 15 |
| Vegetable Soup Mix: | | |
| (Croyden House) | 1 Tbsp. | 7 |
| (Wyler's) | 8 Fl. Ozs. | 9 |
| Beef (Lipton) | 1 Pkg. | 22 |
| Vegetables, Stuffed Celery With Cheese Canape | 1 Serv. | 1 |
| Velveeta Cheese | 1 Oz. | 1 |
| Velvet Parfait | 1 Serv. | 4 |
| Vermicelli | 3/4 Cup | 12 |
| Vermouth | 1 Shot | 2 |
| Dry: | | |
| (C & P) | 3 Fl. Ozs. | 3 |
| (Gallo) | 3 Fl. Ozs. | 2 |
| (Lejon) | 3 Fl. Ozs. | 2 |
| (Noilly Pratt) | 3 Fl. Ozs. | 1 |
| (Taylor) | 3 Fl. Ozs. | 1 |
| Rosso (Gancia) | 3 Fl. Ozs. | 7 |
| Sweet: | | |
| (C & P) | 3 Fl. Ozs. | 14 |
| (Gallo) | 3 Fl. Ozs. | 2 |
| (Lejon) | 3 Fl. Ozs. | 11 |
| (Noilly Pratt) | 3 Fl. Ozs. | 12 |
| (Taylor) | 3 Fl. Ozs. | 10 |
| White (Gancia) | 3 Fl. Ozs. | 8 |
| White (Lejon) | 3 Fl. Ozs. | 3 |
| Vermouth Cooler | 1 | 15 |
| Vermouth, Italian | 1 Shot | 4 |
| Vichysoisse | 1 Cup | 15 |

| FOOD | AMT. | CARB. GRAMS |
|---|---|---|
| (Crosse & Blackwell) | 1 Can | 19 |
| Vienna Bread | 1 Sl. | 10 |
| Vienna Sausage, Canned: | | |
| (Armour Star) | 1 Can | 0 |
| (Armour Star) | 1 Sausage | 0 |
| (Hormel) | 1 Oz. | T |
| (Wilson) | 1 Oz. | T |
| Vienna Sausage Sandwich | 1 | 24 |
| Vienna Souffle Omelet | 1 Serv. | 12 |
| Vinaigreete, Asparagus | Av. Serv. | 4 |
| Vin Chaud Beverage | 1 Serv. | 37 |
| Vinegar | 1 Oz. | 1 |
| Cidar (Hunt's) | 1 Oz. | 1 |
| Distilled (Hunt's) | 1 Oz. | 1 |
| Vin Rouge Cooler | 1 Serv. | 24 |
| Vinespinach or Basella, Raw | 4 Ozs. | 3 |
| Virginia Ham, Baked | Av. Serv. | 0 |
| Vodka | 1 Oz. | T |
| Vodka Cocktail: | | |
| Martini (Calvert) | 3 Fl. Ozs. | T |
| Screwdriver (Old Mr. Boston) | 3 Fl. Ozs. | 10 |
| Vodka, Flavored (Old Mr. Boston): | | |
| Wild Cherry, Grape, Lemon, Lime or Orange | 1 Fl. Oz. | 8 |
| Peppermint | 1 Fl. Oz. | 5 |
| Voigny Wine (Chanson) | 3 Fl. Ozs. | 7 |
| Wackies, Cereal (General Mills) | 1 Oz. | 23 |
| Wafers, Vanilla | Av. Size | 4 |
| Waffle, Cream Cookie | 1 Med. | 7 |
| Waffle, Ham | 1 Med. | 28 |
| Waffles, Blueberry | 1 Med. | 35 |
| Waffles, Cheese | 1 Med. | 28 |
| Waffles, Chocolate | 1 Med. | 48 |
| Waffles, Country (Aunt Jemima) | 1 Section | 8 |
| Wahine Beverage | 1 Serv. | 4 |
| Waldorf Salad | 4 Ozs. | 12 |
| Wall Eyed Pike | 1 | 0 |
| Walnut Cake Mix, Black (Betty Crocker) | 4 Ozs. | 92 |
| Walnut Caramel Squares | 1 Av. | 10 |
| Walnut Cookies | 2 Ozs. | 32 |
| Walnut Creams | 1 Av. | 9 |
| Walnut Ice Cream | 1 Scp. | 14 |
| Walnut Sundae | Av. Serv. | 50 |
| Walnut Sundae, Fancy | 1 Serv. | 57 |
| Walnuts (B1) | 4 | 2 |
| Walnuts, Black | 11 Halves | 8 |
| Kernel (Hammons) | 1 Lb. | 11 |
| Chopped (Diamond) | 1 Tbsp. | 1 |
| Halves (Diamond) | 1 Cup | 16 |

| FOOD | AMT. | CARB. GRAMS | FOOD | AMT. | CARB. GRAMS |
|---|---|---|---|---|---|
| Halves (Diamond) | 8-15 Halves | 2 | (Kellogg's) | 1 Cup | T |
| Walnuts, Persian | 4 Ozs. | 8 | (Quaker) | 1 Cup | 8 |
| Ward Eight | 1 Oz. | 2 | Wheat Rolled Cooked | 4 Ozs. | 20 |
| Warm Or Cold Onion Salad | 1 Serv. | 5 | Wheat, Shredded | 1 | 18 |
| Washington Cream Cake | Av. Pc. | 51 | Wheatena | 1/2 Cup | 15 |
| Water | 1 Cup | 0 | Wheaties | 1 Oz. | 23 |
| Water Cracker | 1 | 3 | Wheat Thin Cracker | 1 | 1 |
| Watercress | 1 Bunch | 3 | Whip, Apricot | 1 Serv. | 24 |
| Watercress | 1 Lb. | 15 | Whip, Lemon | Av. Serv. | 3 |
| Watercress, Raw | 4 Ozs. | 3 | Whip'N Chill (Jell-O): | | |
| Watercress Soup | Av. Serv. | 5 | With Whole Milk | 2 Ozs. | 19 |
| Watermelon | Med. Sl. | 22 | With Skim Milk | 2 Ozs. | 19 |
| Watermelon Cake | Av. Serv. | 71 | Whipped Cream | 1 Tbsp. | T |
| Watermelon Rind, Pickled | 1/2 Cup | 25 | Whiskey, Bourbon | 1 Shot | T |
| (Crosse & Blackwell) | 1 Tbsp. | 9 | Whiskey, Canadian | 1 Shot | T |
| Watermelon Rind Relish | 1/2 Cup | 25 | Whiskey Cocktail | 1-1/2 Ozs. | 6 |
| Water, Seltzer | 8 Ozs. | 0 | Whiskey Fizz | Av. | 5 |
| Water, Quinine | 8 Ozs. | 0 | Whiskey Highball | Av. | 18 |
| Welsh Rabbit | 1 Serv. | 22 | Whiskey, Irish | 1 Shot | T |
| Welsh Rarebit | 1/2 Cup | 22 | Whiskey, Rye | 1 Shot | T |
| Western Omelette | 1 Av. Serv. | 1 | Whiskey Sour | Av. | 6 |
| West Indies Punch | 1/2 Cup | 3 | (Calvert) | 3 Fl. Ozs. | 9 |
| Wheat Chex, Cereal | | | (Hiram Walker) | 3 Fl. Ozs. | 12 |
| (Ralston) | 1/2 Cup | 23 | Whiskey Sour Mix: | | |
| Wheat, Cracked | 3 Tbsp. | 23 | (Bar-Tender's) | 1 Serv. | 17 |
| Wheat, Cream of | 3/4 Cup | 23 | Low Calorie, Sip 'n Slim | 1 Serv. | T |
| Wheat Flakes, Cereal, | | | Whiskey Sour Soft Drink: | | |
| Dietetic (Van Brode) | 1 Oz. | 23 | (Canada Dry) | 8 Fl. Ozs. | 24 |
| Wheat Flour | 1 Cup | 84 | (Shasta) | 8 Fl. Ozs. | 22 |
| Wheat Flour, All Purpose | 1 Cup | 85 | White Bread | 1 Sl. | 12 |
| Wheat Flour, Bread | 1 Cup | 79 | White Bread | 1/4 Lb. | 59 |
| Wheat Flour, Cake or Pastry | 1 Cup | 84 | White Bread: | | |
| Wheat Flour, Pancake Mix | 4 Ozs. | 43 | (2% Non-Fat Solids) | 1 Sl. | 12 |
| Wheat, Flour, Self-Rising | 1 Cup | 79 | (4% Non-Fat Solids) | 1 Sl. | 12 |
| Wheat Flours, Whole 80% | 1 Cup | 84 | (6% Non-Fat Solids) | 1 Sl. | 12 |
| Wheat Germ | 1 Tbsp. | 7 | White Bread Toast | 1 Sl. | 12 |
| Wheat Germ, Cereal: | | | White Enriched Bread | 1 Sl. | 12 |
| (Kretschmer) | 1 Oz. | 12 | White Cake | Av. Pc. | 32 |
| With Sugar & Honey | | | White Fish, Broiled | Av. Serv. | 0 |
| (Kretschmer) | 1 Oz. | 27 | White Fish, Fried | Av. Serv. | 0 |
| Wheat Germ Flakes | 1/4 Oz. | 13 | White Fish, Steamed | Av. Serv. | 0 |
| Wheat Germ, Stirred | 4 Ozs. | 56 | White Flour | 1 Cup | 84 |
| Wheat Honeys, Cereal | 1 Cup | 32 | White Flour | 1 Tbsp. | 6 |
| Wheaties, Cereal | 1 Oz. | 23 | White Marrow Beans, Dried | 4 Ozs. | 62 |
| Wheat & Malted Barley | | | White Muffins | 1 Med. | 21 |
| Cereal | 3/4 Cup | 22 | White Plain Muffin | 1 | 21 |
| Wheat Meal Cereal Cooked | 4 Ozs. | 20 | White Rice, Raw | 4 Ozs. | 91 |
| Wheat Oats, Cereal, Dry | 1 Oz. | 19 | White Sauce, Med. | 1 Tbsp. | 1 |
| Wheat Pancakes | 1-4 In. | 11 | White Turkey Meat | 4 Ozs. | 0 |
| Wheat Pancake, Enriched Flour | 1-4 In. | 11 | White Wine | 1 Gl. | 4 |
| Wheat, Puffed, Cereal: | | | White Wine Cup, Trader Vic's | 1 Cup | 8 |
| (Checker) | 1 Oz. | 11 | Whites, Egg | 1 | T |

| FOOD | AMT. | CARB. GRAMS | FOOD | AMT. | CARB. GRAMS |
|---|---|---|---|---|---|
| Whites, Egg, Dried | 1 Oz. | T | Won Ton Soup | Av. Serv. | 7 |
| Whiting | Av. Serv. | 0 | Worcestershire Sauce | 1 Tbsp. | 2 |
| Whole Meal, Cooked | 8 Ozs. | 22 | (Crosse & Blackwell) | 1 Tbsp. | 3 |
| Whole Meal, Cooked | | | (Heinz) | 1 Tbsp. | 1 |
| Wheat Germ | 8 Ozs. | 27 | (Lea & Perrins) | 1 Tbsp. | T |
| Whole Milk | 1 Cup | 12 | Yam Potatoes | 1 Sm. | 23 |
| Whole Milk, Dry Reconstituted | 8 Ozs. | 39 | Yam Potatoes, Baked | 5 Ozs. | 36 |
| Whole Wheat Bread | 1/4 Lb. | 55 | Yams, Boiled | 6 Ozs. | 45 |
| Whole Wheat Bread | 1 Sl. | 11 | Yams, Canned | 8 Ozs. | 54 |
| Whole Wheat Crackers | 1 | 5 | Yams, Candied | 1 Med. | 60 |
| Whole Wheat Muffin | 1 | 19 | Yankee Doodles (Drake's) | 1 Cake | 18 |
| Whole Wheat Raisin Bread | 1 Sl. | 15 | Yeast, Bakers | 1 Oz. | 3 |
| Whole Wheat Raisin Bread, | | | Compressed (Fleischmann's) | Cake | 2 |
| Toasted | 1 Sl. | 15 | Dry (Fleischmann's) | 1 Oz. | 12 |
| Whole Wheat Toast | 1 Sl. | 11 | Yeast Biscuit | 1 Lg. | 15 |
| Whoopie Pie (Berwick) | 1 Pie | 45 | Yeast Raised | 1 Tbsp. | 3 |
| Wienerschnitzel | Av. Serv. | 7 | Yeast, Dry Brewers | 1 Tbsp. | 3 |
| Wild Berry, | | | Yogurt | 1 Cup | 13 |
| Fruit Drink (Hi-C) | 6 Fl. Ozs. | 22 | Plain: | | |
| Wild Duck Raw | 3-1/2 Ozs. | 0 | Swiss Style (Borden) | 8 Ozs. | 16 |
| Wild Rice, Cooked | 5/8 Cup | 25 | (Breakstone) | 8 Ozs. | 12 |
| Wild Rice, Raw | 4 Ozs. | 91 | (Dannon) | 8 Ozs. | 14 |
| Wine, Bordeaux | 1 Gl. | 4 | Apple, Dutch (Dannon) | 8 Ozs. | 15 |
| Wine, Burgundy | 1 Gl. | 4 | Apricot: | | |
| Wine, Burgundy, Sparkling | 1 Gl. | 4 | (Breakstone) | 8 Ozs. | 37 |
| Wine, Chablis | 1 Gl. | 4 | (Breakstone) Swiss Parfait | 8 Ozs. | 43 |
| Wine, Champagne, Dry: | | | (Dannon) | 8 Ozs. | 51 |
| Domestic | 1 Gl. | 4 | Black Cherry (Breakstone) | | |
| French | 1 Gl. | 4 | Swiss Parfait | 8 Ozs. | 45 |
| Wine, Claret | 1 Gl. | 2 | Blueberry: | | |
| Wine, Dry | 4 Ozs. | 4 | (Breakstone) | 8 Ozs. | 46 |
| Wine, Elderberry | 1 Gl. | 6 | (Breakstone) Swiss Parfait | 8 Ozs. | 53 |
| Wine, Madeira | 1 Gl. | 5 | (Dannon) | 8 Ozs. | 51 |
| Wine, Red | 1 Gl. | 4 | (Sealtest) Light n' Lively | 8 Ozs. | 50 |
| (Great Western) Pleasant | | | Boysenberry (Dannon) | 8 Ozs. | 51 |
| Valley | 3 Fl. Ozs. | 4 | Cherry (Dannon) | 8 Ozs. | 51 |
| Wine, Rhine | 1 Gl. | 4 | Cinnamon Apple (Breakstone) | 8 Ozs. | 39 |
| Wine, Riesling | 1 Gl. | 4 | Coffee (Dannon) | 8 Ozs. | 33 |
| Wine, Sauce | 1 Tbsp. | 2 | Danny (Dannon) Cuplet: | | |
| Wine, Sauterne, Dry | 1 Gl. | 1 | Blueberry | 8 Ozs. | 50 |
| Wine, Sauterne, Sweet | 1 Gl. | 4 | Red Raspberry | 8 Ozs. | 51 |
| Wine, Sherry | 1 Gl. | 5 | Strawberry | 8 Ozs. | 51 |
| Wine Soup | 1 Serv. | 15 | Honey (Breakstone) | | |
| Wine, Sweet | 3-1/2 Ozs. | 4 | Swiss Parfait | 8 Ozs. | 51 |
| Wine, Tokay | 1 Gl. | 6 | Lemon (Breakstone) | | |
| Wine, White | 1 Gl. | 4 | Swiss Parfait | 8 Ozs. | 50 |
| (Great Western) Pleasant | | | Lemon (Sealtest) | | |
| Valley | 3 Fl. Ozs. | 4 | Light n' Lively | 8 Ozs. | 43 |
| Wink, Soft Drink | | | Lime (Breakstone) | | |
| (Canada Dry) | 6 Fl. Ozs. | 23 | Swiss Parfait | 8 Ozs. | 40 |
| Winter Squash, Baked Mashed | 1 Cup | 20 | Mandarin Orange: | | |
| Winter Squash, Boiled Mashed | 1 Cup | 20 | (Borden) | 8 Ozs. | 45 |

| FOOD | AMT. | CARB. GRAMS | FOOD | AMT. | CARB. GRAMS |
|------|------|-------------|------|------|-------------|
| (Breakstone) Swiss Parfait | 8 Ozs. | 48 | Strawberry: | | |
| Peach: | | | (Borden) | 8 Ozs. | 44 |
| (Borden) | 8 Ozs. | 45 | (Breakstone) | 8 Ozs. | 43 |
| (Breakstone) Swiss Parfait | 8 Ozs. | 47 | (Breakstone) Swiss Parfait | 8 Ozs. | 50 |
| (Sealtest) Light n' Lively | 8 Ozs. | 49 | (Dannon) | 8 Ozs. | 51 |
| Peach Melba (Breakstone) | | | (Sealtest) Light n' Lively | 8 Ozs. | 44 |
| Swiss Parfait | 8 Ozs. | 49 | Vanilla: | | |
| Pineapple (Breakstone) | 8 Ozs. | 38 | (Borden) | 8 Ozs. | 45 |
| | | | (Breakstone) | 8 Ozs. | 29 |
| Pineapple (Sealtest) | | | (Dannon) | 8 Ozs. | 33 |
| Light n' Lively | 8 Ozs. | 47 | Yolks, Eggs, Dried | 1 Oz. | T |
| Pineapple-Orange (Dannon) | 8 Ozs. | 51 | Youngberry Jam | 1 Tbsp. | 14 |
| Prune Whip: | | | Zabaglione | 1 | 6 |
| (Breakstone) | 8 Ozs. | 41 | Zinfandel Wine: | | |
| (Dannon) | 8 Ozs. | 51 | (Italian Swiss Colony- | | |
| Raspberry: | | | Gold Medal) | 3 Fl. Ozs. | T |
| (Borden) | 8 Ozs. | 47 | (Louis M. Martini) | 3 Fl. Ozs. | T |
| (Breakstone) | 8 Ozs. | 45 | Zombi | 14 Ozs. | 14 |
| (Sealtest) Light n' Lively | 8 Ozs. | 42 | Zucchini | 1 Cup | 8 |
| Red (Breakstone) | | | Zweibach | 1 Av. | 5 |
| Swiss Parfait | 8 Ozs. | 46 | (Nabisco) | 1 Pc. | 5 |
| Red (Dannon) | 8 Ozs. | 51 | (Sunshine) | 1 Pc. | 5 |
| | | | Zwieback Toast | 1 Sl. | 5 |

# FOODS WITH NO CARBOHYDRATES

Beef, Chuck
Beef, Flank
Beef, Hamburger (Grd. Bf.)
Beef, Hamburger (Ln. Rd.)
Beef, Porterhouse
Beef, Rib Roast
Beef, Round
Beef, Rump
Beef, Sirloin
Beef, Roast Beef, canned
Beef, Canned Infant Foods
Beef, Dried or Chipped
Bouillon Cubes
Brains, All Kinds*
Butter, Sweet or Salt*
Chicken, Broilers
Chicken, Canned
Chicken, Fryers
Chicken, Roasters
Chicken Meat, Breast Only
Chicken Meat, Leg Only
Codfish
Croaker
Eels
Egg, White Only
Egg, Whole
Egg, Yolk Only
Fats, Cooking (Veg. Oil)
Flounder
Frog Legs
Gelatin, Plain
Haddock
Halibut
Lamb, Rib Chops
Lamb, Shoulder Roast
Lamb, Leg Roast
Lard

Mackerel, Fresh or Canned
Margarine
Oils, Salad or Cooking
Pork, Canned Infant Food
Pork Cured, Boiled Ham
Pork Cured, Canned, Spiced
Pork Cured, Ham Smoked
Pork Cured, Salt Pork
Pork Cured, Sausage
  Links or Bulk
Salmon, Fresh Caught
Salmon, Canned Chinook
  or King
Salmon, Canned Chum
Salmon, Canned Coho or
  Silver
Salmon, Canned Pink
  or Humpback
Salmon, Canned Sockeye
  or Bulk
Sausage, Pork Bulk, Canned
Sausage, Pork Vienna,
  Canned
Swordfish, Fresh Caught
Tongue, Beef
Tuna Fish, Canned,
  Incl. Liquids
Tuna Fish, Canned,
  Liquid Drained
Turkey (Med. Fat)
Veal Cuts, Thin
Veal Cuts, Medium, Fat
Veal Cuts, Fat
Veal Cutlet
Veal Shoulder Roast
Veal Stew Meat
Veal, Canned Infant Food

# DAILY CALORIE NEEDS FOR WOMEN

| HEIGHT | SMALL FRAME | MEDIUM FRAME | LARGE FRAME |
|---|---|---|---|
| 4' 11" | 1635 | 1725 | 1845 |
| 5' 0" | 1665 | 1770 | 1890 |
| 5' 1" | 1695 | 1800 | 1935 |
| 5' 2" | 1740 | 1845 | 1995 |
| 5' 3" | 1785 | 1875 | 2040 |
| 5' 4" | 1845 | 1950 | 2100 |
| 5' 5" | 1890 | 1995 | 2145 |
| 5' 6" | 1950 | 2040 | 2220 |
| 5' 7" | 2010 | 2130 | 2280 |
| 5' 8" | 2055 | 2175 | 2340 |
| 5' 9" | 2115 | 2235 | 2400 |
| 5' 10" | 2175 | 2295 | 2460 |
| 5' 11" | 2220 | 2340 | 2505 |
| 6' 0" | 2265 | 2415 | 2580 |

# DAILY CALORIE NEEDS FOR MEN

| HEIGHT | SMALL FRAME | MEDIUM FRAME | LARGE FRAME |
|---|---|---|---|
| 5' 2" | 1845 | 1965 | 2085 |
| 5' 3" | 1890 | 2010 | 2130 |
| 5' 4" | 1950 | 2070 | 2205 |
| 5' 5" | 2010 | 2130 | 2265 |
| 5' 6" | 2045 | 2175 | 2325 |
| 5' 7" | 2115 | 2235 | 2400 |
| 5' 8" | 2175 | 2310 | 2460 |
| 5' 9" | 2235 | 2370 | 2520 |
| 5' 10" | 2295 | 2430 | 2595 |
| 5' 11" | 2355 | 2490 | 2670 |
| 6' 0" | 2430 | 2565 | 2745 |
| 6' 1" | 2505 | 2640 | 2820 |
| 6' 2" | 2595 | 2730 | 2910 |
| 6' 3" | 2670 | 2805 | 3000 |

# CALORIC ENERGY
# REQUIREMENT CHART

| ACTIVITY DONE | CALORIES NEEDED |
|---|---|
| | Per Lb., Per Hr. |
| Sleeping (soundly) | .4 |
| Sleeping (fitfully) | .5 |
| Sitting (no movement) | .6 |
| Standing (relaxed) | .7 |
| Sewing (by hand) | .75 |
| Dressing (or undressing) | .8 |
| Singing | .85 |
| Typewriting (average speed) | .9 |
| Washing Dishes (ironing or dusting) | .95 |
| Sweeping Floors (broom or vacuum) | 1.0 |
| Exercising (lightly) | 1.25 |
| Walking (approx. 2.8 mph) | 1.5 |
| Trade Work (carpentry or plumbing) | 1.75 |
| Exercising (active) | 1.9 |
| Walking Fast (4 mph) | 2.0 |
| Going Down Steps | 2.25 |
| Loading Heavy Objects (or unloading) | 2.5 |
| Exercising (heavy) | 2.75 |
| Active Sports (tennis or swimming) | 3.25 |
| Running (approx. 5.5 mph) | 3.75 |
| Exercising (very heavy) | 4.0 |
| Going Up Steps | 7.0 |

*NOTE:* To find out how many calories are needed per hour by you, multiply your body weight by the figure shown according to the activity listed. Be sure the decimal point is in the correct place after multiplication.

## DESIRABLE WEIGHTS FOR MEN AND WOMEN

### WEIGHTS FOR WOMEN

| HEIGHT (with shoes on) 2-inch heels | SMALL FRAME | MEDIUM FRAME | LARGE FRAME |
|---|---|---|---|
| 4' 10" ...... | 92- 98 | 96-107 | 104-119 |
| 4' 11" ...... | 94-101 | 98-110 | 106-122 |
| 5' 0" ...... | 96-104 | 101-113 | 109-125 |
| 5' 1" ...... | 99-107 | 104-116 | 112-128 |
| 5' 2" ...... | 102-110 | 107-119 | 115-131 |
| 5' 3" ...... | 105-113 | 110-122 | 118-134 |
| 5' 4" ...... | 108-116 | 113-126 | 121-138 |
| 5' 5" ...... | 111-119 | 116-130 | 125-142 |
| 5' 6" ...... | 114-123 | 120-135 | 129-146 |
| 5' 7" ...... | 118-127 | 124-139 | 133-150 |
| 5' 8" ...... | 122-131 | 128-143 | 137-154 |
| 5' 9" ...... | 126-135 | 132-147 | 141-158 |
| 5' 10" ...... | 130-140 | 136-151 | 145-163 |
| 5' 11" ...... | 134-144 | 140-155 | 149-168 |
| 6' 0" ...... | 138-148 | 144-159 | 153-173 |

### WEIGHTS FOR MEN

| HEIGHT (with shoes on) 1-inch heels | SMALL FRAME | MEDIUM FRAME | LARGE FRAME |
|---|---|---|---|
| 5' 2" ...... | 112-120 | 118-129 | 126-141 |
| 5' 3" ...... | 115-123 | 121-133 | 129-144 |
| 5' 4" ...... | 118-126 | 124-136 | 132-148 |
| 5' 5" ...... | 121-129 | 127-139 | 135-152 |
| 5' 6" ...... | 124-133 | 130-143 | 138-156 |
| 5' 7" ...... | 128-137 | 134-147 | 142-161 |
| 5' 8" ...... | 132-141 | 138-152 | 147-166 |
| 5' 9" ...... | 136-145 | 142-156 | 151-170 |
| 5' 10" ...... | 140-150 | 146-160 | 155-174 |
| 5' 11" ...... | 144-154 | 150-165 | 159-179 |
| 6' 0" ...... | 148-158 | 154-170 | 164-184 |
| 6' 1" ...... | 152-162 | 158-175 | 168-189 |
| 6' 2" ...... | 156-167 | 162-180 | 173-194 |
| 6' 3" ...... | 160-171 | 167-185 | 178-199 |
| 6' 4" ...... | 165-175 | 172-190 | 182-204 |

## Weight in Pounds According to Frame (In Indoor Clothing)

Note: Prepared by the Metropolitan Life Insurance Company. Derived primarily from data of the *Build and Blood Pressure Study, 1959*, Society of Actuaries.